# Ngapartji Ngapartji

*In turn in turn: Ego-histoire, Europe and Indigenous Australia*

# Ngapartji Ngapartji

*In turn in turn: Ego-histoire,
Europe and Indigenous Australia*

Edited by Vanessa Castejon, Anna Cole,
Oliver Haag and Karen Hughes

PRESS

Published by ANU Press
The Australian National University
Canberra ACT 0200, Australia
Email: anupress@anu.edu.au
This title is also available online at http://press.anu.edu.au

National Library of Australia Cataloguing-in-Publication entry

Title: Ngapartji ngapartji, in turn, in turn : ego-histoire, Europe and Indigenous Australia / Vanessa Castejon, Anna Cole, Oliver Haag and Karen Hughes, editors.

ISBN: 9781925021721 (paperback) 9781925021738 (ebook)

Subjects: Aboriginal Australians--History.
Aboriginal Australians--Social conditions.
Aboriginal Australians--Politics and government.

Other Authors/Contributors:
Castejon, Vanessa, editor.
Cole, Anna, 1969- editor.
Haag, Oliver, editor.
Hughes, Karen, editor.

Dewey Number: 305.89915

All rights reserved. No part of this publication may be reproduced, stored in a retrieval system or transmitted in any form or by any means, electronic, mechanical, photocopying or otherwise, without the prior permission of the publisher.

Cover image: Artwork by Julie Gough. Detail, Intertidal resulted from an invitation to participate in an exhibition <Abstractions>. My concept was to arrive with raw materials collected during my journey to the Canberra gallery from which new works would be made. One of the four pieces produced was titled Intertidal for which I finely ground-up the materials and applied them to a board surface in linear striations. Each 'stripe' represented my absence from Tasmania as well as the fulfilling exploration of working with and combining new materials to describe my, at the time, nomadic life.

The ANU.Lives Series in Biography is an initiative of the National Centre of Biography at The Australian National University http://ncb.anu.edu.au/.

Cover design by Nic Welbourn and layout by ANU Press

This edition © 2014 ANU Press

www.ingramcontent.com/pod-product-compliance
Lightning Source LLC
Chambersburg PA
CBHW040934240426
43670CB00033B/2980

# Contents

Acknowledgments............................vii
Notes on Contributors........................ix
Preface: Ego-Histoire........................xv
    *Bruce Pascoe*

## Theoretical Introduction

1. Introduction: 'Ngapartji Ngapartji: In Turn, In Turn'—
Ego-histoire and Australian Indigenous Studies ........... 3
    *Vanessa Castejon, Anna Cole, Oliver Haag and Karen Hughes*

2. 'Introduction' from *Essais d'Ego-Histoire* .............. 21
    *Pierre Nora, Translated by Stephen Muecke*

## Self and History

3. Ngarranga Barrangang: Self and History, a Contemporary
Aboriginal Journey.......................... 25
    *Victoria Grieves*

4. A Personal Journey with Anangu History .............. 41
    *Bill Edwards*

5. Layers of Being: Aspects of Researching and Writing
*Professional Savages: Captive Lives and Western Spectacle* . 61
    *Roslyn Poignant*

6. Stories my Grandmother Never Told Me: Recovering
Entangled Family Histories Through Ego-Histoire ......... 75
    *Karen Hughes*

7. 'Start By Telling Your Own Story': On Becoming An
Anthropologist and Performing Anthropology............ 93
    *Franca Tamisari*

8. Yagan, Mrs Dance and Whiteness ................... 109
    *Jan Idle*

9. Becoming Privileged in Australia: Romany Europe,
Indigenous Australia and the Transformation of Race ..... 125
    *Oliver Haag*

## Out of Place

10. From Paris to Papunya: Postcolonial Theory, Australian Indigenous Studies and 'Knowing' 'the Aborigine' . . . . . . . 143
    *Barry Judd*

11. Situated Knowledge or Ego (His)toire?: Memory, History and the She-Migrant in an Imaginary of 'Terra Nullius' . . . . 159
    *Jane Haggis*

12. Genealogy and Derangement. . . . . . . . . . . . . . . . . . . . 173
    *John Docker*

13. Art Works From Home, Out of Place . . . . . . . . . . . . . . . 189
    *Helen Idle*

14. From Bare Feet to Clogs: One Aboriginal Woman's Experience in Holland . . . . . . . . . . . . . . . . . . . . . . . . 197
    *Rosemary van den Berg*

## Tales of Mystery and Imagination

15. Home Talk . . . . . . . . . . . . . . . . . . . . . . . . . . . . . . . 211
    *Jeanine Leane*

16. True Ethnography . . . . . . . . . . . . . . . . . . . . . . . . . . 227
    *Gillian Cowlishaw*

17. Lands of Fire and Ice: From Hi-Story to History in the Lands of Fire and Ice—Our Stories and Embodiment as Indigenous in a Colonised Hemisphere . . . . . . . . . . . . . . 241
    *May-Britt Öhman and Frances Wyld*

18. Turning into a Gardiya . . . . . . . . . . . . . . . . . . . . . . . 259
    *Stephen Muecke*

19. Tales of Mystery and Imagination from the Tweed River: Shaping Historical-Consciousness . . . . . . . . . . . . . . . . . 271
    *Philip Morrissey*

20. Nourishing Terrain: An Afterword . . . . . . . . . . . . . . . . . 281
    *Gillian Whitlock*

## Appendix

Is 'Ego-Histoire' Possible?. . . . . . . . . . . . . . . . . . . . . . . . . 289
  *Pierre Nora, Translated by Stephen Muecke*

# Acknowledgments

The production of this book would not have been possible without the generous funding by Centre de Recherches Interculturelles sur les Domaines (CRIDAF), Pleïade, Université Paris 13, Sorbonne Paris Cité, and the Austrian Centre for Transcultural Studies, Vienna. We are deeply thankful for the trust and faith shown in our project by Melanie Nolan and the National Centre for Biography, ANU. We also wish to thank Francoise Palleau and Gillian Whitlock for commenting on earlier drafts of the manuscript.

We wish to extend our gratitude to the following colleagues for refereeing individual chapters: Margaret Allen, Josie Arnold, Sue Ballyn, Diane Bell, Anne Brewster, Ann Curthoys, Paul Gillen, Victoria Grieves, Jane Haggis, Chris Healy, Ian Henderson, Victoria Haskins, Martina Horakova, Barry Judd, Shino Konishi, Jeanine Leane, Jane Lydon, Ian McLean, Stephen Muecke, Maria Nugent, Suvendrini Perera, Andrew Peters, Cassi Plate, Martin Renes, May-Britt Öhman, Gillian Whitlock, Christine Winter and Frances Wyld. We thank Swinburne University for collegial support and as well as the talented team at ANU Press.

# Notes on Contributors

*Vanessa Castejon* is an Associate Professor at University Paris 13. Her work explores Aboriginal political claims, self-determination and sovereignty, and the image of Aboriginal people in France/Europe. Her recent publications include an article on her ego-histoire, 'Identity and Identification: Aboriginality from the Spanish Civil War to the French Ghettos' in *Passionate Histories: Myth, memory and Indigenous Australia*, (Aboriginal History/ANU E Press, 2010), edited by Frances Peters-Little, Ann Curthoys and John Docker. Her book, *Les Aborigènes et l'apartheid politique australien,* was published by Harmattan in 2005.

*Anna Cole* was born in south west England to Anglo-Irish/Celtic parents. As a child she migrated with her parents and siblings to live on Nyungar land in Western Australia. She began learning about Indigenous history as a student at the University of Western Australia while involved in activism around a sacred Wagyl water source. Her previous edited collections include, *Uncommon Ground: White Women in Aboriginal History* (with Victoria Haskins and Fiona Paisley, Aboriginal Studies Press, 2005) and *Tattoo: Bodies, Art and Exchange in the Pacific and the West* (with Nicholas Thomas and Bronwen Douglas, Duke University Press, 2005). Her co-written film documenting Indigenous debutante balls in urban Sydney, *Dancing with the Prime Minister* (November Films, 2010), was short-listed for a UN Media Peace Award. She has two young children and lives in the UK, where she teaches post-colonial history and literature at Brighton University.

*Gillian Cowlishaw*'s ethnographic work explores structural and interpersonal relations between Indigenous and other Australians. Her publications include the historical ethnography, *Rednecks, Eggheads and Blackfellas* (Michigan University Press, 1999), *Blackfellas, Whitefellas and the Hidden Injuries of Race* (Blackwell, 2004) and *The City's Outback* (UNSW Press, 2009), an adventurous ethnography in the suburbs.

*John Docker* is an honorary Professor at the Department of History, University of Sydney. He is the author of *1492: The Poetics of Diaspora* (Continuum, 2001) and *The Origins of Violence: Religion, history and genocide* (Pluto Press, 2008). He is writing a memoir entitled *Growing Up Communist and Jewish in Bondi: Memoir of a non-Australian Australian.*

*W. H. (Bill) Edwards*, ordained as a Minister of the Presbyterian Church in 1958, was Superintendent of Ernabella Mission (1958–72), Superintendent of Mowanjum Mission (1972–73), and Minister of the Pitjantjatjara Parish based at Fregon (1973) and Amata (1976–80). He has lectured in Aboriginal Studies at the Torrens College of Advanced Education, the South Australian College of Advanced Education, and the University of South Australia. In retirement, he remains an adjunct senior lecturer at the University of South Australia, and interprets Pitjantjatjara in hospitals and courts. In 2008, he was awarded a PhD in history at Flinders University for his thesis, 'Moravian Aboriginal Missions in Australia'. He is the author of *An Introduction to Aboriginal Societies* (Social Science Press, 2004), and editor of *Traditional Aboriginal Society* (Macmillan, 1998). He was awarded membership of the Order of Australia in 2009.

*Victoria Grieves* is ARC Indigenous Research Fellow at the University of Sydney, currently developing the project, *More than Family History: Race, Gender and the Aboriginal family in Australian history*. The most accessed of her published works is the online book, *Aboriginal Spirituality: Aboriginal Philosophy* (Lowitja Publishing, 2009).

*Oliver Haag* has been engaged in Indigenous Studies for almost ten years. He first became interested in the relationship between Indigenous autobiographies and the re/writing of Australian history. He has started to research European translations and marketing of Australian Indigenous literature and the 'translation' of Indigeneity into European contexts. In his ego-histoire, he explores the impact of travelling on his Romany heritage. He is currently working on a research project that investigates the functioning of idealised Indigeneity in German imperialism.

*Jane Haggis* is Associate Professor at the School of International Studies, Flinders University. She has published widely in development and culture, historiography of gender and colonialism, and critical race and whiteness studies. She is currently writing a monograph, *Storying the Borderlands: Transnational imaginaries of modernity in settling the refugee*. She is also collaborating with Margaret Allen on a research project, 'Resistant subjectivities: Alternative trajectories out of empire, a study of liberal religious women in India during the nineteenth and twentieth centuries'.

*Karen Hughes* is Senior Lecturer in Indigenous Studies at Swinburne University of Technology. She has also taught at Monash University and the University of South Australia, and in 2011 was a Visiting Fellow at University Paris 13. Her research focuses on intimate and gendered histories of the contact zone in New World settler-colonial societies, incorporating transnational perspectives. She is currently involved in a cross-cultural collaborative project with Indigenous communities in southern Australia and the United States, as well as an intergenerational study with the Ngukurr community of South East Arnhem Land. Her research pursues de-colonising methodologies through a partnership approach to ethnography.

*Helen Idle* is a PhD candidate at the Menzies Centre for Australian Studies, King's College London. Her research focuses on the experience of the display of Australian Aboriginal art in Europe. This work builds on her MA in Visual Culture, which looked at the displays of work by Spinifex artists from Tjuntjutjara, Western Australia, in Utrecht and London. Helen is Western Australian, born of settler families, and was educated in Perth, Western Australia, and London, UK. She works part-time in marketing and communications and lives in London.

*Jan Idle* was born on the edge of the western desert (Western Australia) to itinerant school teacher parents, and now lives in inner city Sydney. She is a PhD candidate at the Social Policy Research Centre, University of New South Wales, and her research looks at how young people talk about, experience and make community. Jan has lectured in the areas of design and Australian studies. Her research interest is the collision of visual culture, storytelling, whiteness, Indigenous and settler history, and practices of community in contemporary Australia.

*Barry Judd* is a descendent of the Pitjantjatjara people of North West South Australia and British immigrants who settled on the Victorian goldfields in the 1850s. He has a research interest and expertise in explorations of Australian identity and the process of cultural interchange between Indigenous and non-Indigenous peoples in Australia since 1770. He is particularly interested in this interchange in the context of Australian sports and has published several volumes on this topic. He is an Associate Professor at RMIT University in Melbourne, where he teaches Indigenous Studies.

*Jeanine Leane* is a Wiradjuri woman from south west New South Wales. A Doctorate in the literature of Aboriginal representation followed a long teaching career at secondary and tertiary levels. Formerly a Research Fellow at the Australian Institute of Aboriginal and Torres Strait Islander Studies, she currently holds a Post-Doctoral Fellowship in the Australian Centre for Indigenous History at The Australian National University. Her first volume of poetry, *Dark Secrets After Dreaming: AD 1887–1961* (PressPress, 2010) won the 2010 Scanlon Prize for Indigenous Poetry from the Australian Poets' Union. Her book, *Purple Threads* (University of Queensland Press, 2011), won the David Unaipon Award at the Queensland Premier's Literary Awards and was shortlisted for the 2012 Commonwealth Book Prize and the 2012 Victorian Premier's Award for Indigenous Writing. Jeanine is the recipient of an Australian Research Council grant for a proposal called 'Reading the Nation: A critical study of Aboriginal/Settler representations in the contemporary Australian Literary Landscape'. In 2014 she received an ARC Discovery Indigenous Award for the project 'Aboriginal writing through the David Unaipon Award'.

*Philip Morrissey* is the Academic Coordinator of the Faculty of Arts Australian Indigenous Studies program at the University of Melbourne. He developed the University of Melbourne's first Australian Indigenous Studies Major and Honours program. He is a co-editor of *Aesopic Voices: Re-framing truth through concealed ways of presentation in the 20th and 21st centuries* (Cambridge Scholars Publishing, 2011).

*Stephen Muecke* is Professor of Ethnography at the University of New South Wales. He works with Indigenous groups in Broome, and on the Indian Ocean. His recent books include *Butcher Joe* (Hatje Cantz Verlag GmbH & Company KG, 2012) and, with photographer Max Pam, *Contingency in Madagascar* (Intellect, 2012).

*Pierre Nora* has been a member of the Académie Française since 2001. He has shared his life between editing and university. He is one of the directors of Editions Gallimard, where he created the journal *Le Debat*, which he has chaired for 30 years. He directed *Lieux de Memoire*, which contributed to a 'history of the present'. He chairs the association Liberté pour l'Histoire, which is fighting against the multiplication of laws qualifying the past in France which hamper historical research. His publications include *Les Français d'Algérie*, prefaced by Charles-André Julien (Julliard, 1961), *Essais d'Ego-Histoire* (Gallimard, 1987), *Les Lieux de Mémoire* (Gallimard, 1984–1992), and *Public Historian* (Gallimard, 2011).

*May-Britt Öhman* is of Forest Sámi origin (Lule River region), Sápmi, Sweden, and PhD of History of Science and Technology (2007). She is a Research Fellow at the Centre for Gender Research, Uppsala University, leading the research project 'DAMMED: Security, risk and resilience around the dams of Sub-Arctica'.

*Roslyn Poignant* is an independent scholar, writer and exhibition curator who works with Arnhem Land and North Queensland Aboriginal communities. For over two decades her publications and exhibition projects were concerned particularly with the intersections between photography, anthropology, and popular culture, and cross-cultural issues. Roslyn was a Visiting Fellow at the Centre for Cross-Cultural Research, ANU, 1997–1998, and curator of a touring exhibition for the National Library of Australia, 'Captive Lives: Looking for Tambo and his companions', 1997–2001. Her book, *Professional Savages: Captive lives and western spectacle (*Yale University Press, 2004) received the Stanner Award in 2005. She was awarded an honorary D.Litt. from Sydney University in 2006 and is a member of the Australian Institute of Aboriginal and Torres Strait Islander Studies.

*Franca Tamisari* was awarded her PhD in Social Anthropology at the London School of Economics and has taught Cultural Anthropology at the University of Sydney and the University of Queensland. Since 2005, she has been teaching Anthropology at Ca' Foscari University of Venice. She has been conducting ethnographic research in Northeast Arnhem Land, Australia, since 1990 and has published on Australian Indigenous cosmology and performance, with particular attention to dance in ritual and crosscultural contexts, bicultural education, Australian Indigenous contemporary art, and fieldwork methodology.

*Rosemary van den Berg* is a Bindjareb Nyoongar woman from Pinjarra, Western Australia (her mother's country), with affiliations with the Palkyu Aboriginal people from Hillside Station, Marble Bar and Nullagine in the Pilbara region of Western Australia (her father's country). She obtained her BA (Hons) English, MA in English, and Doctorate of Philosophy at Curtin University, Western Australia. In 2010 she as an Associate Professor at Curtin University. She is a writer and historian and has had books and academic papers published in Australia and overseas.

*Gillian Whitlock* is an ARC Professorial Fellow at the University of Queensland, where she is working on archives of asylum seeker materials for her forthcoming book, *The Testimony of Things*. Her book, *Postcolonial Life Narrative*, is currently in press for the Oxford University Press 'Postcolonialism' series.

*Frances Wyld* is a descendent of the Martu People of Western Australia and lecturer at the University of Adelaide. She recently finished a Doctor of Communication with a thesis titled 'In the Time of Lorikeets: Storywork as an academic method'. She has a passion for decolonising education and takes an inter-disciplinary approach centred within Indigenous knowledges and cultural studies championing the methods of storytelling, auto-ethnography and mythography.

# Preface: Ego-histoire

## Bruce Pascoe

Winners write the history but, in the case of colonists, what they most often write is an excuse.

James Kirby, an early commentator on European–Aboriginal contact history on the Murray River, described the massive clay weirs built through the riverine system and only reluctantly admitted that they must have been built by Aboriginal people.

He describes a fishing system based on tension springs placed in purpose-built apertures in the weir walls. He watches as the fish spring the trap which plucks them from the river and deposits them beside the Aboriginal who casually places them in a basket and resets the trap. This process is repeated many times, although the Wati Wati man refuses to notice Kirby's presence. He is showing off, disdainfully.

Kirby has witnessed a dam wall construction which represents a massive labour and technical investment, and is a fishing machine of grand design. Does Kirby reflect on this system from the point of view of the Aboriginal economy? No, he defaults to a position which justifies his theft of the land: 'I had often heard of the indolence of the blacks and soon came to the conclusion after watching a blackfellow catch fish in such a lazy way, that what I had heard was perfectly true.'

This attitude bedevils black–white relations to this day; a deliberate misrepresentation of the Aboriginal economy by Europeans with more than enough education to understand the true position, should it be in their interests to do so.

The History Wars are not only between left and right views of the same event; they are between the perceptions of black and white when each tell the story of the country.

Australia has until recently rarely seen fit to include Aboriginal perceptions in its discussion of history and identity. For an Aboriginal person to open a book and read stories such as those told by Jeanine Leane, Phillip Morrissey, Vicki Grieves and Barry Judd is a remarkable and moving experience. Most historical reflections are written about us, not by us.

Across these essays there is a sense of the writers, black and white, talking together, a rare Australian experience. Jan Idle, Oliver Haag and Karen Hughes tell deeply personal stories of how *their* stories rub up against Aboriginal Australia. They stop becoming observers and become players in the events of Australian racial history.

John Docker's story about his parents is deeply disturbing, not because it mentions Aboriginal people, but because it reveals how quickly ideas can become authoritarian. Docker's mother, fortunately, is the questioner and if she passed anything on to her son it was the glory of doubt. We need to approach the accepted Australian history with doubt, not antagonism, just the clear-minded ability to wonder.

Ego-histoire is a call to patience and reflection, to listen to the stories of others, just as you would if you intended to honour the other with your love rather than your simple, adolescent curiosity.

Ego-histoire has the potential to begin removing the mask of colonial thought, but only if we are prepared to acknowledge the past. And isn't that what historians are supposed to do?

# THEORETICAL INTRODUCTION

# 1. Introduction: 'Ngapartji Ngapartji: In Turn, In Turn'—Ego-histoire and Australian Indigenous Studies

Vanessa Castejon, Anna Cole, Oliver Haag and Karen Hughes

## Beginnings

'To tell the history of another is to be pressed against the limits of your own'. Sara Suleri, 'The Rhetoric of English India' (Ashcroft, Griffiths & Tiffin, 2002).

'When I ask anybody where they are from I expect nowadays to be told an extremely long story'. Stuart Hall (The Stuart Hall Project, 2013).

These are stories, histories. They emerged in part from encounters between scholars from Australia and Europe that offered a transnational way to think about culture, class, ethnicity, identity, inbetweenness and whiteness in Australian Indigenous studies. Our intention was to weave together professional and personal accounts of studies that have Australia and Indigeneity at their heart. The origins of this book lie in a discussion between Anna Cole and Vanessa Castejon that took place after a European Australian Studies conference at the Universitat de Barcelona's Centre d'Estudis Australians in 2008. Over breakfast they wondered why many of the Australian scholars speaking on Indigenous topics at the conference did not reflect on their role in representing Indigenous Australia in and to Europe, despite the achievements of self-determination and self-reflexivity. That this conversation took place one morning in Barcelona— the place that Vanessa's parents had been exiled from during the Spanish civil war—was significant. The power of place to unlock stories and to allow them to be felt and have an impact was something we had learned to articulate from working alongside Indigenous Australian historians and cultural custodians. So Vanessa and Anna started with themselves, trying to understand more about how their histories fed their motivations to work in Australian Indigenous history. Subsequently Anna and Vanessa were invited by John Docker, Ann Curthoys and Frances Peters-Little to publish these ego-histoires in *Passionate Histories* (Peters-Little, Curthoys & Docker, 2010) and so began the process of taking ego-histoire out of its strictly European origins and into 'a broader history of colonialism and postcolonialism' (Curthoys, 2012).

In *Passionate Histories*, Vanessa Castejon wrote of how as a French scholar in Australia she had often been accused of exoticism because of the colonial past of her country (Castejon, 2010). People in Australia, she observed, tried to define her, impose an identity on her, and tell her whether she was French or Spanish (because of her origins). In Australia, as never before, people told her she was 'white', ignoring her feelings of otherness and marginalisation as someone who grew up in the red suburbs (or ghettos) around Paris. In her ego-histoire, she discusses the circumstances of her anarchist family's forced exile from Franco's Spain as a guiding influence on her reasons for choosing to later study Aboriginal political activism (Castejon 2002; Castejon 2003; Castejon 2005a; Castejon 2008), and her abiding interest in issues of conflict, war, violence, and claims of sovereignty. Alongside this, she further locates her interest in identity (Castejon 2005b; Castejon 2007) as coming from the fact that she feels as an 'in-betweener'. Understanding her position has changed her as a researcher, a process she identifies as 'extrospection' rather than introspection, serving to better illuminate facts as well as affects hidden beneath her research.

Anna Cole wrote about the relationship between her research on Indigenous urban cultural politics in 1960s Australia and her personal history of gender, class, migration and ethnicity (Cole 2010; Cole 2009). Part of a family who migrated from Britain to Western Australia in the late 1970s, her upbringing had involved a process of exile, re-invention and assimilation. Anna was curious about how her experiences fuelled her enduring interest in the processes of attempted assimilation of Indigenous Australians (Cole 2000; Cole 2003a; Cole 2003b) and, more recently, how her father's institutionalisation from the age of seven as a child in Britain had fed her long-standing commitment to documenting the processes that led to the institutionalisation of Indigenous children in Australia (Cole 1994; Cole 2005; Cole 2009). Anna and Vanessa went on to co-convene, with Oliver Haag and Karen Hughes, a conference entitled 'Researching the Other, Transfers of Self: Egohistoire, Europe and Indigenous Australia' at the Université Paris 13 in December 2011. We mention this here because, as co-editors of this book, we feel we cannot ask contributors to share their stories without sharing our own. Oliver Haag and Karen Hughes publish their ego-histoires for the first time in this collection.

This project has drawn on many intellectual currents and, in part, on the trajectory of 'new imperial histories'. In the introduction to her book, *Empire in Question*, Antoinette Burton writes, 'I foreground my whiteness, my gender and my class position within the North American academy not as any kind of disclaimer, but as recognition of my own accountability and the ways in which it is shaped, without being fully determined, by the situations I occupy' (Burton 2011, p. 37). In particular, an important influence on this collection stems from the last three decades of life-story writing in a range of academic disciplines and contexts, including, but not limited to, anthropology, cultural studies, oral history, historical anthropology, queer studies and, more recently, auto-ethnographical studies (Kaplan 1999; Kadar 1992; James & Marcus 1986; Alexander & Gibson 2004; Hornung 2013; Reed-Danahay 1997; Okeley & Callaway 2001). In part, this work was inspired in the 1970s and early '80s by women scholars in history and other academic disciplines who sought to reclaim the silences and omissions of 'universal', depersonalised histories by applying personal voices, applying 'situatedness' and 'standpoint' theory to interdisciplinary work, making explicit the standpoint of the 'knower' (including Olsen 1978; Harstock 1998; Harraway 1988; Collins 1991). This 'autobiographical turn' also reflects the interests of critical historiography since the 1980s in the ambiguous relationship between the present, the past, and the writing of history (Docker & Curthoys 2010). Such influences led, in Gillian Whitlock's words, to 'styles of scholarship that address the authority of experience' (Whitlock 2005). At its best, we hope a collective exploration of life history which the process of ego-histoire represents, including unearthing the history of the Stolen Generations in Australia, or the atrocities of the Spanish civil war in Europe, can recognise and value experiences that have been silenced and help individuals and nations heal from painful aspects of the past.

In Australia, Indigenous writers, historians, activists and cultural custodians have led the field in using life-story work to convey the politics of personal history (see Haag 2008 for a survey of this field). While Indigenous life-histories provide invaluable perspectives on Australian and Indigenous history, they expose Indigenous scholars to personal scrutiny in a way that is not comparable to non-Indigenous scholars. This collection hopes to go some way to balancing this, with themes that include Indigenous perceptions of Europe past and present, similarities and differences between Indigenous and/or ethnic groups in Europe, and including non-Indigenous as well as Indigenous reflections on the relationship between personal, family, or ancestral life and professional research.

## Ego-histoire

'Ego, is not a dirty word'. Skyhooks, 1975.

'Ego-histoire' is a term introduced by French historian Pierre Nora in his collection *Essais d'Ego Histoire* (Nora *et al* 1987). Nora's intention was that ego-histoire would be a combination of a personal history, a broader social history and historiographical reflection. His original *Essais* invited seven distinguished French historians to apply their methods to themselves:

> These are not phony literary autobiographies, nor pointless intimate confessions, nor abstract professions of faith, nor attempts at basic

psychoanalysis. The exercise was to clearly set down one's own story [*histoire*] as one would write someone else's; to try to apply to oneself, each with his or her own particular style and methods, the same cool, encompassing and explanatory gaze that one so often directs towards others. To explain, as an historian, the link between the history you have made and the history that has made you. (Nora *et al* 1987, p. 7)

Nora invited the French historical profession to respond to what he called 'the falsity of detachment … revealed through two decades of historiographical debate', and saw ego-histoire as different from conventional autobiography partly because the different life histories are intended to be read side by side. Whereas autobiography can highlight the unique and personal, essays in ego-histoire invite comparison about the relationship and points of dialogue between personal and collective identities. In this way, ego-histoire can demonstrate, elegantly at times, both the close connection between individual and national identity and the inextricable intertwining of research methodology and outcomes, and subjective data.

Nora's short introduction to his original volume is published here in English for the first time, with thanks to Stephen Muecke for the translation. Nora's longer essay, reflecting on the first ego-histoire collection some years after its publication, 'L'Ego-Histoire est-elle possible?' (Nora 2001), is published here as an appendix to this volume. Nora rather grandly claimed ego-histoire as a 'new genre, for a *new age* of historical consciousness'. The 'old age', as Luisa Passerini and Alexander Geppert noted in their 2001 collection, *European Ego-Histoires: Historiography and the self, 1970–2000*, 'had been that of canceling the writing subject of the historian, of dissimulating personality behind knowledge, and of escaping to other epochs, and had been dominated by illusions of impersonality and objectivity' (Passerini & Geppert 2001). Nora's *Essais d'Ego-Histoire* invited just one woman historian to participate and issues of French colonialism were marginalised in his volume. As Richard Vinen notes: 'The Ego-histoire collection … belonged to a specific time and place. It went with a group of historians who belonged to a certain generation (born between 1917 and 1936, with a special concentration of those born around 1930) and who were associated with particular kinds of institutions' (Vinen 2011, p. 553).

We think ego-histoire, in a broader historical and postcolonial context, has insightful application for scholars writing in the area of Australian Indigenous studies. In this volume, we employ ego-histoire as a useful tool for researchers seeking to engage with a range of post-colonial questions. For example: How does our sense of nation, class, gender, and generation, among other identity markers, shift and take on different meanings in Australia and outside it, in Europe, for example? What impact do national histories implicitly have on one's sense of self? How as a non-Indigenous Australian researcher do you find an ethical way to acknowledge your family's personal investment in colonial history and live in Aboriginal country and engage in research that is decolonising, politically purposeful and genuinely collaborative? How as an Indigenous researcher do you find ethical ways to work within academic disciplines, including Indigenous studies, that have sought to 'know' Indigenous Australians? For Indigenous intellectuals, does Europe represent a regressive space, representative of the colonial metropole, or a liberating one, removed from the every-day taken-for-granted racism of settler-colonial countries (although replete with racism all of its own), or something in-between or something else altogether? What could ego-histoire reveal of European researchers' motivations to work in Indigenous Australian studies? Could they be seeking to 'liberate' Indigenous Australians, 'the great white hope', in Frank Doolan's words (see Gillian Cowlishaw, this volume), or themselves from the tyrannies of colonial history? What about those 'in-betweeners' who feel they are not from one culture or another but a mix of many?

We invited scholars from a range of disciplinary backgrounds to write their version of ego-histoire, applying it as a useful methodological tool to explore transnational influences on scholars and their work in Indigenous studies. Unlike Nora's original collection, we eschew a less rigid definition of what or who makes history, inviting anthropologists, literary studies scholars and cultural studies scholars, alongside professional historians from different ages and stages in their careers, to reflect on their 'ego-histoire'. Many of the contributors to this collection reject, either explicitly or implicitly, Nora's 'cool, encompassing and explanatory gaze', yet all seek, in one way or another, to make a link between the history or scholarship they have made, and the history that made them. As Gillian Whitlock observes, 'Nora is speaking specifically about ego-histoire, however his observations about memory work triggering self-reflexive forms of scholarship has wider application' (Whitlock 2005, p. 339).

The project of applying ego-histoire to Australian Indigenous studies has been utilised here by a number of Indigenous scholars drawing on a historical method resonant with long-standing Indigenous pedagogies of telling and interpreting histories from the standpoint of the self and collective self, inclusive of place or country. The application of the concept of 'ego-histoire' to Australian Indigenous studies is not meant as a model for Indigenous scholars to engage in self-reflexivity. Diverse Indigenous cultures have prior and sovereign concepts of storytelling and history that rest on complex relationships to country, genealogies and personal/familial connections (for example, Moreton-Robinson 2002, p. 16; Wilson 2003). As noted, 'autobiographical stories' or 'life writing' have a strong intellectual tradition in Indigenous Australia, and are arguably different in ontological conceptions of relatedness, identity and history from Nora's concept of the 'self' in ego-histoire. But in bringing

European and Indigenous life-story work together, new perspectives are gained. In some Indigenous contributions in this collection, the Eurocentric premise of 'Europeans studying the Aborigines' is turned on its head. Instead, Europe is studied through Indigenous ego-histoires, and in the process 'provincialized' (Chakrabarty 2000).

## Europe and Australia

One of the ideas that motivated this collection was to ask European scholars who work in Australian Indigenous studies why they are committed to a field so geographically removed from Europe? Such geographical distance adds difficulties to research. It is not easy to practice regional and local histories other than in focused field-work trips, nor to sustain personal connections and friendships from the other side of the world, although the digital age has shrunk some of these expanses. Scholars based in Europe researching Indigenous studies are confronted with charges of participating in the European exoticism and primitivism of other cultures that occurred through a long history of colonial objectification in human exhibitions (Bancel et al., 2002), as well as Europe's ubiquitous involvement in the slave trade at the nexus of Empire (Poignant 2004; Jahoda 1999; Hiller 1991; Nederveen Pieterse 1990). Next to outright racial denigration, there is also an escapist tradition from European modernity that seeks notional refuge in different, seemingly 'pre-modern' cultures. Some of the European translations of Marlo Morgan's *Mutant Message Down Under* (Morgan 1991), for example, are still advertised as 'Aboriginal literature', influencing European popular cultural consumption of Indigenous Australia (Haag 2009, p. 8). 'I've read Marlo Morgan', is a frequent, disturbing and earnest comment made by European students when disclosing their knowledge of Indigenous studies. Long-held constructions of Indigenous 'difference', influenced by 'New Age' culture, still abound in Europe. Such claims to difference, resting on primordial and primitivist othering, are different from Indigenous concepts of sovereignty and the politics of self-determination. Translating concepts of self-determination into contemporary European discourse, as Oliver Haag's essay in this volume shows, is complicated by invisible and unspoken boundaries of culture and 'race' that can become visible again through the process of ego-histoire. Ego-histoire, in an Australian context, goes some way to rectifying the imbalance identified by Aileen Moreton-Robinson: 'the writer-knower as subject is racially invisible, while the Aboriginal as object is visible' (Moreton-Robinson 2004, p. 81).

In this collection we ask explicitly, could the distance between Europe and Australia also be productive? European scholars have a range of different motivations for working in Indigenous studies, often precipitated by their different social, class, gender and ethnic backgrounds and their relationships to other colonial or diasporic histories. By analysing these differences through the lens of ego-histoire, different conceptions of social and apparently 'racial' categories in Europe (or, rather, the many Europes) and Australia (or, rather, the many Australias) are brought to the fore. This works to add fresh insight into the rich scholarship on European representations of Indigenous cultures (including Summo-O'Connell 2012; Jurgensen 1995; Thomas 1994). Ego-histoire can render racial and other identifications visible and act as a political strategy of decentring the asymmetrical power-relations in academic knowledge production. It is also of analytic merit for understanding the complexity of constructions of racialised, as well as gendered and classed positions. Ego-histoire, we argue, allows for more complex understandings of European 'writer-knowers' than is given by the cover of invisibility. Racial, cultural and gendered 'opposites', this book shows, simply do not hold. Complexity and reciprocal exchange borne of relationship are at work in our ego-histoires.

## Essays

Ego-histoire is different from conventional autobiography in that different life histories are read side by side, in the spirit of 'serial data', in Nora's words. Essays in ego-histoire invite comparison between individual and collective identities as they explore relationship and points of dialogue. While none of the essays in this book were written to fit into the sub-headings below or explicitly in dialogue with each other, we grouped them together because of their perceived common themes. We invite you to read them as part of a whole, noting that place, relationship and, at times, the ineffable nature of research, plays a part for each. In this volume, essays are grouped into three broad sub-groups. The first, 'Self and History', includes six essays that reflect on influences from early family life and the passage into adulthood on subsequent research and writing. Victoria Grieves's contribution opens this section. Like many of the other writers in this collection, she alludes to the 'outsider status' that has fuelled her intellectual work. Grieves relates theoretical interventions, such as Walter Mignolo's border thinking, to her personal history in order to emphasise the opportunities for critical analysis produced under the intense personal and political pressures of colonial racism and assimilation. Following on from her personal and theoretical account of New South Wales history, Bill Edwards' essay describes his personal journey with Anangu history, a journey that stretches from the late 1950s to the present. He reflects on his role as interpreter, including during the Pitjantjatjara/Yankunytjatjara, Uluru and Maralinga land rights claims, and as a lecturer in the first Indigenous tertiary education unit in Australia. His essay gave us the title for our volume, 'ngapartji, ngapartji, in turn, in turn', a significant and primary concept from Anangu culture expressing the importance of reciprocal exchange.

Roslyn Poignant reflects on her decades of involvement with Indigenous history and sketches a path from Maroubra, 'when the sand dunes opposite our house stretched all the way to Botany Bay', to her training and aptitude for visual literacy and later marriage to Axel Poignant, to the coincidental wrapping of Little Bay on a return trip home to Sydney, and the record of a death found easily in the British Registry Office in the early 1990s. Drawing on memory together with extracts from her research diary, she sketches a historiography of her best-known writing and curatorial work. An entry in her research diary highlights what might be the impossibility of not writing ego-histoire: 'To write the *seeing* 'I' out of the narrative is to represent the mirror-field as if a portion of it has been obliterated by a retinal blind spot'. Karen Hughes reflects on the process of reciprocity of knowledge in settler-colonial contexts, noting at the beginning of her essay that her forgotten or silenced family history of cross-cultural interaction with Indigenous families 'is recuperated not through my family's stories but through the stories of Aboriginal neighbours'. She describes the metamorphosis or transformation of identity and a more complex sense of belonging that came from relating her family stories to those of her Indigenous neighbours. Franca Tamisari sketches her intellectual journey from Italy to remote Australia and back again, and argues for the foundational importance of 'starting from your own story', as Yolngu thinker Keith Lapulung advised her many years ago. Citing the foundational work of Italian ethnographer Ernesto De Martino, she argues that scholars should not hide their passions and choices, but assert them without being afraid of becoming unfaithful to truth: 'On the contrary this attitude [could] open up the research to a new dimension of fidelity to the real' (De Martino 2002, p. 92). This section concludes with Jan Idle's challenge to herself: to feel 'history's breath', to slow down and, amidst the felt-sense of shame for her non-Indigenous family's settler-colonial past, create enough space to 'feel, acknowledge and speak the violence of contact between settlers and Indigenous people'.

The second part of this collection, 'Out of Place', borrows its name both from Helen Idle's essay in this section and from Edward Said's memoir, an intellectual fellow traveller for this volume on ego-histoire. The six essays in this section reflect on the impact of the experience of 'being out of place' on the authors' scholarship. Oliver Haag begins by discussing the difficulties—at times even impossibilities—of translating Australian meanings of 'race' into the German-speaking context in which he became a scholar. The silencing of 'race' in post-Holocaust German-speaking academia, especially in leftist circles, became noisy in Australia where Oliver found he had suddenly 'inherited' more than one race The re-translation of these discourses into German-speaking contexts meant again a loss of 'race' and proved a struggle of cross-historical interpretation. For Barry Judd, a research trip to Papunya and Alice Springs, the open inquiry of an overseas colleague and a new relationship to what is for him an old and known place, opens a space to reflect both on theoretical paradigms as well as his own role of 'native informant', as he dryly calls it, in the university sector. Judd draws attention to the potential of work from earlier postcolonial scholars, such as Fanon and Césaire, in laying the groundwork for decolonising approaches to Indigenous history in Australia. Jane Haggis, a British immigrant to Australia as a child, finds herself unable, as an adult, when requested at a Whiteness studies conference in Queensland, to tell a story of genealogy unknown to her: 'stuck in the mud of the Thames'. She wonders if the 'awkwardness of the contact zone' that her post-migration family story attests to might be a place for entangled knowledges to emerge. John Docker explores ego-histoire from the viewpoint of both his settler-colonial and diasporic consciousness. Diaspora consciousness, he explains, inheres in a sense of relating to more than one history, to more than one time and place, more than one past and future. He relates the story of his family background to make connections between his personal story and wider Australian social history, reflecting along the way on the methodology and historiography of ego-histoire. Helen Idle writes of her embodied experience of viewing artworks from 'home out of place' to wonder aloud at the ways of viewing Aboriginal art available to her from a European perspective. She reflects, from Europe, on her settler-colonial connection to country and the possibility of contributing, from out of place, to new public interpretations and displays of Indigenous Australian art internationally. This section concludes with Rosemary van den Berg's reflections on her experiences of being away from Australia, living in the Netherlands as a young mother, and the decisive impact of this experience on her subsequent career as a scholar back in Australia. Her contribution suggests that Indigenous autobiography and biography need to be understood in familial, local, regional, national and transnational contexts. These contexts are not separate, but interwoven.

Contributions to the third and final section of the collection, 'Tales of Mystery and Imagination', have in common a sense of the vitality and significance of personal relationships to research trajectories, and reflect on the ineffable and, in some cases, numinous aspects of research, which elude straight-forward strictly common sense explanations of research careers. Jeanine Leane's ego-histoire challenges temporal linear versions of progress and alludes to the unexpected reciprocity between the literature of Europe and Indigenous Australia, citing Alexis Wright: 'Non-fiction is often about the writer telling what it is safe to write' (Wright 2002, p. 13). This seems a good way to describe one of the boundaries that ego-histoire, when done well, pushes against in other essays in the volume. Gillian Cowlishaw offers a personal account of the nature of her ethnographic research among Indigenous people in Sydney's western suburbs, precipitated, in this case, by a loud rap on the door of her 'comfortable Glebe home'. Her approach makes a case for ethnography where personal relationships are at the core, 'with all the risks and responsibilities they entail', and accepts the inseparability of knowledge from its knower. As in other essays in this collection, Cowlishaw highlights the central importance of *experiencing*, in her case, particular social conditions and specific social relationships; an embodied experience that is likely to 'change your mind'. The collaborative essay by Frances Wyld and May-Britt Öhman brings together Indigenous intellectual traditions and historical experiences from Aboriginal Australia and Indigenous Europe. Based on the authors' own embodied experiences, this collaborative essay applies the methods of ego-histoire to call for 'a new version of history as academic discipline; a discipline which includes ... embodied vision and experience'. Stephen Muecke's contribution reflects on multi-linguality, metamorphosis and exchange, and builds the challenges of ego-histoire methodologies into the structure and style of his contribution, as does much as his subject-matter, something learned from Paddy Roe and the Kimberley elders he has collaborated with since the 1980s. It captures the distinctive mix of informality and formality, borrowing, homage and learning, which characterises ceremony, relationships and research, and in its shape reflects something of both the writer's experience and the impact of self-reflexivity on research. Philip Morrissey's essay wonders about a book washed up in a river, plays with the stereotype of the custodial elder, and argues against Deleuze and Guttari's presupposition of 'a collective enunciation' to point to the detailed revision of history embedded in fragments of remembered stories from childhood, read against the grain. Morrissey writes both of metamorphosis and of the body as a site of knowledge, felt and understood. This section concludes with Gillian Whitlock's essay, 'Nourishing Terrains: An Afterword', a place to catch our collective breath and reflect on the achievements and difficulties of ego-histoire.

## Endings: Impossible Possibilities

> 'I think identity is an endless, ever unfinished conversation'.
> Stuart Hall, 2013

Editing this book across four countries, Australia, France, Britain and Austria, has presented practical difficulties, and this volume has had a long gestation and production process. Along with the sometimes complex logistics of working together from different time zones, academic semesters and summers, it revealed to us that the word 'transnational', which sounds like a word that might glide, sounding a little like 'trans-fats', is 'in fact' harder to live and work with than to theorise about. Differences in opinion about what was deemed important, even who was deemed important, inside and outside of Australia, led to long conversations, mostly over email, that kept us busy and made us each question our assumptions about what ego-histoire could be and its value. We also found that writing ego-histoire makes us vulnerable in a way that writing about 'the other' does not. Perhaps more than other topics, such as the state, literature, politics, culture, history, or anthropology, writing one's own ego-histoire reminds us of that old post-modern 'truth', that there is no one definitive truth, and that truth and power are in such close proximity that it is often hard to see one for the other.

As authors of our own ego-histoires, we became aware of how we may consciously and unconsciously choose to ignore central aspects of our own stories that we perceive may make us vulnerable in the eyes of our readers. As editors, we saw how a referee's report could at times read less as a critique of an argument and more as a critique of a life, or person. In some cases, we hit upon longer than usual delays in getting re-writes returned, as authors realised the sort of critiques they may be exposing themselves to by publishing in this collection. We conclude from these experiments with ego-histoire that, despite many years now of the 'reflexive' turn in the social sciences and the growth of a high calibre genre of literary memoir, most scholars are still more familiar and comfortable with recording, analysing and writing the lives of others than their own. As editors, we became aware that there still lies, at the heart of much academia, an intolerance for anything that smacks of narcissism. But we remain convinced that, especially in academia, 'in pursuit of selflessness, attention to self can go underground and become an unconscious and corrosive attachment to pet theories and values' (Moore 1994, p. 71).

After a long-haul process, this manuscript is completed the same week that news of Stuart Hall's death reaches us. John Akmofah, director of 'The Stuart Hall Project' (2013), remembered:

> For my generation in the 1970s [Stuart Hall] was one of the few people of colour we saw on television who wasn't crooning, dancing or running. His very iconic presence on this most public of platforms suggested all manner of impossible possibilities. With him and through him we began to ask the indispensable questions: Who are we, what are we, and what could we become?

In essence, these are the questions that initiated the call for papers that formed this collection. We felt we had come to a place, historically, where it was useful—vital, in fact—to ask these kind of questions of ourselves regardless of our skin colour, national position, geographic origin, class, gender, family background or culture, in part to help us move away from the suffocating racial definitions and nationalism that served as a rationale for the brutalities of settler-colonialism that continue to haunt Australian Indigenous studies and scholars to this day. Toward the end of his life, Stuart Hall said: 'we always supposed that something would give us the definition of who we really are. Our class position, or our national position, or our geographic origins, or where our grandparents came from and I don't think that any one thing any longer will let us know who we are.' By undertaking a collective exploration of who we are, we sought to expand received ideas of what it means to be Aboriginal or non-Aboriginal, Australian or European, and to open the field of enquiry, not to forget history, but to look forward to impossible possibilities.

If ego-histoire is an academic tool that applies the historical methods normally used on others to oneself, the form of the exercise here may appear less academic than usual. When Nora reflected some years later on his original ego-histoire volume, he suggested that perhaps ego-histoire's real value lies in its failures, its license to explore, to defamiliarise, to produce forms of writing that do not obey existing generic boundaries. In exploring identity in this volume, some of the chapters are full of passion, some only partially 'unveil' their subjective interest in their research, and some reveal sharply, powerfully and vulnerably how digging around in one's own story to meet the other across diverse cultural and transnational divides can be difficult and sometimes deeply painful. The writing in this volume takes various forms, some autobiographical, some experimental, and some auto-ethnographical, and all are embodied in different ways in the lives of the authors.

Please read these stories with respect and kindness because, uncommonly, you might have a glance at the researchers' souls. We hope they will show you that not only our intellectual perspectives but also our backgrounds influence, but do not define, our identity and writing, and we hope they will give you a fresh scope on Australian Indigenous studies.

Many thanks to all the contributors who generously shared their stories.

## References

Alexander, J & M Gibson 2004, 'Queer Composition(s): Queer theory in the writing classroom', *Journal of Advanced Composition*, vol. 24, no. 1, pp. 1–21.

Ashcroft, B, G Griffiths & H Tiffin 2002, *The Empire Writes Back: Theory and practice in post-colonial literature*, Routledge, London and New York.

Bancel, N, P Blanchard, G Boetsch, É Deroo, S Lemaire, dirs 2002, *Zoos humains. De la Vénus hottentote aux reality shows*, Éd. La Découverte, Paris, coll.

Burton, A 2011, *Empire in Question: Reading, writing, and teaching British imperialism*, Duke University Press, Durham and London.

Castejon, V 2010, 'Identity and Identification: Aboriginality from the Spanish Civil War to the French Ghettos', in F Peters-Little, A Curthoys & J Docker (eds), *Passionate Histories: Myth, memory and Indigenous Australia*, ANU E Press, Canberra.

Castejon, V 2008, 'Une conciliation nécessaire après la Réconciliation ? L' Etat des affaires autochtones en Australie en 2006', Nedeljkovic Maryvonne, Conciliation and Reconciliation – Volume 1: Strategies in the Pacific, L'Harmattan, Paris, pp. 73–84.

Castejon, V 2007, 'L'identité aborigène sous les gouvernements d'Howard: un retour aux définitions imposées de l'Aboriginalité?', *Le Mensuel de l'Université* No. 20.

Castejon, V 2005a, *Les Aborigènes et l'apartheid politique australien*, L'Harmattan, Paris.

Castejon, V 2005b, 'A global Indigeneity?', in Russell West-Pavlov et al., *Who's Australia? – Whose Australia?: Politics, Society and Culture in Contemporary Australia*, WVT, Trier, pp. 99–106.

Castejon, V 2003, 'Aboriginal radical discourse in Australia: a reaction to political marginalisation, a redefinition of Aboriginality?', in J Gifford and G Zezulka-Mailloux (eds), *Culture and the State: Disability Studies and Indigenous Studies*, Canada Research Chair Studio, University of Alberta, Edmonton, pp. 133–140.

Castejon, V 2002, 'Aboriginal affairs: monologue or dialogue?', Journal of Australian Studies (JAS) No. 75, University of Queensland Press, pp. 27–31.

Chakrabarty, D 2000, *Provincializing Europe: Postcolonial thought and historical difference*, Princeton University Press, Princeton.

Cole, A 2010 'Making a Debut: Myths, memories and mimesis', in F Peters-Little, A Curthoys & J Docker (eds), *Passionate Histories: Myth, memory and Indigenous Australia*, ANU E Press, Canberra.

Cole, A 2009, 'Dancing with Myth and History', *Coolabah: Journal of Centre d'Estudis Australians*, vol. 3, pp. 252–258.

Cole, A 2005, '"Would have known it by the smell of it": Ella Hiscocks, uncommon ground — white women in Aboriginal history', in A Cole, V Haskins & F Paisley (eds), *Uncommon Ground: White women in Aboriginal history*, Aboriginal Studies Press, Canberra, pp. 153–171.

Cole, A 2003a, 'Gender and the forced Diaspora of Australian Aboriginal Communities in Australia', *Les Cahiers du CICLaS*, Australian Series Special edition, no. 2, September 2003, pp. 15–25.

Cole, A 2003b, 'Unwitting Soldiers: The working life of Matron Hiscocks at the Cootamundra Girls Home, NSW', *Aboriginal History*, vol. 27, pp. 146–162.

Cole, A 2000, '"The Glorified Flower": Gender, "biological" and "cultural" assimilation in Australia, 1937–69', unpublished PhD thesis, University of Technology, Sydney.

Cole, A 1994, 'Taking the Subordination of Women for Granted?: Aboriginal women's work and the concept of underemployment', in P Hetherington & P Maddern (eds), *Gender and Sexuality in History*, University of Western Australia Press, Nedlands.

Collins, P H 1991, 'Learning from the Outsider Within: The sociological significance of black feminist thought', in J Hartman & E Messer-Davidow (eds), *Gendering Knowledge*, University of Tennessee Press, Knoxville, pp. 40–65.

Curthoys, A 2012, 'Memory, History, and *Ego-Histoire*: Narrating and Re-enacting the Australian Freedom Ride', in A Burton (ed.), 'Writing History for Variety of Publics', special issue, *Historical Reflections/Reflexions Historiques,* vol. 38, no. 2, pp. 25–45.

De Martino, E 2002, 'Promesse e Minacce dell' Etnologia', in E De Martino (ed.), *Furore Simbolo Valore*, Feltrinelli, Campi del sapere, Milano, pp. 84–118.

Docker, J & A Curthoys 2010, *Is History Fiction?,* second edition, University of New South Wales Press, Sydney.

Haag, O 2009, 'Indigenous Australian Literature in German: Some considerations on reception, publication and translation', *Journal of the Association for the Study of Australian Literature*, special issue, *Australian Literature in a Global World,* pp. 1–17.

Haag, O 2008, 'From the Margins to the Mainstream: Towards a History of Published Indigenous Australian Autobiographies and Biographies', in A Haebich, F Peters-Little & P Read (eds), *Indigenous Biography and Autobiography*, ANU E Press and Aboriginal History Incorporated, Canberra, pp. 5–29.

Haraway, D 1988, 'Situated Knowledges: The science question in feminism and the privilege of partial perspectives', *Feminist Studies*, vol. 14, no. 3, pp. 575–599.

Hartsock, N 1998, *The Feminist Standpoint Revisited and Other Essays*, Westview Press, Boulder, Colorado.

Hiller, S 1991, *The Myth of Primitivism: Perspectives on art,* Routledge, London and New York.

Hornung 2013, 'Return Visits: The European background of transcultural life writing', *European Journal of Life Writing*, vol. 2, pp. 27–38.

Hughes, K 2012, 'Microhistories and Things that Matter: Opening spaces of possibility', *Australian Feminist Studies,* vol. 27, no. 73, pp. 269–278.

Hughes, K 2010, 'Fluid Waters: Cultural exchange in the land of the Ngarrindjeri, a poetics and a politics', *Le Simplegadi*, vol. 8, no. 8, pp. 24–35.

Jahoda, G 1999, *Images of Savages: Ancient roots of modern prejudice in western culture,* Routledge, London and New York.

James, C & G Marcus 1986, *Writing Culture: The poetics and politics of ethnography*, University of California Press, Berkeley.

Jurgensen, M 1995 (ed.), *German-Australian Cultural Relations Since 1945,* Peter Lang, Bern.

Kadar, M 1992, *Life Writing: From genre to critical practice*, University of Toronto Press, Toronto.

Kaplan, P 1999, 'Anthropology, History and Personal Narratives: Reflections on writing "African voices", "African Lives"', *Transactions of the Royal Historical Society*, vol. 9, pp. 283–290.

Moore, T 1994, *Care of the Soul*, HarperCollins, New York & London.

Moreton-Robinson, A 2004, 'Whiteness, Epistemology and Indigenous Representation', in A Moreton-Robinson (ed.), *Whitening Race: Essays in social and cultural criticism*, Aboriginal Studies Press, Canberra, pp. 75–88.

Moreton-Robinson, A 2002, *Talkin' Up to the White Woman: Indigenous women and feminism,* University of Queensland Press, St Lucia.

Morgan, M 1991, *Mutant Message Down Under,* Thorndike Press, Thorndike.

Nederveen Pieterse, J 1990, *Wit Over Zwart: Beelden van Afrika en zwarten in the westerse populaire cultuuur,* Koninklijk Instituut voor de Tropen, Amsterdam.

Nora, P 2010, *Rethinking France: Les lieux de memoire, Vol 4—Histories and Memories*, University of Chicago Press, Chicago.

Nora, P 2009, *Rethinking France:Les lieux de memoire, Vol 3—Legacies*, University of Chicago Press, Chicago.

Nora, P 2006, *Rethinking France:Les lieux de memoire, Vol 2—Space*, University of Chicago Press, Chicago.

Nora, P 1999, *Rethinking France: Les lieux de memoire, Vol 1—The State*, University of Chicago Press, Chicago.

Nora, P 2001 'L'Ego-Histoire est-elle Possible ?', *Historein*, vol. 3, pp. 19–26.

Nora, P et al 1987, *Essais d'Ego-Histoire*, Gallimard, Paris.

Okely, J & H Callaway 2001, (eds), *Anthropology and Autobiography*, Routledge, London and New York.

Olsen, T 1978, *Silences*, Delacorte Press, New York.

Passerini, L & A Geppert 2001, 'Historians in Flux: The concept, task, and challenge of ego-histoire', *Historein: A review of the past and other stories*, special issue, *European Ego-Histoires: Historiography and the self, 1970–2000*, vol. 3, pp. 7–18

Peters-Little, F, A Curthoys & J Docker (eds) 2010, *Passionate Histories: Myth, memory and Indigenous Australia*, ANU E Press, Canberra.

Poignant, R 2004, *Professional Savage: Captive lives and western spectacle*, University of New South Wales Press, Sydney.

Popkin, J 2007, 'Ego-Histoire Down Under: Australian historian-autobiographers', *Australian Historical Studies*, vol. 38, issue 129, pp. 106–123.

Reed-Danahay, D (ed.) 1997, *Auto/Ethnography: Rewriting the self and the social*, Berg, Oxford.

Summo-O'Connell, R (ed.) 2012, *Imagined Australia: Reflections around the reciprocal constructions of identity between Australia and Europe*, Peter Lang, Bern.

Thébaud, F 2009, 'Entre Parcours Intellectuel et Essai d'Ego-Histoire: Le poids du genre', *Genre et Histoire*, vol. 4. Available at: http://genrehistoire.revues.org/697?lang=en.

Thomas, N 1994 *Colonialism's Culture: Travel, anthropology and government*, Princeton University Press, Princeton.

Vinen, R 2011, 'The Poisoned Madeleine: The autobiographical turn in historical writing',*Journal of Contemporary History*, vol. 46 no. 3, pp. 531–554.

Whitlock, G L 2005, 'Disciplining the Child: Recent British academic memoir', *Auto/Biography Studies*, vol. 19, no. 1–2, pp. 46–58.

Wilson, N 2003, *Our Identity Is Our History and Our Future: A brief history of the west coast Aboriginal peoples — An extended research of the Tindale and Birdsell collections of genealogies of Indigenous peoples of the west coast of South Australia, 1928, 1939, and 1952,* Aboriginal Family History Project, South Australian Museum, Adelaide.

Wright, A 2002, 'Politics of Writing', *Southerly,* vol. 62, no. 2, pp. 10–21.

# 2. 'Introduction' from *Essais d'Ego-Histoire*

Pierre Nora

Translated by Stephen Muecke

With this volume, Gallimard's *Bibliothèque des Histoires* collection has produced a different kind of book. It is not the product of an investigation; it is more a laboratory experiment in which historians attempt to turn themselves into historians. These are documents, which will be treated as such by future historians, but documents also at one remove; not those that historians normally use, but ones which, for once, they have agreed to write about themselves. These essays can, and should, be read as they were written, independently of each other. But their writing, which has responded to a pressing need, and their collection here are, above all, contributing to the development of a genre: ego-history, a new genre for a new period of historical consciousness.

It begins at the crossroads of two important movements. The first starts by undermining the classical foundations of historical objectivity, the other by investing the historical gaze with the present.

For a century now, the scientific tradition as a whole has forced historians to absent themselves from the scene of their work, to hide their personalities behind their knowledge, to set up barricades with file notes, to run away to some other period, to only express themselves through others. The self is only briefly authorised in the thesis dedication or in the preface to a book. For the last 20 years, historiography has shown up the pretenses of this impersonality and how its guarantees lie on shaky ground. Historians today are, unlike their predecessors, ready to admit there is a close and quite intimate link between themselves and their work. No one is unaware that spelling out one's involvement with the material offers a better protection than vain protests about objectivity. The stumbling block thus turns into an advantage. The unveiling and analysis of existential involvement, rather than moving away from some impartial investigation, becomes instead an instrument for improving understanding.

The same body of traditions feed into a robust mistrust of a contemporary history which is still too recent to deserve any positive assessment. The way in which historians have conquered their own century, or even their present time, is one of the advances the discipline has made in recent decades. It has shown that supposedly prohibitive obstacles have been overcome, and that an historical understanding of the present was not only possible, but necessary. If we follow the line of this critical retreat from what is close at hand, should we not all be drawn into seeing ourselves, and most of all the historian, as objects of inquiry twice over?

This situation led us to ask a group of historians to attempt the experiment that we felt was virtually happening around us.[1] It was essential that they be well known to the public through their books, they had to be writing in enough different idioms to assure the representativeness of the discipline, and they should not have already done a similar job on their own account. Many would not take it on for personal reasons, though without ever denying the methodological interest of the proposal. So I am all the more grateful to Maurice Agulhon, Pierre Chaunu, Georges Duby, Raoul Girardet, Jacques Le Goff, Michelle Perrot and René Rémond for having taken the plunge, well aware of what they were in for and the risks involved. Should someone blurt out their surprise in the face of all this exhibitionism, the complaints should be directed only to the instigator, who was motivated by perfectly disinterested personal curiosity, and who set out the rules of the game.

These are not phony literary autobiographies, pointless intimate confessions, abstract professions of faith, or attempts at basic psychoanalysis. The exercise was to clearly set down one's own story [*histoire*] as one would write someone else's; to try to apply to oneself, each with his or her own particular style and methods, the same cool, encompassing and explanatory gaze that one so often directs towards others. The idea was to explain, as an historian, the link between the history you have made and the history that has made you.

Now, over to the reader to decide how the results bring newness to the tried and true genres, in terms of personal memory and of deepening our understanding of the times.

---

1    The prototype was provided by Philippe Ariès in *Un Historien du Dimanche* (Editions du Seuil, 1980), a work prefigured by Michel Winock, who told the story of two important years for him in *La République se Meurt* (Editions du Seuil, 1978). This was followed by Emmanuel Le Roy Ladurie, with *Paris-Montpellier, P.C.–P.S.U., 1945–1963*, (Gallimard, in the Témoins series, 1982). The genre starts up again, here and there. We could note, in particular, Pierre Goubert, 'Naissance d'un Historien: Hazards et racines', the preface to *La France d'Ancien Régime* (Mélanges Pierre Goubert, 1984), as well as 'L'Image dans le Tapis', an autobiographical introduction very close to ego-histoire that Mona Ozouf offered in *l'Ecole de la France*, (Gallimard, 1984), or, in completely opposite idioms, Ernest Labrousse, 'Entretiens Avec Christophe Charle', *Actes de la Recherche en Sciences Sociales*, April–June 1980, No. 32–33, and Georges Dumezil's *Entretiens*, with Didier Eribon (Gallimard, 1987), as well as the memoirs of Alain Besançon, *Une Génération*, (Julliard, 1987).

# SELF AND HISTORY

# 3. Ngarranga Barrangang:[1]
# Self and History, a Contemporary Aboriginal Journey

## Victoria Grieves

Sometimes I think I was born an historian. I was certainly a child who asked many, many questions. This was often a burden and an embarrassment to my mixed-race mother, who could be identified as Aboriginal in some contexts, and who was anxious to fly under the radar in conformist and settled rural New South Wales of the 1950s and 1960s.

On reflection, this is paradoxical, since it was the stories and memories of my mother, told to me in the isolated life we lived together, that inspired my interest in the past and the forces that shaped our lives. It is also the curious outsider position that I have occupied in various social contexts throughout my life, through the agency of mixed-race, and initially through my mother's choice of isolation from urban contexts, that has led me to reflection and enquiry. Latter day engagements with theoretical approaches to knowledge production, such as the 'border thinking' of Walter Mignolo, emphasise the unique opportunity for critical analysis possible for the *mestizo,* the ubiquitous and transnational person of mixed race. I now understand myself as an insider to particular knowledges and a product of world history.

I am writing this ego-histoire piece in the full sense of a history of self after the work of Pierre Nora that has become accessible to me. I can only read what is available in English and what I have read agrees with me entirely. I have long understood the position that Nora has framed: that when reading history we learn mostly about the person who wrote it. The aim of ego-histoire writing, then, is to uncover more of the person who is the historian by telling a history of the person's relationship to history. I write here of how it is that the person that is me—very close in many ways to others of mixed race origin in Australia—has found the pursuit of history so important in my life's journey and my survival. All of what I write here has been grist for the mill; it is the background to my theoretical approach to history making.

Thus it is that I write selectively for the first time of my formative years, my insatiable appetite for knowledge of the past and the inexorable development of

---

[1] 'Ngarranga Barrangang' is Warraimay for 'listen to me'; the deeper meaning is about having a right to speak, having the authority to speak of the matters at hand.

my identity. However, the experience that has made me is against the stereotype of what it means to be Aboriginal in Australia today. Importantly, even the word 'Aboriginal' and the contemporary meanings attached to it are historical in their nature and formation. I prefer to call myself Warraimay, a word that connects me to the country of my mother through the female line which is powerful in a matrilineal society. And that is what I am from, a family dominated by challenged, frail and wounded, but ultimately strong and surviving women.

My childhood and adolescence in a highly segregated settler colonial society were isolated and often lonely, marked by social isolation and later social ostracism. As an adult I have found that I am not so alone in the world, there are many others who share a similar experience on a national and global scale. The position I occupy is normal for many and some aspects of my being and my position in Australian society are unique and valuable.

My earliest memories are both of the sheep station near West Wyalong where we worked and of the wonderful heady days in the house of my grandparents on the mid-north coast. I say 'we worked' because I was apprenticed to my mother in the kitchen and in domestic work from the earliest age. She first sought work on stations before I was one year old and I generally accompanied her in whatever she was doing.

The first place we went to was a remote station in the vicinity of Brewarrina where my mother had a position as a housemaid. The station owner or manager would not allow her to bring me into the house and so she had to leave me alone in a hut built of rammed earth. She put my cot in the centre of the room, its legs in small tins of water, a barrier against crawling insects, and she went around the room with a stick, attempting to crush any spiders in the cracks in the walls. I asked her if I cried or fretted and she said no, I played happily most of the time. I think too that I was full of milk and a baby photo of the time attests to that. As does an aversion to cow's milk, even to this day.

I remember an idyllic life on the next station we went to, 'Carinyah', on the Ungarie Road near West Wyalong, when, at the age of three or four, I told myself I should never forget one seemingly perfect morning, and I never have. I picture it in my mind's eye like glimpses of another world entirely. The sensations return to me: the crackle of frost on the grass, the clear fresh air, full of scents of sweet pea, lilac, pencil pines, the daphne in huge pots on the verandah, and, later in the heat of summer, the scent of the tomato bushes as I brushed by them, the crush of stones beneath my sandalled feet. My life was full, with pet dog and bird companions, baby chicks, ducks and lambs, and adults who more than indulged me. Except for my mother, who swung unpredictably from indulgence to severe punishment and whose private anger was often frightening. What is important is that I was with her and for this I am now particularly grateful.

My mother and I spent most of the time in or near what was called 'the old kitchen', the original stationhouse that had been retained as an informal dining room where everyone ate together on a workday. In the normal, everyday work life of the station we had access to the whole of the house. When other family members visited from Sydney it became an 'upstairs, downstairs' situation and servant/master relationships were invoked. My mother became a rather reluctant and unhappy waitress for the table, instead of one of the people sitting at it and I was banned to the kitchen. I remember having a tantrum about that on one occasion. I was very small but not happy to be excluded.

The stationhouse proper, built from the profits made from wool and later than the old kitchen, was more formal, with higher ceilings and larger rooms, surrounded by a verandah and almost grand. Beds covered with rugs of fox fur both repelled and fascinated me. This was the domain of the aged and demented patriarch who I worried over. When on occasion he tore around the house naked and screaming, I tried to comfort him: 'Now, now, Poppy. Don't worry about that.' When he died I was heart-broken. I crept out of my room at night to witness the fistfight that occurred between his sons, probably over the inheritance. I adored his daughter, Muriel, who was very sweet, who frequently entered into conversation with this small child, and who had a great sense of fun. Much older than my mother and never married, she was also more relaxed about social mores. She taught me to squat and wee in the wheat shed when I was caught out, too far from the pit-toilet near the house. The blissful relief is also unforgettable.

My life here was full of play and discovery, indulged by the adults around me. I held impromptu concerts on the piano that I could not properly play and waited expectantly for applause that was enthusiastically given. While I was encouraged to play the piano rolls for something more tuneful, my feet could not reach the pedals, so I persisted in my own compositions. It must have been torturous for the small audience of station workers who nonetheless good-naturedly persisted with my childish whims and seemed to enjoy me immensely.

Through all of this, I had a sense of the arrival of these people in this country, from their talk and their demeanour and, after all, my mother and I had also arrived. The contrast of this country to the lush and bountiful coastal land we visited was palpable. In my own childish way I wondered how these outsiders got to be here and where they came from. The answers were that they came by horse and dray, from England. I imagined the place of their origins as a kind of kingdom, with flags flying from turrets, such as existed in the books of fairy tales.

I knew where I was from and that was my grandmother's country on the coast, well worn in my memory and never forgotten, that always seemed to have been there, a part of the natural world that we went out into and lived on when we visited. I really wanted to be there all the time and suffered extreme homesickness when we left. The small timber house by the lake that my grandparents lived in could hardly contain the huge family they had. For all the bareness and poverty, my heart was there with my grandparents, in and around the saltwater of the sea and freshwater of the river and lake. By contrast, I had a sense of the impermanence of the green oasis of the farmstead that we rarely left to go out into the paddocks. There it was dry and brown and often withered and we were always in the shelter of a vehicle and, wearing stout boots, only vicariously in contact with the earth. The impermanence of 'Carinyah' was a fact; it has long been in ruins. That family lasted only three generations on the land that was taken up for farming in the mid-nineteenth century. There is no lasting legacy of their time there. They would be long forgotten with the deaths of their contemporaries and there is no lasting memorial to that farming operation.

Every visitor to that farm in the time I was there, until about seven years of age, is remembered by me. That is not so difficult, as there were not very many. I remember particularly the swaggies who were still on the road long after the depression and the war had ended. Some were old fellas who knew no other life and others were younger, maybe shell-shocked from war experiences, and who now preferred a solitary life. They were not strong, often shy and humble. My mother was always kind to them and they mostly preferred to do some work in exchange for food, so tasks were found for them to do, such as chopping wood, raking or cleaning the yard. They were given food and drink, strong black sweet tea at the station and sandwiches packed for them on the road. There was always the small brown child that was me there, dressed in gathered cotton and lace trimmed dresses, and tiny white-sandalled feet, watching and thinking.

Many years later when I was appointed as the inaugural Koori Teaching Fellow at Charles Sturt University in Bathurst I remembered a colleague from when he was a skinny boy in short khaki shorts, scrambling over the back of a produce truck with his twin brother. Both he and I were intrigued by the history and the social stratification of country towns that put paid to the idea of a completely egalitarian Australia. West Wyalong with its 'Top Town' where the poor lived and Cootamundra with its equivalent 'The Warren' were in contrast to 'The Hill' of the more well-to-do and betrayed the class stratification that underlies the social life of these places. I was never really a part of it. I was apart in the beginning and later in life have felt more comfortable keeping myself apart. Many years later, when I read Jill Ker Conway's celebrated account of an Australian girl's country childhood, *The Road from Coorain*, there was little for me to recognise as similar to the life she led on the farm near Hillston, not so far from West Wyalong and 'Carinyah'. Her family had taken up land further west, more recently than the established squatters that my mother worked for.

Hers was an earlier childhood than mine. However, I do recognise the class nature and male domination of Australian society that she was made aware of and which led her to be active in breaking down barriers for disadvantaged women in her work in the USA. My experience also includes that of racism and epistemic violence in the academy and in the whole of my education.

School for me began in the town of West Wyalong for two years, then one year in Yass, one at Muttama, and the rest in the town of Cootamundra. At the beginning it was truly terrifying and uncomfortable. I never felt settled and was mostly miserable. I was shocked by the aggression and cruelty of the other children to each other, especially in the toilet block and the weathershed. I stayed out of their way as much as I could, though I was called a greasy Greek, partly a play on my surname but also in recognition of my colour. Even without this, I would have much preferred to stay home. Miserable and unhappy is the story of my whole school experience, except for a year at the one-teacher school at Muttama, near Cootamundra. The time with Mr Price at this school was a delight.

Moving from 'Carinyah' and eventually resettling on a farm that included both 'Hamilton' and 'Lochinvar' near Muttama and Cootamundra, where my mother again found work, was a difficult period for me. I became a reader as a way of escaping from the difficulties of my life. During long periods of illness from ear, nose and throat infections I worked my way through a set of encyclopaedias, a fact that fascinated but also alarmed my mother. Newnes Pictorial Knowledge, these quaint British texts were mostly unremarkable except for the stories from ancient Greece and Rome. These stories were framed as foundational to English society and I admit to having trouble working that out from my position. As a child in the colony, far from the metropole, I was perplexed about this. It did not relate to my life in any way.

By the age of ten, when I travelled for an hour and a half each way to school, I was also a daily visitor to the Cootamundra Library in the school lunchtime and was reading as much as a book a day. I remember the books there fondly and I fear going back because the storybooks that I treasured would be long gone. I miss them like old friends and harbour a secret wish that is difficult for me to utter: that they will all be there if ever I do go back. I would treasure them and remember many of them now. Part of my life's work has been the expression of my love of books; the development of a huge personal library that threatens to take over my life.

While many fiction books introduced me to a historical consciousness, at about 13 or 14 years of age I began to read history, fascinated by world events and facts about the past. I was never able to study history at school because it clashed with domestic science on the timetable. At first I wanted to take domestic science as it was easy for me and I was successful at it, having long been tutored by my mother. By senior school, when I received a Commonwealth Secondary Scholarship to continue to years 11 and 12, I agreed to stay at school if I could enrol in history. Perhaps the only time my mother came to my school was at the request of the headmaster to discuss this. They conscripted my mother into the scheme to have me continue with domestic science. The irony of this: my mother, who, by her own admission, had worked like a slave in domestic work. History and domestic work still play a tug of war in my life to this day.

My main engagement with Cootamundra was through school, as we lived 25 miles from the town. At the school there were Aboriginal girls who lived a segregated existence and who resided in the Aboriginal Girls Home on the edge of the town. They had a matron who drove them everywhere, to and from school mostly, in a bus. I asked why they were there and my mother told me they were orphans. 'Orphans!' I exclaimed in alarm. 'What happened to their parents?' I was struck by the thought of all these people dying at the same time. My mother did not want to answer questions about them. Maybe she did not really know the full story. Maybe she did.

It was not possible for me to mention to my mother that I was called racist names by other children at school, names that had me feel tense all over my body, especially in my stomach, instantly hot in my face, and the tears spring to my eyes. I had no idea what it meant to be a 'coon', or a 'boong', or to have a 'touch of the tar', or that all I needed was 'a bone in the nose' to be fully black and recognisable as such. I also had to endure the most obscene and profane racist 'jokes' about Aboriginal people, and when I did not see the humour I was derided for being a bad sport and too serious. I had nothing to say when this happened and just hoped it would go away. I can't describe my feelings and there was no support for me. At school I was very anxious, sometimes burst into tears, and stuttered so badly that I could not really speak from eight until 14 years of age. I had unexplainable health problems. I was confused and bewildered.

How could I report to the teachers harassment that was commonplace and also somehow a shameful thing about me? The environment at school actively discouraged me from achievement. Sometimes when I was in the town after school, running errands for my mother (who preferred not to leave the house) people would ask me if I was 'one of the little girls from the home'. Only recently did I realise with a start that if I had said yes, they would have called the police. It was always the police who dealt with the girls when they tried to run away or to take the liberty of movement around the town.

Even now I find the prospect of telling of my friendships with girls from the home then and since very painful and I won't go into those stories here. Suffice to say that any friendships were more than difficult across the race divide, and they were more divided from society than anyone. As for my understanding of the reality of the Aboriginal Girls Home at Cootamundra, it was not until some ten years later, when I was finally in Redfern in Sydney and Peter Read had published a booklet 'The Stolen Generations: The removal of Aboriginal children in New South Wales, 1883–1969' through the NSW Department of Aboriginal Affairs, that I began to learn the truth about child removal. A realisation hit me with full force: that the parents must have really died, but died inside, under the full impact of this genocidal policy. More recently, I have been overcome and wept over growing up in a town with a concentration camp for girls on the edge of it. That is what it was, a fascist conceit of white Australia, and the way it was in Cootamundra, it was alarmingly normal.

There were several of us who were coloured and who were flying under the radar as much as possible as children in school. For me, this was not conscious and I only acted on hints and concerns of my mother. There was some unspoken recognition between us coloured kids at school, but any tentative attempts I made to seek common ground were not taken up. I remember not only girls from school but some older boys that were around town and surveilled closely by the law, who I suspected shared my position, whatever that was. However, there was only a deep fear of recognition, no solidarity. Now I know that some have family names that are recognisable as Aboriginal, such as Roberts, Little, Sutton and Buckley from the Wiradjuri.

Many other (white) people asked me if I was Aboriginal or not—in school, down the street, at the tennis—and I did not know how to answer it. This may have been construed as evasion at the time, but I was a child whose identity was forming, and I was not really informed by my mother. I am sure the people who asked me did so because I was a child and I might have let something out. Asking my mother was a difficult matter because, as most children do, I instinctively knew her no-go zones of discussion. There was a conversation I initiated, after a long period of people asking me if I was Aboriginal, when I was about fourteen. They did not and would not ask my mother. It was extraordinarily stressful for me to raise the topic; I felt it in my stomach and a loud beating sound in my head. The conversation went something like this:

'Mum, what are we?'

'What are we? What do you mean?'

'Well, we are different aren't we?'

'Different? In what way?'

'Well, the colour of our skin. You know how you said we have olive skin.'

'Have you heard of the Black Irish?'

'No.'

'Pop's grandmother was Irish. That's where it comes from. The Black Irish'.

Now I wonder, what was I to do with that? I went back and dutifully told the people who had asked me that I was, in fact, one of the Black Irish!

Twelve years later I caught up with a friend who had lived on a farm nearby. She had her own set of family difficulties and fled to England when she could. There she met and married a black man from Trinidad. They had a young family when my children were also small. When we met at this time, I told her I had important news:

'I am Aboriginal. My mother and I, we're Aboriginal!'

'Of course you are. Everyone at Muttama and Cootamundra knew you were Aboriginal.'

'Why didn't you tell me?'

'I thought you knew. And anyway I didn't think it made any difference.'

I was in awe of her strength of character, and the memory of her acceptance of me makes me emotional even now. I stay in touch with her and will always enjoy her wonderful soul. Because it did matter to other people, and I did feel discrimination and unfair judgements. The impact of this was as deficiencies on my part and in such a context it is very difficult to retain self-esteem. This is what it means to be an Aboriginal person living within a settler colonial regime. I know this from my own life experience. That I am Aboriginal made a difference to others but not to her. She was a person who sat next to me on the school bus where I often sat alone.

The times that I spent with the farmer who became my (step)father have become precious memories for me. He was gaunt and lean, no stranger to hard work, patient, understanding and fostered a deep independence in me. Though I did not know it at the time, he was a man who embodied decency; quiet, humble, capable and kind. He was hard when he needed to be. There was no way that he would be flash. There was always a subtext of dry humour when you were around him. Everything in the seemingly ordinary days, including the antics of dogs, horses, chickens and sheep, contributed to a deep but understated sense of fun. He had also spent many years shearing, on the Hay, Hell and Booligal run amongst others, and was a gun in his time. I enjoyed immensely travelling about the paddocks with him in the blue Dodge truck he drove. He spoke to it as if it had a personality and of course I began to speak to it too; the truck was there as a third person in our halted conversations and made its opinion known by various splutters and jerks. He gave me a licence for freedom on a horse or on a bike and I explored the extent of the 2,000 acres or so and the laneway that went by the properties, seeking and absorbing the personality and history of that land as if a sponge. He introduced me to responsibility by giving me the tasks to do with medicating the stock, including injecting pigs when to everyone's great amusement I found out the toughness of bacon rind. I learnt some mechanics, as all of the machinery for cropping was continually breaking down, and I was the one standing by handing over the tools as assistant or wielding the grease gun. I learnt how to trap foxes and rabbits and how to use a rifle and shotgun to shoot ducks, rabbits and snakes. Once he took me with him to shoot the dying sheep in the midst of drought when many farmers would not waste the bullets; he could not see them suffering with no hope of recovery.

Through my time with him, the past of the farm became alive to me. There were paddocks named after the Aboriginal shepherds who were once there, Paul and Barmy. I have come to understand the latter was no doubt *Biami*, from the name of the creation ancestor for Wiradjuri people. This would have been a man of high degree. When the rest of the Aboriginal people who worked on the station left, (the question of where they went haunts me to this day), the old fella wanted to stay. His name is the clue to his status; this man may have embodied Law as a senior lawman. He lived in a shack in the back paddock by a spring of groundwater and my father and his family would bring him food from time to time. I spent many hours searching for a vestige of the old hut when I was an adolescent. I would ask, 'Was it here?' And he would answer, 'No, up a bit further'. I would say, 'Are you sure?' And here I was, walking up and down and across the side of a big hill, looking for some remains of the hut, while he was at the bottom mending a fence or doing something similar.

It was in this vicinity that I was riding the old creamy mare right on dusk and she reared up all of a sudden and headed for home. At that moment, while clutching wildly at the saddle pommel, I saw small lights dancing around on the top of a ridge nearby. I can't describe my feeling of awe, fear and wonderment. My father was highly amused at the unusual speed of old Creamy and as we entered the house paddock asked what had happened. Yes, he said, that's what spooked her, the Min-Min lights. He went on to explain the phenomenon as if it was ordinary and everyday. Amongst other things I learnt how animals are more sensitive to these spiritual experiences, ruptures of the Dreaming, than people. My father knew many things, could predict rain a week ahead by observing the movements in the natural environment. My white father had grown up amongst Aboriginal people on what was at that time an isolated farm. He learnt from them and then he was also teaching me. He was in tune with something of the deep spiritual movement of this country and this was the reason why he found it possible to marry my mother. When I read Patrick White's *The Tree of Man* I thought he could have modelled Stan and Amy at least to some extent, on my parents.

Our lives on the farm were not centred on the radio but it was there at mealtimes, especially in school holidays. I enjoyed the ABC News at breakfast, 'Dad and Dave' at lunchtime, and the news and various serials on some evenings. Whenever girls tried to escape from the Aboriginal Girls Home in Cootamundra and ran out along one of the roads, heading home or just heading anywhere else I guess, it was reported on the radio. I was perplexed and worried by this, wondering who it was, why she had run away, and if she was safe.

My interest was piqued at the time of the Freedom Rides through northwest NSW in 1965. A student action group from the University of Sydney had hired a bus and invited a prominent Aboriginal spokesperson, Charles Perkins, to join them. Each day I would be listening for this news. I was excited by it and not sure why. I felt as if I was busting inside. I could not talk about it much to anyone, but those around me must have sensed my excitement. I remember my mother at the sink with her back to me, clattering the washing-up as the news report of the Freedom Rides was broadcast. Then, without even turning, she said, 'It won't make any difference to anything'. There was such a note of defeat and resignation in her voice; it felt like death to me. In more recent years I have begun to think she was right, so little has improved, and there have been backwards steps. As for the Freedom Riders, I was all the time wondering if they were going to get to Cootamundra. In fact I still don't understand why they did not get there and protest, since that Aboriginal Girls Home was a site of huge cruelty and injustice.

My mother fed me tantalising titbits of information, stories of her life as a child, and a sprinkling of words from our language, whetting my appetite for our family history. Paradoxically, perhaps, she did not want me to explore it. She wanted me to leave well enough alone. In the spirit of the child who always takes direction from the life of the parent, even against the express wishes of the parent, I did eventually set out on that road. The journey to establish the truth of my family history, over 35 years of off and on research, culminated when I was given a photograph of the Aboriginal woman from whom we are all descended, Anne Butler. All these years the photo had been in an old biscuit tin in someone's back shed. She looked so familiar to me and to other family members. I thought, 'Yes, that is her'. That recognition, very deep, I do not understand. Every picture tells a story but this one more than most for me.

**The woman in this photograph is Mrs Anne McClymont nee Butler and the children are from left John Alexander and Mary Wilhelmina, who is the author's great grandmother.**

Source: Courtesy of Eric Dates.

This photograph dates from the mid-1860s and is not of the genre of the formal posed photographs of the time. It looks like a homegrown photograph, perhaps taken by her husband, William McClymont, or by another member of his family. She is seated in grass that forms a wild and unusual background. She has my great-grandmother, Mary Wilhelmina, on her lap and a son, John Alexander, beside them. She has a very cute small hat on, with a voile veil draped around it and her face. Her blouse has sleeves to the wrist and ruffles at the wrist and neck. Maybe it is made of silk. The children are also dressed very well in the hand-made, elaborate velvet dresses of the day, worn by boys as well as girls. Her wedding ring is visible on elegant hands that I recognise as like mine but more my mother's. She looks content and in love.

Much of what passes for Aboriginal history which has developed since then has been sometimes exciting, but overall difficult for me to relate to personally. I am aware that it barely reaches members of my family and my countrymen and women, many of whom remain illiterate. My engagement with history has become an attempt to address aspects of my wellbeing and that of my family and kin. This puts me outside of the institution of history in Australia.

Surprisingly, I graduated with honours and a double major in history in 1981, the first Aboriginal graduate with honours and the first with a degree in history. In this, I owe a great deal to my supervisor, Professor Beverley Kingston, whose work is celebrated in women's history and who I credit with teaching me to think critically. She met my questions only with more questions, forcing awareness of the complexity of the past. The natural progression for me was into a PhD program, and I did enrol, but was racially vilified by my supervisor so promptly did a disappearing act. I was recruited into Tranby Aboriginal College in Glebe as the first head teacher of a tertiary preparation course and shared responsibility for coordinating the Aboriginal Studies program.

Tranby met all of my expectations. It was cutting edge in terms of teaching methodologies and curriculum development. There was an opportunity to learn from the students and community people from across the whole of the country who dropped into our Aboriginal home and haven. Regular visitors that I was able to engage with included John Newfong, Oodgeroo Noonuccal, Jack Davis, Joe McGuinness, Jim Everett, Garry Williams, Gary Foley, Mick Miller, Jack Walker, Shorty O'Neill, and Harry Mumbulla. We were cossetted by the wonderful Kevin Cook, the lynchpin of the vast connections that nurtured Tranby. Kevin told me they had known of me over at the University of NSW for some time. I asked him why they had not come and got me earlier! So many bright and dedicated staff members, both Aboriginal and non-Aboriginal, made the programs excellent, relevant and rigorous, arguably equal to a cutting-edge university.

Employed at a university, I am a marginal academic in Australia; it is an enormous struggle to produce Indigenous knowledges within the western academy. Somehow I have held on to my engagement with history in spite of uncertain employment prospects. I have a strong conviction that it is our Aboriginal understanding of history that will bring about change for social justice. It has not been easy, but I would not have it any other way. Everything that has occurred has been valuable including being made unwelcome on racial grounds, especially within PhD programs at two universities, whereby I was awarded the degree much later than I should have been in a just world.

I have been extremely fortunate to have met and learned from people of great worth including my kin, the late Patricia Davis Hurst, Mae Simon, Norma Fisher, Vilma Simon and others too many to mention. Others include Louise Campbell, Jean Carter, John Heath, Grace Close, and Micko and Neville Donovan, lawmen. Then there are some of the first of the Aboriginal health workers at community level in NSW who taught me while I was ostensibly teaching them. The time I spent with them in 1986 was my first experience as a lecturer in a university and I am immensely grateful to them for much of what I have learnt and now understand as important in our knowledge production.

3. Ngarranga Barrangang

Photograph of students and staff in the Diploma of Aboriginal Health and Community Development 1986. Some people in this photograph are now deceased and very much missed by all of us. The people whose names could not be remembered are not forgotten. My thanks to Edna Craigie who helped me to name the people in the photograph, who are as follows: Back row from the left: David Nean, Quirindi/Newcastle; Terry Doolan, Dubbo/Wilcannia; Vicki Grieves, Forster/ Redfern (staff); Lurline Ardler, Wreck Bay; Jan Yow Yeh, Redfern; Minnie lane. Goodooga; Margaret Morgan, Deniliquin; Cheryl Cowan, Nowra; Pamela Duncan, Toomelah; Vince Quayle, Dareton; Jenny Beale, Western Sydney (staff); Hal – (staff). Middle row: unknown; unknown (staff); Vince Kennedy, Walgett. Front row: unknown; Carl McGrady, Toomelah/ Tenterfield; Teresa Ellis, Western Sydney; Graeme Skinner, Lismore; Edna Craigie, Terry Hie Hie/ Moree; ? Fay Williams, La Perouse.

Source: Victoria Grieves.

There are also many others who influence my history writing, such as Steven Tjampitjinpa Patrick of the Walpiri, and Jim Everett from Tasmania. My network is nationwide, international and also deep. Laurelyn Whitt, a Choctaw scholar, has been my friend and colleague for 20 years and first gave me the opportunity to publish. I have had the opportunity to learn about the important philosophical underpinnings to many Aboriginal cultures and knowledge bases and I am grateful (Grieves 2009).

The process of writing history has sometimes been an immense emotional burden, such as when writing of my mother's great uncles, Billy and Johnny (Grieves 2011). This project had me cloistered in a house in my country for six weeks with the research evidence and my own fragile being. A local elder was practically the only person I spoke to at length during this time, she would call by and have me talk to her about what I was writing. She was the best of counsellors who then reported to the others, who have been a wonderful support. There were times when I felt the burden of this history as unbearable, the realisation that we as a family and as a people were actually struggling to come out of the institution of slavery. How this explained the existential angst of my mother's generation and the effects on me. I changed as a person through this experience.

History has taken me into the belly of the beast, into the netherworld of genocide and brutality, secrets and lies, the complexity and mystery of interracial sexual attraction and intimacies and the social consequences for the mothers, fathers and the children. It has taught me about gender relationships that betray slavery and fascist social organisation. As a descendant of survivors of these regimes along with others, I am as they are, extraordinarily well equipped to explore and develop these histories that get to the nub of colonial relations and colonial aspirations. I want to bring the histories that spring from our own world-view into the academy.

Paradoxically, my survival is through an engagement with history and this, as I have outlined here, is the best side of my life, it overshadows all of the worst experiences and gives me a reason to be alive. It is also this historical endeavour that has made me what I am, that has helped to forge my identity over time. I was asked today, as I often am, which community I feel most accepts me in Australia, the black or the white. I often find such questions intrusive. They come from an acceptance of the binary of segregationist ideologies that I do not share. Nonetheless, I am often obliged to respond, given that I do live in a highly segregated, race-conscious society. My answer was honest, not wishful thinking, which would have me say both communities accept me equally. The truth is that I am black I can never be white, only white blackfellas, coconuts, are truly accepted by white society. I have to say, in closing, that this settler colonial nation is most marked by the lack of a just and proper settlement or any vestige of fair dealing for my people. If this were different then my identity would also be different. Perhaps, all too late, history will be the judge.

## References

Conway, J K 1990, *The Road from Coorain,* Vintage, New York.

Grieves, V 2009, 'Aboriginal Spirituality: Aboriginal philosophy, the basis of Aboriginal social and emotional wellbeing', Discussion Paper No. 9, Cooperative Research Centre for Aboriginal Health (CRCAH), Darwin.

Grieves, V 2011, 'The McClymonts of Nabiac: Interracial marriage, inheritance and dispossession in nineteenth century New South Wales society', in A Hollan and B Brookes (eds), *Rethinking the Racial Moment: Essays on the colonial encounter*, Cambridge Scholars Publishing, Cambridge, pp. 125–156.

Mignolo, W 2000 *Local Histories/Global Designs: Coloniality, subaltern knowledges and border thinking*, Princeton University Press, Princeton.

Read, P 1981, 'The Stolen Generations: The removal of Aboriginal children in New South Wales, 1883–1969', NSW Department of Aboriginal Affairs, Sydney.

White, P 1955, *The Tree of Man,* Random House, New York.

# 4. A Personal Journey with Anangu History[1]

Bill Edwards

## Early Life

Despite an interest in history during school years, my engagement in postgraduate historical research was delayed until retirement. My childhood home was in the town of Lubeck, in the Wimmera district of Victoria, where my paternal grandparents, having migrated from Wales, opened a general store in 1877. My parents later conducted this business until retirement in 1952. In the 1930s, the population of Lubeck, with its store, post office, hotel, school, hall, two churches and railway station, was approximately 75, with a similar number living on farms in the surrounding area. Living in this small country town, it was beyond imagination that one might progress to university. I left school in 1946 to work in a bank, just as had my three older siblings. A feeling of call to train for the Presbyterian Church ministry led to enrolment in the University of Melbourne in 1950. Appointed to an Aboriginal mission in 1958, I worked for two decades with Anangu Aboriginal people. This experience not only shaped my subsequent life and work on every level, but also prepared me to lecture in Aboriginal Studies in the first Indigenous tertiary education unit in Australia. In this role, I confronted the tendency of some academics to negatively stereotype Aboriginal missions.

As a child in the Wimmera, my knowledge of and contact with Aboriginal people was extremely limited. Before white settlement, this region was occupied by the Jardwadjali people (Clark 1990, p. 256). A century later, these people had been largely forgotten. The only reminders of their earlier presence were grindstones at a sandhill west of Lubeck which had been a campsite, and tree trunks from which bark had been cut to make artefacts. Monuments on nearby roadsides in the 1930s bore inscriptions: 'Major Mitchell passed by here'. These implied that Mitchell's exploratory expedition was the beginning of history in the region, reflecting what W. E. H. Stanner identified as 'the great Australian silence' in Australian history (Stanner 1969, p. 18). I knew that Aboriginal men played for Dimboola in the Wimmera Football League. They were descendants of the Wergaia people who found refuge at Ebenezer Mission, established on the

---

[1] I would like to thank Karen Hughes for her editorial advice and insightful comments on earlier drafts of this chapter.

banks of the Wimmera River approximately 70 kilometres north-west of Lubeck in 1863. Later, in retirement, I researched the history of Ebenezer as part of a thesis on Moravian Aboriginal Missions in Australia (Edwards 2007). A feature of the Great Depression period of my early years was the movement of swagmen travelling from town to town on goods-trains, camping in railway sheds and obtaining food by doing odd jobs. I recall one of them being Aboriginal, probably descended from Ebenezer residents. In return for food, he gave my father an incised boomerang, now one of my prized possessions. The community service of my parents in this small town and my early observation of their assistance to struggling families in that post-depression period provided a model for my later commitment to support Indigenous people in their struggles.

In that era, few Aboriginal people were household names in mainstream Australia. In the 1930s, David Unaipon from Port McLeay near the mouth of the River Murray in South Australia toured that state and Victoria to speak in churches and other places about his people. In 1945, the Aboriginal Tenor, Harold Blair, sang on the Australian Amateur Hour radio program. In 1949, I attended an Easter Convention in the Wimmera town of Warracknabeal. We camped at the local showgrounds. On a pavilion wall was a photograph of a short stocky Aboriginal man, Doug Nicholls, who won the Warracknabeal Gift footrace in 1929, the year of my birth. As a boy, I collected cards with pictures of Australian Rules footballers. These included Doug Nicholls as a Fitzroy footballer, probably the first Aboriginal player in the Victorian Football League. By the 1940s, the Central Australian landscape painter, Albert Namatjira, was receiving national recognition.

University studies in the 1950s did little to enlarge my knowledge of Aboriginal people. They were ignored in history and other disciplines, and there were probably no Aboriginal students enrolled at the university. My studies in history were confined to Ancient, British, Modern and Church history subjects. However, limited association with Aboriginal people deepened my interest and led eventually to my involvement with them. In 1954, I visited universities around Australia as a staff-worker with a student Christian organisation, the Inter-Varsity Fellowship. A visit to Adelaide in March coincided with the royal tour of Queen Elizabeth and Prince Phillip. Pitjantjatjara people from Ernabella Mission in the north-west of South Australia expressed interest in seeing this couple. They sold dingo scalps for the government bounty to pay for petrol and were driven 1,500 kilometres on the back of a truck, mostly on dirt roads.

This group of young Pitjantjatjara people learned western part singing in the Ernabella School and sang as the Ernabella Choir. I heard them sing in the Adelaide Teachers College and visited them at their accommodation at the Tusmore Presbyterian Church. I could not have imagined that four years later I would be conducting this choir. In 1955, I visited Alice Springs with a work party that laid a forecourt for the John Flynn Memorial Church. On the road we met an Ernabella staff member and a Pitjantjatjara man, Andy Tjilari, who were travelling from the Finke railway township to Ernabella. I had met Tjilari in Adelaide with the choir. He was to become a close colleague and lifelong friend as we reciprocally taught each other deeper aspects of our respective cultures. Our relationship reflected a basic Anangu concept, *ngapartji ngapartji*, 'in turn in turn'.

Two events at university furthered my interest in Aboriginal people. First, students, concerned at the lack of Aboriginal students, raised funds to provide scholarships. This culminated in the establishment of Abschol (Attwood 2003, p. 283). I screened a film on Ernabella, *Men of the Mulga,* as a fund raiser for Abschol. Secondly, in my final year, I attended a university meeting at which Doug Nicholls, then pastor of an Aboriginal church in Fitzroy, Melbourne, reported on his visit to Western Australia to investigate the effects of the Woomera rocket range on Aboriginal people in the Western Desert region. His report alerted me to ways in which the rights of Aboriginal people were ignored by governments and deepened my interest in the people of this remote region (Clark, 1972). Although this interest was initially motivated by evangelical concerns, contact with students whose concerns were more political broadened my focus as we discussed the burning issues of the 1950s, such as the Korean War and the spread of communist influence in Asia. Doug Nicholls' talk in particular was pivotal to growing my awareness of the dispossession suffered by Aboriginal people and my later involvement interpreting in land rights negotiations. While there was nothing in my university courses to inform me about Aboriginal culture and history, these contacts awakened my interest in Indigenous issues.

During this final year, I heard that there was a vacancy on a north Queensland mission and was invited to meet the Mission Board Secretary during the 1957 Presbyterian Church General Assembly in Melbourne. As an emergency situation had arisen at Ernabella, I was invited to go there. Having had those earlier contacts with Ernabella people and knowing something of the history and policies of the mission through these contacts, I had no hesitation in accepting this offer.

After working at Ernabella for a while, I suspected that the Board appointed me not on the grounds of my tertiary studies but because of my experiences in a country store and in banking. At Ernabella, I was to act as store-keeper and book-keeper among many other tasks. In Melbourne, I was unable to study anthropology to prepare for work in another cultural context, as the universities of Sydney and Western Australia were the only Australian universities offering regular courses in the discipline. Donald Thomson offered a short course in anthropology to honours history students, but when I inquired about auditing this course in 1957 it was unavailable because Thomson was embarking on one of his expeditions to the 'Bindabus' (Pintubi) in Central Australia (Batty 2006, p. iv). There were few textbooks on Aboriginal culture available. I went armed with A. P. Elkin's *The Australian Aborigines: How to understand them* (Elkin 1956) which gave me insights into basic Aboriginal concepts related to the Dreaming and into the intricacies of their kinship systems.

**Bill Edwards serving in the Ernabella trading store.**

Source: Photograph from Bill Edwards collection. Courtesy Ara Irititja Project Netley, South Australia.

In January 1958 I commenced a summer Institute of Linguistics course offered by the Wycliffe Bible Translators. This course, held at Belgrave Heights, east of Melbourne, provided training in phonetics, phonemics and grammar in order to assist missionaries to learn a previously unwritten language and devise an alphabet. It also provided some preparation for engagement in a cross-cultural context.

## Ernabella Mission

Ernabella Mission was established in 1937 in the lands of the Yankunytjatjara and Pitjantjanytjara peoples. These were two dialects of the Western Desert language group who refer to themselves as Anangu, a term meaning person or body. They occupy the Musgrave, Mann and Tomkinson ranges which stretch along the South Australia/Northern Territory border and sandhill country to the north and south of the ranges. Living as hunter-gatherers in small groups associated with the totemic centres related to the various species of the region such as the *malu* (kangaroo), *kalaya* (emu), *ngintaka* (perentie) and *ili* (native fig), they exploited the resources of the land as they moved from one water supply to another (Edwards 2004, pp. 37–47). Rituals were designed to ensure the continued supply of these resources.

The role of a Scottish-born surgeon, Dr Charles Duguid, was central to the establishment of Ernabella in 1937 (Kerin 2011). He and his wife Phyllis (née Lade) became strong advocates for the rights of Aboriginal people. In 1934, in his Adelaide practice, Duguid heard from a patient who had worked in Arnhem Land of abuses suffered by Aboriginal people in that region. He travelled to Alice Springs to investigate and was appalled by the living conditions of Aborigines and by stories of mistreatment (Duguid 1963, pp. 20–25). At Hermannsburg Mission, Pastor F. W. Albrecht suggested that Duguid examine the situation in the far north-west of South Australia. Duguid envisaged that:

> An intelligent Christian mission, in my mind, is the only way, but those who attempt the task must have a knowledge of anthropology, must learn the language of the natives, and must have in them the spirit of Christ (Advertiser, 1934, p. 6).

Driving to Ernabella in 1935, Duguid observed discrimination on cattle stations and frontier settlements and heard reports of abuse of Aboriginal men's labour and the sexual abuse of women. He advocated the establishment of a mission to act as a buffer between the Aborigines and the encroaching white settlers and in 1936 persuaded the General Assembly of the Presbyterian Church to purchase the Ernabella lease. Ernabella Mission was thus administered by the Presbyterian Board of Missions from 1937 until 1973, when control was transferred to the Ernabella Community Council Inc.

Sheep work was central to the economy and the employment of Anangu residents who worked as shepherds, shearers, fencing contractors, well-sinkers and boring contractors. Women adapted a traditional method of spinning fibres to make hooked floor rugs, woven scarves and knee rugs from wool. Thus a craft industry was established in 1948. A school based on a vernacular education policy was opened in 1940. From 1945, a clinic was staffed by a nursing sister. Anangu were employed as aides in the school and clinic. Women baked bread and cooked meals for workers and school children. Men worked in the garden to provide vegetables for the kitchen, butchered sheep to supply meat and were employed in brick-making, maintenance and building work.

Following shearing, the people left on an annual 'walkabout' holiday, travelling west and south-west on camels, donkeys and on foot to visit traditional totemic areas. A similar holiday was taken after Christmas. These breaks enabled Anangu to maintain contact with traditional sites and the related knowledge and ceremony.

Although Ernabella was established as a Christian mission, little pressure was exerted for immediate results in the form of religious conversion. It was 15 years before the first baptisms were celebrated. Solid foundations were laid through learning the language, the example of staff, translation of the Gospel of Mark, and conducting regular services. As interest in the Christian story increased, a catechism was prepared in Pitjantjatjara. Early reports emphasised the role of singing in worship and the development of the choir. Several hymns were translated.

A report in December 1952 described the establishment of the Church at Ernabella, recalling that tribal sanctions had not been interfered with and that contact with the mission and engagement in the activities had been voluntary. A cement-block church building was erected in 1952. Local men were employed making and laying the blocks. On Sunday, 9 November, 1952, 400 people gathered for the dedication of the new church and in the afternoon 20 young people were baptised (Ernabella Newsletter 1952, pp. 5–6). Church members soon participated in church services by leading in prayer, reading Bible passages and preaching.

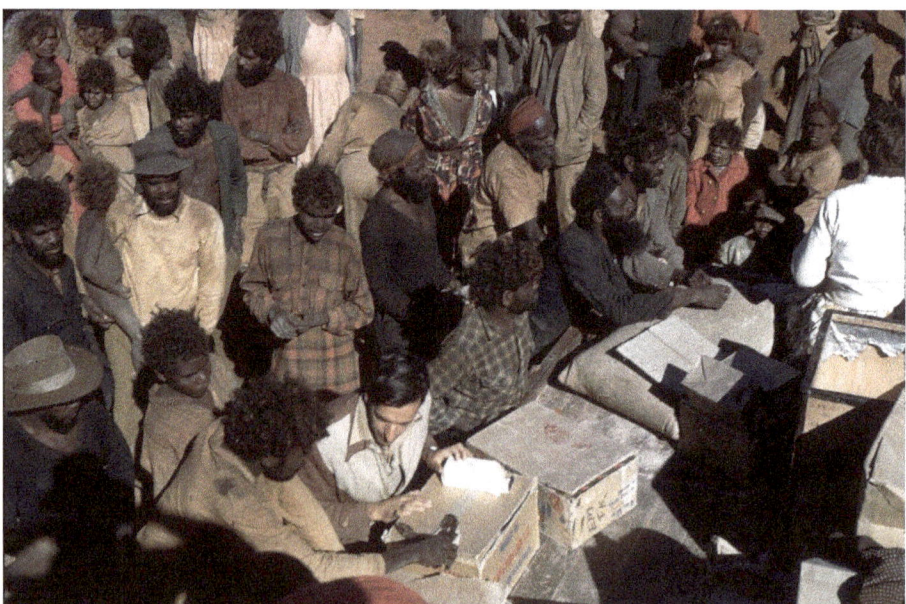

**Bill Edwards trading food with Anangu people in return for dingo scalps, Yulpartji, 1958.**

Source: Photograph from Bill Edwards collection. Courtesy Ara Irititja Project Netley, South Australia.

As superintendent of Ernabella from 1958 to 1972, my tasks were varied as I pastored the church, managed the office and store, maintained financial records, coordinated the various departments of the mission, and supervised the local people in the garden, butchery and general maintenance. In 1961, Fregon cattle outstation was established 60 kilometres south-west of Ernabella to provide a home and employment for people who belonged to the sandhill country. The South Australian Government opened Amata settlement to the west of Ernabella in 1961, and Indulkana settlement, approximately 190 kilometres south-east of Ernabella, in 1968. I visited these stations monthly to conduct church services. Andy Tjilari resided at Fregon to preach and teach the catechism. In line with the mission's policy of respecting traditional culture and language, I visited traditional sites with Anangu people to learn some of the stories and observe ceremonies associated with the *Tjukurpa* or Dreaming heritage of the Anangu.

On a visit to a remote area in 1966, while walking across a sandhill I observed the footprints of dingoes and euros (hill kangaroos). Andy Tjilari joined me and pointed out from the tracks that a dingo had followed a euro, tackled it and dragged it towards a nearby rocky hill to feed its young. While I had seen some tracks, Andy, because of his long training in the bush, had observed a story. I thus gained a deeper understanding of the meaning of the words of Jeremiah, later cited by Jesus: 'Do you have eyes but fail to see, and ears but fail to hear?' (Jeremiah 5.21; Mark 8.18). For Anangu, the ground is a book from which they read the signs of what has taken place. My earlier education was based on learning from written records. Andy and other Anangu were teaching me to read the stories embedded in the landscape. As I gained increasing knowledge of fundamental concepts in Anangu thought and expression, I was able to apply this to my analysis of history and issues.

I completed a Bachelor of Education by external studies during my early years at Ernabella. Living in an isolated community, it would have been easy to lose touch with academic life. This study helped me to maintain contact. My first published paper was based on an assignment. I continued to reflect on my work, built up my own library and wrote papers on Aboriginal issues, often with an historical focus (for example, Edwards 1961, 1966, 1967, 1969). I had the advantage when writing about Aboriginal issues and history that I wrote from a grassroots position and from direct involvement. Day-to-day discussions with the mission's teacher, sheep overseer, church leaders and other colleagues were reflected in my writing of papers on education, employment and the relationship between culture and gospel.

While reflection and writing provided some relief from the pressures of the daily work, another fulfilling outlet was the role of training the Ernabella Choir. In line with the Anangu tradition of being participants rather than spectators, there was no separate choir in normal services as all people sang and learned parts. However, a choir sang for special Christmas and Easter pageants (in which real donkeys and camels featured) and when visiting other centres such as Alice Springs. Having worked with the choir for a few years, and remembering my first meeting with them in Adelaide in 1954, I arranged a tour to Adelaide, Melbourne and several provincial centres in Victoria and South Australia in 1966. This choir was comprised of 12 women and 12 men. The program included western hymns and folk songs, and performances of Anangu songs and dances. The response was overwhelming. Having envisaged singing in church halls to audiences of approximately 200, local committees in provincial centres organised concerts in town halls with 700–900 attending. When a cancellation left a free night in the Melbourne Town Hall during the Moomba Festival, the choir was invited to perform before an enthusiastic audience of approximately 2,000. A broad smile beamed from the centre of the front row. It was Doug Nicholls, who I had heard speak at the university a decade earlier. In Adelaide, the choir was invited to attend a practice of the London Symphony Orchestra. Having finished their practice, the Orchestra played a Dvořák Slavonic Dance especially for the choir. In response, the choir sang the Pitjantjatjara version of 'The Lord is my Shepherd'.

**Bill Edwards conducting the Ernabella Mission Choir, Scots Church, Adelaide March 1966.**

Source: Photograph from Bill Edwards collection. Courtesy Ara Irititja Project Netley, South Australia.

Another enriching aspect of work at Ernabella was learning and speaking the Pitjantjatjara language. As well as communicating with Anangu in daily tasks and preaching in the language, I recorded and translated stories of their contact experiences with intruding white explorers and settlers, including reactions to first sightings of camels, horses and motor vehicles. Andy Tjilari's stories were evocative of the changing world he had experienced (Tjilari 2006). This added another perspective to my involvement in historical research, enabling me to bring Aboriginal experiences to the centre of historical analysis.

From the late 1960s, external and internal pressures forced changes in Aboriginal affairs as the policy of assimilation gave way to self-management and self-determination. In 1972, I moved to Mowanjum Mission in Western Australia to oversee the incorporation of the Aboriginal community and transfer of administration from mission to community. This became the prototype for this initiative. The same process took place at Ernabella and Fregon in 1973. I returned to the Anangu region to live at Fregon in 1973 as parish minister. In 1974, I studied theology at the Pacific Theological College and sociology at the University of the South Pacific in Fiji. Interacting with people from Pacific Island nations and learning of the structures and values of their societies enabled me to bring fresh insights to understanding Anangu society when I returned to the region in 1976. For example, reading Marshall Sahlins on social stratification in Pacific societies with his analysis of ascribed and achieved status in Polynesian societies and the role of Bigmen in Melanesia made me more aware of the problems confronting people from the egalitarian Anangu society as they encountered challenges in establishing new political structures (Edwards 1998, pp. 161–181). In 1975, I studied anthropology at the University of Adelaide and lectured in Aboriginal Studies at the Torrens College of Advanced Education.

## Return to the Anangu Lands

In 1976, I returned to Anangu country to reside at Amata to minister in a parish that now stretched for 600 kilometres from east to west. Changes in government policies relating to Aboriginal people encouraged some Anangu to establish outstation or homeland communities in traditional totemic areas. Amata was near the centre of the total area. I was able therefore to intimately observe the development of the homeland movement in the region, a topic I have subsequently written of when changing government policies placed homelands under threat (Edwards 1993, 2013).

While I was occupied with conducting services, teaching, translating and training church elders, including my close friend Andy Tjilari, I increased my knowledge of Anangu Dreaming stories as I camped with people on the land.

These experiences gave me new insights into the meaning of some Bible stories in a cross-cultural perspective, for the people of Israel had also at times gone 'walkabout' in deserts. Biblical references to God and the Holy Spirit as rock, fire and wind were meaningful for Anangu, who lived in close proximity to these elements. Soon after my arrival at Ernabella, when I was wearing sandals, a young woman exclaimed to her friends, *'Nyawa! Tjina wiru'*, 'Look at his beautiful feet'. Normally protected by shoes and socks, my feet contrasted markedly with their feet, which suffered injuries as they walked barefoot across rocks, hot sand, ashes and thorns. For the first time, I understood the mundane nature of the imagery expressed by Isaiah: 'How beautiful on the mountains are the feet of those who bring good news' (Isaiah, 52: 7). The feet of the messengers who brought Israelite captives news of their release were enclosed in sandals, whereas the feet of the Israelites had suffered as they walked across the hot desert sands. Singularities in the feet of Anangu contributed to their acclaimed ability as police trackers, as they could identify offenders by their footprints. For example, one person might be known to have bad cracking in the left heel while another had a bunion on the big toe of the right foot.

South Australian Premier Don Dunstan, who instituted sweeping changes in Aboriginal affairs at this time, had a long engagement with Aboriginal people and organisations. For example, he had Doug Nicholls appointed Governor of South Australia in 1976, the year of our move to Amata. Unfortunately, ill-health forced Nicholls to resign from the position before he had opportunity to visit Anangu communities.

Representatives from Anangu communities met at Amata in July 1976 to form the Pitjantjatjara Council as a forum for discussing issues and making representations to governments. At bi-monthly meetings they pressed for recognition of their right to ownership of the land. At the first meeting, I was invited to act as secretary and interpreter. Although I handed over the role of secretary to an Anangu person, I continued to record minutes of meetings in English and Pitjantjatjara and to interpret for four years. This latter task was crucial, as Anangu expressed their demands to Premier Dunstan and other politicians, public servants, lawyers and anthropologists whose cultural understandings were vastly different to those of the Anangu people. Negotiations between the South Australian Government and the Pitjantjatjara Council culminated in the enacting of legislation in March 1981 which granted inalienable freehold title to 102,360 square kilometres of land to Anangu Pitjantjatjara Inc.

**Bill Edwards interpreting with the Premier of South Australia, John Bannon, at the handover of title for the Maralinga lands to Maralinga Tjarutja Inc, December 1984.**

Source: Photograph from Bill Edwards collection. Courtesy Ara Irititja Project Netley, South Australia.

Over this period, I wrote papers on various topics related to my involvement in these landmark political and social changes in Aboriginal affairs (for example, Edwards 1973, 1983). I was fortunate to have a close association with Anangu people who held strongly to traditional knowledge, values and practices while adjusting to the impact of European culture, and to be involved in the processes of change. I was part of the history and, as I reflected on what was happening about me, I was increasingly recording details in my diary, correspondence and minutes. After two decades of residence in the Anangu lands, my wife Valerie and I moved to Adelaide. Our sons commenced their schooling in Anangu schools, but needed to be nearer other schools for their secondary education. I had confidence too, that the 25 Anangu men and women ordained as Church Elders could fulfill the ministry in the churches across the Anangu lands. One of them, Peter Nyaningu, was undertaking studies for ordination as a minister of the Uniting Church of Australia. Having studied and lectured in Adelaide in 1975, we returned there in 1981 so that I could continue studies in anthropology and lecture in Aboriginal studies at what was to become the South Australian College of Advanced Education, which was incorporated into the newly established University of South Australia in 1991.

## Teaching and Researching in Adelaide

My main areas of teaching were traditional Aboriginal culture and Pitjantjatjara language. I also lectured on land rights, traditional Aboriginal education and health. As there was a growing awareness of the need for students enrolled in other courses to learn about Aboriginal culture, I pioneered the teaching of Aboriginal culture subjects in nursing, parks and wildlife, education and other courses. I also conducted cultural awareness workshops for police trainees, librarians, teachers and hospital staff. While I structured these workshops and taught about the Anangu concept of the Dreaming and the basic structures of their kinship system, I invited Aboriginal people to share their personal knowledge and experiences. Andy Tjilari's younger brother, Gordon Ingakatji, who had assisted me in the store and office at Ernabella and been my principal language teacher, came to Adelaide periodically to assist in teaching Pitjantjatjara. Mona Tur, a Yankunytjatjara woman, who came to Adelaide as a teenager and later married there, also worked with me in language teaching.

At that time, there were few Indigenous academics in Australia. Most Aboriginal Studies teaching was done by non-Indigenous people. Some Aboriginal students in these courses later became leaders in Aboriginal education and Indigenous studies around Australia. Most of the Aboriginal students came from urban or rural backgrounds and had limited experience of 'traditional' cultural life. Most respected that I had some experience of this and were willing to learn from me. On the other hand, I learned much from them about their cultural life as people of mixed descent whose families had often suffered discrimination. It was another case of *ngapartji ngapartji,* reciprocal engagement. Some of these Aboriginal students commented in their assignments that they had lost their culture. I reminded them that as human beings they had been enculturated and that, although their particular culture differed to that of their Aboriginal forebears, it was a culture to be equally valued. I encouraged them to build on the positive values of that culture and to recall things told to them by their parents or grandparents, to consider whether these stories reflected elements of traditional culture.

While my residence in the Anangu lands for two decades provided a wealth of knowledge and experience to share with students, I continued to have active involvement and advocacy in Aboriginal issues. Before leaving the Anangu lands, I interpreted in negotiations which led eventually to the granting of land rights over Uluru (Ayers Rock) National Park in 1984. I interpreted for the Maralinga Tjarutja people, whose land lies south of the Pitjantjatjara lands, in their land rights claim. I also interpreted for the Maralinga people during the Royal Commission into British Nuclear Testing in Australia. I was called upon to interpret for Anangu people in the legal and health sectors, a task that took me into courts, prisons, forensic mental health institutions, hospitals and other institutions. I visited the Anangu lands annually to conduct workshops, interpret, attend funerals and celebrations and to meet old friends. I continued my association with the Ernabella Choir, conducting them on a visit to Sydney and other centres in New South Wales in 1984 and at a performance in the Adelaide Town Hall during the 2004 Adelaide Festival of Arts, half a century after my first encounter with them in Adelaide.

As a lecturer in Aboriginal studies, I was confronted by critical comments about the role of missions in Aboriginal experience in Australia. While I was well aware of the shortcomings of some mission policies and practices, I was concerned at the stereotyping and lack of detailed research which often underlay these criticisms. Earlier romanticised depictions of missions had given way to distorted presentations. Eric Sharpe expressed this change as follows:

From confident assurance before 1914, the record has proceeded by way of paradox and ambiguity in a general direction of a gloomy but superficial catalogue of failure. In the first phase, the missionary seemingly could do no wrong; in the last, one sometimes wonders whether the missionary can ever be given credit for doing anything right (Sharpe 1989, p. 79).

An example of this negative view is found in the entry on 'Missions' by historian Ian Clark in *The Encyclopaedia of Aboriginal Australia*, where he writes that 'the word means a place where many of our people were "imprisoned"'(Clark 1994, vol. 2. p. 706). The entry continues in this vein with little reference to specific missions and stereotypes are reinforced. No account is taken of the very positive comments expressed by many Aboriginal people about their experiences of mission life (Edwards 2007, p. 23, fn 63), albeit in a system that, like all non-Indigenous institutions, was imbricated in colonialism. Dennis Ingram, May O'Brien and Denzil Humphries, for example, have written positively about the care, example and training provided by missionaries and of the opportunities this opened up for them in later life (Taylor 1998, pp. 240, 332, 333). Another aspect often overlooked is the involvement of Aboriginal people themselves in this enterprise, for example, David Unaipon, Nathaniel Pepper, Doug Nicholls, Blind Moses and other Arrente evangelists in Central Australia, Reverend Lazarus Lamilami, James and Angelina Noble, and Pastor Ben Mason. While missionaries are sometimes validly accused of removing people from their lands and destroying their culture, in many instances it was missions that enabled people to remain in their country and maintain their language and cultural practices. Marcia Langton noted that 'if it had not been for missions, there would be no Aboriginal people alive in Victoria today' (Perkins 2008) and Noel Pearson similarly stated that 'missions did not destroy the culture that remains, as some often allege' (Pearson 1998, p. 147).

My venture into post-graduate research in mission historiography was partly motivated by a concern to counter such inaccuracies as identified by Langton and Pearson. I was encouraged by the publication of several books which provided a more balanced approach to the study of mission history (for example, McDonald 2001; Choo 2001; Loos 2007; Kenny 2007). Writing of the massacre of Aborigines in Western Australia, Neville Green provided an example of a missionary, Ernest Gribble, who sought justice on behalf of Indigenous people despite facing hostile opposition (Green 1995).

In 1991, a seven-week sabbatical at the Centre for the Study of Christianity in the Non-Western World at the University of Edinburgh broadened my understanding of mission history. I came across references to Moravian missions. Missionaries from the Moravian church in Saxony pioneered several Protestant mission fields from the early eighteenth century and from the 1890s provided staff for Presbyterian missions in north Queensland. As I wrote papers on Presbyterian missions in which I had been involved, I was referring to Moravians. In 1994, I spent a week at a Moravian College and Archive in Bethlehem, Pennsylvania. The archivist produced a box of letters written from 1866 to 1874 by Mary Hartmann, wife of a Moravian missionary, from Ebenezer in Victoria, to her parents in England. To my knowledge, no writer on Aboriginal history had accessed these letters previously. They gave vivid descriptions of the complex daily interaction of missionaries and Aboriginal people in their homes and gardens and on picnics, details often overlooked in the stereotyped presentations of Aboriginal missions.

Two 1870 letters record the care given by the Hartmanns in their home to a dying man named Dick-a-Dick. Two years earlier, Dick-a-Dick played for the first Australian cricket team to tour England, a team comprised of Aboriginal players. In 1864, Dick-a-Dick was one of three Aboriginal trackers who found three young children, Jane, Isaac and Frank Duff, who wandered from a station near Apsley in western Victoria and were lost in the bush for nine days. As a child, I read an account of this in Victoria's Grade IV Reader. My mother, as a child in Horsham, visited the home of Jane Turnbull (formerly Jane Duff), to hear her recount this experience (Edwards 1999b, pp. 59–61).

A Professor of History at Flinders University in Adelaide commented favourably on some of my publications and this encouraged me to undertake doctoral research on the history of Moravian missions in Australia under his supervision. I intended, in retirement, to write on the work in which I had been involved. However, I chose the Moravian missions for my thesis in order to enable me to engage with Aboriginal mission historiography more 'objectively'. I intended returning to writing about Ernabella after honing my skills in mission history by researching the Moravians.

At one stage of my writing, when I was feeling uncertain, a colleague who had gained her doctorate in anthropology offered to read drafts of my chapters. She suggested I was too reticent about intruding my own experience when writing about the Moravians, of deploying this as a methodology. There were many correspondences between the work at Ebenezer and Ernabella and I had written a seminar paper entitled 'A Moravian Mission in Australia, Ebenezer Through Ernabella Eyes'. I began to realise that my experiences gave me unique insights into situations in which Moravian missionaries had been involved a century earlier. This enhanced my practice as a historian. My colleague's suggestion contributed to the successful completion of my thesis.

# Conclusion

**Bill Edwards and Andy Tjilari, 2012, a lifelong friendship.**

Source: Photograph from Bill Edwards collection. Courtesy Ara Irititja Project Netley, South Australia.

I am now proceeding with research, reflection and writing on Ernabella. The year in which I write this is the 75th anniversary of Ernabella's establishment. To celebrate this, I gave a lecture to the Uniting Church Historical Society in Adelaide in May 2012 entitled 'Mission in the Musgrave: Ernabella Mission 1937–73, a place of relationships' (Edwards 2012). I was concerned that much of the writing about Christian missions in Australia was clouded by stereotypes which overlooked the daily interaction of mission staff and Aboriginal residents and their influence on each other in a co-created world. Having researched the relationships between women missionaries and Indigenous women, Patricia Grimshaw contends that theorists dismissive about the entire mission enterprise conflate 'the outcomes of missionary endeavours with the destructiveness of other colonial intruders' (Grimshaw 2011, p. 10). Grimshaw concluded that the outcomes of joint endeavours in the fields of education and health were 'negated largely because of the specific nature of settler colonialism in Australia and its sharply racialised boundaries' (Grimshaw 2011, p. 24).

As I read contemporary reports of social problems and dysfunction in remote Indigenous communities and am confronted by these issues as I interpret in courts, prisons and hospitals, the words of the anthropologists, John and Jean Comaroff, writing of post-colonial southern Africa, resonate with my experience. They refer to 'the inherent contradictions of colonialism' in Africa and the problems encountered by missions in their 'campaign to refashion the African personhood' as 'a study in ambiguity, contradiction, and the sheer perversity of the unintended in history' (Comaroff J L & J Comaroff 1997, p. 368).

Discovering the letters written by Polly Hartmann, from Ebenezer Mission in Victoria, to her parents in England, with their insights into the relationships between missionaries and Aborigines, further prompted my interest in this aspect of mission history and lent insight into my role as an historian shaped by the worlds I was writing about. After my parents died, I discovered not only the etched boomerang referred to earlier, but that they had kept my weekly letters to them. Thus, as I return to recording the history of Ernabella, I have documents that provide details of dates, events and people. My writing of this history cannot be objective, as I have been a participant in these events as well as in the negotiations that culminated in the recognition of land rights for the Pitjantjatjara/Yankunytjatjara, Uluru and Maralinga lands. My writing of Anangu history is inextricably bound to my personal story, a project that is both autobiographical and historical in which my development as an historian has been influenced directly by the history in which I was immersed, and thus an example of ego-histoire.

# References

Advertiser 1934, 'Treatment of Aborigines: Criticism by Dr. Duguid', *The Advertiser,* Adelaide, 28 December, 1934.

Attwood, B 2003, *Rights for Aborigines,* Allen & Unwin, Crows Nest.

Batty, P (ed.), 2006, *Colliding Worlds: First contact in the Western Desert, 1932–1984,* Museum Victoria, Melbourne.

Choo, C 2001, *Mission Girls: Aboriginal women on Catholic Missions in the Kimberley, Western Australia,* University of Western Australia Press, Crawley.

Clark, I D 1994, 'Missions', in D Horton (ed.), *The Encyclopaedia of Aboriginal Australia,* 2 vols, Aboriginal Studies Press, Canberra.

Clark, I D 1990, *Aboriginal Languages and Clans: An historical atlas of western and central Victoria, 1800–1900,* Monash University, Melbourne.

Clark, M 1972, *Pastor Doug: The Story of Sir Douglas Nicholls, Aboriginal Leader,* Landsdowne, Melbourne.

Comaroff J L & J Comaroff 1997, *Of Revelation and Revolution,* vol. 2: The Dialectics of Modernity on a South African Frontier, The University of Chicago Press, Chicago.

Duguid, C 1963, *No Dying Race,* Rigby Ltd, Adelaide.

Edwards, B 1999a, *Moravian Aboriginal Missions in Australia, 1850–1919,* Uniting Church Historical Society (S.A.), Adelaide.

Edwards, B 1999b, 'The Fate of an Aboriginal Cricketer: When and where did Dick-a-Dick die', *Australian Aboriginal Studies,* no. 2, 1999.

Edwards, B & B Clarke 1988, 'From Missions to Aboriginal Churches: The Uniting Church in Australia and Aboriginal Missions', in T Swain and D B Rose (eds), *Aboriginal Australians and Christian Missions,* Australian Association for Religious Studies, Bedford Park.

Edwards, W H 2013, 'From Coombes to Coombs: Reflections on the Pitjantjatjara outstation movement', paper presented at workshop on the Aboriginal Outstation Movement, The Australian National University.

Edwards, W H 2012, *Mission in the Musgrave: Ernabella Mission 1937–73, a place of relationships,* Uniting Church Historical Society (S.A.), Adelaide.

Edwards, W H 2007, 'Moravian Aboriginal Missions in Australia', unpublished PhD thesis, Flinders University, Adelaide.

Edwards. W H 2005, 'Tjukurpa Palya: The Good Word: Pitjantjatjara responses to Christianity', in Peggy Brock (ed.), *Indigenous Peoples and Religious Change,* Brill, Leiden.

Edwards, W H 2004, *An Introduction to Aboriginal Societies,* second edition, Thomson Social Science Press, South Melbourne.

Edwards, W H 1998, 'Leadership in Aboriginal Societies', in W H Edwards (ed.), *Traditional Aboriginal Society,* Macmillan Education Australia, Melbourne.

Edwards, W H 1993, 'Patterns of Aboriginal Residence in the North-West of South Australia', *Journal of the Anthropological Society of South Australia,* vol. 30, no. 1–2.

Edwards, W H 1983, 'Pitjantjatjara Land Rights', in N Peterson and M Langton (eds), *Aborigines, Land and Land Rights,* Australian Institute for Aboriginal Studies, Canberra.

Edwards, W H 1978, 'The Gospel and Aboriginal Culture'. *Interchange,* no. 24, pp. 195–204.

Edwards, W H 1973, 'The Changing Climate of Aboriginal Development', *Interchange,* no. 14, pp. 70–80.

Edwards, W H 1969, 'Experience in the Use of the Vernacular as an Introductory Medium of Instruction', in S S Dunn and C M Tatz (eds), *Aborigines and Education,* Sun Books, Melbourne.

Edwards, W H 1967, 'Communicating the Gospel to Australian Aborigines', *The Bulletin,* Christian Institute for Ethnic Studies in Asia, vol. 1, no. 1.

Edwards, W H 1966, 'Report on Ernabella Labour Export Project, 1965–66', in I G Sharp and C M Tatz (eds), *Aborigines in the Economy*, Jacaranda Press, Melbourne.

Edwards, W H 1961, 'Aboriginal Education: Aims and principles', *Journal of Christian Education,* vol. 4, no. 1.

Elkin, A P 1956, *The Australian Aborigines: How to understand them,* second edition, Angus & Robertson, Sydney.

*Ernabella Newsletter,* December 1952, Australian Presbyterian Board of Missions, Sydney.

Giles, E 1889, *Australia Twice Traversed,* 2 vols, Sampson Low, Marston, Searle & Rivington.

Green, N 1995, *The Forrest River Massacres,* Fremantle Arts Centre Press, South Fremantle.

Grimshaw, P 2011, 'Rethinking Approaches to Women and Missions: The case of colonial Australia', *History Australia,* vol. 8, no. 3.

Hilliard, W 1968, *The People in Between: The Pitjantjatjara People of Ernabella,* Hodder and Stoughton, London.

Kenny, R 2007, *The Lamb Enters the Dreaming: Nathanael Pepper and the ruptured world,* Scribe Publications, Carlton North.

Kerin, R 2011, *Doctor Do-Good: Charles Duguid and Aboriginal advancement, 1930s–1970s,* Australian Scholarly Publishing, North Melbourne.

Loos, N 2007, *White Christ Black Cross: The emergence of a black church,* Aboriginal Studies Press, Canberra.

McDonald, H 2001, *Blood, Bones and Spirit: Aboriginal Christianity,* Melbourne University Press, Carlton South.

Neill, S 1964, *A History of Christian Missions,* Penguin Books, Harmondsworth.

Pearson, N 1998, 'Ngamu-Ngaadyari, Muuri-Bunggaga and Midha Mini in Guugu Yimidhirr History', in Jan Kociumbas (ed.), *Maps, Dreams, History: Race and representation in Australia,* University of Sydney, Sydney.

Perkins R 2008, 'Episode 3: Freedom for our lifetime', *The First Australians,* Blackfella Films.

Sharpe, E J 1989, 'Reflections on Missionary Historiography', *International Bulletin of Missionary Research,* vol. 13, no. 2.

Stanner, W E H 1969, 'After the Dreaming', The Boyer Lectures 1968, ABC, Sydney.

Taylor, P 1988, *After 200 Years: Photographic Essays of Aboriginal and Islander Australia today,* Aboriginal Studies Press, Canberra.

Tjilari, A 2006, *Learning as a Pitjantjatjara Child/Ngayulu Iriti Tjitji Nintiringkunytja,* (originally recorded and translated by Bill Edwards), Department of Education and Children's Services, Adelaide.

# 5. Layers of Being: Aspects of Researching and Writing *Professional Savages: Captive Lives and Western Spectacle*

Roslyn Poignant

My book, *Professional Savages: Captive Lives and western Spectacle,* was the outcome of a project that extended over many years in which I aimed to make sense of, and make a narrative of, what happened to a group of nine Manbarra and Biyaygirri Aborigines from North Queensland—Billy, Toby, Jenny, Tambo, Sussy, Jimmy, and the others—who were removed overseas by the showman R. A. Cunningham in 1883, and who toured extensively through America and Europe. By following the routes they had taken, and by drawing on sources, ranging from unreliable newspaper accounts of the period to culturally blinkered anthropological reports, as part of the process of interpretation, the visual material that I gradually assembled—photographs, circus ads, posters, newspaper sketches and cartoons—frequently functioned as crystallising images in which the dynamics of interaction were exposed, thereby shaping both the processes of 'looking for'—that is, the research—and the 'telling about' of their story. But first something about ego.

In early 2011, I attended a seminar in the October Gallery, London, led by three Indigenous Australian performance artists. One of the speakers, Fiona Foley, a Batjala woman from Fraser Island, referenced *Professional Savages* for the well-illustrated account it gave of the frontier wars in Queensland that had decimated her people and their more northerly neighbours. Afterwards, when she asked me why I had made so few references to my personal involvement in the story, I reminded her of the 'History Wars' of the 1990s and 2000s, and told her that I thought the best way to counter Keith Windshuttle's representation of the postcolonial rethinking of the colonial project as a *Fabrication of Aboriginal History* was with as carefully researched, detailed and non-partisan an account as possible.

Billy, Jenny and her son Toby—the survivors of the group of nine removed from North Queensland—Paris, November 1885.

Source: Photograph by Prince Roland Bonaparte. Courtesy of the Royal Anthropological Institute, London.

Fiona also asked me how and why I had become the teller of the story of Tambo and his companions. This was a question I had reframed for myself about halfway through my research in a note filed on my computer on February 12, 2001 as 'Layers RP', 'as being not a simple matter of my self-imposed exile giving me insight into their displacement. It is more layered than that. An Australian exile in London is only one layer of my being. There are deeper layers of displacement in my family histories'. 'I can choose', I wrote, 'from a range of identities from Scottish Protestant, signalled by my name Roslyn, bestowed by my father who had migrated to Australia in the first decade of the twentieth century, to Jewish from my mother, whose forbears migrated to Australia from a shtetl in the Russian/Polish borderlands in the early nineteenth century, and settled in northern NSW, where my grandfather was a builder of hotels, hospitals and schools.' So I was personally aware of Jewish displacement and exclusion on account of race. More important, perhaps, an early awareness of difference had fuelled my curiosity about others.[1] To take a different time and tack:

In 1969, my partner Axel and I arrived back in Sydney after a 13-year absence. For many months we had made our way slowly across the Pacific, staying and photographing in several different island communities. Wherever we went we encountered independence movements that were rippling out from the events of '68 in France and Europe. Flying on to Sydney, we found the Aboriginal Land Rights Movement in full swing. It was an exciting moment in history. On our first morning there I opened the paper and saw a photo of the artist Cristo and his wife, Jeanne-Claude, in the process of wrapping the rocky shoreline of Little Bay, a small sheltered cove just north of Botany Bay, Captain Cook's first landfall in Australia. The small beach at the foot of those cliffs was where I had spent some of the happiest hours of my childhood, and I saw the wrapping of a site of such personal significance to me as a gift: a welcome home to the place of my Dreaming. Little Bay lay several miles south of my childhood home in Maroubra, a straggling suburban encroachment on a shifting landscape of sand dunes and reedy swamps. A tramline, linking the inner city to the northern shore of Botany Bay, passed our front door, and then continued on past the concrete undulations of the speedway (a car-racing track) and the whitewashed walls and watchtowers of Long Bay Gaol, to the 'coast' hospital, leprosarium and quarantine station at the end of the line. There, in this liminal zone of Sydney, on the other side of the line, up the slope from Little Bay was the Aboriginal Reserve.

My father, who was a nurse at the hospital, had contact with the community, and one of my earliest memories is of his Aboriginal friend, Bill, who entertained

---

1  Docker identifies Leopold Bloom's 'diasporic consciousness' in Joyce's *Ulysses* as 'an attentiveness to other and previous histories, a worldly ease of reference and multiple habitation, a lack of fear of the elsewhere' (Docker 2001, p. 106).

the crowds with his skill as a boomerang thrower. After a performance, Bill took us back to his humpy, a large domed structure made of curved branches and covered in pieces of canvas, where I was seated on an upturned bucket and given a mug of milky tea. There was also some conventional housing but during the worst depression years of the 1930s, many more Aborigines had drifted to Sydney from other districts in search of work, and had put up their temporary structures. A neighbouring gully, known as Happy Valley, was where the homeless unemployed set up their camps. Having now looked at the period photos online, I see it was even bleaker than the memory, remarkably accurate, of my five- or six-year-old self.[2]

A few years later, as times improved, an Art-Deco cinema was built across the tramline from us. On Saturdays the Aboriginal children would ride into Maroubra on the offside running board of the trams, out of reach of the conductors. Small dark figures would slide quietly behind the ushers into the cinema. Inside, all of us, Aboriginal and white kids, would riot up and down the aisles until the lights went down, then we would grab the nearest seats. When, a few years later, I stayed with family friends in the outer Sydney suburb of North Ryde, I was surprised to find there was a roped-off area for the Aborigines in the small open air cinema. As the lights went down they entered silently. Looking back, I recognise the distancing in both situations, for I had merely been one of the crowd.

Growing up in the economically tough 1930s, but having a sense of stability of family and place, my identity was also shaped by an awareness of being the product of two diasporas. I was also politicised by the depression and the arrival of refugees from Nazi oppression. Although my sister and I attended Presbyterian Sunday School, when I turned 12 in 1939 I decided not to be confirmed. It wasn't a matter of choosing between parental religions, but a conscious decision of my own made with the minister's encouragement. Nor was it a fixed position, but a shifting one that engendered a profound scepticism about all religions and a strong sense of justice. I was beginning to position myself as an outsider.

In time, this position also fuelled a curiosity about other cultures that would lead me to study history and anthropology at university. In 1947, in my final year, unable to choose between the two subjects, I undertook combined honours while 'majoring' in political protest. The issue was support for Indonesian independence, and our demonstration outside the Dutch Embassy was brutally broken up by Police Squad 21, which had been set up during the war to control the soldiers of several nations on leave in Sydney. It became a civil liberties

---

2  An extensive collection of over 200 photographs of Little Bay is available at http://www.photosau.com.au/Randwick/scripts/home.asp.

issue, and my task as secretary of the University Labour Club was to gather statements from members of the public who had witnessed police violence (Barcan 2002). So I spent my days and nights divided between court hearings and the calm of the Mitchell Library, researching for my thesis. There in the quiet of the Library, inhaling the dust of disintegrating newsprint, I read an account of an aging Aboriginal man standing in downtown Melbourne, crying for his lost people and land—a powerfully haunting image to conjure up. It was also in that defining moment that I realised my future was in the archives and not in the streets. With the passage of time, I came to appreciate that the archive can also be a place for protest and resistance.

Unexpectedly, my combination of subjects, plus a strong interest in film, led to my first proper employment at the Commonwealth Film Division and thus began my lifelong engagement not only with film, but also still photography as both process and project, and, more particularly, since the 1970s, with a concern for the visual representations of 'the other' as a subject for interrogation and interpretation. This I pursued through publications and exhibitions, beginning with 'Observers of Man' in 1980 for the Royal Anthropological Institute, London. Included in that exhibition was a photograph of Billy, Jenny and her son Toby taken by Prince Roland Bonaparte in 1885 in Paris. At the same time the elder (husband and father) Toby was dying in a Paris hospital. In an already disturbing image, the point to which the eye is drawn is the stuffed dog in the foreground, undoubtedly placed there deliberately. The shock of this cruel visual pun on death and embalmment activates what Roland Barthes has described as 'the obtuse—as opposed to the obvious meaning … Indifferent to moral or aesthetic categories it is on the side of carnival' (Barthes 1977, p. 55). As I have written elsewhere (Poignant 2004), it was the power of this particular image to compel an interrogative reading that launched my research project.

These three, Billy, Jenny and Toby, were the survivors of a group of nine North Queensland Aborigines removed abroad by the showman, Robert Cunningham. The first paper in which I attempted to tell their story more fully, *Captive Aboriginal Lives: Billy, Jenny, Little Toby and their companions,* was published by the Sir Robert Menzies Centre for Australian Studies, University of London, in 1993 (Poignant 1993). Writing in a milieu of involvement in activities of an Aboriginal Support Group in London, I addressed Aboriginal writer Henrietta Fourmiles' assertion that 'the hegemony of dominant culture continues to make Indigenous Australians captives of the archives and of discourse' (Fourmile 1989). I argued that 'the reclaiming of this suppressed history [of Aboriginal resistance to invasion] is urgent for all of us', and that '[t]here is also a sense in which archives are not the source, but the product of research; frequently they are formed in the process of ferreting out the evidence on the margins of history' (Poignant 1993, p. 43).[3]

My ferreting out of the details of the Aboriginal travellers' lives continued as a consequence of the entanglement of two projects. In the 1990s, I made several field trips to the Maningrida community in Arnhem Land by way of making cultural returns of Axel Poignant's photographs of the different language groups living in the area in the 1950s, the outcome of which, in 1996, was an exhibition and the book *Encounter at Nagalarramba* (Poignant & Poignant 1996). Although unable to get funded support for the 'Captive Lives' project, on each of my exits from Arnhem Land I routed myself via North Queensland and then home to London across America, in order to follow their trail. Meanwhile, the small publication, *Captive Aboriginal Lives,* had made its way to Nicolaas Heijm, an anthropologist working with the Palm Island community, and in Brisbane in 1993 I at last made contact with Nick and Walter Palm Island. I had already learnt of a genealogical record made by the anthropologist N. B. Tindale that mentioned a brother of Walter's grandfather, Dick, who 'had gone to America for a show' and died there.[4] This was the critical evidence that would later establish that Walter was a collateral descendant of Tambo. While we were together, I received news that the British Academy had come good with support for a research trip to America. So, by October, I had just arrived to research the circus collection in San Antonio, Texas, when a phone call came through from a newspaper in Cleveland, Ohio, with information about an Australian Aboriginal circus performer called Tambo. It seems, they said, his mummified body had been found in the basement of a funeral home in Cleveland. I won't retell the story of this serendipitous event here, except to say that the outcome—it seemed Tambo's special gift to me—was extra research time in America. Funded by the Aboriginal and Torres Strait Islander Commission's rapidly formed 'Bring Tambo Home' committee, I was able to stay on in America, continuing to research, while I waited for Walter Palm Island and his brother, Reg, to arrive in Cleveland and, after due ceremony, take their ancestor, Tambo, home.

Antonis Liakos has observed that, in history, writing our own experiences comes through like the rising damp surfacing through a newly painted wall. To paraphrase: It comes through, even as we write the experience of historical otherness; the more we try to separate our sympathies and antipathies, the more

---

3 'Ferreting' on the margins had also led me to write 'The Grid on Contested Ground' about the handover of Aboriginal skeletal remains from the Anatomy Museum at the University of Edinburgh, at Pickford's freight store, London Airport, in 1991, for *The Olive Pink Society Bulletin*, a short-lived journal concerned with 'the interaction of race and gender with the practices of Anthropology within Australia' (Poignant 1992).
4 Genealogical Sheet 63, Palm Island, Queensland, 28 October, 1938. Norman B. Tindale's papers, Museum of South Australia. Dick Palm Island (Walter's grandfather), born circa 1880, was about two when Tambo and the others were taken, so the knowledge would have been transmitted orally until Tindale wrote it down.

we try to distance ourselves from our experience, the more it comes out from us in the writing of history (Liakos 2001). Obviously, I had begun my search for what happened to the Aboriginal travellers in the most accessible of the great libraries and archives. But as I extended the 'field' of my 'work' from the home places of Tambo and his companions in North Queensland to follow the routes of their journeys in America and Europe, I began to think of my research strategy as 'walking their walk': covering the same ground they had covered.

Although Guy Debord came up with the idea of psychogeography as a corollary to the 'society of the spectacle' (DeBord 2013), the relationship between the two became evident to me in the course of my research into the spectacle of the circus in America. This was especially so when I explored a town such as Bridgeport, once the winter quarters of Barnum & Bailey's circus, and I noted on a postcard of the museum sent to a friend:

> This surreality is a real building in a real street — not a model! It is set in a de Chirico townscape of elegant fortress bank buildings — the 19th century prosperity is over — and they are no longer occupied — in deserted streets alongside the concreted wall of the elevated railway tracks. No signs or services on the station. At the foot of a graffitied stairway leading to the road I ran into a family of dwarfs (elevated disadvantaged). It seemed somehow only to be expected in the town where Tom Thumb had been born and raised. That was way back at the beginning of the journey. It has been like that all the way, a shadow journey, catching reflections from the past through a shattered and fragmented mirror. Tambo is only one piece …

While travelling alone, sometimes chance factors, coupled with a tiny budget, exposed me to experiences that heightened my awareness of the existential predicament of the Aboriginal travellers in America. From time to time, I filed diary notes on my laptop where I teased out some of the researching/writing/living issues that preoccupied me. Here are two extracts. The first, concerned with attitude and how to represent, was written sometime between mid-1993 and September of that year, just before leaving for the US:

> I suppose in the way in which I relate to others — all others — I am locked into a-sort-of-voyeuristic engagement, the participatory nature of which foregrounds issues of ethics of representation. To write the *seeing* 'I' out of the narrative is to represent the mirror-field as if a portion of it has been obliterated by a retinal blind spot. To see, know, acknowledge oneself within the mirror-field is to represent, in varying degrees, autobiographically. Whatever the degree, is there any escape from the narcissistic trap? Is there life beyond the mirror?

Fiction beckons. The refractory process. Yet, apart from the difficulties of *how to make the fictional,* the possibility of the trauma of betrayal remains contained within it. The very effectiveness of fiction — the projected image — depends on this dangerous edge of recognition and identification and on its power to reflect. There it is all done with mirrors. Is fiction perhaps the ultimate distancing mechanism? Or is all representation betrayal?

The second extract records experience and is written at the end of my stay in America, after the return of Tambo's body to Queensland. Titled "Dec. 12th New York", it is written after 8 December, 1993, when the ceremony for the release of Tambo's spirit took place in Cleveland, Ohio, followed by the repatriation of his body. After the Palm Islanders departed for Australia, I flew to New York, with only a few days before my plane left for London. Undecided about how to usefully advance my research in the remaining days, I wrote:

> I'm too exhausted — emotionally drained to write it down [i.e. the events of the past few days in Cleveland]. I know I must risk not getting it down now. These are my last days in New York and choices to be made: Do I go to the New York Performing Arts to read New York clippers or to the Public Library to try a sampling of Californian papers? And back to Brooklyn for the clippings file. A choice between ruining my eyes on microfiche or microfilm. I opt instead for looking at techniques for printing the ads in the newspapers in an attempt to understand how printing techniques shaped the forms of representation. Who were the anonymous craftsmen in Cincinnati or Baltimore who took the cuts of newspaper entertainment ads and developed the circus ads, particularly for shows of Indigenous people?
>
> One last day in the NY Public Library — by now I must look like a regular because the man next to me asked me how to adjust the machine.

[Later, in the same entry, I am describing the following day, 11 December.]

> Outside it begins to sleet and snow … On the way to the airport: the snow falls in great enveloping swirls of white out of a foggy sky. I sit straight behind the driver's radio listening to a constant commentary on the developing chaos at Kennedy airport … 'Which way will I go', the disembodied voice asks. The reply cuts in 'there's only one way: Slow and easy'. The flight — all flights have been cancelled for 24 hours. The amenity desk helps me to book a bed at YMCA West 23rd St. I discover it is not a bit like West Central [where I had stayed on a previous occasion]. I pay for my bed, 44 $ (5$ refund on the key). The lift is not working and a middle-aged black man quickly guides me on what he describes

as a short-cut across a large unlit hall to the service lift. I am a late night gift. The possibility of earning something. The corridor walls are dark green and the cisterns from the lavatory block are running noisily. The room is shabby, but clean. The TV — as is usual — is suspended high up on the wall.

There are two pairs of metal, tiered, bunk beds, and a single bed. One lamp. I slip into bed trying to distinguish the street noises. Sleep fitfully. Read Toni Morrison. But it all comes flooding back to me. The strangeness of the way in which my journey shadows their journey. It is as if the disturbance of the surface uncovers and penetrates the deep layers. I tentatively grasp again the idea of 'fiction' or 'fact' — the notion of a shared history. The reach of the imagination required. It is as if the difficulties of my journey bring me in touch with the experiences of their journey. Should I allow myself to be submerged in the experience so deeply?

I switch on the television:

'Prime Time. Keeping you connected to those you care about.'

Obsessive compulsion of the flow of ads. 'Five have died in a Long Island train massacre …', we are told. Apparently the shoot-out took place Tuesday last (Dec 7th) the same day as Tambo's ceremony. They are interviewing people in the street about stricter gun control laws. Then comes: A pink doll in a walking frame. She giggles as she bounces. I switch her off and try to go to sleep. Night cries from the street enter my dreams. I switch the light on and see a cockroach scuttling along the top bed rail of the two-tiered-bunk on the other side of the room.

…

Daylight — 7.30 or 8 am I go down to telephone the airline. Yes, the plane will go at 2 pm, but I should get to the airport. And why not? There's not much else to do. I walk the corridors, lugging my bag up and down runs of stairs, until I find myself in the proper entrance hall that I'd missed the night before. There is a queue of about a dozen people, mostly men, in a subdued and orderly line at the desk. A tired man sits there dispensing soap and towel for a few coins, as they shuffle by. I haven't the gall to recover my five dollars for the key. Pushing the bag ahead of me onto the broken ice of the deserted street, and past the boarded-up housing estate, I come to a main thoroughfare on which the traffic is going uptown. I wait a long time before a taxi picks me up.

After America, I knew the story-gathering was incomplete and I wanted to get on with the research of what happened to the Aboriginal travellers in Europe, but the pressure for a piece of public history-telling was too great. The outcome was the 'Captive Lives' exhibition for the National Library of Australia in 1996. One strand of the exhibition sought to recover the individual identities of the Aboriginal travellers from performance roles. The other examined the mechanisms of their obliteration, particularly the consolidation, by the late nineteenth century, of the savage stereotype, which was imprinted both through performance, in what I called the 'show-space', and in graphic and photographic forms of representation, examples of which I had assembled along the way.

Key to the development of the exhibition was the Library's agreement to the appointment of four Indigenous advisors, each one representing one of the related language groups from which the Aboriginal travellers had come, led by Walter Palm Island, who was representing both his family and the Manbarra of Palm Island. Certainly, one of the most emotionally difficult things I have ever done—though also among the most rewarding—was to take the layout of the whole exhibition back to the Palm Island community, where it was discussed by a large gathering of the residents. The experience of removal, and the fear of it, loomed large in the collective memory of everyone present and, one after the other, they began, quietly and with dignity, to testify to personal recollections and experiences of removal from Aboriginal communities throughout Queensland to Palm Island. Yes, they wanted this earlier history of removal to be told. The meeting went on for the best part of the day.

After Canberra, the exhibition toured widely, including several centres in Queensland, and it has had an afterlife as a permanent installation at the Aboriginal Centre, Mungalla, the heartland of the Nyawaygi-speaking clans on Halifax Bay, Queensland. In the 1990s, Australia seemed to be at an historical moment of reformulation of national identity, central to which was an endeavour, as a community, to forge a new contract with the original owners of the land. But such moments are difficult to sustain in the face of continuing prejudice. In 1998, the London *Sunday Times* published a feature article about the high suicide rate of the young men of Palm Island, which they described as the 'most violent place on Earth' and 'Devil's Island' (Scott & Levy 1998, pp. 14–25). Without concern for the inaccuracy of the statistics they printed, or for historical accuracy, the writers chose to frame their story, 'This Spectred Isle', within a retelling of Tambo's removal and the apparent return of his ghost. The picture editor obligingly provided a red image of the ghost by digitally manipulating the photo of Jimmy, not Tambo, copied from the 'Captive Lives' exhibition broadsheet (Scott & Levy 1998, p. 14). Photographic manipulation has always featured as a visual narrative device, and the issues, as always, are to do not only with aesthetics but also ethics, moral rights, and power relations. The digitised transformation of a nineteenth century photograph had facilitated the persistence of an old stereotype of savagery in the service of continued discriminatory practices: the careless demonisation of an Aboriginal community. My protests to the Murdoch press went largely unsupported, even by institutions that had hosted the exhibition.

**Captive Lives exhibition opening at National Library, Canberra 1996. From left to right: Alan Palm Island, Josephine Giea, Walter Palm Island, Reg Palm Island, Ernest Grant and Maurice Bligh.**

Source: Photograph by Louis Seselja. Courtesy of the National Library of Australia, exhibition section.

**The Palm Island delegates visiting the Captive Lives exhibition.**

Source: Photograph courtesy of Roslyn Poignant.

In spite of the exhibition, from my point of view the story of the Aboriginal travellers remained incomplete. It was not until after 2000 that I was able to obtain funding to pursue what happened to the ever-diminishing group of Aboriginal travellers in Europe, where their transformation into professional show people was completed as they honed their performance skills. Indeed, for me, there was no sense of closure until 15 September, 2000, when, on an unusually warm autumn day, I sat in the sunshine in a cemetery in Darmstadt by some marker stones that indicated the spot where Jimmy had once been buried. Cemetery documentation showed that his remains had long since been removed to a communal burial area.[5] Nearby was a line of taps and a row of watering cans on hooks, all around me people were quietly tending graves. I absorbed the quiet beauty of the spot where Jimmy had been laid to rest by strangers. Jimmy, who had made my search for what happened to the Aboriginal traveller seem not only possible but irresistible, when I so easily found the record of his death in the Registry of Deaths Abroad, in the British Registry Office in the early 1990s.

## Acknowledgements

My thanks to a younger generation of scholars who welcomed me to their conference in December 2011. Thanks also to my patient readers, Christopher Wright, Ian Henderson and Lynette Russell. Thanks always to the Indigenous advisers for the 'Captive Lives' exhibition, Walter Palm Island, Reg Palm Island, Maurice Bligh, the descendants of the original travellers, and to Josephine Giea, Ernest Grant and Nicolaas Heijm.

## References

Barcan, A 2002, *Radical Students: The old left at Sydney University*, Melbourne University Press, Melbourne.

Barthes, R 1977, *Image, Music, Text*, translated by Stephen Heath, Fontana Press, London.

DeBord G 2013, *The Society of the Spectacle*, Notting Hill Editions, London.

Docker, J 2001, *1492: The Poetics of Diaspora*, Continuum, New York.

---

[5] In Germany grave sites are usually cleared after 25 years. I was reassured that, in this case, the rate of decay was related to soil composition.

Foley, F (ed.) 2006, *The Art of Politics the Politics of Art: The place of indigenous contemporary art*, Keeaira Press, Brisbane.

Fourmile H 1989, 'Who Owns The Past?: Aborigines as captive of the archives', *Aboriginal History*, vol. 13, no. 1.

Liakos, A 2001, 'History Writing as the Return of the Repressed', *Historein*, vol. 3, pp. 47–58.

Poignant R 2004, *Professional Savages: Captive lives and western spectacle*, Yale University Press, New Haven.

Poignant R 1993, 'Captive Lives: Australian captivity narratives', in K Darian-Smith K, R Poignant & K Schaffer, working papers in Australian studies no. 85–87, Sir Robert Menzies Centre for Australian Studies, University of London.

Poignant R 1992 'The Grid on Contested Ground', *The Olive Pink Society Bulletin*, vol. 4, no. 1.

Poignant R and Poignant A 1996, *Encounter at Nagalarramba*, National Library of Australia, Canberra.

Scott, C C & A Levy 1998, 'This Spectred Isle', *Sunday Times*, 1 February, 1998.

# 6. Stories my Grandmother Never Told Me: Recovering Entangled Family Histories Through Ego-Histoire[1]

### Karen Hughes

In 1997, I accompanied the oldest Ngarrindjeri person, the distinguished storyteller, Aunty Hilda Wilson, then aged 86 and becoming a staunch friend, home to Country, to the Aboriginal community of Raukkan, the former Point McLeay Mission on the southern edge of Lake Alexandrina. Aunty Hilda was born there in 1911, a year that marked the legal separation of South Australian Aboriginal and settler peoples with the passing of the *SA Aborigines Act 1911*.[2] As we stepped onto the shore of Lake Alexandrina, she led me to a clump of rushes in the sand, where her mother, Olive Varcoe (née Rankine), once sat and picked the fine but sturdy fibres with her sisters and Country-women, weaving the famous Ngarrindjeri baskets for sale and personal use. The women washed clothes here in a kerosene-tin over an open fire, gossiped and laughed, cared for little ones, and discussed important *business*. Aunty Hilda soon told me of sitting patiently alongside her great-grandmother, Ellen Sumner (1842–1925), at large ceremonial gatherings near this site during the 1910s and 1920s. From Ellen Sumner, renowned composer and singer, she also learnt *Pata Winema*, 'the old corroboree song'. Hilda claimed to discern the meaning of only one of its lyrics, *lieuwen*: to 'lay down', 'sleep' or 'rest'. Many believe this was adapted as a sorcery song against settlers for the destruction their intrusion brought (Bell 1998, p. 155).

Looking across the Lake in the blue haze of late afternoon, I suddenly recognised a familiar outline of pine trees, a miniature jetty, and the small rise of the town of Milang. Twenty kilometres north, Milang was the place of my grandmother's childhood, and of significant parts of mine. I had not been there for many years, after a decade and a half of living away, first in Sydney, then Italy and the United States. My maternal grandmother, Dorothy Johnson (née Pavy) (1909–2003), a third-generation descendant of French-English migrants from the 1850s, was born at Milang just 18 months before Hilda Wilson's birth on the mission. My

---

[1] My grateful thanks to Glenda Ballantyne, Margaret Allen, Eleanor Hogan (and the anonymous peer-reviewers) for insightful comments on this and earlier drafts.
[2] Aboriginal people were subjected to similar 'Aborigines Acts' in other states over this period via which they were segregated and controlled.

grandmother's birth narrowly preceded the passing of the Apartheid-style *Aborigines Act SA 1911,* which aimed to segregate the localities and lives of Aboriginal and settler peoples, in the wake of Australian Federation's 'whitening imperative'.[3] Subsequently, it served to separate their histories.

## Up Close and Dangerous: *De-familiarisation* and the Making of a Settler-Colonial Historian

That distinct moment at the end of 1997 began to radically shift my understanding of the interrelationship between history and self. Drawing on Pierre Nora's notion of *ego-histoire*, I explore the broader context of this moment and its impact on the way I have come to write and think about particular histories since. I also acknowledge the very significant methodological influence of feminist and Indigenous scholars (both community-based and in the academe) that predates and parallels Nora's work, in which the value of situatedness and standpoint is shown to be primary in producing more transparent, accountable scholarship (for example, Allen 2012; Rigney 2006; Harding 1991; Collins 1991; and Olsen 1978). I am long familiar with Nora's incisive work on memory. However, it is only with the publication of this volume that his analysis of ego-histoire has become widely available to English-speaking scholars through its first English-language translation. What registers as particularly useful to me as a non-Indigenous scholar doing history within the specific anxieties of the settler-colonial contact zone is Nora's identification of ego-histoire's capacity 'to *defamiliarise* a subject which we spontaneously inhabit' [emphasis mine].[4] Indeed, the shock of the familiar in my encounter with Aunty Hilda Wilson ultimately spurred my course as an historian and with it refigured my sense of belonging in a landscape I had previously assumed 'known'.

As a child in Adelaide, I frequently witnessed Aboriginal people in the outdoor spaces of the city, yet rarely found myself in situations of interpersonal contact. Although my parents had enjoyed somewhat limited contact with Aboriginal children in the classrooms and on the sporting fields of rural South Australia, by the time I came along we lived in Adelaide in a white, lower-middle-class suburb without Aboriginal friends. As Marcia Langton so famously and aptly said, 'most Australians do not know and relate to Aboriginal people. They relate to stories told by former colonists' (Langton 1993, p. 33).

---

3   See Grimshaw 2002, and Hughes 2012 on Federation's impact on Indigenous-settler relations and patterns of absence and presence in historiography.
4   Nora's 'L'Ego-Histoire est-elle Possible?' appears as an appendix to this volume.

During my early twenties in Sydney, when writing about the city's music and arts scene for *The Australian* (for example, Hughes 2006), something compelled me to want to better understand Aboriginal cultures. Although difficult to pinpoint, it followed a spiritual experience on waking during a meditation retreat in Goulburn in 1981. When wondering how best to pursue this, an acquaintance encouraged me to contact Uncle Guboo Ted Thomas (1909–2002), the respected Yuin land rights activist and cultural educator at Wallaga Lake Aboriginal community on the New South Wales south coast (Goodall 1996, pp. 335–351). Generously responding to my telephone call, Ted Thomas, then in his mid-seventies, invited me to spend Easter of 1981 in the community with his family. He immersed me in a living history of palpable deep time, contrasting a half-day trek up sacred Gulaga Mountain, and the stories of ancient beings actively inhabiting its crevices, with documentary evidence archived in his personal filing cabinet of colonial and state atrocities. He interwove this with personal accounts of the resilience, enterprise and activism of Yuin people and culture. Later, Ted Thomas stayed with me on two short trips to Sydney for speaking invitations I had arranged. His main focus was on helping me see and understand differently, through a different historical paradigm and cultural lens drawn from Indigenous ways of speaking about the past, rather than merely consuming historical evidence. I am immensely fortunate to have begun my study in Aboriginal history with such an exceptional teacher. Ted Thomas's nephew, Burnum Burnum (1936–1997) (see Farnsworth 1997), also visited my house in Darlinghurst, sometimes with gifts of firewood and tea-tree leaves from the bush from which we brewed tea to fuel afternoons of conversation. He shared his concerns over cultural heritage and intellectual property protection, and the plans he was hatching to bring issues of Aboriginal sovereignty into the public arena, which culminated in his spectacular planting of the Aboriginal flag on English soil on Invasion Day, 1988 (historychannel.com.au 2014). Burnum Burnum, in particular, introduced me to the shocking, bitter history of the Stolen Generations, drawing on the sadness of his personal experience of being forcibly removed from his family in 1936 as a three-month-old baby, growing up in Bomaderry, and then the horrific Kinchella boys home (see Ramsland 2004). He gave me a copy of Peter Read's first treatise on the Stolen Generations (Read 1981). The now faded slim monograph has travelled with me across continents, a provocative reminder of why collaborative history is important, and a pointer of what still needs to be unearthed. The bookshop at Tranby Aboriginal Co-operative College became a further source of self-education and contact over this period, and in my journalism I began to publish interviews with Aboriginal musicians, film-workers and broadcasters.

Returning to Adelaide in 1983 to work with the Aboriginal Jubilee 150 Committee[5] and architect Ian Hannaford on an Aboriginal Heritage Centre for South Australia,[6] I was introduced to Ruth Heathcock (1901–1995), a remarkable non-Aboriginal nurse, a friend of former South Australian premier Don Dunstan. A decade older than my grandmother, Ruth was similarly raised around Lake Alexandrina. Yet, in contrast, Ruth had lived against the grain of her times, profoundly engaged with Aboriginal people and politics, mostly as a leprosy nurse in the Northern Territory (Hughes 2005). I wondered why Ruth's experience so differed to my grandmothers', and came to realise that such engagement was only really possible before the 1911 *Act*. Ruth had lived her first ten years before its passage, forming life-changing friendships with Ngarrindjeri children and families.

I directed a documentary about Ruth Heathcock's collaboration with Aboriginal women in the Northern Territory in 1984 (Hughes 1986), and through this I began a number of deep—now intergenerational—friendships with the family who adopted Ruth in the 1930s, and who later adopted me (Hughes 2013a). My classificatory-mother, the Ngukurr elder Rosalind Munur (1931–2005), significantly influenced my perspective and subjectivity over this decade, expanding the historical paradigm Ted Thomas had instilled during our trek up Gulaga Mountain. Over the years that followed, Rosalind patiently taught me ways of understanding and doing history from an expressly Indigenous epistemological and pedagogical base. She approached history holistically, seeing caring for stories as intrinsic to active custodianship of Country,[7] and overall family and community well-being. It was her firm belief that histories resided in the bodies of people and in the land, and that historical knowledge is inalienable from this nexus. She showed me how knowledge travelled intergenerationally through genealogies, linked to specific Dreaming tracks and belonging to place. By adopting me as a daughter, Rosalind drew me into a correct relationship with that knowledge and began instructing me in an ethics of working and being by which it might be possible to begin to move toward a cross-cultural approach to history: as much socio-political and scholarly as deeply personal (Hughes 2013a).

---

5   The committee included Vi Deuschle (chair), Doreen Kartinyeri, Judy Lucas, Lewis O'Brien, and Val Power.
6   This later became Tandanya: National Aboriginal Cultural Institute, after Premier John Bannon refused to grant specific land on the River Torrens for the larger, purpose-built structure the committee had requested.
7   Throughout, I use the Aboriginal-English term 'Country' (as distinct from the standard Australian-English meaning), which encompasses home, clan estate, and the powerful complex of spiritual, animate and inanimate forces which bind people and place.

## Elemental Forces and Purposeful Ghosts

Pointing to Freud's concept of 'the uncanny' as a trope fundamental to settler experience, Ken Gelder and Jane Jacobs contend that an 'uncanny' experience occurs when 'one's home — one's place — is rendered somehow and in some sense unfamiliar; one has the experience, in other words, of being in place and "out of place" simultaneously. This happens precisely at the moment when one is made aware that one has unfinished business with the past, at the moment when the past returns as an *"elemental" force* [emphasis mine] ... to haunt the present day' (Gelder & Jacobs 1996, p. 111).

When I saw my grandmother's birthplace and the site of my childhood from the 'othered' shore, history for me became an elemental force. It was at that point that I began to fully perceive my family history and Ngarrindjeri history recalibrated in the same geo-social space—intersubjective and entangled.

Before, Lake Alexandrina had floated in my earliest memories as a mythic childhood place of creamy limestone cottages, hypnotic silvery water and elderly relatives—a site of great but un-investigated power, in which emanations of a deeper ancestral past resided, yet without clear articulation. I now began to question what exactly those traces were, and how they were constituted. What were the implications of my family's past in the Lower Murray lakes for Ngarrindjeri? My questions acted as 'purposeful ghosts', urging me to re-search this past as a way of explaining a now defamiliarised present.

The cultural theorist, Gail Jones, described the significance of an 'imagined real' in navigating through subterranean histories, suggesting that 'any child, who imagines her own history, re-dreams it, enters impossible perspectives ... performs the transitive and transferential, recognises in an almost intuitive way that her nation has various and diverse "situated knowledges" within it' (Jones 2006, p. 14).

Perhaps because my mother died when I was in adolescence, I retain heightened memories of her stories. Many of these belonged to Milang and the Lake, centering on vivid recollections of my mother's great-grandmother Louisa Coad (née Mott) (1851–1946), a lithe, strict woman in Victorian black, who stitched delicate 'log-cabin' patchworks and chased my mother around the veranda with a broomstick for eating almonds she was supposed to be shelling. Louisa's personal qualities of matrilineal authority, independence and creativity were discussed widely among our family. These stories mostly emphasised how Louisa, as an old woman, came back to the flat watery landscape of Milang from an even more mythic place, 'Ned Kelly country' in Victoria, to help out after her daughter (my great-grandmother) was widowed in 1935.

**Louisa Coad at Tawonga, Victoria, c. 1940, painted photograph.**

Source: Courtesy of Mrs Amy Ladson, collection of the author.

6. Stories my Grandmother Never Told Me

**Louisa Karpany (on right), c. 1910.**

Source: Courtesy of Ellen Trevorrow and the South Australian Museum.

As a child of seven, I would float on the Lake's brackish waters on hot summer afternoons and extend these sparse memory-fragments to imagine that Louisa (before her white hair and widows' gowns) had been Ned Kelly's lover. I remained convinced that, in time, a secret letter would emerge, hidden in an attic, verifying my great-great grandmother's agency in history. She was 'the woman behind the man', the only place she could have occupied in the Australia of that time, as well as the Australia of my 1960s imagination.

My creative dream-space, with its impossible leaps of agency and place, was indelibly linked to 'remembering' the Lake, and indeed my maternal lineage, through an improbable white male resistance history, embodied in the mythic figure of Kelly. Yet it was this listening for deeper layers of meaning, as Gail Jones suggests, that inspired my search for 'situated knowledges' and continuity of story as I grew. It also revealed much of my childish positioning of self in a suburban nuclear family during Australia's deeply assimilationist 1950s and early 1960s, in which powerful women were marginalised and Aboriginal peoples barely visible (Stanner 2011, pp. 182–191), Kelly's dislocated mask, superimposed across the Lake's surface, usurped the space where localised stories of strong, skilled women and enduring Aboriginal presence continued. Later, I was told of another Louisa, the Ngarrindjeri woman 'Queen' Louisa Karpany (née Kontinyeri) (c.1821–1921), who also dressed in black Victorian gowns, and whose presence in the landscape is still tangible. Eventually, I would come to work closely with some of her descendants (see Hughes & Trevorrow 2014).

## A Place of Sorcery

Gazing across to my grandmother's birthplace while standing beside the oldest living Ngarrindjeri woman from Point McLeay, I wondered at the possibilities for interconnectedness in these women's lives, which had paralleled each other over most of the twentieth century. Overwhelmingly I grasped the sense of missed encounters and lost possibilities. As children on opposite sides of Lake Alexandrina, and with the far wider gulf imposed by the *Aborigines Act SA 1911*, each was quite differently caught in the vortex of its ongoing consequences. In listening to the stories of Aunty Hilda Wilson and the other elders she introduced me to in the decade that followed, I became aware of how these consequences continued to unfold for the subsequent generations of their families, as for Australian society at large. The name 'Milang' itself, I discovered, was appropriated from the displaced Ngarrindjeri name, *Milangk*: 'place of sorcery'. Now Milang and Lake Alexandrina became a site of defamiliarisation and transformation, contributing to a revised identity and more complex sense of belonging and historical understanding.

6. Stories my Grandmother Never Told Me

I hoped a visit to my grandmother Dorothy might shed further light on our interwoven, intersecting pasts. In 1997, Dorothy was living just north of Milang in Strathalbyn. She possessed a lucid memory, although rarely one to indulge in the 'country of the past'.[8] Excited by my discoveries, I bombarded her with a torrent of questions, beginning with:

> 'Nanna, do you remember Aboriginal people living around Milang when you were a child?'
>
> 'There weren't any', she replied.

As I told her about accompanying Aunty Hilda Wilson to the former Point McLeay Mission she became animated, interrupting excitedly:

> 'I've been to Point McLeay'.
>
> 'What for?'
>
> 'The football!' she exclaimed.

On a number of occasions, my grandmother revealed, she had crossed Lake Alexandrina as a child to watch her father, her brothers and cousins in the Milang football team. Staggeringly, I was to discover they were competing against Hilda Wilson's brothers and cousins in the Point McLeay team, which was captained by Aunty Hilda's father, Wilfred Varcoe, in a game umpired by her grandfather, William Rankine (personal communication with Hilda Wilson, 1998). Dorothy described these Milang vs Point McLeay matches as 'wild', suggestive of the boundary-crossing inherent in the engagement of the occasion. Remarkably, I realised, rather than actively remembering the spectacle of the oval and its players, the act of crossing the Lake by wood-powered steamer boat, and the pleasure of these culturally transgressive intercommunity events, my grandmother had internalised a construction of settler-colonialism's grand narrative that there 'weren't any' Aboriginal people around Milang. So strong was this fiction, that it was only when I regaled her with Aunty Hilda's stories that she began to relate vivid memories of football matches between the two communities, often followed by picnics and dances—at a time when she said 'football was all there was'—with an Aboriginal presence (Hughes 2012, pp. 270–273).

Browsing the local history book, *Alexandrina's Shore*, lent by my mother's sister, I found a photograph of the Milang football team taken in 1897, a century earlier. It portrays Dorothy's father, my great-grandfather Tom Pavy, and Aunty Hilda's grandfather William Rankine, together in the frame. The photo

---

8   I refer to David Lowenthal's (and L P Hartley's) celebrated phrase, 'the past is another country' (Lowenthal 1985).

also reveals a third of the players in the 1897 Milang team to be Ngarrindjeri, although the Ngarrindjeri players are not named in the caption. Another prominent Ngarrindjeri elder, Ben Rigney, (who ran the mission butcher shop in conjunction with Milang's butcher, Ted Burgess, my grandmother's cousin-in-law), is also in the team. Elsewhere in the book, relegated to a chapter entitled 'Aborigines, Explorers and Wild-Life', was a photograph of Hilda's grandfather, William Rankine, with his infant daughter, Hilda's mother, Olive, on his lap. Later, exploring these photographs at my aunt's house, Aunty Hilda and I were able to put some of our overlapping stories together. These compelling images from more than a century before provided a valuable window into a more culturally diverse and interconnected world, hinting at biculturalism, negotiation and coexistence largely overwritten in later remembrance and localised constructions of settler identity (Hughes 2012, p. 273).

My grandmother also summoned a very early memory of Ngarrindjeri *ngowanthi* or wurlies on the Lake edge, where the Milang caravan park now sits, stretching across the foreshore to Lake Plains where her family had farmed. Late nineteenth-century drawings, too, record these Ngarrindjeri homes, but little is written of the everyday relations between the Ngarrindgeri families, estimated to comprise around 200 people (Burgess c.1980), and the recently arrived European townspeople, the *kringkari*, who 'shared' this space from the late 1840s until at least several years after *the Act*. In my grandmother's memory, the wurlies 'disappeared' by the late 1910s, but Aunty Hilda was able to provide names, faces and voices to at least one of the families in the Milang wurlies: that of her great-grandparents, Ellen Sumner and John Rankine, and their five children, including Aunty Hilda's grandfather, William Rankine. Theirs is a rich family story that stretches forward to descendants who now flourish in contemporary Australian society and public life, such as the former AFL football player Michael O'Loughlin and 2014 Australian of the Year, Adam Goodes.

Questions raised by the patterns of absence and presence in settler memory drove my doctoral research at Flinders University, exploring the intersection of Ngarrindjeri and settler history (Hughes 2009). This held broader implications for the way racialised, gendered and classed histories in Australia are locally and intimately constituted (Hughes 2012, 2013). Retracing my maternal genealogy, I sifted through signs that remained in letters, photos, household objects, in the landscape itself, and, most fruitfully, in conversations with those in the present. Surprisingly, it was mostly Ngarrindjeri people's recollections that enabled me to fill the gaps in my family's history.

Reputedly well-regarded across the cultural divide (personal communication with Madge Williams, 2000), my maternal grandfather, Hughie Keough, was a travelling picture-showman who brought the first silent films to the Lower

Murray towns, including the Point McLeay Mission, from the 1910s to the 1930s. Unfortunately, I was never able to hear his stories, for he died just months before I was born. Moreover, Dorothy, my grandmother, burnt most of his belongings (including films that he had made), but I treasure his small box brownie camera handed on from my mother. Ngarrindjeri loved the new medium of cinema so much that when they first travelled the two kilometres from Point McLeay to Narrung to see the movies, they filled and spilled out of the hall, soon building their own hall for the movies beside the mission church (personal communication with Leta Padman, 2009). At this time, the knowledgeable and respected Ngarrindjeri elder, Albert Karloan, in 1919 had an enterprising plan to make his own films and travel with his son Clem, showing movies, telling stories. This likely would have been the first Indigenous filmmaking venture in the world, but Albert Karloan was refused a loan to buy a cinematograph by the chief 'protector' of Aborigines, R. D. South, despite a letter of resounding support from Point McLeay's superintendent (Mattingly 1988, p. 125). It was quite possibly my grandfather who encouraged this venture and offered to procure a cinematograph. Whenever my grandfather pulled up to the mission hall, a small boy, Matthew Kartinyeri, waited to greet him and help carry his bag up the stairs to set up the reels in the projectionist's aerie. Matthew was never known by his birth-name, only by his nickname, Pictureman, which he continued to be called throughout his life, and which is now on his headstone (personal communication with Noreen Kartinyeri & Verna Koolmatrie, 2011). Although my aunt had earlier told me about her father taking the movies to Point McLeay, these were not stories told by my grandmother, but by Ngarrindjeri living today at Raukkan, and from Pictureman's daughter, Aunty Noreen Kartinyeri.

Other connections emerged that had been edited from my family's active remembering, including a marriage between my grandmother's second-cousin, Irene Coad, and the Ngarrindjeri man Walter McHughes early in the twentieth century. I was delighted that some of their 13 children were living. Their 80-year-old son, John McHughes, embraced me as 'cuz', describing the racism his mother endured—including from some of her sisters—for marrying black. I have to still meet John McHughes's sister, Betty Lorraine, who bears the same Christian names as my mother, Betty Loraine Hughes, living in parallel.

Another woman, Christina Black, further back in time, intrigued me. A great-aunt to my grandfather, Hughie Keough, she lived at Lake Plains in the 1840s, close to where Milang was later established. Thought to be an Irish-born servant, and known as 'generous hearted Christie', Christina broke ranks and openly sympathised with Ngarrindjeri dispossession, 'freely sharing her provisions with them'. 'Poor people', she is recorded to have said, 'we have taken their land' (Donald and Christina McLean Genealogical Council 1995, p. 203).

The reason for Christina's husband's explicit disinheritance from the large estate, amassed by his Scottish-born father Donald McLean, in the nascent years of the colony, however, is not stated, but perhaps implied by her renegade actions. Living against the currents of her times, her voice was a rarity. Intriguingly too, a Ngarrindjeri child born in the 1850s shares her name (Kartinyeri 2007, p. 80).

My father, Dean Hughes, was born elsewhere, in the dry mallee country inland from the Murray river-town of Loxton. His family walked off the land during the Great Depression drought in 1939. They leased a dairy-farm on Hindmarsh Island, in the Murray Mouth—an island with special significance for Ngarrindjeri women, at the centre of a distressing legal case in the 1990s (see Bell 1998). My father played football for the mainland town, Goolwa, alongside Ngarrindjeri sporting legend Herbert Rigney and, during the Second World War, shared a military hospital-ward and combat stories with Tim Hughes, the highly decorated Kaurna/Narrunga soldier. Yet his primary-school history book from a one-room school house in Wanbi in the 1930s (which I coveted as a child) makes only a single mention of Aboriginal peoples, as being 'extinct', while Captain Cook beams majestically from the cover (Granger n.d., p. 31). Moreover, his father, Alfred Hughes, was delivered in a tent under several inches of rising floodwaters on the Teetupla goldfields at Waukaringa on New Year's Day, 1888, by a skillful Aboriginal midwife, probably an Adnyamathanha woman. Such textual and material fragments allude to richer intersubjectivities and the potentiality of possible encounters, in 'unpicking of imperial histories' (Hall 1996, p. 76), but also to the missed encounters and lost social relationships found in cross-cultural reweaving.

## 'Learning to fall in love with your country'

In the decade that followed my 'epiphany' by the Lake at Raukkan, Aunty Hilda Wilson periodically fuelled my sense to know more, instructing me in histories, genealogies, stories and songs of her Country, and ancestors, which shaped my subsequent work. As with Rosalind Munur, history, Country and kin were inseparable. Stories were revealed where events had occurred as we travelled to visit friends and relations and to places of significance along the Coorong and in Adelaide homes. Slowly, too, I became part of a wider sense of kin as our relationship became family-like. Aunty Hilda passed away in 2007 at the age of 96, ten years after that first trip to Raukkan with her. She remained in good health until her death, singing songs and telling stories to her family and the hospital-nurses even in her final hours. For her, too, history had remained an elemental force.

Moreover, she had never allowed colonial intrusion to erode her sense of cultural sovereignty and Aboriginal identity (Hughes 2013b). Her granddaughter, Aunty Ellen Trevorrow, the renowned Ngarrindjeri weaver and cultural educator, and I now collaborate on a range of projects, as my learning continues (Hughes & Trevorrow 2014). But more than this, we have become an integral part of each other's family life, sharing the joys and the crises life throws before us.

Deploying ego-histoire as an historical method enabled a finely granulated appreciation of settler-colonial histories as a complex interweave of localised, intimate and intersubjective family histories (Haskins 1999). This encouraged me to pursue a microhistorical approach and a cross-cultural sensibility in my subsequent work, drawing in particular on Minoru Hokari's call for the need to cross-culturalise the discipline of history itself (Hokari 2011). The contact zone is co-creative and without closure, reaching across time, generations and space. Things can be otherwise. My sense of place is entirely different than before, and it is no longer possible to tell one story without the other, or to write histories of here or elsewhere to which I am disconnected. Bruce Pascoe calls this coming into knowledge of the settler-colonial atrocities, the unexpected ruptures of kindness, the injustices, the misunderstandings, the whole wham-bam thing, as 'learning to fall in love with your country' (Pascoe 2007).

## Epilogue: 'Time-travelling'

Not long ago, after moving to Melbourne, I met one of Louisa Coad's few surviving grandchildren, Amy Ladson, a younger cousin of my grandmother, Dorothy. Amy had cared for Louisa in her final years, when she could barely walk, during the 1940s, in the small Alpine community of Tawonga in northeastern Victoria. One long weekend, I drove there with Aunty Amy to meet others descended from Louisa. As night fell, family members assembled at the home of Louisa's great-grandson, Harold Coad. Many brought photographs inherited from Louisa's personal collection. These were shared around the dining table along with stories of the various photographic subjects and their connections to each of us. I gasped aloud with excitement as a large image caught my attention. Cardboard-backed and fraying at the edges, taken by a professional photographer in the 1890s, it featured a young non-Aboriginal man sharing a picnic outdoors with an Aboriginal man of similar age on a rural property. They sit together comfortably; their pose is unusual, hinting at a social relationship as much as a working one. Turning it over, I found written the names of its actors, likely written by Louisa's hand: Bill Bartholomew (Louisa's older brother's son) and Bob Pinkey, a name I instantly recognised as being Ngarrindjeri/Boandik from the Bordertown region in south-eastern South Australia. I felt as if I had been waiting for this photo for most of my life.

**Bob Pinkey and Bill Bartholomew, Bordertown, South Australia, c. 1890.**

Source: Photographer unknown, courtesy of Mrs Hazel Coad.

# References

Allen, M 2012, 'Impeccable Timing: A personal reflection', *Australian Feminist Studies*, vol. 27, no. 73.

Bell, D 1998, *Ngarrindjeri Wurruwarrin*, Spinifex, Melbourne.

Burgess, E c.1980, taped interview, Milang and District Historical Society.

Collins, P H 1991, 'Learning from the Outsider Within: The sociological significance of black feminist thought', in J Hartman & E Messer-Davidow (eds), *Gendering Knowledge*, University of Tennessee Press, Knoxville.

Donald and Christina McLean Genealogical Council 1995, *History of Donald and Christina McLean and their Descendants: First wheat crop growers in South Australia, 1838*, Milang, South Australia.

Farnsworth, C 1997, 'Burnum Burnum, 61, Fighter For Australia's Aborigines', *The New York Times*, August 20, 1997. Available at: http://www.nytimes.com/1997/08/20/world/burnum-burnum-61-fighter-for-australia-s-aborigines.html.

Gelder, K & J M Jacobs 1996, 'The Postcolonial Ghost Story,' *Journal of the Association for the Study of Australian Literature*, special issue, 'Current Tensions: Proceedings of the 18th Annual conference 6–11 July 1996', pp. 110–120.

Goodall, H 1996, *From Invasion to Embassy: Land in Aboriginal politics in NSW from 1770 to 1972*, Allen & Unwin, Sydney.

Granger, W (ed) n.d., *Australia's Story Told in Pictures*, John Sands, Sydney.

Grimshaw, P 2002, 'Federation as a Turning Point in Australian History', *Australian Historical Studies*, vol. 33, no. 118, pp. 25–41.

Hall, C 1996, 'Histories, Empires and the Post-Colonial Moment', in I Chambers & L Curtis (eds), *The Postcolonial Question: Common skies, divided horizons*, Routledge, London.

Harding, S 1991, Whose Science? Whose Knowledge?: Thinking from women's lives, Cornell University Press, New York.

Haskins, V 1999, 'Family Histories, Personal Narratives and Race Relations History in Australia', *Canberra Historical Journal*, vol. 45, pp. 25–29.

historychannel.com.au 2014, 'The Burnum Burnum Declaration of 26 January 1988'. Available at: http://thepeoplespeak.thehistorychannel.com.au/speeches/burnum-burnum/.

Hokari, M 2011, *Gurindji Journey: A Japanese historian in the outback*, UNSW Press, Sydney.

Hughes, K 2013, 'I'd Grown up as a Child Amongst Natives: Ruth Heathcock', *Outskirts: Feminisms along the Edge*, vol. 28. Available at: http://www.outskirts.arts.uwa.edu.au/volumes/volume-28/karen-hughes.

Hughes, K 2013a, 'Becoming Rosalind's Daughter: Reflections on intercultural kinship and embodied histories,' *Journal of the European Association for the Study of Australasia*, vol. 4, no. 1, pp. 76–91.

Hughes, K 2013b, 'Resilience, Agency and Resistance in the Storytelling Practice of Aunty Hilda Wilson (1911–2007), Ngarrindjeri Aboriginal Elder', *Media-Culture Journal*, vol. 16, no. 5. Available at: http://journal.media-culture.org.au/index.php/mcjournal/article/viewArticle/714.

Hughes, K 2012, 'Microhistories and Things that Matter: Opening spaces of possibility', *Australian Feminist Studies*, vol. 27, no. 73, pp. 269–278.

Hughes, K 2010, 'Fluid Waters: Cultural exchange in the land of the Ngarrindjeri, a poetics and a politics', *Le Simplegadi*, vol. 8, no. 8, pp. 24–35.

Hughes, K 2009, 'My Grandmother on the Other Side of the Lake', unpublished PhD thesis, Department of Australian Studies and Department of History, Flinders University.

Hughes, K 2006, 'Bob Dylan: The Sydney interview', in J Cott (ed.), *Bob Dylan: The essential interviews*, Hyperion, New York, pp. 237–251.

Hughes, K 2005, '"Same Bodies, Different Skin": Ruth Heathcock', in A Cole *et al.* (eds), *Uncommon Ground: White women in Aboriginal history*, Aboriginal Studies Press, Canberra, pp. 83–106.

Hughes, K 1986, *Pitjiri: The snake that will not sink*, (DVD re-release 2008), Ronin Films, Canberra.

Hughes, K and E Trevorrow 2014, '"It's that Reflection": Ngarrindjeri photography as recuperative practice', in J Lydon & S Braithwaite (eds), *Calling the Shots: Aboriginal photographies*, Aboriginal Studies Press, Canberra, pp. 175–204.

Jones, G 2006, 'A Dreaming, a Sauntering: Re-imagining critical paradigms', *Journal of the Association for the Study of Australian Literature*, vol. 5, pp 11–24.

Kartinyeri, D 2007, *Ngarrindjeri Nation*, Wakefield Press, Adelaide.

Langton, M 1983, 'Well, I Heard it on the Radio and I Saw it on the Television: An essay for the Australian Film Commission on the politics and aesthetics of filmmaking by and about Aboriginal people and things', Australian Film Commission, Sydney.

Lowenthal, D 1985, *The Past is a Foreign Country*, Cambridge University Press, Cambridge.

Mattingly, C, *et al.* 1988, *Survival in Our Own Land*, Wakefield Press, Adelaide.

McKenna, M 2002, *Looking for Blackfellas' Point: An Australian history of place*, UNSW Press, Sydney.

Olsen, T 1978, *Silences*, Delacorte Press, New York.

Pascoe, B 2007, *Convincing Ground: Learning to fall in love with your country*, Aboriginal Studies Press, Canberra.

Ramsland, J 2004, 'Bringing up Harry Penrith: Injustice and becoming Burnum Burnum — the formative years of a child of the Stolen Generation', Education Research and Perspectives, vol. 31, no. 2, pp. 94–106.

Read, P 1981, 'The Stolen Generations: The removal of Aboriginal children in New South Wales, 1883 to 1969', New South Wales Ministry of Aboriginal Affairs, Sydney.

Rigney, L 2006, 'Indigenist Research and Aboriginal Australia', in J Kunnie & N Goduka (eds), *Indigenous Peoples' Wisdom And Power: Affirming our knowledge through narratives*, Ashgate, Bodmin, pp. 32–50.

Stanner, W E H 2011, 'The Great Australian Silence', in *The Dreaming and Other Essays*, Black Inc, Melbourne, pp. 182–191.

# 7. 'Start By Telling Your Own Story': On Becoming An Anthropologist and Performing Anthropology

### Franca Tamisari

'Start from your own story, from your own experience, what brought you here from far away and what you learnt.' Keith Lapulung to the author, Milingimbi 1999.

*'Life as the product of life*. However far man may extend himself with his knowledge, however objective he may appear to himself — ultimately he reaps nothing but his own biography.' Friedrich Nietzsche, *Human All Too Human*, Section IX, 'Man Alone with Himself', aphorism 513.

## Introduction

Since the beginning of my career as an anthropology undergraduate in the mid-80s, and then as a PhD student in the early 90s at the London School of Economics, I have been aware of the issues raised by the so-called reflexive turn in the discipline. I was, in fact, particularly affected by the methodological and ethical concerns of what is known as 'cultural critique' or more generally the 'politics of representation': dismantling the power of the interpreter, the strategies of othering, as well as debunking the pitfalls of essentialism, the illusion of objective truth, and the partiality of ethnography (Clifford 1988; Fabian 1983; Marcus & Fisher 1987; Rosaldo 1989; Torgonvick 1991). I was equally exposed to some of the proposed solutions to these questions, such as the shift to embodied experience, and intersubjectivity in everyday life and in fieldwork research (Jackson 1983, 1989, 1998; Stoller 1989). My past interest and ongoing commitment to these issues in my current practice as a fieldworker, author, and lecturer also stem from personal, as well as professional motivations, choices, experiences and encounters which have brought me to anthropology.

I am reminded of the words that my Yolngu friend, Keith Lapulung, told me a few years ago, on the occasion of one of my return visits to Milingimbi, the Indigenous community in Northeast Arnhem Land where I have been conducting most of my fieldwork research since 1990. In one of our long conversations, I asked him to advise me on what aspects of my research I should write a book. Without hesitation, he told me not only to focus on what I learnt over the years in Milingimbi but also to 'start from your own story, from your own experience, what brought you here from far away'. This perspective would not only start including others as our public, as Lapulung's suggestion might have implied, but could also offer us other means to shift from what has been termed knowledge *about* to knowledge *with* the other (Jackson 1989, p. 8; von Sturmer 1999, 2001). In anthropology, knowledge *about* the other requires detachment or distance, objectivity, pre-established criteria and theoretical frameworks according to which ideas, objects and people are arrayed; in other words, it is conceived as separate from the sociality and intimacy in which it is embedded. In contrast, knowledge *with* is the more intuitive, face to face, coeval (Fabian 1983, p. 156), immediate and personal ways of knowing others in the field that cannot be reduced to the impersonal reality in the languages of theoretical reflexions and generalisations (De Monticelli 1998, p. 88; Jackson 1996, p. 8). Knowledge *with* is a 'being alongside with' that strengthens as well as makes one vulnerable (von Sturmer 2001, p. 104; De Monticelli 1998, pp. 181–182; Jackson 1989, p. 1; Tamisari 2006). In other words, encounters should be conceived in terms of the reality of a person in her own singularity, diversity, originality, creativity and unpredictability: an individuality 'incarnated in the lived actualisation of one's feelings—and in the passions, decisions and actions that follow' (De Monticelli 2003, p. 168).

With his clear and compelling words, Lapulung expressed one of the premises of a 'new ethnology', as identified by Ernesto De Martino (De Martino 2002, p. 86), an Italian ethnologist who, since the 1950s, incisively questioned the epistemological basis of positivist anthropological representations, including the ethnographer's positioning.[1] Criticising ahistorical approaches and 'objectivity' in anthropological descriptive accounts, as early as 1961, De Martino states that it is necessary to reveal the genesis of one's own research and/or 'consider the problem' of the authors' cultural history in order to acknowledge the other. In proposing a 'new anthropology', Fabian makes a similar point. In contrast to an 'informing ethnography' conceived of as a process of collection, selection and classification of data mainly through verbal communication, he advances the notion of a 'performing ethnography' (Fabian 1990, p. xv). In order to challenge 'the power of the hermeneut, the authoritative interpreter of texts', he affirms that 'ethnographies are questionable representations unless they show their own genesis', and ethnographers should recognise that any social phenomenon under scrutiny 'is not principally what they perform and we observe', but a reality in which we are engaged (Fabian 1990, p.p xiv–xv). These are the same

---

1  Ernesto De Martino is almost unknown in English-speaking anthropological traditions. His first monograph, *The Land of Remorse: A study of Southern Italian Tarantism*, was translated into English by D.L. Zinn in 2005. The book was first published in Italian in 1961 as *La Terra del Rimorso: Contributo a una storia religiosa del Sud*. On the 'promises and threats of anthropology', see also (De Martino 2002, pp. 84–118; De Martino 1977, pp. 389–423).

questions at the basis of Pierre Nora's project for a 'new history' that would break with a long scientific tradition which forced historians to 'disguise their personality behind their knowledge … and express themselves only through others' (Nora 1987, p. 5).

Nora's project, Fabian's performing ethnography, Lapulung's advice, and especially De Martino's warning, say the same thing in different yet complementary ways: if we deny ourselves we deny the other, if we do not start from our own story, we debase that of the other, if we do not start by unveiling the genesis of our own research as well as the passions and motivations informing and sustaining it, we will diminish the passion and the individuality of the other. The problem is not only due to having taken the other's individuality for granted—a shortcoming that has been recognised and partially addressed— but also to having systematically hidden the ethnographer's 'personal reality' (De Monticelli 1998, p. 98) and 'cultural history' (De Martino 2002, p. 1) that, with the individuality of the other, equally constitutes the grounds of any engagement. As 'the miniaturists of the social sciences' (Geertz 1971, p. 4), anthropologists should not only put others' 'individual lives under the microscope as a route to elucidating the nature of human social life' (Rapport 2003, p. 6), but also trace their own personal and intellectual trajectories by telling their stories. With some exceptions, as Popkin notes for historians (Popkin 1999, p. 727), anthropologists have been reluctant to engage in autoethnography (see Ellis, Adams & Bochner 2011) mainly because exposing their personal selves 'could undermine the authority of their scholarship'. As De Martino insists, scholars should not hide their own passions and choices but assert them without being afraid of becoming unfaithful to truth: 'On the contrary this attitude [could] open up the research to a new dimension of fidelity to the real' (De Martino 2002, p. 92).

## Either-Or: From Philosophy to Anthropology via a Tearoom

For me, anthropology has brought together four great passions: my political commitment, my fascination for philosophy, the real pleasure of learning foreign languages, and my intense life-long love for dancing. I was born in Genoa but, at the age of 12, moved with my family to Venice, where my father had found a job as a shipping clerk in a government-owned company. At the beginning, I took the move to Venice very badly but I soon grew to love my new city, as it offered me an independence and autonomy that would have been impossible in other places. Now that I have returned to live in Venice, I like to think I am a Venetian by adoption, as I spent here the most forming years of my adolescence.

From my first year at high school I was fascinated by philosophy, thanks to the teaching of Professor Aldo Cardin, who was able to capture our restless attention by presenting us key topics in an accessible yet sophisticated and rigorous way. One of the philosophers I was introduced to was Søren Kierkegaard. His book, *Either-Or: A fragment of life*, had a deep influence on me, although I read this text in an idiosyncratic manner, picking and focusing on the specific concepts and ideas that most resonated with the impetuous and impatient adolescent I was. I completely identified with the dilemma of choosing, as I was anxiously looking for ways of asserting and shaping my personality and future. What struck me in this work and has remained with me since was the way in which the 'reality of choosing' (Kierkegaard 1976, p. 52) was not determined by the 'rightness' of the choice, but was defined by the passion of the act of choosing itself. Picking up the very copy of this book I read so eagerly, I have found what I had underlined when I was around 16:

> ... I can say that in choosing it is not important to choose right but rather the energy, seriousness and pathos with which one chooses (Kierkegaard 1976, p. 43, my translation).

From the very beginning of high school, I started gravitating around the student movement that was very active in those years. In fact, my political commitment started in my first year in high school, on the 11th of September, 1973, the day in which President Salvador Allende, we claimed, was assassinated, and did not commit suicide.[2] I joined the other students walking out of the school to participate in an almost spontaneous demonstration of indignation and protest without any doubt.

My political commitment was also influenced and informed, at least at the beginning, by the political education I received from my father at home. A supporter of the Italian Communist Party, my father often lectured us on social justice, workers' rights and especially his firm opposition to the Catholic Church's meddling in State affairs. Almost every Sunday, my father used to initiate a heated discussion on current political debates with his own father, who was a republican, and his father-in-law, who had remained a convinced fascist and member of the Italian Social Movement Party (MSI). Although my mother asked us to leave the table as soon as the fierce altercations would start, I could hear my father screaming and swearing at the top of his voice until the front door would slam shut behind the theatrical exit of one of my two grandfathers.

I remember a particular speech my father made to me when I was around ten, in a moment that I could only properly contextualise later. It must have been

---

2 Despite the fact that President Salvador Allende's suicide was confirmed by the Chilean Government following the exhumation of his body in 2011, there are still speculations that he was assassinated in the aftermath of Pinochet's coup d'état.

just after the unrests of 1968 when he summoned me, and, in a solemn and concerned tone of voice, warned that I should value events 'always thinking with my own mind'. To be able to do that, he added, I had 'to read a lot and go on studying'. I followed closely all the modest yet highly-principled battles he waged with the unions against his employer in order to have some of his rights recognised. During high school, however, I started arguing with my father over a series of issues, mainly due to my sympathies for extra-parliamentary political movements and particularly my assiduous participation in a local feminist group. Despite his communist ideals, my father, like most men of his generation, was steeped in, and kept on reproducing sexist and racist attitudes towards everything different or new. For instance, he was in favour of divorce—legalised in Italy with the referendum of 1974—but opposed the legalisation of abortion that was passed after the referendum of 1978. My thirst for independence and the escalating tension and frequent arguments with my father led me to leave home and move into a small shared flat in Venice as soon as I turned 18.

At the end of high school, I started a degree in philosophy at Ca' Foscari University of Venice, which I did not complete. It was then the end of the 70s, a period of social political turmoil also known as *gli anni di piombo,* literally 'the years of lead', in reference to the number of lead bullets shot in both right-wing and left-wing terrorist attacks. State control increased through the enforcing of a series of anti-terrorist laws after the Red Brigades kidnapped and assassinated Aldo Moro, then President of the Christian Democratic Party, in 1978.

My involvement in the student movement, especially a local feminist group, distanced me from university and the way in which philosophy was taught at the time. Despite my passion for the discipline, philosophy was taught, as Bourdieu puts it in his 'self-analysis', in a 'closed, separate world, set apart from the vicissitudes of the real world' (Bourdieu 2007, pp. 8–9), and it seemed to me, as Lévi-Strauss notes, 'a kind of aesthetic contemplation of consciousness by itself'(Lévi-Strauss 1989, p. 63). I kept on studying philosophy outside the university, but opted for Foucault's *Discipline and Punish* (Foucault 1976), which I read avidly in 1979. At the same time, I continued to read Sartre's novels, which affected me deeply. I particularly recall *Nausea* and *Dirty Hands*, as the latter dealt with political engagement. However, my total energies were completely absorbed by the ideas, initiatives and events aimed at claiming justice, democracy and freedom. Looking for an activity that could allow the enactment of this real effervescence towards political change, in 1979 I left university and, with four other 18-year-old women, I opened a tearoom called *La Zucca* (The Pumpkin). This name was decided upon in reference to the feminist re-readings of the Cinderella tale, to stress the capacity for political transformation leading to women's emancipation.

Following the model of similar initiatives in Florence and Bologna, the tearoom was not only a commercial activity but represented the possibility of creating a meeting point or, better, a sort of refuge from the oppressing policing enforced by the State in those years. We saw the tearoom as an alternative place where we could discuss politics, read poetry or simply gather in a free and creative space. After a few months, however, the tearoom went bankrupt for a number of reasons: many of our prospective clients were, in fact, only interested in boozing; in addition, most of the shopkeepers around, mainly men, derided us for our inexperience and ingenuousness; finally, a group of drug addicts who lived in the neighbourhood started being aggressive. Soon I realised that our initiative was completely foreign to the cultural and social reality in which it was set, or, as I would have said in those days, 'the tearoom was bourgeois', as it went against the cultural grain of everyday life in Venice. Those who knew Venice back then, when the local taverns (*bacari*) were the privileged gathering places for bean soup-eating, card-playing and soccer-talking workers, will certainly smile at the notion of a place where only tea and cakes were served.

I decided to go back to studying. Perhaps, I thought, this was the only thing I could do properly. I chose to dedicate myself to the study of languages, English and French, a practical study that could keep me in touch with people and life. In 1980, I enrolled in a private interpreting school in Florence where I lived for three years. During this period, I travelled and lived for long periods in France and England in order to become proficient in the languages I was studying. Perhaps, without knowing it, my anthropological career started from my travel experiences in these countries, when I realised that the only way of learning a language was with others, mainly in the streets. I used to spend many hours listening to the different ways and accents in which people spoke English around me, trying to understand what was happening and attempting to participate. I finally felt at ease when I could effortlessly reply to a young woman who had asked me for directions with a thick London accent.

As soon as I established myself as a freelance translator and interpreter in London, however, I started feeling unsatisfied, as I was missing the intellectual stimulus and the rigorous critique I had known when studying philosophy. With the exception of some interesting jobs (interpreting at the international meetings of the World Council of Churches, and in some court cases, for example) most of my work dealt with boring translations of technical instruction manuals which, once again, made me feel isolated from the people and life around me.

In 1986, looking at university curricula, I came across social anthropology, a subject I had never heard of before. In my ignorance, I believed that anthropology united the study of the philosophy of non-western societies and the study of a language necessary to understand and document their knowledge system, values, symbols and practices. In addition, from my quixotic perspective, it offered the potential of dealing with, or, at least, learning and denouncing the consequences of what, at the time, I termed as the imperialist domination and destructive capitalist influence of the 'West over the rest'. Thanks to a scholarship, I enrolled as an undergraduate student in the Social Anthropology Department at the London School of Economics (LSE) in 1986.

At LSE my studies were guided by a group of academics who stimulated my intellectual curiosity and developed my research potential in different ways.[3] However, in hindsight, I am grateful to my teachers not only for their intellectual rigour, but also for the contagious enthusiasm for critical thinking that they transmitted in their teaching. Paradoxically, it was this very passion they passed on that motivated and sustained me especially when I made important choices in my student career so openly against their judgment and advice.

## Sticking To My Decision: Doing Fieldwork on Dance

In my third year as an undergraduate, I took a course taught by David McKnight, who had conducted his fieldwork among the Lardil in the Gulf of Carpentaria in Australia. McKnight's introduction to his course struck a chord with me. In a few broad and dismissive sentences that sounded like a challenge, he said something like: 'I'm going to teach a course on my own research on ritual and dance and I only want students who are interested'. His lectures inspired me not only for their informality but also because, for the first time, I could start appreciating that anthropology is a modality of knowledge based on first-hand experience and encountering people. More significantly, McKnight's lectures awoke another of my passions that had remained dormant up to then: dance. From a very young age I loved dancing and over the years I practiced a varieties of styles: rhythmic, classical, and modern dance. I have always danced and I could not live without practicing some form of dancing. My latest discovery is Argentine tango, which I've been assiduously practicing for the last nine years.

In talking about Lardil ceremonies, McKnight insisted that dance in ritual contexts is an 'intellectual activity', and, in order to capture what perhaps could not be said in words, would turn on the music and start dancing. He would explain to us the meanings of dance steps and gestures. Most importantly, through his impromptu and energetic executions, he enacted the intensity or 'feeling' of movement as a way of engaging attention. This expressive aspect and sensual understanding of dance performance—what is immediately

---

3   I would like to acknowledge the following lecturers in particular: Maurice Bloch, Chris Fuller, Alfred Gell, David McKnight, Joanna Overing, Jonathan Parry, Michael Sallnow and James Woodburn.

experienced yet escapes analysis (Dufrenne 1973, p. 263)—was to be a central concern in my research (Tamisari 2000, 2005a, 2005b, 2014). Thanks to my dance practice, those unusual lectures on Lardil dance made me understand—on a pre-objective, experiential level—that the 'how' adds meaning to the 'what' of performance, or, in other words, expression overflows and gives life to representation (Tamisari 2005a, p. 194; see also Schieffelin 1985). What resonated with me in those lectures was that, as I argued much later, 'feeling [is] a mode of attention [that] revives knowledge and it is knowledge which makes this feeling intelligent' (Tamisari 2005b, p. 54). From that time, I started reading whatever I could find on Australian Indigenous studies in general and dance in particular. The dearth of material then available in London further increased my intellectual curiosity.

My proposal to focus on ceremonial dance and carry out fieldwork in Australia did not, however, meet my other lecturers' wishes. The head of department was opposed to my choice. He said that Aboriginal people were 'dead', as they had been completely assimilated by the colonial regime, and dismissively added that studying dance in this context would be equivalent to studying embroidery in the Catholic Church. Another of my lecturers who had exercised a strong influence during my undergraduate years discouraged me from carrying out research in Australia, saying 'I wouldn't be seen dead there'. This time, however, I was not prepared to give up, and, defying my teachers, I stuck to my decision.

The difficulties I encountered did not end with my return from the field, when, like other PhD students, I was to present my research results. Around 1992 at LSE, most lecturers were not attuned to ethical concerns in general, and were oblivious of the particular processes of recognition and protocol that research in Indigenous studies could not avoid considering. In what follows, I would like to recall a series of events that informed my approach and practice in teaching Indigenous studies. As Fabian notes, the notion of performance does not only refer to what, beyond discourse, can be 'made present only through action [and] enactment' in which the ethnographer is engaged, but also implies the 'communication of our finding, mostly through writing', and, I would add, teaching (Fabian 1990, p. 6). During my fieldwork I was not only taught many aspects of Yolngu knowledge but was also educated to become and be accountable for the knowledge I had learnt. In other words, I was given and expected to take up the responsibility of performing that knowledge according to Yolngu Law (*rom*) both in the community and elsewhere (Tamisari 2005b).

## The Responsibility of Performance

As soon as I arrived in Milinbimbi in 1990, I realised that I had been naïve and rather arrogant in wanting to study Yolngu ritual in general, and dance in particular, in isolation from the complexities of a highly sophisticated political system expressed in a religious and aesthetic idiom, and as such, a highly sensitive sphere of power and authority negotiations in gender, generational and cross-cultural interactions. Very soon I recognised that, in order to approach the significance of Yolngu ritual dance, I had to learn the language, transcribe the songs, understand the principles and dynamics of the land tenure organisation, and orient myself in the intricate network of rights and duties in everyday life and ceremonial performance. Ceremony is not simply a specific context, but rather provides a frame and logic of Yolngu Law (see Christie 1992, p. 12; Tamisari & Milmilany 2003, p. 6), namely the correct social and moral behaviour to establish, reproduce and sustain relationships with others, both human and ancestral, animate and inanimate (Tamisari & Bradley 2005). Most importantly, as I was gradually taught in subtle yet consistent ways, the law is also a modality of knowledge, which, always actualised through consenting and dissenting with another person or 'quasi-person' in specific encounters (De Monticelli 2003, p. 168), needs to be experienced and felt in order to be observed and applied (Tamisari 2006, 2014).

When, on my return from the my first period of fieldwork (1990–1992), I was asked to report on my research results, I strongly felt that there was some information that I could not mention—in this case a series of proper individual and group names. At the time, fresh from the field, I had not as yet elaborated the cultural and political significance of proper names (Tamisari 2002), but I knew that I could not present that information. The lecturer who was organising the seminars criticised me, saying that these concerns were not relevant and that I should relate all the data I collected without hesitation 'in the name of science'. Although at the time I could not fully articulate the reasons behind my ethical position, I replied that in pronouncing those proper names I would have betrayed the people who entrusted me with that knowledge. With the wisdom of hindsight, this was the first occasion in which I realised that, along with the knowledge, I was also given the responsibility to handle it without contravening Yolngu rules and sensibilities.

On several occasions during my fieldwork I had received direct instructions on what I should not document and reproduce in any form because of its sacred/secret nature. More informally, I understood what constitutes intimate and personal knowledge that cannot be divulged. However, it was only at the end of my first stay in Milingimbi that I officially received precise instructions on how to handle the knowledge I had acquired. A few days before my departure from the field and return to London in 1992, I was summoned by Charles Manydjari, my 'mother's brother' (*ngapipi*) and Liwagawumirr elder who presented me with a precious gift after a short but intense dance organised for the occasion. The feather crownlet I was given is one of the sacred objects embodying the ancestral knowledge and land ownership of his group.

At the end of the dance, sitting next to him with the crownlet firmly around my head, Ngapipi said to me: 'This is your mother, it is private, and it is for you to take away. I give it to you to take to London where you should not forget that you can always put your Yolngu cap on. However, you should only wear it on important occasions.'

The meaning of this event, which I recall in detail elsewhere (Tamisari 2005b), was a way of consolidating the passion of our relationship (Sansom 1995, p. 308), acknowledging my stay in the community, marking my departure, and a manner of stressing our 'mutuality of being' (Stasch 2009, p. 132; see also Sahlins 2011) which bonded us and all other living and deceased kin of my adoptive family. The dance and the gift I received also marked the beginning of a new relationship, a welcome rather than a farewell. Only now, however, almost 20 years from that day and after many returns, can I begin to appreciate the meaning of this gift in terms of the ongoing fulfilment of the responsibilities that such a mutual engagement engenders. Ngapipi stated that the gift I received was the potential—in its meaning of having the power and authority—'to put my Yolngu cap on', but I did not fully understand it at the time. As Ngapipi instructed me, I took the feather circlet with me to London where I returned to write up my PhD thesis. The first opportunity to wear it presented itself at my viva, which took place at the London School of Economics in 1994. At the end of the viva, I took the circlet out of my bag and posed for a photograph tall and proud with it firmly on my head standing between my two examiners, Professors Howard Morphy and Bruce Kapferer. The second opportunity was in 1999, when I received Australian citizenship at the Leichhardt Town Hall in Sydney. I donned the crownlet during the ceremony. In displaying this object on important occasions, as instructed by Ngapipi, I continued to learn about the significance of the performative from a Yolngu perspective. At the time, I thought that these occasions warranted the display of this object because the circlet would be the Yolngu equivalent of a PhD award and citizenship certificate. I now understand that the significance of this gift does not only reside in the object as a token of my membership in Yolngu society, nor is it merely the equivalent of a degree in Yolngu knowledge. The significance of this gift resides in the responsibility of performance, the possibility I was given to display it, and the rights and duties I was granted in handling Yolngu knowledge. Every time I look at the crownlet, which I jealously keep in my bedroom, I remember and understand what Charles Manydjari told me when he bestowed it upon me.

The crownlet is not simply an object to be worn at important occasions but, most importantly, stands for a way of thinking, a mode of knowing and doing I was taught and asked to employ whenever I dealt with and presented Yolngu knowledge in my performances as a writer and a teacher.

## Teaching Indigenous Studies

When I arrived in Sydney to take up my first lecturing appointment, I was disoriented. It was the first time that I lived in an Australian city, having spent most of the previous two and a half years in the Indigenous community of Milingimbi. I planned, wrote and delivered several courses, including the large introductory class in Indigenous studies that I co-taught with Gillian Cowlishaw. I will never forget the first lecture I gave in this course, entitled 'Aborigines in Australia'. Despite my scrupulous preparation, my heart throbbed in my throat and I was almost paralysed in front of hundreds of students who were eagerly looking at me in anticipation. Today I can say that what made me so insecure was not so much my inexperience in addressing a large student audience for the first time, but the responsibility of performance that my teaching involved. From this moment, I became aware that, as Charles Manydjari told me, teaching was one of the occasions where I had to test and find out what 'to put my Yolngu cap on' meant, not only in terms of the trust I was given in handling Yolngu knowledge, but also in dealing with Indigenous realities, with all their ethical risks and possibilities. One of the major issues I have had to confront throughout my teaching in Australia, as well as now in Italy, was students' stereotypical representations of Indigenous realities: a superficial knowledge of Australian colonial past and an almost total ignorance of the history and extent of the country's racial conflict. After the first lectures on aspects of this history, some students accused me of not telling the truth, while others were sincerely shocked and asked me, as in Reynolds' book title 'why weren't we told?' (Reynolds' 1999). Although many studies on this hidden history had been published and political events had been drastically changing the political scene throughout the 90s, it seemed to me that 'the Great Australian Silence' (Stanner 1979, p. 207) was still carrying on in subtle yet powerful ways. Given the complicity of anthropology in reproducing and transforming 'the Great Australian Silence' into 'a cult of forgetfulness' of past and present racial relations (Stanner 1979, p. 214), it was, for me, a priority to make students critically reflect on these historical and cultural representations by focusing on what I referred to as 'the politics of representation' (Langton 1983, 2003, pp. 109ff). It is from this perspective that I enthusiastically collaborated with the colleagues of the Koori

Centre at the University of Sydney who were struggling to gain control over the teaching of the courses in Indigenous Studies in order to develop the Centre, which had been established in 1992 (Mooney & Cleverly 2011).[4]

In 2001 at the University of Queensland I found myself again co-teaching the introductory course in Indigenous studies ('Aboriginal and Islander Australia', which was renamed 'Contested Realities' in 2003) this time in collaboration with John Bradley, with whom I shared my concerns.

Thanks to the discussions I had with John throughout these years of close collaboration, I could start identifying and fully elaborating the ways in which our personal encounters with specific persons in the field are at the basis of the knowledge we produce in our performances as teachers and authors. It was from this time that I began courses by 'telling my story', thus expanding the notion of the ethnographer's 'positioning' to include my motivations, choices, experience and passions inevitably stemming from specific encounters with other persons through the gradual and never-ending process of personal acquaintance (Tamisari 2006).

In the field, we neither meet a culture as system of values and ideas, nor do we meet a(ny)body with its biological functions and rhythms. In the field we do not happen to come across a 'habitus' (Bourdieu 1972, p. 72), but a person with her essential individuality 'which is the story of a person, one's experiences, one's formation, encounters, choices, adventures and misadventures' (De Monticelli 1998, p. 121). If it is impossible to conceive a world without this sense of personal reality (De Monticelli, p. 98), I would argue that it is possible to encounter another person only by exposing one's own essential individuality. Thus, in order to encounter another person—in the field, in a classroom or in writing—it is not sufficient to focus on the other's essential individuality without also including our own as ethnographers, teachers and authors. Elaborating on De Monticelli, I maintain that the encounter is not only the experience in which an essential individuality announces itself to us, but also the manner in which we are prepared to announce ourselves to them, or the willingness of disclosing our personal and cultural history (De Monticelli 1998, p. 134). 'Starting by my own story'—what brought me to become an anthropologist as well the passions behind my choices and motivations—has allowed me to fulfil the responsibility implicit in the trust and accountability that a mutual engagement with other persons engenders. Continuously challenged by my performance as a writer and a teacher, I keep exposing myself to all the risks of relationships in order to renew the full potential of encountering the other.

---

4   I am particularly grateful to Janet Mooney, Michelle Blanchard, Katherine Thorpe and Wendy Brady, who gave me the possibility of participating in their discussions and plans aimed at realising this project.

# References

Amit, V & N Rapport 2002, *The Trouble with Community: Anthropological reflections on movement, identity and collectivity*, Pluto Press, London.

Bourdieu, P 2007, *Sketch for a Self-Analysis*, Polity Press, Cambridge.

Bourdieu, P 1972, *Outline of a Theory of Practice*, Cambridge University Press, Cambridge.

Clifford, J 1988, *The Predicament of Culture: Twentieth-century ethnography, literature, and art*, Harvard University Press, Cambridge.

Cohen, P A 1994, *Self Consciousness: An alternative anthropology of identity*, Routledge, London and New York.

Cohen, P A & N Rapport 1995, 'Introduction: Consciousness in Anthropology', in A P Cohen & N Rapport (eds), *Questions of Consciousness*, Routledge, London and New York, pp. 1–18.

Christie, M 1992, 'Grounded and Ex-centric Knowledges: Exploring Aboriginal alternatives to western thinking', paper presented at 'Thinking Conference', James Cook University, Townsville.

De Martino, E 2005, *The Land of Remorse: A study of Southern Italian Tarantism*, translated by D L Zinn, Free Association Books, London.

De Martino, E 2002, 'Promesse e Minacce dell' Etnologia', in E De Martino (ed.), *Furore Simbolo Valore*, Feltrinelli, Milano, pp. 84–118.

De Martino E 1977, 'L'Umanesimo Etnografico', in C Gallini (ed.), *La Fine del Mondo: Contributo all'analisi delle apocalissi culturali*, Biblioteca Einaudi, Torino, pp. 389–413.

De Monticelli, R 2003, *L'Ordine del Cuore: Etica e teoria del sentire*, Garzanti, Milano.

De Monticelli, R 1998, *La Conoscenza Personale: Introduzione alla fenomenologia*, Guerrini Studio, Milano.

Dufrenne M 1973, *The Phenomenology of Aesthetic Experience*, translated by E L Casey, Northwestern University Press, Evanston.

Ellis, C, T E Adams & A P Bochner 2011, 'Autoethnography: An Overview', in *Forum: Qualitative Social Research*, vol. 12, no. 1. Available at: http://www.qualitative-research.net/index.php/fqs/article/view/1589/3095.

Fabian, J 1990, *Power and Performance: Ethnographic explorations through proverbial wisdom and theatre in Shaba, Zaire*, The University of Wisconsin Press, Madison.

Fabian, J 1983, *Time and the Other: How anthropology makes its object*, Columbia University Press, New York.

Foucault, M 1976, *Sorvegliare e Punir:, Nascita della prigione*, translated by A Tarchetti, Einaudi, Torino.

Geertz, C 1971, *Islam Observed: Religious development in Morocco and Indonesia*, University of Chicago Press, Chicago.

Jackson, M 1998, *Mimima Etnographica: Intersubjectivity and the ethnographic project*, University of Chicago Press, Chicago.

Jackson, M 1996, 'Introduction', in M. Jackson (ed.), *Things as They Are: New directions in phenomenological anthropology*, Indiana University Press, Bloomington, pp. 1–50.

Jackson, M 1989, 'Introduction', in M. Jackson (ed.), *Paths Towards a Clearing: Radical empiricism and ethnographic inquiry*, Indiana University Press, Bloomington, pp. 1–18.

Jackson, M 1983, 'Thinking Through the Body: An essay on understanding metaphor', *Social Analysis*, vol. 14, pp. 127–148.

Kierkegaard, S 1976, *Aut-Aut: Estetica ed etica nella formazione della personalità*, Mondadori, Milano.

Langton, M 2003, 'Aboriginal Art and Film: The politics of representation', in I Anderson & M Grossman (eds), *Blacklines: Contemporary Critical Writing by Indigenous Australians*, Melbourne University Press, Melbourne, pp. 109–121.

Langton, M 1983, 'Well, I Heard it on the Radio and I Saw it on the Television: An essay for the Australian Film Commission on the politics and aesthetics of filmmaking by and about Aboriginal people and things', Australian Film Commission, Sydney.

Lévi-Strauss, C 1989, *Tristes Tropiques*, Picador Classics, London.

Marcus, G E & M J Fischer 1987, *Anthropology as Cultural Critique: An experimental moment in the human sciences*, Chicago University Press, Chicago.

Mooney, J & J Cleverly 2009, *Taking Our Place: Aboriginal education and the story of the Koori Centre at the University of Sydney*, Sydney University Press, Sydney.

Nietzsche, F 1996, *Human All Too Human: A book for free spirits*, translated by M Faber and S Lehmann, University of Nebraska Press, Lincoln.

Nora, P 1987, 'Présentation', in P Nora (ed.), *Essais d'Ego-Histore*, Gallimard, Paris, pp. 5–7.

Popkin, J D 1999, 'Historians On An Autobiographical Frontier', *The American Historical Review*, vol. 104, no. 3, pp. 725–748.

Rapport, N 2003, *I Am Dynamite: An alternative anthropology of power*, Routledge, London and New York.

Reynolds, H 1999, *Why Weren't We Told?*, Penguin Books, Melbourne.

Rosaldo, R 1989, *Culture and Truth: The remaking of social analysis*, Beacon Press, Boston.

Sahlins, M 2011, 'What Kinship Is (Part One)', *Journal of the Royal Anthropological Institute*, vol. 17, no. 1, pp. 2–19.

Sansom, B 1995, 'The Wrong, the Rough and the Fancy: About immortality and an Aboriginal aesthetic of the singular', *Anthropological Forum*, vol. 7, no. 2, pp. 259–314.

Schieffelin, E L 1985, 'Performance and the Cultural Construction of Reality', *American Ethnologist*, vol. 12, no. 4, pp. 707–724.

Stasch, R 2009, *Society of Others: Kinship and mourning in a West Papuan place*, University of Califorrnia Press, Berkeley.

Stanner, W E H 1979, 'After The Dreaming', in W E H Stanner (ed.), *White Man Got No Dreaming: Essays 1938–1973*, ANU Press, Canberra, pp.198–248.

Stoller, P 1989, *The Taste of Ethnographic Things: The senses in anthropology*, University of Pennsylvania Press, Philadelphia.

Tamisari, F 2014 'Feeling, Motion and Attention in the Display of Emotions in Yolngu Law, Song and Dance Performance', *Journal for the Anthropological Study of Human Movement*, vol. 21, no. 2.

Tamisari, F 2006, 'Personal Acquaintance: Essential Individuality and the Possibilities of Encounters', in T Lea, E Kowal & G Cowlishaw (eds), *Provoking Ideas: Critical Indigenous studies*, Darwin University Press, Darwin, pp. 17–36.

Tamisari, F 2005a, 'Writing Close to Dance: Reflexions on an experiment' in E Mackinlay, D Collins & S Owens (eds), *Aesthetics and Experience in Music Performance*, Cambridge Scholars Press, Newcastle, pp. 174–203.

Tamisari, F 2005b, 'Responsibility of Performance: The Interweaving of politics and aesthetics in intercultural contexts', *Visual Anthropology Review*, vol. 21, no. 1–2 University of California Press, Berkley, pp. 47–62.

Tamisari, F 2002, 'Names and Naming: Speaking forms into place', in L Hercus, F Hodges & J Simpson (eds), *The Land is a Map: Placenames of Indigenous origin in Australia*, Pandanus Books, Canberra, pp. 87–102.

Tamisari, F 2000, 'The Meaning of the Steps is in Between: Dancing and the curse of compliments', in *The Australian Journal of Anthropology*, vol. 11, no. 3, pp. 36–48.

Tamisari F & J Bradley 2005, 'To Have and to Give the Law: Animal names, place and event', in A Minelli, G Ortalli & G Sanga (eds), *Animal Names*, Istituto Veneto delle Scienze, Lettere ed Arti, Venice, pp. 419–438.

Tamisari F & E Milmilany 2003, 'Dhinthun Wayawu: Looking for a pathway to knowledge — Towards a vision of Yolngu Education', *The Australian Journal of Indigenous Education*, vol. 23, pp. 1–10.

Torgonvick, M 1991, *Gone Primitive: Savage intellects, modern lives*, Chicago University Press, Chicago.

von Sturmer, J 1999, 'Aborigines in Australia', unpublished manuscript, The University of Sydney.

von Sturmer, J 2001, 'Hot Diggidy Dog or Stomaching the Truth or One Way Passage', *UTS Review*, vol. 7, no. 1, pp. 96–105.

# 8. Yagan, Mrs Dance and Whiteness

Jan Idle

## Perth

It is a very hot day in the northern suburbs of Perth, Western Australia; really hot and very dry. It is the kind of day when the shimmer of the temperature distorts the horizon line of the Indian Ocean that I can see when we go to swim. The beach is ten minutes walk from my parents' house, a 1970s dream home, originally with shag pile carpet, which has long been replaced. On days like this it is too hot to walk, and we drive for our mid-morning swim, the second swim of the day. The heat from the bitumen makes the air shimmer and the sand sears our feet, so we get as close to the sea as possible before running shoeless for the water and gentle waves. It is perfect weather for drying laundry, yesterday's dirty washing is white, pristine, folded and put away before lunch. It is Perth and this is Christmas. We return 'home' regularly to visit relatives and old friends, to reconnect with our shared history, but by the end of two weeks I am always ready to go back to the east coast, where my real life is disconnected from my Western Australian past, which is how I prefer it. Besides, all that swimming gives me water brain and all I can imagine is immersing myself in the salty water of the Indian Ocean in order to get cool, and I cannot think. The distance between there and here is geographically and psychically great, and 'home' pulls in both directions. That past continues to live into my present, hounding my academic endeavours, luring me into remembering history and acknowledging it.

When it is this hot, we go to the Karrinyup Shopping Centre, a 20-minute drive south, or to the Art Gallery of Western Australia, which takes about the same time but on the freeway, to enjoy the air-conditioning until the sea breeze, affectionately referred to as the 'Fremantle Doctor', comes in, offering some relief from the relentlessness of dry and hot. The shopping centre can be too crowded and too awful, claustrophobic, and you can be swallowed up by the consumerism of Christmas or the frenzy of the Boxing Day sales, or encounter fierce parking anger as the drivers try to park close to the entrance of the centre to minimise the transfer from air-conditioned car to air-conditioned shops and avoid the barren walk across the bitumen. A trip to the gallery is usually more pleasant, entertaining and diverse. No parking problems there and it gives us (that is, the extended family and me) something to talk about. But when it is this hot it is too hard to think.

The heat is nostalgic and familiar, pulling me back into this place, returning me to what I left behind. The sense of longing to belong and a conflicted connection with the past and its heritage persists in post-colonial, non-Indigenous Australia, and is acted out through a 'haunted community', a community haunted by the deaths of others (Secomb 2002, pp. 131–150), and 'white paranoia', the anxiety of white settlers' possession of territory (Hage 2003, pp. 47–66). It is a community that continues to negotiate: the history and lie of *terra nullius*, the 2008 apology to the Stolen Generation, the intervention into Indigenous communities in the Northern Territory, and the gap between Indigenous and non-Indigenous lives. Australian concepts of identity are underpinned by their complex relationships with the past, marked by 'discontinuity' where 'what we choose to call the past is reflexive: the past is not so much that which has already happened as it is a label to be applied to that which we wish to finish and forget, from which we wish to differentiate ourselves and thus to absolve ourselves from responsibility' (Rose 2004, p. 18). 'Many Aboriginal people in the Victoria River District ... indicated they believed Whitefellas were in a state of epistemological crisis ... [not knowing] what to remember and what to forget' (Rose 1997, p. 101). The promise of this amnesia, this archiving of memory, is that an Australian identity can be imagined and arise from a clean, working space with all the tools and the messy ingredients of colonising country and nation put away, neatly contained by labels and timeframes, and separate from us. That past is done, but not here in the gallery, here there is only respite from the heat (Connerton 2008, pp. 59–71).

Artefacts and visual culture display a form of institutionalised heritage, engaging us with what we can know or understand of the past. It prompts us to revisit and articulate the haunted community, whiteness, disconnection, and shame of the past and the present in the Australian context, bringing history into the everyday. I return to look at two paintings from the permanent collection in the Art Gallery of Western Australia. These paintings help me to think about the representations of shared (and contradictory) meanings of historic events through paying attention to a local, idiomatic and experiential or 'vernacular heritage', to engage with constructions of (my) identity and history (Healy 2008, p.105). One painting, of Mrs Dance, the boat captain's wife, and the other, of Yagan, a local Indigenous leader, illustrate historic events of Western Australia that took place in 1829 and 1833, approximately two to three kilometres from each other, a similar distance from where the gallery now stands. *The foundation of Perth, Mrs Dance strikes the first cut August 12, 1829* was painted in 1929 by George Pitt Morison, former curator at the Western Australia Museum and Art Gallery, and *Yagan (1833)* was painted by contemporary Indigenous artist Julie Dowling in 2006. Completed long after the events they depict, these images form conversations between the histories that have made me and the history I make, conversations between the paintings and the events themselves and between a younger and older self (Muecke, this volume). Both paintings reflect the political climate at the time of their execution, flowing with the 'tides of remembering and forgetting', where 'one moment Aboriginality seems to be enormously significant and in the next, of historical interest only' (Healy 2008, p. 204). Here history is performed at the command of the painter, 'something like a script that is at one's command as an assignment', coming forward and returning elsewhere (Spivak 1989, p. 114).

## Painting

Inside the cool gallery, memory returns. We have escaped from the sun and the shopping centre. I have been looking at and thinking about these pictures, Yagan and Mrs Dance, for some time and return to see them with my family. The one I am more familiar with, Mrs Dance, holds recollections of my naïve childhood understanding of the founding of the colony. My introduction to the events in the painting and Mrs Dance's story coincided with the feminist political climate of the early 1970s (Idle 2010, pp. 527–541). It answered simplistically the perplexing question of how I came to be here, it helped me feel at home, comfortable, settled, clear not confused, the transition from Aboriginal land to white settlement smooth and non-violent. Looking at the white woman courageously chopping down a tree, I belonged. The other picture of Yagan was painted almost 80 years later and challenges everything that was then so explicit and easily explained by the first. It disrupts the easy, unsophisticated understandings of colonial history depicted in Mrs Dance, and draws attention to an Indigenous narrative at a time when cultural institutions and their (white) audiences were ready to hear and see them. The paintings can be found not quite side-by-side but near to each other in a postcolonial display in the permanent collection. I am drawn to them both. Pitt Morison, painting at a time when white settlers were calling for the expulsion of Indigenous children from public schools, has, consciously or not, overlooked Indigenous presence and documents a moment in white colonial history (Haebich 2004, pp. 267–289). Dowling's picture reflects the political climate of remembering Indigenous presence and mimics a romantic narrative she describes as influenced by looking at Hogarth paintings. She portrays a story of an important Indigenous leader and defender of Indigenous land and culture, and her work is one of the many 'distinctive and strong Indigenous voice(s)' that have come to be celebrated in Australian cultural institutions in the flow of remembering Indigenous heritage that has become 'a catalyst for a re-evaluation of Australian history' (Perkins in Isaacs 2011, Introduction). Like Gordon Bennett and Daniel Boyd, Dowling's work provokes a political revisiting of Indigenous history in Australia. Dowling's imagery draws on historic narratives, diaries and oral history, while Boyd and Bennett rework well known colonial imagery 'answering back' to their (colonial) message (Nugent 2009).

Here in the cool gallery, I can think about painting and history, my history and that of the paintings and painters, Julie Dowling and Mrs Dance, George Pitt Morison and Yagan. Critic Ian Burn writes that a landscape 'is not something that you look at it is something you look through' (Stephen 2006, p. 220), and it makes sense. The labour of these images is in performing the public role of narrating the settler nation, telling stories of our colonial past back to us, interrupting our historical understanding and the present. Standing here looking, this past comes back shaped differently and always incomplete. This telling of history pushes me into thinking about Indigenous presence, then in the 1800s, in my childhood of the 1960s and 1970s, and now. Moving from country town to country town, I started school in a small wheat-belt town with lots of Indigenous kids and after three years we moved south to the coast, where it was whiter and even more English; it rained and the country was green. We moved again to a milling town, and then again. The nomadic nature of this childhood meant that any relationships were fleeting: Eric, who drowned in the pool aged seven; Jenny, who had the first colour TV in town; Heather, whose old English father drove a Rolls Royce, Nancy at the birthday party; and Hedley at the school gate teasing us as we walked across the road home to the headmaster's house. No Captain Cook here. He didn't fit into our colonial mythology. In Western Australia, our history was more Dutch, and our belonging transient. My focus was always on surviving the alienating climate of a new school, wondering how we came to be here and how long we would stay. Perceptions of colonialisation were constructed through fleeting glimpses of contradictory observations, pushed to the back of memory, pushed to the outside of town. In the public cultural institution of the art gallery, through the stories of Yagan and Mrs Dance, I am called to remember the habits of my forgetting and my will to remember (Healy 2008, p. 35, 204), to pay attention to the shared and sometimes contradictory meanings of objects and images, a vernacular heritage.

# Mrs Dance

'The Foundation of Perth, Mrs Dance strikes the first cut', George Pitt Morison (1929) Art Gallery of Western Australia.

Source: National Library of Australia, nla.pic-an7748217.

> In white people's history white women are mythologised as the brave woman who fought against the harsh climate, but no mention is made about how they lived and profited from the land stolen from Indigenous women. (Moreton-Robinson 2000, p. 174).

And here she is, Mrs Helena Dance, 1829, accompanied by Captains James Stirling, Charles Fremantle, Frederick Irwin, Mark Currie and William Dance, Peter Brown, Lieutenant J Septimus Roe and Dr William Milligan, as well as members of the 63 Regiment, and some of the crew from the HMS Challenger who travelled up river to mark the foundation of Perth. As recorded by Fremantle, 'there being no stone' to turn, Mrs Dance was enlisted to 'strike the first cut' into the felling of a tree (Cygnet 1935). The historic record shows that, within five years, at least two of these officiating white men, Stirling and Roe, would take part in the ambush and bloody massacre of Indigenous people in Pinjarra, south of Perth, in order that Thomas Peel could take up good farming land along the Murray River with impunity (Perth Gazette 1834, pp. 382–383; Fletcher 1984). Early in the morning on the Murray River it is cool, even if the day promises to be hot. The water keeps the heat down until slightly later in the day and it is a popular place for camping and canoeing, which I did as a teenager, only reading about Stirling, Roe, and the massacre later when I had moved to the other side of the continent. But here, in this painting, Stirling and Roe are on their best public behaviour, well-dressed and gentlemanly, this colonising project is ceremonial. Pitt Morison's painting was well received when it was donated and displayed in 1929. The scene is passive, despite the axe and the armed men. The process of colonisation is neat and nice, almost dull, the founding of Perth a matter of formal arrangement that neglected the original inhabitants. In 2012, Mrs Dance maintains her position in the gallery collection, holding a space for colonisation, neat in her bonnet, a solo white woman surrounded by Indigenous absence and men in ceremonial dress, braving the heat—fighting against the 'harsh climate'. She performs the task of white female icon, brave and visible; she made space for a white girl growing up in a masculine rural environment in Western Australia and connected my presence in the settler state with the past (Idle 2010). Following the sequicentenial celebrations of 1979, Janda Gooding wrote that this painting had 'come to be accepted as a true and accurate record of the past' (Gooding 1989, p. 115) and, in 2011, my friend Karen Fisher reported to me that the gallery guide still carefully described the scene as an 'authentic' reproduction of the event. Mrs Dance's story endures.

Whiteness is displayed and maintained as the base from which otherness is defined. Being non-Indigenous is not spoken, it is a given. Encountering Mrs Dance in my childhood as a representative of the colonising of the state in this somewhat mediocre but much reproduced image smoothed over the unsettling state of understanding colonialism. Mrs Dance stood in for the good, white woman, and she held the axe, she made up my past, neat and contained, and I imagined how I came to be here through what I mistook for feminist presence. Katrina Schlunke writes of 'an environment of systemic whiteness. "White" endures in a way that other categories or ways of knowing do not, but "white" is also a kind of silence written into how we know the past and how we see the land around us' (Schlunke 2005, p. 234). In the painting of Mrs Dance, this whiteness is performed through Indigenous absence. Moreton-Robinson writes: 'White women have privileges accorded them by their membership of the dominant group ... They have access to more resources, enjoy a better standard of living, earn more money and are better educated than Indigenous women' (Moreton-Robinson 2000, p. 174). This assumed privilege is reinforced by the position, place and reproduction of Pitt Morison's painting and I wonder if it will return, or come out again for the bicentennial of Perth in 2029.

In *Bluff Rock: Autobiography of a massacre*, Katrina Schlunke begins by describing how she had always 'known that Aboriginal people were killed as a part of the taking of land in Australia. I learnt this in New England, where I was born, as I learnt to walk. It seems it was never a shock' (Schlunke 2005, p. vi). Knowing is different from feeling, and Schlunke writes the story of the Bluff Rock massacre through retelling the past in her present and draws out how that past informs and is felt. Walking through the dense scrub and bush of Bluff Rock with her partner Susan, Schlunke recounts historic records of the massacre, wondering how the pursued Indigenous people were thrown off the top or jumped to their deaths; how could the horses scramble up those rocks? Her book disallows the present to be fleeting and moving into the future but stays still, embodying the history of place. This future is within the past via the present—the thick bush and sharp rocks. We are held *by* place and temporality is held *in* place, helping us to know what to remember. Her challenge to us is to feel history's breath, to feel, acknowledge and speak the violence of contact between settlers and Indigenous people in the colonising of Australia; history's breath into the writing of the white researcher and into the present. In the gallery, in front of Mrs Dance is the airless heat of white history.

Unlike Schlunke, who had always known of the settler–Indigenous conflicts, retribution sorties and massacres, on the other side of the continent, in Western Australia, this wasn't the case for me. I was not preoccupied with Indigenous presence, but with more self-centred concerns. Later, when I was listening more closely, I heard the stories of resistance and massacre. This is not to say that these were unspoken. The Indigenous absence from my family storytelling came from being cosseted in a white environment, sitting politely at the quiet dinner table, watching our manners. Indigenous presence was a part of school, but not home. Indigenous people were out there, beyond the edge of town. We had seen them as we drove across the Simpson and Great Sandy Deserts in 1969. We had artefacts: the carved wooden souvenirs from Docker River on the mantelpiece and the shield from cousin Clem's shed. Indigenous people were there but, as if by magic, not known. Not-knowing or asking was an affect of being good and a product of the political climate in our house. Ross Gibson writes: 'Knowing is an after-effect of understanding' (Gibson 2010, p. 4). This not-knowing is an after-effect of not-understanding, a part of Stanner's 'great Australian silence' (Stanner 1991). For me, in Western Australia the transition from Indigenous ownership and presence to white colonial possession and Indigenous absence was as straightforward as a white woman striking a blow at a native tree, everything else was unspoken. The painting held the narrative tightly in the myth of non-violent transition, reinforcing Indigenous invisibility from 'settler' view, hiding, what novelist Alexis Wright has called, 'stories too shameful to tell', haunting memories and frightening silences (Wright 2007).

Often when I am thinking about this past and memory, I call my mother. She quite likes a conversation, especially one that helps her to think. My childhood recollection of her is detached and distant, but she is a willing communicator these days. She will happily engage in a conversation about the past and takes seriously my interest in Mrs Dance and Yagan. Recently, she has been keen to discuss an exhibition of Indigenous painting from the travelling exhibition 'Yiwarra Kuju, the Canning Stock Route' (Davenport, La Fontaine & Carty 2011), which she has been to see three times. She is struck by the story of the stock route's construction and the violence; she wants to talk about Indigenous perspectives.

This visual display has triggered different knowing and understanding for her, and our conversation leads me to ask about the Indigenous-settler relationships in the rural community of her childhood. A time marked by the brutal assimilationist policies of A. O. Neville, Chief Protector of Aborigines in Western Australia, who was key in 'shaping policy from 1915–1940' (Haebich 1988). So I draw up my courage: when she was growing up, did she know about the violence, the conflict? Sometimes these 'tricky' questions have not been well received; sometimes my tone and our relationship interferes with our conversation and, as she always has, she starts by replying to a different question: 'We hadn't even known how badly they bombed Darwin during the war.' (Her father was based in Darwin during World War Two.) She went on to say she was aware of racial conflict, and sometimes she and her sister would play with the Aboriginal kids, but at other times, fight. Sometimes this meant being prevented from using the bridge and they would wade through the river to get home from school. She tells me a story I hadn't heard previously—a 'story too shameful to tell'—of my great-great-grandmother, Grannie Norrish, wielding the shotgun on the verandah of the farm near Kojonup, Western Australia, to keep the Indigenous locals away from the water on the farm, our white advantage built on Indigenous deprivation (Moreton-Robinson 2000). I had wanted my history to be different from this shame, to keep an academic distance, but here it is, that past now into my present. Robyn Ferrell describes the impossibility of community in the Australian settler state as a product of the embodied shame of non-Indigenous people (Ferrell 2004, pp. 29–46). Memory and shame of the past is repeated in the boredom and shame of the present, and the collision of the will to remember and the longing to forget plays out in the shared space or shared heritage of community, alongside debates about who 'makes' or controls public memory (Healy 2008).

When I ask Mum if she knew about Yagan, she replied that she had only heard of him when vandals attacked the statue at Matagarup on Heirrison Island. It seems that neither of us remembers the children's story written by Mary Durack, *The Courteous Savage: Yagan of Swan River* (Durack 1964), which describes the relationships between Yagan and white settlers as a series of cultural misunderstandings leading to his death. Instead, Yagan (re)appeared through a contemporary violent encounter that mimicked his murder in 1833.

The search for, and repatriation of Yagan's head to the Noongar people began sometime in the early 1950s, finally located and exhumed from the Everton Cemetery in Liverpool, UK in 1997 (National Museum of Australia n.d.). This repatriation triggered a racist and symbolic re-enactment when the head of a memorial statue was removed with an angle grinder. These modern day headhunters attacked the statue, beheading it twice and invoking 'the power of mimesis to invigorate our modern memorials and monuments with a lie of their own' (Martin 2007, p. 316). Indigenous writer Archie Weller responded to this (post-) colonial violence in *Confessions of a Headhunter* (Weller and Riley 2000). Weller's film shows two young Indigenous men 'beheading' memorials of white colonial heroes around the country, beginning with Stirling and ending with Cook. It is

> a film that speaks about the conflict between Indigenous people or Noongar of the Perth area, and colonial culture. The symbolic violence that is the artefact of an actual war that took place—and as the film suggests—is still taking place, is represented here by the Indigenous characters, who retaliate to the disrespect shown to their ancestor warrior Yagan, an important part of Noongar heritage and culture (Moreton-Robinson 2000).

# Yagan

**'Yagan', Julie Dowling (2006).**

Source: Julie Dowling/Licensed by Viscopy 2014.

The visual portrayal of historic moments for mass consumption has been a successful method for producing history and telling stories, standing in for public memory, and is instrumental in constructing cultural knowledge (Edwards 2001, p. 149). In 2006, Julie Dowling's painted image of Yagan, the Indigenous leader, works to reinsert Indigenous presence into the visual records of history. Painted 170 years after his murder, Dowling's painting does not tell us of the violence of Yagan's death, but of the power and impact of his life. While Pitt Morison's painting reinforces an idea of Indigenous absence, Dowling's twenty-first-century image tells the story of first contact differently, recalibrating Indigenous presence into colonial history (Smith 1998). In this picture, Yagan is taking part in a public competition in a display of strength. Neville Green describes the event that took place on 13 March, 1833: 'The theme of the corroboree was a kangaroo hunt and Yagan, the master of ceremonies, acquitted himself with a grace and dignity that surprised those who had regarded him only as an implacable ruffian' (Green 1984, p. 82).

Julie Dowling writes:

> Yagan was an outlaw leader by that stage and he walked into the scene with his small female black and white mutt that he picked up somewhere and trained as a hunting dog.
>
> The swans in the area were at extinction (and they are now because the black swans you see aren't the original ones that lived in Perth) so he was making a statement about his moral will over their invasions with guns etc. He simply joined in the tournament and won every contest ... it started early in the day till late afternoon and by the end of the day everyone knew it was Yagan but they couldn't arrest him because the Noongars outnumbered the non-indigenous by about ten to one ... the rest is that he simply walked through the parting crowd and back up to the hills many km away ... I guess they wanted to see the character of the 'native' but what they found was a crew of Spartans laconically treating them to a good honest moral display of strength with no violence.
>
> The place where the Perth entertainment centre is located now used to be (and still is by many Noongars today) as a great place for meetings and a good feed of shellfish. This place was where they initially met but because the crowd grew it seems that the tournament took place on the foreshore near where the Narrows Bridge is today.
>
> The oral history goes that when people found out it was Yagan they all were in awe because he was taller than most of them and very handsome.
>
> So I modelled him on some of his known descendants the Wyatt's and Bodney's I grew up with in Belmont and Redcliff not far from Perth (personal communication).

Killed by William Keats in 1833, Yagan's skin markings were sliced from his body and his head severed and smoked. A young James Keats was rewarded for his brother's successful headhunting, and Robert Dale took this 'trophy' to England to be displayed as a parlour curiosity (Perth Gazette 1834). An etching of Yagan's smoked head is held in the National Library of Australia and this image accompanies his entry in the Australian Dictionary of Biography (Havell 1834). The reproduction of this image shows Yagan as a 'prize' of white colonisation, not the respected and fierce Indigenous leader described in accounts of his life. Hannah McGlade describes the history around Yagan as 'an extremely powerful story: it is a story of invasion, and early contact between two cultures; of colonialism and its racist bloody nature. It is, to the dominant culture a threatening story' (McGlade 1998, p. 252).

Dowling's painting in the state collection at the Art Gallery of Western Australia brings Yagan's story into the colonial conversation next to Mrs Dance. Standing in front of this picture I am relieved. Is that the right word, is it relief? Here is Yagan and over there is Mrs Dance. Yagan is witnessing us, in the present, Mrs Dance and me, we are unsettled, he stands looking at me. I enter into an 'imaginative engagement' (Wilder 2007) with these pictures, starting a conversation between both the pictures and my fellow onlookers, a cacophony of possible histories rush at us, if we sit down here in the gallery we can talk, and think, it is too hot outside. Here we all are in the same space, at the same time, remembering our forgetfulness (Haebich 2011, pp. 1033–1044). Perhaps we should have a break from history, sit down to share a meal and a cool drink in the café.

Dowling writes:

> First contact relationships between Aboriginal and non-Aboriginal people in the colonies reveal much about the divide that continues to exist today and this painting is about what we can learn from such engagements (Dowling 2006).

Her work demands us to engage with history now, to bring the past into our present, to think about what to remember. In the gallery, Yagan enlivens Mrs Dance, 'answering back'. Dowling's rendering includes Indigenous onlookers and early settlers, whose diaries and writings have informed her work. 'By using the colonial romantic imagery of Aboriginal people as a tool, I can inform non-Aboriginal people of the denial of Aboriginal culture in current representations of Australian history' (C. Dowling 2006). Pitt Morison's hero, Governor Stirling, is transformed in Dowling's painting into the perplexed onlooker (in the red shirt). Carol Dowling, Julie's sister, writes: 'We reach across generations, trying to understand what had happened to our people, feeling what we have in common with them and where we differ, so that we can see who we are and see what we might become' (C. Dowling 2006). In a process that mimics and enchants, Dowling's painting returns an Indigenous past to me, part of a dialogue, a 'disruptive form of encounter' (Rose 2008, p. 157). Yagan stands triumphantly on the hot sand, challenging me, my whiteness, my understanding, returning my gaze. This past is not complete and neatly packaged, disconnected from the present, it is here, in the ongoing conversation of place, in the cool gallery and on the hot sand.

## History's Breath

> This is the problem with history, isn't it? If you think you can know it by simply reading it as a discrete entity, an independent body that can be walked around, wholly mapped, wholly disciplined, then you will never feel its breath (Schlunke 2004, p. 167).

Julie Dowling's painting repatriates Yagan and Indigenous presence to the everyday of the twenty-first century, next to a slightly uneasy Mrs Dance, who is losing her grasp on the national narrative. Yagan's story destabilises and unsettles white settler history and a past that is too shameful to tell. In the context of the art gallery, his presence facilitates thinking about perceptions of time, identity and history. The white onlooker and researcher is drawn into the conversation, moral accountability and responsibility. In the comfort of the cultural institution, we look again at the visual representation of these events and the making of history, now displayed in close proximity. The past, our past here returning to the present, a past held in place through storytelling and painting. These pictures demand that we attend to the 'whitefella crises' of 'what to remember and what to forget', questioning what we think we know and how we remember. Here in the gallery, escaping the heat of a Perth summer day and waiting for the sea breeze, we might feel history's breath.

## Acknowledgements

Thank you to Katrina Schlunke for early comments on the ideas in this paper, Prudence Black for her comments, Anna Cole for her editorial responses, the conference and editorial team, Oliver Haag, Vanessa Castejon and Karen Hughes, and to the anonymous reviewers for their thoughtful suggestions to this paper. Importantly, thanks to Julie Dowling for sharing her thoughts and her painting about Yagan.

# References

Bulbeck, C 2007, 'Aborigines, Memorials and the History of the Frontier', *Australian Historical Studies,* vol. 24, no. 97, pp. 168–178.

Connerton, P 2008, 'Seven Types of Forgetting', *Memory Studies,* vol. 1, pp. 59–71.

Cygnet, 1935, *The Story of the Birth of Perth: Early days in Western Australia,* Swan River Booklets no. 4, Paterson Brokensha, Perth.

Davenport, C, M La Fontaine & J Carty 2011, 'Yiwarra Kuju, The Canning Stock Route', National Museum of Australia travelling exhibition, Perth Convention Centre, 2–27 November, 2011.

Dowling, C 2006, 'Bal Goort Gootun Gunyuing (Her Heart Has Broken)' in J Dowling, *Widi Boornoo (Wild Message)*. Available at: http://members.iinet.net.au/~artplace/catalogs/WidiBorno.pdf.

Dowling, J 2006, *Australian National Indigenous Triennial: Culture Warriors,* National Gallery of Australia. Available at: http://nga.gov.au/Exhibition/NIAT07/Detail.cfm?IRN=144778.

Durack, M 1964, *The Courteous Savage: Yagan of the Swan River,* Thomas Nelson, Melbourne.

Edwards, E 2001, *Raw Histories,* Berg, Oxford.

Ferrell, R 2004, *The Real Desire,* Indra Publishing, Melbourne, pp. 29–46.

Fletcher, 1984, 'The Battle for Pinjarra: A revisionist view', *Studies in Western Australian History*, vol. 8, pp. 1–6.

Gibson, R 2010, 'The Known World', *TEXT,* special issue no. 8, 'Creative and Practice-Led Research: Current status, future plans'.

Gooding, J 1989, 'The Foundation of Perth: George Pitt Morison's persistent image', *Studies in Western Australian History,* vol. 10, pp. 114–120.

Green, N 1984, *Broken Spears: Aborigines and Europeans in the southwest of Australia,* Focus Education Services, Perth.

Haebich, A 2011, 'Forgetting Indigenous Histories: Cases from the history of Australia's Stolen Generations', *Journal of Social History,* vol. 44, no. 4, pp.1033–1044.

Haebich, A 2004, '"Clearing the Wheatbelt": Erasing Indigenous presence in the southwest of Western Australia, in A D Moses (ed.), *Genocide and Settler Society*, Berghahn Books, Oxford, pp. 267–289.

Haebich, A 1988, 'Neville, Auber Octavius (1875–1954)', *Australian Dictionary of Biography*, National Centre of Biography, The Australian National University. Available at: http://adb.anu.edu.au/biography/neville-auber-octavius-7821/text13575.

Hage, G 2003, *Against Paranoid Nationalism: Searching for hope in a shrinking society*, Pluto Press, Annandale, pp.47–66.

Havell, R 1834, 'Yagan', *Australian Dictionary of Biography*, National Centre of Biography, The Australian National University. Available at http://adb.anu.edu.au/biography/yagan-2826.

Hawke, S & M Gallagher, M 1989, *Noonkanbah: Whose land, whose law*, Fremantle Arts Centre Press, Fremantle.

Healy, C 2008, *Forgetting Aborigines*, UNSW Press, Sydney.

Idle, J 2010, 'Mrs Dance Strikes the First Cut: Visual storytelling and girlhood', *Journal of Australian Studies*, vol. 34, no. 4, pp. 527–541.

Isaacs, J 2011, *Spirit Country: Contemporary Australian Aboriginal art*, Hardie Grant, Melbourne.

Martin, D 2007, 'Of Monuments and Masks: Historiography in the time of curiosity's ruin', *Postcolonial Studies*, vol. 10, no. 3, pp. 311–320.

McGlade, H 1998, 'The Repatriation of Yagan: A story of manufacturing dissent', *Law Text Culture*, vol. 4, no. 1, pp. 245–255.

Moreton, R n.d., 'Confessions of a Headhunter', curator's notes, Australian Screen, National Film and Screen Archives. Available at: http://aso.gov.au/titles/shorts/confessions-headhunter/notes/.

Moreton-Robinson, A 2000, 'Talkin' Up to the White Woman: Indigenous women and white feminism', in M Grossman (ed.), *Blacklines: Contemporary critical writing by Indigenous Australians*, University of Queensland Press, St Lucia, pp. 66–77.

National Museum of Australia n.d., 'Yagan's story'. Available at: http://www.nma.gov.au/exhibitions/first_australians/resistance/yagan.

Nugent, M 2009, *Captain Cook Was Here*, Cambridge University Press, Melbourne.

Perth Gazette 1834, 'Yagan's Head', 13 December, 1834. Available at: http://trove.nla.gov.au/ndp/del/article/641141.

Rose, D B 2008, 'On History, Trees and Ethical Proximity', *Postcolonial Studies,* vol. 11, no. 2, pp. 157–167.

Rose, D B 2004, *Reports From a Wild Country: Ethics for decolonisation,* UNSW Press, Sydney.

Rose, D B 1997, 'Dark Times and Excluded Bodies in the Colonisation of Australia', in G Gray & C Winter (eds), *The Resurgence of Racism: Howard, Hanson and the race debate,* Department of History Monash University, Melbourne, pp.97–116.

Schlunke, K 2005, *Bluff Rock: Autobiography of a massacre,* Fremantle Arts Centre Press, Perth.

Schlunke, K 2004, 'Useless History', *Cultural Studies Review,* vol. 10, no. 2, pp.165–167.

Secomb, L 2002, 'Haunted Community', in M Strysick (ed.), *The Politics of Community,* The Davies Group, Aurora, pp. 131–150.

Smith, T 1998, 'Visual Regimes of Colonisation: Aboriginal seeing and European vision in Australia', in Nicholas Mirzoeff (ed.), *The Visual Culture Reader,* Routledge, London and New York, pp. 483–494.

Spivak, G 1989, 'The Intervention Interview', in S Harasym (ed.), *The Post-Colonial Critic: Interviews, strategies, dialogues,* Routledge, New York.

Stanner, W E H 1991, 'The Great Australian Silence: Stanner after the dreaming' Boyer Lecture Series, ABC.

Stephen, A 2006, *On Looking at Looking: The art and politics of Ian Burn,* Miegunyah Press, Melbourne.

Weller, A & S Riley 2000, *Confessions of a Headhunter,* Scarlett Pictures. Available at: http://aso.gov.au/titles/shorts/confessions-headhunter/.

Wilder, K 2007, Negotiating Painting's Two Perspectives: A role for the imagination, *Image[&]Narrative,* vol. 18. Available at: http://www.imageandnarrative.be/inarchive/thinking_pictures/wilder.htm.

Wright, A 2007, 'AWAYE!', ABC radio. Available at: http://www.abc.net.au/radionational/programs/awaye/2007-07-28/3669386.

# 9. Becoming Privileged in Australia: Romany Europe, Indigenous Australia and the Transformation of Race

### Oliver Haag

This chapter explores the different discourses of race as they affected my position as a German-speaking scholar of Indigenous Australian studies. There are difficulties, at times even impossibilities, in translating Australian meanings of race into a German-speaking context. The silencing of 'race' in German-speaking academia, especially in leftist circles, has led to a difficulty to reclaim difference. This silencing was cracked in Australia, where I had suddenly 'inherited' more than one race. The retranslation of these discourses into German-speaking contexts meant, again, a loss of my race and proved a difficulty for German-speaking scholars to handle a concept so profound for (Indigenous) Australian studies: race.

'What is the gain for scholarship if the world knows that you like pasta, stay up late and have a love for French movies?', commented an Austrian historian sarcastically on my efforts to engage in ego-histoire. I answered that I was not planning to write merely about myself but also about Australia and Europe. I was intrigued by the different discourses of race, I said, and reflecting on my own 'race', or what in German would be called *ethnischer Hintergrund* ('ethnic background'), would illuminate some of the mechanisms and assumptions of writing about race in different cultural contexts. 'This is pretty essentialist', he said. 'So I shouldn't have a race?', I replied. 'You are white anyway.'

This answer is informed by the privilege of deracialising not only white people but also white researchers. The idea of researchers being free of any race due to their perceived whiteness is, in this event, backed by the moralising argument of not engaging in seemingly essentialist rhetoric, hence not to speak of racial positioning. 'Let's just leave this and return to serious research', was the reply I received. Such hidden privileges in academic research have undergone critical assessment in the humanities and social sciences which has entailed, at least on a theoretical level, an increasing dissolution of the hierarchical relationship between informant and interpreter, object and subject (for example, Devereux 1967; Erdheim 1982, pp. 9–40). Along with this dissolution, the postulates of objectivity in the production of knowledge have been dismantled as an epistemological impossibility (von Glasersfeld 1995), and a tendency has evolved to highlight the ethical implications for academic research (for example,

Hesse-Biber & Leavy 2006, pp. 59–92; Christians 2005). Critical whiteness and Indigenous studies in particular have deflected attention towards highlighting racial privilege in the production of knowledge (for example, Smith 1999; Janke 1997; Denzin *et al.* 2008; Riggs 2006, pp. 91–113).

When Pierre Nora edited the collection *Essais d'Ego-Histoire* in 1987, the scrutiny of researchers was in its infancy, especially so in German-speaking academia. The term 'I' had to be strictly avoided in scholarly texts; as an undergraduate student in Vienna I was still taught that passive constructions and the plural 'we' had to be employed. *Essais d'Ego-Histoire* is deeply ethnocentric and 'colour-blind': all contributors to the volume are white, there is only one female contributor, and race is not made an issue. In Europe, despite a translation into German, *Essais d'ego-histoire* has not been as widely received as Nora's other works, especially *Les Lieux dé Mémoire*. Nora speculates that this is perhaps because the time was not ready for the book (Nora 1984) because western academics still grapple with how to integrate personal stories into a generalised and abstract narrative. Perhaps this is also because personal narratives, other than those of the 'other', the 'Indigenous', for example, sound too trivial for academic purposes? The interest in self-reflection seems to be much stronger with Australian than European historians. As Jeremy Popkin observes, Australian historians have published more works in the genre of ego-histoire than any other historians, including the French (Popkin 2007).

Despite its ethnocentric origin, ego-histoire is nonetheless a useful tool, especially so for a biographically-orientated study of researchers. This question is all the more important in relation to the European contributions to Indigenous studies, which are evident yet remain largely unexplored (Peters-Little, Curthoys & Docker 2010). There are, for one, more books on Indigenous Australian life histories that have originated from Europe than from Australia. Europeans, I had been told in Australia, have it easier in collaborating with Indigenous people. A recent biographical study by Fiona Paisley has uncovered that some Indigenous political activists not only put more hope into Europe than into Britain but also evinced more admiration for Europe (Paisley 2012). European–Indigenous relations seem to be of different character than Anglo-Saxon–Indigenous relations. I can only speak for myself, without making any generalisations about other European scholars: what was my incentive to undertake research in Indigenous studies and how do I relate my 'self' to my research? Ego-histoire fills an important gap in the understanding of the practices of Indigenous studies from the distance of Europe.

Ego-histoire, however, needs to be removed from its original context in order to make sense for a transnational approach to Indigenous studies. The first step to such an approach is to explain what ego-histoire is not. It is commonly understood as an autobiography written by an academically trained historian (Popkin 1996; Schulze 1996, p. 13). This specialist authorship makes ego-histoire, by definition, different from conventional autobiographies: ego-histoire does not ponder the entire spectrum of a life but focuses on professional life. Henry Reynolds' *Why Weren't We Told* (Reynolds 1999) and Ann Curthoys' *Freedom Ride* (Curthoys 2002)—the latter being possibly less autobiographical but nonetheless relying on personal remembrances—count among the most distinguished contributions to what can be termed ego-histoire in Indigenous Australian studies. Such ego-histoires are written by established scholars who can reflect on the full scale of their academic careers. In this, I argue, these autobiographical works constitute a distinct genre of history. This chapter is far from being such an 'autobiographical history'.

As an emerging scholar, unable to reflect on an entire academic life but rather on a comparatively short period of professional work, I regard my project of ego-histoire as a method rather than a genre of history—even if Pierre Nora stresses the importance of not conceiving of ego-histoire as a method. Still, as German historian Lutz Niethammer suggests, ego-histoire can be seen as a tool of deconstructing the social categories which affect scholars and influence researchers in their work (Niethammer 2002). The project of telling my ego-histoire is thus not concerned with exposing my life in the way a conventional European autobiography would do, but is rather about assessing those social categories that affect my research and ask how they have been reshaping my work. Hence I consider it important to differentiate between autobiography and ego-histoire, on one hand, and ego-histoire as a genre and ego-histoire as a method, on the other.

Gillian Cowlishaw addresses Aileen Moreton-Robinson's demand for white researchers to reflect on their racial privileges thusly: 'How can we respond? How can those privileged by racial power divest themselves of privilege and engage in a decolonising enterprise?' (Cowlishaw 2004, p. 66). Ego-histoire is one possibility, I think, to divest of privilege. Although certainly selective, ego-histoire has the potential to uncover the hidden privileges of researchers by exposing personal motivations, family histories, political and academic ambitions, all of which can be potentially hurtful processes.

## From Austria to Australia

My academic journey to Australia started on a rainy day in Vienna in the northern summer of 2003. I had completed a seminar on 'Autobiography, Gender and History', and came across an article that mentioned the phenomenon of Australian history being rewritten by Indigenous autobiographies. I cannot remember the details of the article—it might have been one of Sidonie Smith's works—but I clearly remember that I started a search of the library catalogue for Indigenous autobiographies, which eventually returned a few titles, including *Don't Take Your Love to Town* and *Auntie Rita*. The first Indigenous book I read was Rita Huggins' biography *Auntie Rita* (Huggins 1994), followed by Ruby Langford Ginibi's *Don't Take Your Love to Town* (Ginibi 1988). I had very thin knowledge of Australian history and did not know the names of Indigenous intellectuals, writers and artists. Despite my lack of knowledge, I was immensely impressed by *Auntie Rita*. The rewriting of history and the courage of talking-up to academic historians, without moralising and victimising, impressed me the most. My reading experience of *Don't Take Your Love to Town* was similar. I was impressed by Ginibi's fiery and clear style. I liked the sense of resilience and the agency in both authors.

Despite the otherwise unfamiliar contexts of Indigenous autobiographies, their rewriting of history offered a familiar reference for personal connection. As I have argued elsewhere, German audiences tend to read Indigenous films and literature according to culturally familiar and recognisable codes of reference (Haag 2010, 2012). *Rabbit Proof-Fence*, for example, has been interpreted in Germany through the lens of the Holocaust. I too initially related my perception of Indigenous cultures to codes familiar to my own cultural contexts. Having grown up as the grandchild of a Romany grandmother, the first time I was confronted with Romany people in Austrian history was at university. A lecturer mentioned that Romany people—he derogatively called them 'gypsies'—had been his most 'difficult' interview partners because, as he said, they lied all the time. More well-intentioned academics talked about the fate of the 'gypsies' as the most disadvantaged group in Europe. Romany people were subject to racial persecution throughout the past and even today they count among the most discriminated groups in the European Union (see, for example, Rose 2007; Zimmermann 1989). Romany people lead the statistics as the least educated and poorest Europeans, with the lowest life expectancy and highest unemployment rates. Romany history, it seemed, was one of destitution and misery. It was only after reading *Auntie Rita* and *Don't Take Your Love to Town* that I became angry with what I started to perceive as the misrepresentation of Romany people and a glaring absence of scholarly self-reflection. 'Romany people are not merely problems and poor victims', I told my mother, who replied in her sarcastic way, 'Relax, boy, we are immensely rich in being misrepresented'.

My mother was the first in her family to be born in Austria. My father is originally from Slovenia. My mother's parents came from Romania. Her father belonged to the German minority of the Banat, a region inhabited mainly by Romanian and Hungarian nationals but also settled by Germans during the seventeenth and nineteenth centuries. Part of the Austro-Hungarian Empire, the Banat region comprised several ethnic minorities, including Romany people.

My grandmother was Romany, but had concealed her racial heritage for almost her entire life. 'Who wants to be someone like that?', she commented on my mother's desire to unearth her roots. My grandmother left Romania before the coming of communist rule. Barred from her relatives, she left her native country for good and never reconnected with her people (partly because this was almost impossible in light of travel restrictions, but she also rejected any contact with her kin).

There were also national divisions in my family line: my maternal grandfather, though part of the German minority in Romania, chose to stay in Austria and started to hate Germans. What a contradiction, I thought. But he was adamant and declared my uncle a *persona non grata* for marrying a German woman. My mother was made unwelcome by my Yugoslav grandfather who, as a former resistance fighter against the Nazis, considered all Austrian women fascist sluts. Ironically, he was one of the few people to consider my mother Austrian; her darker skin colour (much darker than mine) made Austrians tend to classify her as a foreigner and occasionally as a 'gypsy'. I have grown up with national categories which were ubiquitous in spreading agony across my family. Only my Romany heritage could bridge the family divisions: everyone agreed that Romany people were lazy *Sozialschmarotzer* (social parasites).

A German studies scholar once asked me whether my interest in Indigenous Australia reflected my effort of forging a Romany identity. 'How could I?', was my reply. 'I don't identify as Romany.' I did not grow-up in Romany culture. For most of my life I was not even aware of this heritage (on the demand of my grandmother, my mother silenced our racial origin until a few years before my grandmother's death). After having read *Auntie Rita*, I contacted Jackie Huggins and told her how much I enjoyed her book. Her welcoming hospitality and my many positive experiences with Indigenous writers encouraged me to remain in the field of Indigenous studies (I hasten to add that I also write about Australian topics generally, as well as Romany studies). Out of my initial fascination with the rewriting of history, I have started to explore new fields, including Indigenous book production and the European interest in Indigenous cultures.

My Romany heritage had never dominated my interest in Indigenous Australia. Rather, Indigenous intellectuals have influenced some of my views on racial representations in Europe. I recently joined an activist event in Berlin directed against antiziganism (a term coined to refer to the patterns of prejudice against Romany and Sinti people). The activists in the forum (all non-Romany) remarked that Romany people were a construction of antiziganist discourse, and hence passive victims of racism. Although the audience was well-intentioned, I could not suppress uttering critical remarks which had been inspired from what I have heard in Australia:

I am an Aboriginal woman who was raised by two Aboriginal parents, who was just too determined and proud of being Aboriginal and lucky and I don't wear my oppression. You know. Other people may dispose me and deny me opportunity but, you know, come on, the reality of it is that we are sitting in my office right now and I have my salary, you know, I am a deputy director of a centre in a university, I am doing my PhD, I've travelled around the world, I've written, I've made several films, I'll be writing in several books in the future, I've had several careers as a film maker, historian and a writer and a singer-musician and so if that means being oppressed, then fine (personal communication with F Peters-Little, Canberra, 13 August, 2004).

Drawing on this critique of oppression, I asked the participants whether they detected any construction of victimhood in their political agenda which might unconsciously replicate antiziganism in their antiziganist critique. While my critique largely fell on deaf ears, with only partial acknowledgment, the salient point is that my question has been profoundly influenced by an Indigenous Australian intellectual whose critique offered an utterly transnational dimension to connect to racial representations in Europe. Whether this influence is regarded as an impetus for forging my own identity as a person of Romany descent is of secondary importance. (I think we all reshape our personality with recourse to biographical experiences). Of primary importance is the circumstance of Indigenous Australia having become part of my intellectual and political stance in Europe. As a famous quote in *Ulysses* reads, 'I am a part of all that I have met'. Although written in different context, I have become, in a sense, a part of all that I have met. The Australia that I have met transformed into a biographical journey, a journey as much academic as it is personal.

## Gaining a Race

In 2004, as part of my research on published Indigenous Australian autobiographies, I conducted 22 interviews with Indigenous and non-Indigenous Australians. This was the first of my journeys to Australia in which 'race' became a vital part. In this chapter, I will therefore dwell on the unfolding of 'race' during this transnational journey. The informal talks and interviews related to my position as a researcher in which I had been confronted with my race. I had been aware of ethical protocols and speaking positions in Indigenous studies, mainly through Jackie Huggins's *Sister Girl* (Huggins 1998) and later through the writings of Terri Janke. But I had not been prepared with how to deal with my own 'race'. Indigenous respondents seemed to have questioned my race differently from non-Indigenous respondents: the former asking about my biographical background, while the latter usually took my belonging to the white race for granted. Although I have frequently travelled to Australia since 2004, these interviews were the most intense situation in which my 'race' had been discussed.

The interviews with emerging non-Indigenous scholars proved to be the most complex. In more than half of all cases I could feel distrust. One respondent even refused to have her interview recorded because, as she said, she loathed being 'misrepresented'. Two non-Indigenous interviewees reminded me how to behave correctly when interviewing Indigenous persons, advising me that Indigenous people were much stricter concerning consent papers, and that I would need to clearly indicate my intentions and background. None of the non-Indigenous respondents inquired about my background; their witnessing of me coming from Europe seemed to be enough of a biographical background. One respondent, after having explained what she termed the 'difficulties' in interviewing Indigenous persons, eventually tried to put my mind at ease with a reassuring 'but don't be afraid of *them*'.

This anxiety and distrust reflects the debates about the legitimacy of non-Indigenous research as well as debates about the ethics of cross-cultural research in Australia (Bell 2004, pp. 26–27; Huggins 1998, pp. 83–84). It also mirrors the reversed constellation between interviewee and interviewer: one respondent who had regularly interviewed Indigenous persons confessed to me that the situation of being interviewed made her feel extremely unconfident—it was the first time that the researcher had become the researched. I regularly encountered anxiety and self-doubt among emerging non-Indigenous researchers:

> I would never say I write Aboriginal history for myself because I am not Indigenous, but I stay in a field because at present there is pressing research that needs to be done particularly on oral histories that you need to catch people before the generation has died and there is just not enough Indigenous researchers to replace me. I'd love to replace myself and do something else because I know there is this material I just can't access. Because there is no good reason an Indigenous person should trust me. I am just another whitefella. I might be well intentioned but good intentions have done some terrible things in the past (personal communication with J Jones, Melbourne, 4 August 2004).

I was impressed by the power that Indigenous intellectuals have gained over academic research in Australia (despite this power being limited). Such a situation was utterly unfamiliar to the Austrian context, where Romany studies are almost completely in the hands of non-Romany people (or, in the Romany language, *gadje* people). I liked the expression made by the respondent and imagined what a relief it would be to hear a similar response in Austria of a *gadje* person considering her- or himself just another *gadje*. This decentres white hegemony. The 'just another whitefalla' category also, as far as non-Indigenous scholars were concerned, included me. I was not sure how to handle this newly inherited category, being considered implicitly a member of the white race. In Austria, because of my physical size and darker skin colour, I have often been considered a 'migrant', and in the region where I grew up—the southern Burgenland, which has a large Romany population—a 'gypsy'. I was never classified as a member of the majority population in Austria.

Race has an entirely biologistic meaning in Germany, mainly because human groups had been racialised and persecuted on grounds of their construed race (Fehrenbach 2005, pp. 6–7). As Gillian Cowlishaw argues, the concept of race was also rendered silent in Australia and has often been substituted for 'culture' (Cowlishaw 2004, pp. 59–60). In Germany, however, the concept of race has never regained acceptable status among scholars, even though Austria and Germany continue to be fundamentally racialised. For example, citizenship laws in both countries still premise primarily on the *jus sanguinis*, an utterly blood-based concept of citizenship transferred by the birth of a citizen parent (Yuval-Davis 2011, pp. 68, 72–73). Paradoxically, although the German-speaking world remains extremely racialised, the language of race has been erased. *Rasse*, the German equivalent of 'race', denotes something similarly degrading to 'breed' and 'species' in English (Brewster 2009), without any complexity that would allow a social understanding of race. The category of 'white' races has a similarly problematic connotation and been largely excised from political parlance, although both countries are deeply engrained in whiteness.

In Austria, I have usually been excluded from Austrianness on the grounds of my physical appearance, which does not seem Austrian enough. In Australia, by way of contrast, I was implicitly included as a fellow member of the white race. Non-Indigenous interviewees implicitly considered me to be 'one of them'. While nobody explicitly said 'be aware of *them* because you are white', my perceived whiteness was nonetheless inherent in their reactions. This remark is not meant as a moralising critique, as I do not consider the racialisation of my person as necessarily evil. I harbour many positive memories of non-Indigenous Australian colleagues and friends.

My race was questioned differently by Indigenous interviewees, mainly they asked me biographical questions. Surprisingly, after having heard all the warnings, my interviews with Indigenous respondents proved to be the easiest to conduct. I encountered interest and immense support, which I had not expected. I received a very interesting comment: 'Why can't Australia be like Germany?' It was a time when the official apology for the Stolen Generations still seemed far away. My national background—with which I do not identify—has been regarded as something positive by many of the Indigenous Australians I interviewed and have since worked with. But I remember another, more critical comment: 'Racism in Germany is quite bad.' 'Hallelujah, the first Aussie who is critical of Germany!', I replied, and we started to make fun of Germans. This broke the ice.

To the Indigenous Australians I interviewed, my racial heritage has proven to be of greater relevance than the national one. Many Indigenous respondents became interested in my Romany heritage. In Austria, I had entirely negative experiences with my Romany descent. No one wishes to be a 'gypsy' in Austria. In Indigenous Australia, it made connections easier and became a bridge between the different narratives of race in Europe and Australia. During discussions with Indigenous intellectuals, my 'race' had become increasingly transformed. Indigenous Australians treated my Romany heritage on first view as a racial category, just as white Australians treated my whiteness as a racial category. All of them were at ease in referring to me (and themselves) racially, but this racialisation was neither fixed nor essentialist, it was restricted to biographical and less racially determined questions. The question about my biography suggested flexibility for my racial identity. For the first time in my life, my Romany heritage was not related to my physical appearance. It was rather my biography-in-the-making that informed cross-cultural encounters. Journeying to (Indigenous) Australia has become a part of me, a part of all that I have met.

An Indigenous woman with Austrian ancestry asked whether Romany people were black, that is, whether they designated themselves as 'black'. 'My grandmother didn't really look very black', was my naive reply. 'Blackness isn't about the colour of the skin', answered my Indigenous host, uncovering my unconscious replication of Austrian racial narratives as deeply steeped in physiognomy. Romany scholar Ian Hancock argues that, linguistically, the self-designation in Romany language, *kalé,* denotes blackness, while *gadje* refers to Caucasian non-Romanies (Hancock 2008, p. 186). But neither in Austria nor in Romania would most Romany people self-identify with a global blackness. The remark of blackness was not merely abstract in relating to a racial group, but also applied to my grandmother (and indirectly to me). My answer was 'no', my grandmother was not black. But did this make her (or me) white? I am in-between Romany and white. I suddenly realised that I had no words to designate my race: a typical sign for privilege.

I have never self-identified as Romany because I do not have any connection to Romany people in Romania. There is also a veritable difference between being Romany and being of Romany descent. My journey to Australia uncovered some of the transnational narratives of race that impacted so differently between Austria and Australia. Having 'inherited' a race in Indigenous Australia meant an escape from an immensely racialising world in Austria that has stripped itself of the language of race. The 'inheritance' of race, however, was not of an essentialist nature but showed a profound flexibility in conceptions of race as a biographical journey and conferred a positive perception of Romany people. It was in Indigenous Australia that I saw, for the first time in my life, Romany people being perceived just as humans, not as problems or as exponents of a romanticised world. Moreover, apart from the question of whether Romany people self-identified as black, my whiteness was treated with surprising flexibility, which could indicate an inclusion of my Romany descent in my whiteness without reducing my biography to merely one racial category. There is a profound critique of Indigenous essentialism which Vicki Grieves has recently rebutted as an extension of Indigenous kin and country (Grieves 2008, p. 301). My biographical journey, although resting on individual experiences that might not be readily generalised, shows a view of Indigenous narratives of race as containing highly different connotations from western essentialism. Categories were important to make connections, but they were neither dominating nor excluding.

## Losing a Race

In many of my encounters with Indigenous and non-Indigenous Australians my perceived race proved to be a dominant category determining our mutual relationship. This conception of race was not necessarily biologistic. In Europe, I would not simply use the concept of *Rasse*. Some things remain impossible to translate. But meanings of race as a social category are not completely untranslatable. Subjected to forcible assimilation, Indigenous people in Australia had often been denied the right to be different. In German history, (racial) difference had not been suppressed but established. In Australia, Indigenous claims to difference are part of Indigenous sovereignty and reflect the history of forcible assimilation, dispossession and colonialism. Such claims are difficult, yet not impossible to translate into a German-speaking context. Without translating the cultural contexts, Indigenous sovereignty is likely to be misconceived as a form of essentialism. Ego-histoire shows the importance of such a translation to render visible the common misunderstanding between different cultural contexts (Haag 2010, 2012).

Upon my return to Austria, I presented some of my findings to my academic peers. I reported on the protocols of ethical conduct and the issues of sovereignty. I argued that Indigenous autobiographies were also histories. It was recommended that I write my thesis in German to avoid what was called the political demands of ethical conduct. I was told that autobiographies could never be considered history; historians were professional writers (supposedly not Indigenous people following sovereign intellectual traditions). Based on the Indigenous critiques I encountered in Australia, I argued for the need to deracialise German history, feminism and autobiography. 'It's a question of race', I said. (I did not use the term 'whiteness', due to the lack of a German equivalent). I was told that it wasn't. 'Race doesn't exist, so drop this dangerous argument.' 'There's nothing to be deracialised.' 'If the Australians are obsessed with race, that's their problem. You shouldn't be.'

I was home and had lost my race again. Last year, I submitted a semi-autobiographical article on Romany history in which I criticised some of the scholarship that construed Romany people as deplorable victims of the past. I did not like the moralising and patronising rhetoric employed in this scholarship. Reading referee reports on the article, I recognised how much I had become influenced by Australian debates of racial representation and essentialism (for example, Anderson 1995, p. 37; Moreton-Robinson 2003, p. 32; Birch 1993, p. 21; Lattas 1993, pp. 244–246). Referees had criticised my employment of the terms 'cross-cultural' and 'inter-cultural' to designate the differences between Romany and non-Romany people. This, it was argued, was essentialist rhetoric. 'Cross-cultural' implied the idea of two opposite cultures, which was regarded as essentialist. It is impossible to write about racial prejudice and privilege without using the terms that illuminate the patterns of racial normalisation (Haggis 2004, pp. 51–52). A mere moralising of essentialism (actually imposed by white people) is analytically unconvincing and oversimplifies the complexity of politics of race.

Non-Indigenous people frequently ask me why I had not had made negative experiences in Australia—I had received constructive critique but never been urged to leave the field. Some think that my perspective as an outsider, especially so as a European, has been helpful. But aren't Europeans part of the problem? Aileen Moreton-Robinson, Maryrose Casey and Fiona Nicoll argue for a transnational theorisation of whiteness, implying that Europe is still part of the domination of Indigenous people around the world (Moreton-Robinson, Casey & Nicoll 2008). My Europeanness thus offers a burdened rather than liberating position. I was asked if my Romany heritage had been central. I do not think so. Despite a few similarities, Romany and Indigenous cultures are far too different to be compared. My age and gender are also deemed influential. 'It's rather rare that white European boys are fascinated by the power of black Australian women's writing', was one of the comments a feminist friend made. True, the first texts I read were authored by women, but my fascination did not derive from the authors' gender but from their self-determination. In the end, I think the positive experiences were mostly coincidental, and disappointing experiences may come.

During the journey to my ego-histoire I have discovered that speaking about race can be relieving. I have discovered how much Australia has become an intellectual home. Not that I always agree. I have gained the impression that white people are sometimes homogenised in interracial debates in Australia, just as Indigenous people often are. The idea of forgetting about one's race is principally an act of privilege. Yet this is not always the case, especially where white people have hybrid heritage. As Nell Irvin Painter has pointed out, the history of white races is complex and is not distinguished by privilege in all contexts (Painter 2010). In Europe, it is not a racial privilege to be part-Romany. Yet in Australia it is. My perceived whiteness, the fact that I can pass easily, is a privilege. I am part of white academic practice and power relations. Whiteness, if taken out of its local and national contexts, transforms privilege.

The practice of ego-histoire is one of recognising the complex interplay between whiteness, nationality, age, gender and personality in the mutual relationships between Indigenous and non-Indigenous people. There are no simple categories at work that decide on one's personal experiences in cross-collaborations and engagement. As diverse as Indigenous and white people are, so are the relationships between Europeans and Indigenous Australians. It was neither my race nor my national origin that were truly decisive of my position in Australia. The reactions shown by the Indigenous respondents proved that all these categories were of importance merely during the first encounter in establishing a common relationship. Soon, however, these categories slipped into relative unimportance. Apart from encounters with my Romany friends, I have never felt so comfortable with my Romany heritage than among Indigenous Australians, not because my Romany heritage had been racialised as determined, but rather because it had become seen as undetermined through journeying between different worlds. Undetermined in its openness and non-physiology, race appeared highly different between its occasionally harsh rhetoric and its lived practice. Race matters. But it does not always matter.

# References

Anderson, I 1995, 'Reclaiming Tru-ger-nan-ner: De-colonising the symbol', in P van Toorn & D English (eds), *Speaking Positions: Aboriginality, gender and ethnicity in Australian cultural studies,* Department of Humanities, Victoria University of Technology, Melbourne, pp. 31–42.

Bell, R 2004, 'Aboriginal Art: It's a white thing', in M West (ed.), *Telstra National Aboriginal & Torres Strait Islander Art Award: Celebrating 20 years,* Museum and Art Gallery of the Northern Territory, Darwin, pp. 20–29.

Birch, T 1993, '"Real Aborigines": Colonial attempts to re-imagine and re-create the identities of Aboriginal people', *Ulitarra*, vol. 4, pp. 13–21.

Brewster, A 2009, 'Teaching the Tracker in Germany: A journal of whiteness', in B Baird and D Riggs (eds), *The Racial Politics of Bodies, Nations and Knowledges*, Cambridge Scholars Publishing, Newcastle upon Tyne.

Christians, C 2005, 'Ethics and Politics in Qualitative Research', in N Denzin & Y Lincoln (eds), *The SAGE Handbook of Qualitative Research*, third edition, Sage, Thousand Oaks, pp. 139–164.

Cowlishaw, G 2004, *Blackfellas, Whitefellas and the Hidden Injuries of Race*, Blackwell, Oxford.

Curthoys, A 2002, *Freedom Ride: A freedom rider remembers*, Allen & Unwin, Crows Nest.

Denzin, N, et al. (eds) 2008, *Handbook of Critical and Indigenous Methodologies*, Sage, Thousand Oaks.

Devereux, G 1967, *From Anxiety to Method in the Behavioral Sciences*, Mouton, Paris.

Erdheim, M 1982, *Die Gesellschaftliche Produktion von Unbewußtheit: Eine Einführung in den ethnopsychoanalytischen Prozeß*, Suhrkamp, Frankfurt/Main.

Fehrenbach, H 2005, *Race After Hitler: Black occupation children in postwar Germany and America*, Princeton University Press, Princeton.

Ginibi, R L 1988, *Don't Take Your Love to Town*, Penguin Australia, Ringwood.

Grieves, V 2008, 'The "Battlefields": Identity, authenticity and Aboriginal knowledges in Australia', in H Minde (ed.), *Indigenous Peoples: Self-determination, knowledge*, Eburon, Delft, pp. 287–311.

Haag, O 2013, '"Was sind denn Nicht-Roma, wenn ich Sie fragen darf?": Eine Untersuchung zu Bildern von Oberwart', in M End et al. (eds), *Antiziganistische Zustände 2*, Unrast Verlag, Münster, pp. 274–290.

Haag, O 2012, 'Bumping Some Bloody Heads Together: A qualitative study of German-speaking readers of Ruby Langford Ginibi's texts', *Journal of the European Association of Studies on Australia*, vol. 3, no. 1, pp. 114–125.

Haag, O 2010, 'Tasteless, Romantic, and Full of History: The German reception of *Australia* and *Rabbit-Proof Fence*', *Studies in Australasian Cinema*, vol. 4, no. 2, pp. 115–129.

Haggis, J 2004, 'Thoughts on a Politics of Whiteness in a (Never Quite Post) Colonial Country: Abolitionism, essentialism and incommensurability', in A Moreton-Robinson (ed.), *Whitening Race,* Aboriginal Studies Press, Canberra, pp. 48–58.

Hancock, I 2008, 'The "Gypsy" Stereotype and the Sexualization of Romani Women', in V Glajar & D Radulescu (eds), *'Gypsies' in European Literature and Culture,* Palgrave Macmillan, New York, pp. 181–191.

Hesse-Biber, S & P Leavy 2006, *The Practice of Qualitative Research,* Sage, Thousand Oaks.

Huggins, J 1998, *Sister Girl: The writings of Aboriginal activist and historian Jackie Huggins,* University of Queensland Press, St Lucia.

Huggins, J & R 1994, *Auntie Rita*, Aboriginal Studies Press, Canberra.

Janke, T 1997, *Our Culture, Our Future: Proposals for recognition and protection of Indigenous cultural and intellectual property rights*, AIATSIS, Canberra.

Lattas, A 1993, 'Essentialism, Memory and Resistance: Aboriginality and the politics of resistance', *Oceania*, vol. 63, no. 3, pp. 240–267.

Moreton-Robinson, A 2003, 'I Still Call Australia Home: Indigenous belonging and place in a white postcolonizing society', in S Ahmed (ed.), *Uprootings-Regroundings: Questions of home and migration*, Berg, Oxford, pp. 23–40.

Moreton-Robinson, A, M Casey & F Nicoll 2008, (eds), *Transnational Whiteness Matters,* Lexington Books, Lanham.

Niethammer, L 2002, *Ego-Histoire?: Und andere Erinnerungsversuche,* Böhlau, Vienna.

Nora, P 1984, *Les lieux dé mémoire,* Gallimard, Paris.

Nora, P *et al*. 1987, *Essais d'Ego-Histoire,* Gallimard, Paris.

Painter, N I, 2010, *The History of White People*, New York, Norton.

Paisley, F 2012, *The Lone Protestor: A M Fernando in Australia and Europe,* Aboriginal Studies Press, Canberra.

Peters-Little, F, A Curthoys & J Docker (eds) 2010, *Passionate Histories. Myth, Memory and Indigenous Australia,* ANU E Press, Canberra.

Popkin, J 1996, '*Ego-Histoire* and Beyond: Contemporary French historian-autobiographers', *French Historical Studies,* vol. 19, no. 4, pp. 1139–1167.

Popkin, J 2007, 'Ego-Histoire Down Under: Australian historian-autobiographers', *Australian Historical Studies,* vol. 38, no. 29, pp. 106–123.

Reynolds, H 1999, *Why Weren't We Told?: A personal search for the truth about our history,* Penguin, Ringwood.

Riggs, D 2006, *Priscilla, (White) Queen of the Desert: Queer rights/race, privilege,* Peter Lang, New York.

Rose, R 2007, *Roma and Sinti: Human rights for Europe's largest minority,* Documentation and Cultural Centre of German Sinti and Roma, Heidelberg.

Schulze, W 1996, *Ego-Dokumente: Annäherungen an die Geschichte,* Akademischer Verlag, Berlin.

Smith, L T 1999, *Decolonizing Methodologies: Research and Indigenous peoples,* Sage, Thousand Oaks.

von Glasersfeld, E 1995, *Radical Constructivism: A way of knowing and learning,* Routledge, London.

Yuval-Davis, N 2011, *The Politics of Belonging: Intersectional contestations,* Sage, Los Angeles.

Zimmermann, M 1989, *Verfolgt, Vertrieben, Vernichtet: Die nationalsozialistische Vernichtungspolitik gegen Sinti und Roma,* Klartext-Verlag, Essen.

# OUT OF PLACE

# 10. From Paris to Papunya: Postcolonial Theory, Australian Indigenous Studies and 'Knowing' 'the Aborigine'

Barry Judd

## Introduction

As a scholar from an Aboriginal background who is deeply embedded in the western academe and its claims to universal truth, in this chapter I consider the possibility that Australian Indigenous studies may simply function to re-inscribe the power/knowledge claims of European ideas. This outcome is contrary to the stated claims of the field, which proclaims to offer an anti-colonial platform from which Indigenous peoples can be heard within the academe. Seeking to expose the problematic relationship that exists between Australian Indigenous studies and the European ideas that underpin its critical gaze, my discussion takes place in the context of my own research on the historical and contemporary involvement of Aboriginal people in Australian Football. Applying the notion that Europe exists as an idea that is implicit in the western academe, this chapter develops a critical discussion of key ways in which European understandings of self and other are applied in the research of Aboriginal peoples in Australia. Referencing the work of Gayatri Spivak, I offer a personal and self-reflective insight into the paradoxical nature of research generated in Australian Indigenous studies. This chapter challenges readers to consider if Australian Indigenous studies, instead of disrupting the power of the western academe, has assumed the status of the new anthropology.

I first became motivated to engage with the questions outlined above in the wake of a research trip made to the Aboriginal community of Papunya in September 2011. Located 240 kilometres northwest of Alice Springs, a colleague and I had been asked to Papunya by elders involved in the organisation of the local Australian Football team. The elders wished to use our research skills to help them reinstate a regional football competition that would operate across the western desert in *Luritja* and *Pintupi* country. The elders' desire to restore a league of their own was driven by the deeply held concern that current arrangements, requiring the team to play in Alice Springs, had significant negative consequences for the young footballers and their community.

According to the elders, 'the law of the town' was destroying young men. They wanted to reinstate *Luritja* and *Pintupi* law ('the law of the land') by instituting an 'on country' football league in an effort to redirect the young men of Papunya away from the destructive influence of Alice Springs, the bad law of violence, drug and alcohol abuse and imprisonment that characterise their experience of town. After visiting Papunya, I made my way back to Alice Springs, where I spent a morning at the Magistrates Court. Here I saw first-hand why the elders were so concerned to redirect their young men away from the 'law of the town'. I watched defendant after defendant—all young, male and Aboriginal—being sent to prison on remand for a variety of petty offences.

These experiences left me wondering how my professional expertise could possibly benefit the elders of Papunya, a community of artists renowned world over, yet still forced to struggle for even their most basic social and political rights to be recognised and upheld. In the months that followed, these initial doubts deepened, as I began to question how theories and ideas originating in Europe, especially those from the United Kingdom, France and Germany, which provide the basis for scholarship in Australian Indigenous studies, could deliver useful and practical outcomes for the elders I had met.

This chapter represents a first attempt to raise such fundamental questions about the nature of contemporary Australian Indigenous studies in a serious and considered manner. Such questioning casts a critical spotlight on Indigenous studies in order to explore whether the relationship between a theoretical basis made in Europe, imbued with the cultural cachet of the western academe, is or can ever be capable of improving the substantive life experiences of Indigenous people in Australia? While not seeking to provide definitive answers to these questions, the reflections outlined in this chapter are designed to shed more light upon the various characteristics that have come to define Australian Indigenous studies and its relationship, assumed to be positive and productive, with the Indigenous peoples of Australia. In many respects, the idea of ego-histoire developed by Nora provides the perfect framework for critically reconsidering the historical trajectory and current truth claims of Australian Indigenous studies. The notion of ego-histoire is highly relevant because Australian Indigenous studies increasingly rely upon a way of recalling the past that seeks to go beyond history, defined conservatively as that contained in archival documents, to one inclusive of story-telling, which contains an intimacy, specificity and authenticity of understanding drawn from the wellspring of personal experience and its memory. For the Indigenous studies academic who identifies as 'Indigenous' or 'Aboriginal', the growing demand for ego-histoire can be a force for both liberation and entrapment as one finds oneself increasingly positioned as 'native informant' within the confines of the western academe. In keeping with the spirit of this volume, the critical discussion that follows is set out as an ego-histoire, as thoughts and reflections drawn from the memory of personal experience intersect with the history of Indigenous studies in Australia, and those of the European ideas that provide its philosophical and theoretical underpinnings.

## What is Australian Indigenous Studies?

In recent decades Indigenous studies has increasingly acquired the status and trappings of an academic discipline. Australian Indigenous studies appear in a variety of forms: as major or minor study components of generalist degree programs, as elective studies in professional degree programs, and as bachelors, masters and PhD degree programs that exist in their own right. As a formal part of the university curricula, new academic career paths as teachers and researchers of Australian Indigenous studies have emerged. The rise of the specialist academic has in turn witnessed the advent of a diverse and growing body of scholarly writings promoted under the aegis of Australian Indigenous studies. Publications such as the *International Journal of Critical Indigenous Studies*, the *Australian Aboriginal Studies Journal* and the *Journal of Australian Indigenous Issues* have emerged to provide a distribution outlet for this burgeoning scholarship. Professional associations have likewise emerged. Furthermore, an expansive conference circuit which is global in scope and ambition has created transnational relationships between Indigenous studies scholars in Australia and academic peers in Europe, Canada, New Zealand, Hawaii, Asia, and the United States of America.

Despite recent claims that Australian Indigenous studies is an academic discipline in its own right, significant questions remain about whether this is the case. Having worked in teaching and research for a decade and a half I remain uncertain about where the epistemological boundaries of Australian Indigenous studies rest. Australian Indigenous studies are, I think, best conceived not as an academic discipline but as an area of studies. Rather than being an established discipline, Australian Indigenous studies is, in practice, characterised by a lack of its own theories and methods. As a result, Australian Indigenous studies lacks definitive theoretical and methodological boundaries. It is this lack of definition that allows scholars drawn from a wide variety of academic backgrounds to find a home and claim expertise in this field. The absence of definitive boundaries paradoxically functions to define Australian Indigenous studies as an area marked by scholarship that is inherently interdisciplinary and cross-disciplinary; produced by academics who are likely to identify themselves as anthropologists, historians, archaeologists, sociologists, economists, political scientists, cultural theorists, gender theorists, environmental scientists, nurses, medical doctors, lawyers, journalists, artists, and social workers.

The interdisciplinary and cross-disciplinary nature of contemporary Australian Indigenous studies, I believe, makes this area of studies highly dynamic and innovative in a way that academic disciplines often are not. It is these attributes that explain the historic rise of Indigenous studies within the Australian university system. Although accounts vary, the development of Australian Indigenous studies can be traced to the politics of the late 1960s, a period that saw a referendum end the racial exclusion of Aborigines from the Australian Constitution and the policy of Aboriginal self-determination commence (see McGrath 1995).

In scholarly circles this period witnessed W. E. H. Stanner coin the term 'the great Australian silence' in his landmark 1968 Boyer lecture, 'After the Dreaming' (Stanner 1969). Stanner pointed to the near complete absence of Aborigines in the national histories of Australia that had been written in the period since federation in 1901. Stanner challenged historians and other academics to consider the place Aborigines have occupied in the past and will continue to occupy in Australian society. Although an anthropologist himself, the challenge Stanner posed was in part a critique of the monopoly anthropology had assumed in the 'study of the Aborigine'. It was, after all, the 'scientific truths' uncovered by anthropology that defined Aborigines according to measures of blood quantum, confirmed the intellectual and physical inferiority of the 'full-blood' Aborigine and consigned the Aboriginal 'race' in the collective imagination of white Australia to a prehistorical stone age, timeless past and non-synchronous present (see Birch 2005).

The origins of contemporary Australian Indigenous studies are located in the way that scholars responded to Stanner's challenge. In keeping with the progressive mood of Australian society at this time, the new studies of Aboriginal people that developed deliberately adopted a critical stance designed to question, challenge and disrupt old truths about 'the Aborigine' that had come to shape scholarly, governmental and popular understandings of Indigenous peoples. In contrast to the theories and methods employed by anthropology, which imagined the Aborigine as an object of 'scientific study', much of the new scholarship sought instead to position Indigenous people as active agents of history and contemporary social and political movements.

The scholarly response to the authority of anthropology is characterised in the writings of Charles Dunford Rowley, whose works sought to re-position the Aborigine within the grand narratives of Australian history and those of contemporary Australian politics (Rowley 1970, 1972). Later scholarly works, including most notably those by Henry Reynolds, built upon the project commenced by Rowley (Reynolds 1981, 1987, 1989, 1990, 1996, 1998, 2000, 2001, 2003, 2004). Reynolds put questions about the place that Indigenous people occupied in the past, and the implications this has for the present and the future, at the very centre of national debates about what it means to be Australian. Although some Indigenous-focused programs have existed in Australian universities since the 1960s, the wide spread popularity of Reynolds' writings played a significant role in the growth and proliferation of Indigenous studies from the 1980s to the present day.

While the home-grown engagements of Rowley and Reynolds initiated a growing interest in what became known as Australian Indigenous studies, the theoretical foundations that have come to be most closely associated with the contemporary field have their basis in a diffuse range of critical ideas imported from Europe. Reflecting on racial ideologies of fascism, in the 1940s western philosophy adopted a critical gaze, as the truth claim of European humanism to universalism became the subject of widespread intellectual doubt. In Germany, Walter Benjamin and Hannah Arendt questioned the ethical basis of human actions and pointed to the limitations inherent in political systems that based morality in external forms of authority (Benjamin 1969; Arendt 2004). In France, Jean-Paul Sartre raised similar ethical questions. In *Anti-Semite and Jew*, for example, Sartre asks how a committed French nationalist who believes in the reason of the Enlightenment, the Republic and its constitutional pronouncements on the rights of man can at the same time also exist as a self-proclaimed anti-Semite? (Sartre 1995). Sartre in particular encouraged the development of a colonial-based critical philosophy that focused attention on the shortcomings of European humanism as it applied in the context of Europe's overseas colonial empires.

Among those directly influenced by the ideas of Sartre was Frantz Fanon (Fanon 1967, 2007). Fanon, a black colonial intellectual from the French 'overseas department' of Martinique, fused the existentialism of Sartre, the négritude of Aimé Césaire, the psychology of Jacques Lacan, and the political economy of Karl Marx in order to develop his critique of colonialism. According to Fanon, the systematic political and economic process embodied in European colonial domination succeeds in de-humanising both the native and the settler. His most renowned works, *Black Skin, White Mask* and *The Wretched of the Earth*, became foundational texts of what has become known as anti-colonial theory. The writings of Fanon and those of his contemporaries, Césaire and Albert Memmi, created a critical mass of scholarship written from the point of view of colonised natives. The natives spoke back to Europe using a critical philosophical voice to do so. Writers such as Fanon were pivotal intellectual leaders who succeeded in forging an ongoing critical dialogue with the mainstream currents of European intellectual culture. In the decades that followed new voices from the colonies built on the foundational work of Fanon (see Said 1978; Nandy 1992, 1995; Chatterjee 1986, 1993; Bhabha 1994). Just as Fanon and his contemporaries created a philosophical dialogue with Europe, subsequent post-colonial theorists have continued to engage with the work of leading European thinkers (see Derrida 1998; Deleuze 1994; Foucault 1972, 1981).

## A Mechanism for Academic Accountability

This brief historical account suggests that contemporary Indigenous studies in Australia can trace its foundations to a disparate range of origins. While the practical imperative for the development of Indigenous studies may be traced to the particular and growing concerns of Australian scholars, its theoretical underpinnings rest at the heart of Europe and the various post-colonial intellectuals who from mid-twentieth century spoke back to the colonial metropole in their 'masters' voice using the language and ideas of the western philosophic tradition. This chequered history furthermore suggests that claims to position Indigenous studies as an academic discipline are misplaced, as the field exists as an academic scavenger, an adept hunter and gatherer of theories and methods devised elsewhere. Fashioned together in a multitude of ways, this scavenged intellectual material enables Australian Indigenous studies to explore every imaginable aspect of colonialism in order to give action and voice to Indigenous people and their perspectives, understandings and worldviews. Importantly, it is these qualities that provide Indigenous studies with the *potential* to critique and scrutinise the claims to power, knowledge, truth and objectivity that academic disciplines continue to make in respect to Australia's Indigenous people. At its best, Indigenous studies can act as a self-reflexive mechanism to actively question, disrupt and render problematic the assertions made by anthropologists, historians, political scientists and many other areas of expertise to know and speak the truth about Aborigines. The role that Indigenous studies can undertake in placing claims to 'truth' and 'expertise' under critical scrutiny justifies the continued growth of the field within Australian higher education. However, recognition by the field that the truth claims of the western academe have limits and are often specific rather than universal raises fundamental problems for those who claim knowledge and expertise from Australian Indigenous studies itself.

## A Theoretical Paradox

Recognising that Indigenous studies is not the product of Indigenous traditions of knowledge, but rather those of Europe, raises a fundamental paradox for those who claim expert authority under the imprimatur of the field. How can Indigenous studies, as the product of Europe, come to know and claim expert understanding of Australia's Indigenous peoples with any more validity and effectiveness than the similar claims of scholars who have become regular targets of critique and interrogation from Indigenous studies?

Such questions and the paradoxes these raise are rarely admitted by those with established careers in the field of Australian Indigenous studies and its counterparts elsewhere. In 2009, I attended a conference of the Native American and Indigenous Studies Association (NAISA). After listening to a series of highly theoretical papers that sought to grapple with the nature of contemporary Indigeneity, I asked the panel members if they had ever considered the possibility that Native American and Indigenous studies might have become the new anthropology, as its debates about Indigenous peoples appeared to be far removed from the everyday realities of the people that we academics purported to represent? My question was memorable because it was met with an almost unanimous blank stare from those in the audience and with an equally unanimous silence from the panel. Clearly such a question touched a raw nerve with my colleagues as they allude to the stark differences that exist between the world of international conference attendees, marked by global air travel, high-end hotels and corporate credit cards, and the world of Indigenous peoples, a world too often marked by immobility, isolation, poverty, hunger, despair and death. Despite these silences, questions about the ability of Australian Indigenous studies to know Indigenous peoples and re-present their perspectives within the Western Academe remain of critical importance.

## The Ability of Postcolonial Reason to Know and (Re)-Present the Subaltern Native

In the broader project of post-colonial studies the importance of the questions I asked of my colleagues at the NAISA conference is underlined in the work of Gayatri Chakravorty Spivak (Spivak 1988, 1999). Spivak has placed questions of representation at the centre of her scholarly engagements with the colonial and post-colonial. In her highly influential essay, 'Can the Subaltern Speak?', Spivak explores the political campaign to outlaw the practice of *sati*. While the vast colonial archive of the British Raj enables Spivak to hear the voices of colonial authority, the voices of the women who actually participated in the practice of *sati* remain silent to history. The silence that met Spivak in her study of the colonial politics of *sati* suggested that the subaltern might only be traceable as a lack, absence or apparent 'gap' in the historical record. Written as a critical response to the claims of the Subaltern Studies Group that a people's history of colonial India is readily available for retrieval, Spivak shows that the subaltern 'native' is a creation of colonial administration whose act inaugurates only figures of hybridity. 'Can the Subaltern Speak?' contains multiple messages about the status of the subaltern native and her production by the western academe. Pointing out how 'progressive' European intellectuals, such as Foucault and Deleuze, tend to engage in gross universalisations when speaking on behalf of the third world 'masses', Spivak shows how colonial and 'native' representations are similarly problematic. Focussing on widow sacrifice (*sati*) in colonial India, she concludes that, '[b]etween patriarchy and imperialism, subject-constitution and object formation, the figure of woman disappears ... There is no space from which the sexed subaltern can speak' (Kapoor 2004).

The themes of representation first raised in 'Can the Subaltern Speak?' are developed further in *A Critique of Postcolonial Reason: Toward a history of the vanishing present*. Here Spivak seeks to retrace and recapture the ethnographic figure of the native informant as a particular notion of subaltern that is commonly applied by western academics. Spivak pursues the figure of the native informant through the European disciplines of philosophy, literature, cultural studies and history. The search for the native informant is a journey without end. The informant that Spivak seeks turns out to be both a necessary and a necessarily foreclosed figure which is required to inaugurate 'the name of Man' in those key texts of Western philosophy (Kant, Hegel, Marx) that were to inaugurate the ethical, political subject of European Enlightenment. Importantly, Spivak claims the native informant to be an imaginary device that exists as a figure of (im)possibility:

> The native informant is imagined a-temporally. It is also a prosopopoeia, a strategic 'personification' as well as a 'character' that substitutes for the imaginary or absent figure ... The native informant is also 'a blank' that only 'the North-western European' tradition and it's 'Western model disciplines' commencing in the eighteenth and nineteenth centuries could inscribe (Bhatt 2001).

In her discussion on the three great figures of Western philosophy, Spivak concludes that the native informant is the prime condition of being required for the inauguration of European rationalism and humanism.

In seeking to expose the limitations inherent in postcolonial reason, Spivak retraces how the philosopher Immanuel Kant comes to define human culture and reason (which he defined exclusively as a European domain) through the imaginary figure of *der rohe Mensch* (man in raw nature or humanity, without culture, philosophy, god, purpose or reason). Inspired by eighteenth-century tales of discovery, Kant located the figure of 'man in the raw' as the New Hollander (the Australian Aborigine) and the man from Terra del Fuego (the Native South American *Selk'nam* people). Spivak's analysis of Kantian philosophy underscores that the Enlightenment project he helped inaugurate actually functions to obliterate the 'man in the raw'.

The native informant cannot therefore inhabit the frameworks of colonialism/imperialism to function as a manifestation of absolute other but rather functions as a para-subject positioned someplace in-between man in the raw and man cooked by culture – a medium rare man in the process of being cooked – a hybrid creation of colonial/imperial interactions, engagements and entanglements. Echoing Kant's critical approach to knowledge, Spivak's *Critique of Postcolonial Reason* is motivated by the need of the postcolonial (and Indigenous studies) theorist and practitioner to acknowledge the native informant as an illusionary figure, a figment of '(European) Man's' imagination. Sounding the alert, Spivak notes the continuity between Kant's idea of *der rohe Mensch* and her own figure of the native informant. In 'mainstream' western thought, both figures continue to operate as necessary and necessarily-foreclosed figures of absolute otherness that provides perpetual justifications for the projects of colonialism and imperialism. In the present day, it is the figure of the native informant that becomes the object of postcolonial imperialism. In what Spivak dubs 'The New Empire', NGOs, the United Nations and the World Bank imagine the native informant to be located in the universal figure of the woman of the south.

Principally concerned with the production of representation and the tendency of the western academe to conflate the acts of 'speaking for' and 'speaking about', in *A Critique of Postcolonial Reason*, Spivak concludes somewhat pessimistically that, even if the subaltern can speak, nobody (in Europe and/or the western academe) is listening. The ability of the so-called subaltern to speak constitutes an important question for all who seek to articulate anti-colonial understandings of history, culture and politics, and in particular those who claim to represent the perspectives of the subaltern native within the field of Indigenous studies in Australia and elsewhere.

Insistence that the subaltern as native informant exists as an illusionary product of the colonial/imperial project also makes *A Critique of Postcolonial Reason* of fundamental importance as for the ability of Australian Indigenous studies to represent, speak for and speak about Indigenous people. If there exists a true subaltern (as sign of absolute other), Spivak admits she is unable to locate her in a definitive sense. Instead her ongoing search for alterity yields only members of the native ruling and middle classes, known to posterity because of their relationship with colonial rule, and noted in the archives of the imperial power as footnotes in the history of empire.

Returning to the archive of British imperial India in an attempt to locate the elusive character of the subaltern native, Spivak comes to focus on the liminal figure of the Rani of Sirmur. The Rani appears only briefly in the imperial archive as a woman whose self-immolation the British sought to avert. Spivak as postcolonial critic demonstrates how the figure of the Rani and the circumstances of her life, her character and her relationships become known to us only through the eyes of the imperial functionary. It is in this sense that the subaltern/native informant exists only as a construct of colonial/imperial concern—the archive taken to constitute the stuff of human history. The Rani's place in the archive shows her to be implicated in the project of the British Raj: a 'native' who is both 'known' to the imperial functionary and whose interaction with the British paradoxically transforms her into the hybrid, her identity no longer that of the uncontaminated subaltern native but existing someplace in between colonised and coloniser. But as Spivak shows, her true identity remains impossibly always out of reach despite the best efforts of the anti-colonial or post-colonial writer to know her.

Frustrated by the narrow lens of British historical records, Spivak visits the Rani's palace in an effort to know her identity. Unlike the archives, where the past is already digested as the raw material for history writing, the past here is a past of memory, which constitutes itself differently in different subjects interconnecting:

> As I approached her house after a long series of detective manoeuvres, I was miming the route of an unknowing, a progressive différence, an 'experience' of how I could not know her. Nothing unusual here, and therefore never considered worthy of mention, of notice ... I was halted by my own ideological formations as a child of a Kali-worshipping sect, an East Indian phenomenon imbricated with the so-called Bengal Renaissance, as clearly out of the Rani's reach. There were no papers, the ostensible reason for my visit, and of course, no trace of the Rani. Again, a reaching and an un-grasping ... These are the familiar limits of knowing; why do we resist it when deconstruction points to them? (Spivak 1999, pp. 239–242).

The story of the Rani of Sirmur and the attempt of Spivak to retrieve her as subaltern native indicate that the figures left to us by history are in actuality the faux native. Significantly, according to Spivak, the subaltern and its particular manifestation within the contemporary western academe, the native informant, exist at the very margins of colonial history, her occurrence as almost-other, providing this figure with the ghost-like qualities of the uncanny. The native informant can therefore not ever be fully known and understood by the application of postcolonial reason of the type that informs and directs Australian Indigenous studies (see Fourmile 1989).

## Papunya and Knowing Indigenous Australia

The story of the Rani so eloquently outlined in Spivak's critique resonates strongly with my own engagement with Indigenous Australia. In much of my research I too have scanned the colonial archives seeking to know and understand the truth about the subaltern natives who inhabited the recent colonial past. In researching the historical development of football and the instrumental role of Thomas Wentworth Wills in originating 'the Australian game', I sought to find the *Djabwurrung*. Wills had grown up among these people and had probably been aware of and possibility played their game of football called *marn-grook*. Although his cousin, Henry Harrison, reported that Wills had come to know the language, dance and something about the culture of the *Djabwurrung* in a way few whites on the colonial frontier did, my archival search for this Aboriginal people failed to yield any of the intimate knowledge Tom Wills had known. In the pages of human history, the *Djabwurrung* now exist only as a sad footnote seen through the eyes of George Augustus Robinson, the Chief Protector of Aborigines, as the victims of frontier violence and massacre. Later, the colonial functionaries that succeed Robinson as protectors of Aborigines no longer see the *Djabwurrung* as a distinctive group. Rather they note the presence of 'remnant individuals' who survive at mission stations and are identified by the non-specific label 'western Kulin'. In other research, I went searching for the Aboriginal footballer Joe Johnson, the first 'native' to play Australian Football at the elite VFL/AFL level. Johnson also existed as a footnote in human history. When Johnson volunteers to join the Australian army during World War One, the colonial functionaries note his nationality only as 'British subject'. Later, in Egypt, the archive notes that he is reprimanded for challenging a superior. The ill-discipline displayed by Johnson is considered the outcome of a 'drinking problem'.

When I searched for Sydney Jackson, another Aboriginal footballer still living, I found his life referenced in the archives as a footnote in Western Australia's policy of removing 'mixed blood' children from their Aboriginal mothers. The colonial functionaries only see Jackson within the frame of cultural assimilation. When Jackson is reported for striking in the Western Australian Football League (WAFL), the colonial archive records that elimination of his native traits is not yet complete. My experience in researching Indigenous people in Australia confirms much of what Spivak has to say about the limits and inadequacies inherent in postcolonial reason and the field of Australian Indigenous studies that is informed by it. Human history, as outlined in the colonial archive of Australia, makes the prospect of knowing and understanding Aboriginal people in anything approaching the absolute truth an impossible objective (Judd 2007, 2008).

Having become frustrated with the fact that an Aboriginal presence in the history of colonial Australia is generally only apparent through a lack, an absence and a silence in the archival records, I have in recent research forays gone into the field in search of contemporary Indigenous Australia. As outlined above, I have lately commenced a research engagement with elders at the central Australian Aboriginal community of Papunya. I saw the opportunity to come to know and understand something of the people who live at Papunya and their ongoing relationship with the sport of Australian Football, as a gift, a godsend. I assume that the opportunity to engage with Papunya people arose because colleagues at my university have come to designate me their very own resident native informant. My unstated role as native informant is also, I assume, based on the fact that I am both a recognised scholar in the field of Australian Indigenous studies and, more importantly, one of few academics to claim an Aboriginal heritage. My assumed status as native informant is, then, symptomatic of an Australian higher education sector that continues to lack the critical mass of Indigenous intellectuals who are necessary for the academe to develop a productive, sustainable and ethical engagement with Indigenous Australia. In the absence of a critical mass of Indigenous scholars, the few Indigenous people who work as academics within the Australian university system are assigned the role of native informant, in the sense that they become contemporary representations of 'native otherness' in the way the writings of Spivak describe.

In my professional life, I am viewed as knowing the otherness of the Aborigine because as an Indigenous academic most of my colleagues, I suspect, view me as belonging to the otherness of the Aborigine in an absolute sense. My suspicion that I have come to occupy the position of native informant stems from my everyday experience of being called upon to solve, advise and intervene in any business of the university that requires an engagement with Indigenous Australia or that assumes the prefix 'Aboriginal'. Although I claim a very limited expertise, which is reflective of the qualifications I hold, the teaching experience I have had, and the research interests I am driven to pursue, non-Indigenous colleagues assume that my knowledge and understanding of Indigenous Australia is boundless. Because I am burdened with the role of native informant, those I work with have expectations that I can 'fix' everything 'Indigenous', from the ad hoc complaints of individual students, to curricula and research grant development in areas that lie far beyond my own areas of expertise, to providing advice and feedback to strategic planning activities concerning student services and employment issues, to advice about undertaking ethical engagements with Aboriginal communities and providing cultural awareness sessions to my colleagues.

Although the opportunity to engage with Papunya likely arose from peer and institutional constructions of me as resident native informant I embraced this new research opportunity for personal reasons. My family connections on my mother's side are with central Australia. My grandmother was a Pitjantjatjara woman and my grandfather a whitefella of Scottish and Afghan descent. My mother was born at the cattle station Maryvale, about 100 kilometres south of Alice Springs. Since the age of five, I have made numerous trips to central Australia. Camping out, hunting kangaroo and goanna, collecting wild onions and honey ants, and swimming in water holes remain among my most cherished memories of childhood. These childhood visits also established a lifelong interest in Australian race relations as I attempted to make sense of the fact that I had grown up in an Anglo-Australian suburb in relative affluence while members of my family who were designated Aborigines lived in conditions characterised by poverty, unemployment, and sub-standard housing and education.

Personal experience combined with a professional designation as native informant meant that, for me, the engagement with Papunya would not be without some points of reference. My prior knowledge of and experiences with Aboriginal Australia stood in sharp contrast to that of my colleague who has become my primary research partner in this venture. Newly arrived in Australia from the United Kingdom and with no professional knowledge or personal experience of Indigenous Australia, Papunya existed as an absolute unknown to him. I observed his unease and apprehension as we arrived at the township and were introduced for the first time to the elders who had invited us into their community. His obvious self-doubt succeeded in bringing my own critical questions, about what role and effectiveness 'expert' proponents of Australian Indigenous studies such as myself can have in solving the very real problems that Aboriginal communities face, to the forefront of my thoughts. These remain very serious questions, because the present day reality for communities such as Papunya appears little different to what these same communities faced when I visited as a child in the 1970s.

The questions that my colleague raised in expressing feelings of being 'out of his depth' directly led to drafting this chapter and its critical questioning of Australian Indigenous studies. Re-reading Spivak and her critique of postcolonial reason reconfirms both the strengths and the limitations that characterise Indigenous studies. Its greatest strength remains the possibility that the critical self-reflexive stance of the field may call scholarly engagements with Indigenous people to account, by pointing to the limits of knowledge, truth, objectivity and expertise that are inherent in the claims of the western academe. The other great strength of Australian Indigenous studies is the possibility that its foundational theoretical texts will communicate the complexity of identity that emerges in the colonial or postcolonial context. The native informant, the subaltern native and man in the raw do not exist in reality, but only in the imagination of Europe as a philosophical sleight of hand, used to confirm its own humanity at the expense of all others. In this respect Australian Indigenous studies has an important role to play in educating both the western academe and the broader public that Aboriginal identities are and always have been defined by their complexity, dynamism and multi-cultural characteristics.

In this way, Australian Indigenous studies can therefore communicate that Aborigines commonly designated the role of the subaltern native, the native informant, or man in the raw, exist not as absolute other, but in hybrid spaces that are traditional and modern at the same time, and which render popular stereotypes and scholarly categories of difference meaningless in their universal simplicity. Such insights and understanding of Indigeneity, native-ness, alterity and difference can trace their genealogy to the philosophical insights of European thinkers, and to writers among the former colonials who have responded to new ideas originating in the metropoles of Europe. In this qualified sense, then, the relationship between Europe and the great metropolitan centres of London, Berlin and Paris, and places such as Papunya, can be a productive one as it reminds researchers such as myself to consider the limitations of our knowledge, and therefore of our own abilities to know Aboriginal people in a way that would deserve the label of 'expert' being applied.

The great weakness of Australian Indigenous studies is that those who work in the field start to uncritically accept the superiority of their own knowledge and expertise, in contrast to the traditional academic disciplines it competes with for credibility and authority in 'knowing Indigenous people'. To ignore the insights of anti- and post-colonial theory is to risk the field of Indigenous studies becoming the new anthropology. In working with a colleague brave enough to admit no prior knowledge or understanding of Indigenous Australia, I have been reminded of the value of the critical work of Spivak and of my own professional limitations. More than this, I have been reminded, on our visits to Papunya, that open-mindedness, a willingness to listen to, and be directed by the agendas of Indigenous people themselves, a commitment to commence a long-term relationship, and, above all, an honesty to admit that we don't know, counts for just as much.

# References

Arendt, H 2004, *Eichmann in Jerusalem*, Penguin Books, London.

Benjamin, W 1969, *Illuminations/Selections*, edited by H Arendt, Schocken Books, New York.

Bhabha, H 1994, *The Location of Culture*, Routledge, London.

Bhatt, C 2001,'Kant's "Raw Man" and the Miming of Primitivisim: Spivak's critique of postcolonial peason', *Radical Philosophy*, vol. 105, pp. 37–45.

Birch, T, 2005, 'Death is Forgotten in Victory: Colonial landscapes and narratives of emptiness', in J Lydon & T Ireland (eds), *Object Lessons: Archaeology and heritage in Australia*, Australian Scholarly Publishing, Melbourne, pp. 186–200.

Chatterjee, P 1993, *The Nation and its Fragments: Colonial and postcolonial histories,* Princeton University Press, Princeton.

Chatterjee, P 1986, *Nationalist Thought and the Colonial World,* Zed Books, London.

Deleuze, G 1994, *Difference and Repetition,* Continuum, London.

Derrida, J 1998, *Of Grammatology,* Johns Hopkins University Press, Baltimore.

Fanon, F 2007, *Black Skin, White Masks,* Grove Press, New York.

Fanon, F, 1967, *The Wretched of the Earth,* Penguin, London.

Foucault, M 1981, *Power/Knowledge: Selected interviews and other writings, 1972–1977,* Pantheon Books, New York.

Foucault, M 1972, *The Archaeology of Knowledge,* Tavistock Publications, London.

Fourmile, H 1989, 'Who Owns the Past?: Aborigines as captives of the archives', *Aboriginal History,* vol. 13, pp. 1–8.

Judd, B A 2008, *On the Boundary Line: Colonial identity in football,* Australian Scholarly Publishing, Melbourne.

Judd, B A 2007, 'Australian Game, Australian Identity:(Post)colonial identity in football', unpublished PhD Thesis, Monash University, Melbourne.

Kapoor, I 2004, 'Hyper-Self-Reflexive-Development?: Spivak on representing the third world "Other"', *Third World Quarterly,* vol. 25, no. 4, pp. 627–647.

McGrath, A. 1995 (ed.), *Contested Ground: Australian Aborigines under the British Crown,* Allen & Unwin, Sydney.

Nandy, A 1995, *Creating a Nationality: the Ramjanmabhumi movement and fear of the self,* Oxford University Press, Delhi.

Nandy, A 1992, *Traditions, Tyranny and Utopias: Essays in the politics of awareness,* Oxford University Press, Delhi.

Reynolds, H 2004, *Fate of a Free People,* Penguin, Melbourne.

Reynolds, H 2003, *The Law Of The Land,* Penguin, Melbourne.

Reynolds, H 2001, *An Indelible Stain?: The question of genocide in Australia's history,* Penguin, Melbourne.

Reynolds, H 2000, *Why Weren't We Told?,* Penguin, Melbourne.

Reynolds, H 1998, *This Whispering in Our Hearts*, Allen and Unwin, Sydney.

Reynolds, H 1996, *Aboriginal Sovereignty: Reflections on race, state and nation*, Allen & Unwin, Sydney.

Reynolds, H 1990, *With the White People*, Penguin, Melbourne.

Reynolds, H 1989, *Dispossession. Black Australia and white invaders*, Allen & Unwin, Sydney.

Reynolds, H 1987, *Frontier: Aborigines, settlers and land*, Allen & Unwin, Sydney.

Reynolds, H 1981, *The Other Side of the Frontier: Aboriginal resistance to the European invasion of Australia*, James Cook University, Townsville.

Rowley, C H 1972, *Outcasts in White Australia*, Pelican Books, Melbourne.

Rowley, C H 1970, *The Destruction of Aboriginal Society*, ANU Press, Canberra.

Said, E 1978, *Orientalism*, Vintage Books, London.

Sartre, J-P 1995, *Anti-Semite and Jew: An exploration of the etiology of hate*, Schocken Books, New York.

Spivak, G C 1999, *A Critique of Postcolonial Reason: Toward a history of the vanishing present*, Harvard University Press, Cambridge.

Spivak, G C 1988, 'Can the Subaltern Speak?', in C Nelson & L Grossberg (eds), *Marxism and the Interpretation of Culture*, University of Illinois Press, Chicago.

Stanner, W E H 1969, *After the Dreaming: Black and white Australians — An anthropologist's view*, Australian Broadcasting Commission, Sydney.

# 11. Situated Knowledge or Ego (His)toire?: Memory, History and the She-Migrant in an Imaginary of 'Terra Nullius'

Jane Haggis

## En/countering Ego-Histoire

I admit I had not come across the term ego-histoire until sent a flier for the conference that stimulated this volume. My attention was caught immediately, however, as I crudely translated the subtlety of the French phrase into English as 'self-history'. This seemed to echo precisely my own broad methodological engagements with the relationship between myself as feminist scholar and the subjects of my writing. What story was I telling, from where, and whose? Did ego-histoire offer another avenue to pursue my politico-intellectual search for an ethical writing practice sufficient to render the past and present in tones appropriate to a post-colonising and (hopefully) cosmopolitan future?

My questions reflect an early and long engagement with feminist scholarship concerned to query the universalising that had written women out of 'His/ story', science, social science and the humanities. All these institutionalised disciplines distinguished narratives of evidence and objectivity that scripted out the partiality of the male viewpoints it privileged (see, for example, Bock 1989; Haraway 1988; Scott 1988; Bordo 1987; Harding 1986; Hartsok 1998; Fox-Genovese 1982; Okin 1979) This awareness of the particularity buried under universalising claims led feminist scholars in the 1980s to engage with reflexivity and the methodological implications of partiality buried in claims to knowledge (Lather 1988; Smith 2008; Stanley & Wise 1983). An acute awareness of difference propelled out of the political and intellectual engagement between white women and women of colour (for example, Mohanty 1984; Amos & Parmar 1984; Anzaldua 1987; hooks 1982; Minh-ha 1989) both presaged and meshed with the post-colonial and postmodern critiques of western-centric universalising in knowledge production (Spivak 1985; Said 1978; Butler & Scott 1992). This intellectual genealogy affirmed the particularity of knowledge—the scholarly exegesis was always a view *from somewhere*; specific, particular and partial, rather than omniscient. The trick is authorial—replacing the god-like 'voice from everywhere and nowhere' with a transparent awareness of multiplicity—what Ellen Barklay-Brown, drawing on African American English, referred to as 'gumbo ya ya' to describe histories 'occurring simultaneously, in connection, in dialogue with each other. To relate their tales separately would be to obliterate the connection' (Barklay-Brown 1992, p. 297).

Nora's concept of ego-histoire thus piqued my interest in terms of my existing engagement with the challenge of perspective and writing engaged with in the interstices between history, feminism and post-structuralism. As I look back across two decades of writing and publishing in the specific areas of gender and imperialism and critical race and whiteness studies, the consistent thread is a concern to explicate the link between 'history' and (my)self. Or, to put it another way, the thread has been between private biography and social inquiry within which social and cultural history, along with sociology, anthropology and psychology, take shape (Mills 1970; Clifford 1986; Steedman 1986). This project seems to echo Nora's own—to rework, rethink, reimagine the relationships between the past and the present. Ien Ang's trope of entanglement encompasses the sense in which the methodological imperative is not simply an awareness of how self connects with one's 'History', but the ways in which both self and History are constrained by the entanglements with those other stories Barklay-Brown captures in 'gumbo ya ya'. The methodological journey is from a disruption of singularity to an awareness of partiality, plurality and perspective that does not reconstitute a unity. My narrative of self necessarily demands to be deconstructed to reveal its 'entanglements', complicit and resistant, with other stories of class, race, geography and nation, that work to take the singularity out of History and replace it with a messy tale, unsure of its origins or its trajectory beyond the objective of transparency and (perhaps) an ethical accountability for the 'H/his/her story' so produced.

## Situating The Un-disciplined Her-storian and History

In hindsight, history shapes my intellectual journey but always in ways that skirt the formal discipline of History. I am a scholar of no fixed disciplinary abode, who writes and teaches across the past and the present, sometimes conveniently labelling my work as historical sociology/anthropology, feminist historiography, critical race scholarship, cultural studies, and so forth, but always knowing it somehow refuses the neat labels of institutionalised knowledge-production (Wallerstein 2001). This refusal is wilful—a conscious act, not of rebellion however, but of perspective; itself a consequence of a marginality constituted through class, gender and migration that re-centres around racial privilege.

The first of my transnational extended family to enter university, I did so out of an inchoate ambition shaped by a family respect for 'cleverness' formed by a BBC attempting a broader engagement beyond the confines of class; a grandmother sent out to scrub doorsteps at 12 rather than take up a school scholarship; and a mother who was of the first generation to benefit from a public secondary education in the immediate post-war years. A primary education informed and funded by a London County Council committed to foster an aspirational working class provided a more personal engagement with learning for its own sake, beyond utilitarian concerns of earning a living. Somehow this sensibility survived the journey to rural Australia and subsequent immersion in an education system uneasily transforming itself from a civilising antidote to the savagery of the bush, into an integrated system of socio-economic mobility focused on civility, urbanity and profession. Arriving at university by virtue of a scholarship required a refusal of the teaching pathway—female and paid—to embark on a journey into a campus still largely untouched by mass immigration or the incursions of a publicly educated working class. I am still able to conjure up the overpowering feeling that permeated that first university year: of being a stranger without compass or language, rendered dumb. Failure and retreat completed that first encounter with academe. Retreat into a family faith in the autodidact redolent perhaps of an organic intellectualism figured through workers education and unionism.

Second time round that same campus was transformed into a polyglot of migrants or their offspring, women, and mature age students all grappling with a politics and history curriculum informed by the academic New Left, and the beginnings of institutionalised women's and feminist studies. A new maturity acquired through work, travel and marriage, gave me a voracious appetite for learning. I read every item on each reading list; endlessly discussing ideas in the 'Women's Room' with friends who had cut their teeth on Greek or Italian communist and anarchist ideas argued over family dinner tables; or anti-imperialism inspired by Lebanese and Palestinian diasporas. Histories of anti-colonialism and revolution, political theory immersed in the debates of the Anglo-European New Left, Virginia Woolf, Rosa Luxembourg and contemporary socialist-feminists stoked the fire of my indignation and intellectual curiosity. Where marginality remained was in my identification with the usual objects of study: the 'workers', the 'people', 'ordinary people'. Translating analysis back to my other life, as a family member of an unskilled worker's family in a semi-industrial rural town, I felt the oppression of 'false consciousness', that they— the writers, lecturers, intellectuals and activists—knew us better than we knew ourselves. Family debates about my ideas and our lived realities taught me to look underneath the categories, to value the resistant complicities, talking back, and anterior knowing of everyday popular cultures.

I was ripe for the Birmingham School of cultural studies which, coupled with post-colonial feminisms and subaltern studies, shaped my postgraduate years.

Those years were themselves a kind of reverse migration, to a northern university in the land of my birth where the familiarity of institutional class cultures, replete with southern privilege, gave a regional dissonance to another layer of marginality, as I was viewed as a parochial colonial always '20 years behind'.[1] The working class migrant now found herself fixed by a metropolitan gaze that refuted her 'being at home' and confused any sense of belonging. I seemed caught in a never-ending in between, not quite there, never fully here, which inflected my intellectual pathway into colonial studies via history, sociology and anthropology. Situating the intersections of class, gender and racial hierarchies methodologically and analytically within feminist historiography drove my doctoral studies. Early publications (Haggis 1998a, 1998b) document my struggle to write history dialogically, as an interpellation between text, subjects and authorial representation that might resist the seductions of colonising the other as historical subject or contemporary representation.

Ironically, being misrecognised as a colonial myself kick-started a belated awareness of my own situated knowledge at the heart of empire. Eventual relocation to Australia made this more rather than less awkward to address. The culture wars of history and belonging that stalked the 1990s begged the question how the 'white queen' (Haggis & Schech 2001) was to situate herself in the settler-colony that stubbornly resisted the post-colonising. Professionally, exigencies of geography, opportunity and un-discipline meant I found myself teaching and researching in the field of Australian sociology, then largely untouched by postcolonial studies, Indigenous scholarship or critical race and whiteness studies. Multiculturalism and ethnicity marked the disciplinary borders, as one Australian Sociological Association committee informed me 'race' was too controversial, by implication best left to the anthropologists. On the other hand, more than one Australian historian commented that my work was 'too theoretical' to be 'proper history'. Thus a focus on privilege and racialising the white self reinscribed a sense of, as one colleague couched it, 'being on the margins' of discipline and profession. This sense of marginality and un-discipline is descriptive of my discomfort in a neo-liberal professionalised academy that thrives on borders and boundaries. It is not dissimilar to the sense of being outsiders that Passerini and Geppert identify in their contributors, including Pierre Nora himself. Quite plausibly, they see this 'self-fashioned marginality' as both historically specific to the '1968 generation' and perhaps 'a *leitmotiv* of the entire genre' (Passerini & Geppert). I cannot claim a temporal affinity with Nora and his peers, but do suggest marginality, whether self-fashioned, structural or (most likely) a bit of both, is what gives ego-histoire and situated knowledge

---

1  This quote is verbatim from a conversation with a leading academic about whether my Australian honours prepared me for doctoral studies at an English university.

their critical edge as methodologies of interrogation. To demonstrate this point, in the rest of this paper, I explicate how I situate the 'white queen' in the (never quite) postcolonial of Australia.

## Re-routing/Rooting the She-Migrant

In the early 2000s I attended a whiteness studies conference in Queensland where a workshop was run by Indigenous and non-Indigenous scholars. To start the conference, and reflecting Indigenous protocols of placement and yarning, as well as feminist politics of situating selves, we were asked to break into small groups and tell our stories of genealogy.[2] In my group, both Indigenous and white women briefly recounted their life pathways in terms of origins. For the Indigenous women these turned on country and language-group, interrupted for some by the brutalities of the stolen generations and/or removal from ancestral country, occasionally complicated by border crossings of marriage with German, Irish, Maori, Pacific Islander, Polish or Chinese (great-)(grand-)fathers. The white women told themselves through their connections with that same Aboriginal narrative, the tempo paced around hints of Aboriginal relatives and/or a guilty complicity in colonialism's terrors of massacre, incarceration and loss as well as a knowledge of antecedents buried in the migrancy of convicts, gold, land or persecution from which pioneer legends are construed. I found myself stuck; stuck in the mud of the Thames. I had no connection with the Australian pasts, Indigenous or pioneer. Nor did I have any multi-generational sense of belonging, place and origin as a migrant. Like many of the urban English working class of the early and mid-twentieth century, we had no origin story beyond the imperial and war time narratives of a jingoistic parochialism that averred our sense that this place (South London) was for us and not them.[3] My paternal grandmother, on returning to England in the early 1970s from Australia and being told that her social housing entitlements were attenuated because of her overseas sojourn, retorted in outrage to the young 'Pakistani' clerk: 'I've been through two world wars for this country', which indeed she had; making bombs as a 14-year-old in the first and driving a crane through the Blitz in the second. This slip of memory is revealing in so far as it shows both the source of her sense of entitlement and ownership—in a national narrative of

---

2   As an anonymous reviewer of this chapter pointed out, this form of personal chronological recounting of self is a post-conquest form of Indigenous storying, at least in part a response to the expectations of the non-indigenous inquiry system.
3   Alistair Bonnett's argument about the whitening of the working class reflects my familial history, that those once referred to as the 'heathen' of the urban slums were gradually brought within the auspices of the state's project of a raced modernity and the nation's sense of imperial mission during the late-nineteenth and early-twentieth century (Bonnet 2000).

war rather than 'race' pure and simple (although 'Pakistani' refuses the possible claim of that clerk through birth, empire or citizenship)—and its limits for my ego-histoire.

My history of oozing from the London mud went no further than grandparents and stories of a 'foreign woman' to explain the 'touch of the other' that might be revealed in black hair, brown eyes, sallow skin. The phrase is one from my South London childhood, which I have been unable to track down beyond a memory of my paternal grandmother using it to refer to people who looked a bit different and to her own (or perhaps her deceased husband's) story of the 'foreign woman' to explain the 'dark' features of her own children, and 'the family madness' referring to the 'highly strung' volatile aspects of family personalities. My mother—also from South London and a somewhat more respectable 'steady wage' segment of the working class—recalls the phrase being used to refer to people who were perhaps suffering imaginary illness symptoms or acting 'a bit mad', but has no recollections of it ever being used with racial or 'colour' overtones. It is easy to imagine how the two meanings might blur, if one thinks of those tropes in nineteenth and early-twentieth century English culture in regard to miscegenation and madness indelibly rendered by Charlotte Brontë in Jane Eyre. How does such a narrative place me, the she-migrant, as her-storian in an Australian narrative of origin and belonging? I am caught between the imperialist jingoism of the working class England I claim birth right to and the imaginary of terra-nullius shaping Australia's national histoire/History. A worn-out template of English indigenousness deployed by the likes of the National Front that denies the hybridity of its History/histoire, or a neurotically possessive whiteness (Moreton-Robinson 2004) constantly attending to its 'border wars', whether figured as those who come by boat, or the 'priority of the prior' (Povinelli 2011, p. 15). Is it possible to have a histoire/history that has no start or finish? No sense of being in the right (or my) place?

Invasion and migration mark my sense of histoire differently. Tracked through feminisms' emphatic refusal of objectivity, Nora's concept is caught on a positivist assumption of externality as necessary for the Historian to make History out of her ego-histoire. This assumes the power is in the eye of the beholder (the alter-ego?) but, as Dorothy E. Smith observed of sociology, the power is in the 'language practices … that achieve the transition from being among people to being above them' (Smith 2008, p. 418). Yet, as the work of Foucault, Said, Scott and White demonstrates, no simple demotic of democracy can frame even the feminist's text. The her/historian is rendered not outside, or at one, with the self of histoire or History, but the creator of meaning in both her histoire and history. White argues for an ethical practice of historiography that (re)embraces the 'ethically rich traditions of literary expression' (White 2005, p. 338). There can be no 'History', only histories informed by a poetic sensibility—the rhetorical styles chosen by the historian with which to plot the 'facts'. These are histories that claim meaning rather than knowledge for their artefact. This renders ego-histoire very differently to Nora. From such a post-structuralist and feminist standpoint, the ego-histoire of the historian is not external to the History Nora hopes it will rework. History does not make the ego-histoire. Instead, the self-story becomes a constitutive part of both the H(h)istorian and her 'H/history'. The very first seminar I gave on my then doctoral work, subsequently published in a volume on feminist methodologies (Haggis 1990), described the intersection of biography and history that shaped my intellectual journey to that point. Separating out my history from my histoire was unimaginable to me. My task, methodologically, was not to remove my 'self' in some kind of objective facticity, but to make transparent the way my story, as ego-histoire, necessarily constructs the history I produce as partial, not all-knowing.[4] In Nora's ego-histoire there is no positioning of the H(h)istorian beyond the tension between the individual and the collective. Who is the 'we' that the 'I' belongs to?

## Moon-landing

In 1964 'swinging London' was apparent even in Lower Tooting. Youth's pop culture already ensured my younger sister and I had our first Beatles albums, reflecting our parents' earlier engagements in the nascent teen culture of the immediate post-war years. We sat around the TV as a family and watched Jukebox Jury and Ready, Steady Go! as well as the more sedate London Palladium and, of course, Dr Who. Knock down Ginger on bright summer nights and tea parties on the pavement marked our play time, along with visits to museums and holidays with donkey rides and Norman ruins to shoot arrows from, not to mention Charlie Drake's facile hit song, 'My Boomerang Won't Come Back', to sing in the motor bike's side-car on the way there.

What to make of a place then, with no television, a stuffy BBC clone for a radio, unpaved roads and wood-fired baths? Of a place where, even in those first few months, ghosts flitted past us—Boandik Drive, Blackfella's Caves, Piccaninny Ponds, a dusty window full of strange artefacts, new words in the school yard such as 'lubra lips' and 'Abo'. A place where a talk, dark-skinned girl defiantly refused the shaming imposed by the Grade Five teacher on her standing in the front of the class, her face blank and fierce in the eyes of the alien child, myself, already fearful of a state school culture of corporal punishment administered freely in the classroom.

---

4   For a fuller discussion of this point, see (Haggis 1998, 2012b).

What to make of a school-friend who whispered about her great-great-grandmother's diary recounting how she walked for days through the bush, accompanied only by an Aboriginal guide, as we learned our history lessons about Cook and Gold and Simpson's Donkey. Of a youth culture mired in illicit sex and not so illicit drinking, in which 'gangbangs' were openly talked about and 'shotgun weddings' struggled to survive against the lure of the 'widow's pension' and a kind of independence as a 'mole', always liable to predatory invasions into their housing trust ghetto by men on the lookout for easy sex; outcastes from small town respectability. This at the same time as a different stolen generation, of white babies taken from their young mothers, was secreted away.

What to make of this as a histoire for my History? The memory of that tall girl in my grade five class indelibly impressed on my emotional retina infused with shame—my shame for bearing witness in silence but the discomfort of not knowing from whence I earned this shame. A child's response, perhaps, to an injustice s/he does not understand; the vocabularies that animate it, she is ignorant of; the discomfort of the migrant turned settler. What is the relationship of the migrant to the past? Ghassan Hage convincingly argues that the failure of the colonial project in Australia captures the migrant, even the non-Anglo, 'not quite white' migrant, in the never quite decolonised stasis of the nation-state (Hage 2001). A similar point is made by Nicolacopoulos and Vassilacopoulos, although they centre race possessiveness rather than, as Hage argues in *White Nation*, a conflated nationalist sense of ownership. Both arguments pin the late- or new-comer as coloniser in relation to the dispossessed Indigene just as much as the multi-generational 'Aussie' (Hage 1998). Of course, through the articulation of my working class memories of belonging in a jingoistic imaginary of empire, I am already implicated in this failed colonial project, even before I make my moon-landing.

My gaze is fractured between the imperial metropolitan who already 'knows' the colonial, and the parochial colonial herself. How do I position myself and plot this in terms of those eerie place-names and that tall dark girl in my Year Five memory? The tropes available have already been mapped through the contours of critical race and whiteness studies: the benevolent goodness of whiteness, the guilty burden of the traitorous white, and the moral smugness of the politically correct (Haggis 2004). None engage sufficiently with the complicity embedded in my histoire or the shame infusing my memory, shame tinged with a kind of horror. As I look back to that moonscape of rural Australia I found myself transported to, I seem to discern the longue durée of the colonial frontier; how else to understand the atmospherics of violence that suffuse my memories of classroom and school yard, of late childhood and early youth. How else to understand the predatory and rapacious heterosexual masculinity such that 'black velvet' and 'lubra lips' not only continued their savage racism, but easily transplanted onto the mole, slut and unmarried mother a fearsome sexual conquest that made pre-pubescent girls fair game. This, in part, explains for me the depth of silence and secrecy that haunts the stories of maternity for many young women of that era, especially from 'respectable' families inhabiting the borderland between grazier-ocracy and those white trash/blackfella creolised spaces productive not of positive hybridity (Hughes 2012) but the sordid violence of degradation and marginality.

## (Un)Settled Entanglements

The little extended family of six that arrived by plane as 'ten pound tourists' is now a mob of 20 radiating out from those south London streets to encompass Ngarrindjeri, Illongot, Scottish and multi-generational, Anglo-Celtic pioneer stock. My family's rootedness now encompasses blackness as well as whiteness in ways that 'talk up' to the she-migrant's histoire, extending the frontier trope to a new kind of guerrilla war across the lines of fractured families.

'Hey Granma. Look! Dirty blackfellas.' My four-year-old nephew's words stopped us. Silenced, our eyes clung to each other's as we motored lazily down the hot Sunday morning quiet of the Adelaide highway. 'Hmmm, yeah, look over there, d'ya see that cop car? See the light on top and the big writing? Who do you reckon they're after?' Tension released as the child and his brother turn to see the police vehicle pulled up beside us at the traffic lights. Later, once the child is asleep, we pick at the entrails of that moment, furtive, unsure. 'G– told me once that her mum whacked her over the head and sent her flying, at a pub in M– when she was about thirteen, when this really dark bloke came up to talk to her. Her mum told her to stay away from the "bush blacks", said they were wild and went after young girls to marry.' This seemed to explain the child's words as he watched the two Aboriginal men, beanies on head, their dress, demeanour and embodiment marking them on the Adelaide street as 'remote', from 'up north'. But what if behind his words lurked the overheard racisms repeated by a child still unmindful of the gaze that fixes him as 'dirty blackfella' too? Or, perish the thought, perhaps this was the vocabulary he thought you spoke in whitefella land, with 'us', another language learned from that spoken in his Nunga family. What then of our silence? I recall another access weekend spent with my mother and her two Nunga grandsons: 'Granma, Nanna says you're just a dumb white.' 'She's probably right', the response came with nary a pause. About being dumb or being white or both? I puzzle, reluctant to ask my mother to recollect her words and their meaning-memory. And what of that comment, relayed with a wide-eyed curiosity as to its effect. The wilful wanting to know of a child caught between family wars captures the essence of the 'history wars' also rendered in the language of colour as black or white.

As I write, years have passed; two strong young Nunga lads come of age. Time, tragedy and great-grandchildren work their magic. Two families meet at births, weddings, anniversaries, festivals and those other comings and goings of keeping in touch. Photos litter Facebook along with shout-outs to 'the Haggis mob'. Facebook also brings long-distant half-remembered cousins into focus, on a visit from an England they blog in terms of St George's Day and a visceral ethnic patriotism. Kin proves thicker than terroir, however, as they warmly greet this polyglot extended family, stretched now not only over the temporal reach of Indigeneity but an(other) migrancy that also produces great-grandchildren, rooted deep in the intricate mosaics of Mindanao and a half-forgotten Spanish empire. An empire remembered in a great-great-great-grandmother whose effect within my histoire is uncanny, paralleling the 'foreign woman' conjured by my grandmother to explain that 'touch of the other'. Is my ego-histoire replotted then? Does it shift from the brutality of frontier to the ease of reconciliation and a twenty-first-century cosmopolitanism? Is it suggesting a post-(colonial) nation as a 'contemporary history'? (Nora 2001).

The unease embedded in my recollections of my Nunga nephew's childhood remains however, caught in the hyper-reflexivity of my mother, as she rakes over the coals of another happy gathering. The echo of that early epithet, quite possibly now gone from an elderly memory, caught in her 'did I put my foot in it?' Or the awkward, 'shall we ring them or wait for them to ring us?' conversations between her and I as we set up another Christmas. A different set of tensions emerge in the interstices of a wedding held between southern Mindanao and the western suburbs of Adelaide. Embracing the exotic in the Australian-Pilipina bride leaves a mother bemused and offended by the reverse-racism of a mail-order mother-in-law, perhaps inured in the protective husk of the always-already-raced 'Asian woman' (Ang 1996). Entanglement brings not reconciliation but the awkwardness of the contact zone to my ego-histoire.

My ego-histoire must remain fraught with doubt, anxiety and unease in order to escape the frontier and enter at least the possibility of the impossible (Watson 2007). 'History' as a discrete, defined disciplinary practice or collective structure does not serve. I refuse 'Historian' and claim, perhaps, 'historian', writing always from the particularity of some one's history, a history never external to the narrator or the narrated. Slowly, this is evolving into a method of historiography grounded in an ethics of entanglement: of partiality and incompleteness approximating perhaps Joan Scott's prescription:

> For the historian to ignore the stories themselves ... It is to refuse to engage with the novelty of the old, the strangeness of the new, or the irreducible difference of the other — to insist instead on sameness, on the comfortable familiarity of the already known (Scott 2011, pp. 204–205).

# References

Amos, V & P Parmar 1984, 'Challenging Imperial Feminism', *Feminist Review*, vol. 17, pp. 3–9.

Ang, I 1996, 'The Curse of the Smile: Ambivalence and the "Asian" woman in Australian multiculturalism', *Feminist Review*, vol. 52, pp. 36–49.

Anzaldua, G 1987, *Borderlands: La frontera — The new mestiza*, Spinsters/Aunt Lute Book Company, San Francisco.

Barkley-Brown, E 1992, '"What Has Happened Here": The politics of difference in women's history and feminist politics', *Feminist Studies*, vol. 18, no. 2, pp. 295–312.

Bock, G 1989, 'Women's History and Gender History: Aspects of an international debate', *Gender and History*, vol.1, no. 1, pp. 7–30.

Bonnett, A 2000, *White Identities: Historical and international perspectives*, Prentice Hall, Harlow.

Bordo, S 1987, *The Flight to Objectivity: Essays on Cartesianism and culture*, State University of New York Press, Albany.

Butler, J & J W Scott 1992 (eds), *Feminists Theorize the Political*, Routledge, New York and London.

Clifford, J 1986, *Writing Culture: The poetics and politics of ethnography*, University of California Press, Berkeley.

Curthoys, A 1999, 'Expulsion, Exodus and Exile in White Australian Historical Mythology', *Journal of Australian Studies*, vol. 23, no. 61, pp. 1–19.

Derrida, J 2001, 'Time and Memory, Messianicity, and the Name of God', in P Paton & W Smith (eds), *Deconstruction Engaged. The Sydney Seminars*. Sydney, Power Publication, p. 67.

Fox-Genovese, E 1982, 'Placing Women's History in History', *New Left Review*, vol. 133, pp. 5–29.

Hage, G 2001, 'Polluting Memories: Migration and colonial responsibility in Australia', in M Morris & B de Bary (eds), *'Race' Panic and the Memory of Migration*, Hong Kong University Press, Hong Kong, pp. 323–62.

Hage, G 1998, *White Nation: Fantasies of white supremacy in a multicultural society*, Pluto Press, Annandale.

Haggis, J 1998a, '"A heart that has felt the love of God and longs for others to know it": Conventions of Gender, Tensions of Self and Constructions of Difference in Offering to be a Lady Missionary', *Women's History Review*, vol. 7, no. 2, pp. 171–192.

Haggis, J 1998b, 'White Women and Colonialism: Towards a non-recuperative history', in C. Midgley (ed), *Gender and Imperialism, Studies in Imperialism series*, ed. John McKenzie, Manchester, Manchester University Press, pp. 45–75.

Haggis, J 2004, 'Beyond Race and Whiteness?: Reflections on the new abolitionists and an Australian critical whiteness studies', *Borderlands*, vol. 3, no. 2, Available at: http://www.borderlands.net.au/vol3no2_2004/haggis_beyond.htm.

Haggis, J 2012a, 'White Australia and Otherness: The Limits to Hospitality', in A Hayes & R Mason (eds), *Cultures in Refuge: Seeking sanctuary in modern Australia*, Ashgate, Surrey, pp. 15–30.

Haggis, J 2012b, 'What an "Archive Rat" Reveals to Us About Storying Theory and the Nature of History', *Australian Feminist Studies*, vol. 27, no. 73, pp. 289–295.

Haggis, J 1990, 'Gendering Colonialism or Colonising Gender?: Recent women's studies' approaches to white women and the historical sociology of British colonialism', *Women's Studies International Forum*, vol. 13, No. 1–2, pp. 105–115.

Haggis, J & S Schech 2001, 'Meaning Well and Global Good Manners: Reflections on white western feminist cross-cultural praxis', *Australian Feminist Studies*, vol. 15, no. 33, pp. 387–399.

Haraway, D 1988, 'Situated Knowledges: The science question in feminism and the privilege of perspective', *Feminist Studies,* vol. 14, no. 3, pp. 575–599.

Harding, S G 1986, *The Science Question in Feminism*, Cornell University Press, Ithaca.

Hartsock, N 1998, *The Feminist Standpoint Revisited and Other Essays*, Westview Press, Boulder.

Hooks, Bell 1982, *Ain't I a Woman: Black women and feminism*, Pluto, London.

Hughes, K 2012, 'Microhistories and Things that Matter: Opening spaces of possibility in Ngarrindjeri country,' *Australian Feminist Studies*, vol. 27, no. 73, pp. 269–278.

Hunter, J 2010, 'Women's Mission in Historical Perspective: American Identity and Christian Internationalism', in B Reeves-Ellington *et.al.* (eds), *Competing Kingdoms: Women, mission, nation, and the American Protestant empire, 1812-1960*, Duke University Press, Durham and London.

Lake, M & H Reynolds 2008, *Drawing the Global Colour Line: White men's countries and the question of racial equality*, Melbourne University Press, Carlton.

Lather, P 1988, 'Feminist Perspectives on Empowering Research Methodologies', *Women's Studies International Forum*, vol. 11, no. 6, pp. 569–581.

Mills, C W 1970, *The Sociological Imagination*, Penguin, Harmondsworth.

Minh-ha, T T 1989, *Woman, Native, Other: Writing, postcoloniality and feminism*, Indiana University Press, Bloomington and Indianapolis.

Mohanty, C T 1984, 'Under Western Eyes: Feminist scholarship and colonial discourses', *Boundary 2* vol. 12–13, pp. 333–358.

Moraga, C & G Anzaldua 1981 (eds), *This Bridge Called My Back*, Kitchen Table, Women of Color Press, New York.

Moreton-Robinson, A 2004, 'The Possessive Logic of Patriarchal White Sovereignty: The High Court and the Yorta Yorta Decision', *Borderlands e-Journal*, vol. 3, no. 2. Available at: http://www.borderlands.net.au/vol3no2_2004/moreton_possessive.htm.

Nora, P 2001 'L'Ego-Histoire est-elle Possible ?', *Historein*, vol. 3, pp. 19–26.

Okin, S M 1979, *Women in Western Political Thought*, Princeton University Press, Princeton.

Papastergiadis, N 2004, 'The Invasion Complex in Australian Political Culture', *Thesis Eleven*, vol. 78, pp. 8–27.

Passerini, L & A C T Geppert 2001, 'Historians in Flux: The concept, task and challenge of ego-histoire', *Historein*, vol. 3, pp. 7–18.

Povinelli, E 2011, 'The Governance of the Prior', *Interventions*, vol. 13, no. 1, pp. 13–30.

Ravenscroft, A 2012, *The Postcolonial Eye: White Australian desire and the visual field of race*, Ashgate, Surrey.

Said, E W 1978, *Orientalism*, Pantheon Books, New York.

Schech, S & J Haggis 2004, 'Terrains of Migrancy and Whiteness: How British migrants locate themselves in Australia' in A Moreton-Robinson (ed.), *Whitening Race: Essays in social and cultural criticism*, Aboriginal Studies Press, Canberra, pp. 32–47.

Scott, J W 1988, *Gender and the Politics of History*, Columbia University Press, New York.

Scott, J 2011, 'Storytelling', *History and Theory*, vol. 50, pp. 203–209.

Smith, D E 2008, 'From the 14th Floor to the Sidewalk: Writing sociology at ground level', *Sociological Inquiry*, vol. 78, no. 3, pp. 417–422.

Spivak, G C 1985, 'Three Women's Texts and a Critique of Imperialism', *Critical Inquiry* vol. 12, no. 1, pp. 243–261.

Stanley, L & S Wise 1983, *Breaking Out: Feminist consciousness and feminist research*, Routledge & Kegan Paul, London and Boston.

Steedman, C 1986, *Landscape for a Good Woman: A story of two lives*, Virago, London.

Watson, I 2007, 'Aboriginal Sovereignties: Past, present and future (im)possibilities', in S Perera (ed.), *Our Patch: Enacting Australian sovereignty post-2001*, Network Books, Perth, pp. 23–43.

Wallerstein, I 2001, *Unthinking Social Science: The limits of nineteenth-century paradigms*, Temple University Press, Philadelphia.

White, H 2005, 'The Public Relevance of Historical Studies: A reply to Dirk Moses', *History and Theory*, vol. 44, no. 10, pp. 333–338.

# 12. Genealogy and Derangement

## John Docker

I am a cultural historian, which I feel gives me a licence to wander. Over the decades I have been interested in literary and cultural theory, popular culture, postmodernism and poststructuralism, monotheism and polytheism, diaspora, historiography, Jewish identity, and Gandhian non-violence. I have always written personally, mixing theory and analysis with life stories and family history, and am currently writing an ego-histoire, *Growing Up Communist and Jewish in Bondi: Memoir of a non-Australian Australian*. Since the mid-1980s, I have written critiques of Zionist nationalism and settler colonialism, and reflected on partition in Palestine and India, and Martin Buber's idea of a bi-national Palestine. I have devoted the last several years to genocide and massacre studies, exploring Raphaël Lemkin's suggestion in his originating definition in 1944 that genocide is constitutively linked to settler colonialism (Docker 2008a, 2012b). My most recent books are *The Origins of Violence: Religion, History and Genocide* (Docker 2008b) and (with Ann Curthoys), *Is History Fiction?* (Docker & Curthoys 2006).

As far back as I can recall, I have always thought it was and is completely wrong of a people to come from afar and take away another people's land and world. Its name is settler colonialism, and I am as passionately opposed to settler colonialism in Australia as in Palestine/Israel. Settler colonialism, genocide and massacres are entwined historical processes, by which all settler-colonists, including myself in Australia, have been advantaged. After such knowledge, how can one talk of belonging? Why should we not feel guilt and shame?

I agree with Pierre Nora in 'L'Ego-Histoire est-elle Possible?' that the I who writes ego-histoire will always be enlivened and inspired by failure, the failure of the ego-historian to possess a single coherent successfully positive identity, the failure of the texts we produce to possess a single generic character (Nora 2001). The ego-historian and ego-historical text are always off-balance, always close to vertigo and derangement. Genre in ego-histoire tosses about like a drunken boat, to adapt a famous image of Rimbaud, an important figure for my 1960s generation who appreciated his sentiment in a letter of 1871 that we strive to reach 'the unknown by the derangement of *all the senses*' (Il s'agit d'arriver à l'inconnu par le dérèglement de *tous les sens*) (Rimbaud 2005, pp. 370–371).

## Diaspora and Identity

I will follow ego-histoire's methodological suggestion that personal and family histories are interventions into contemporary history; they are both intensive and lead outwards to wider perspectives (Curthoys A, 2012). *Je est un autre*, said Rimbaud in the same letter, I is someone else (Rimbaud 2005, pp. 370–371). I am an other, or others. My father and mother gifted me wildly divergent diasporic family histories, Protestant Irish and London Jewish. My father's mother, Susan Nash, from a Protestant family in County Clare, on the west coast of Ireland, migrated to Australia in 1881. In Sydney, Susan Nash established an Anglican, English monarchy-loving family, from which my father, as a young carpenter, born in 1894, rebelled to become part of the political left for the rest of his life. As a young man he was in the IWW, the anarchist and syndicalist Industrial Workers of the World, the notorious or wonderful Wobblies, destroyed by the state during the First World War. In 1920 he became a foundation member of the Communist Party of Australia. Over the next three decades he occupied high positions in the Party, in the Central Committee and also the Political Committee, a kind of inspectorate responsible for trouble-shooting within the Party and also for expulsions from it, of which more soon.

As I record in my *1492: The poetics of diaspora*, my mother Elsie Levy and her Jewish family migrated from the East End of London in 1926 (Docker 2001, pp. 20–33). My mother, born in 1912, was then 14. At some time in the 1930s this young woman Elsie Levy became a political radical and joined a Jewish branch of the Communist Party, along with her two younger brothers, Lew Levy and Jock Levy; the two brothers and my mother then helped form a Jewish Youth Theatre, where, in Lew's words, 'We played and read Sholom Aleichem, [Isaac Leib] Peretz and Israel Zangwill'. (Peretz, 1851–1915, was a Polish-Jewish author who wrote in Yiddish; Zangwill, 1864–1926, was an Anglo-Jewish writer; of Sholom Aleichem, 1859–1916, more later.) Jock Levy would become an important figure in Australian radical theatre and film history, in the latter 1930s acting and directing in the Jewish Youth Theatre and later in the New Theatre and then the Waterside Workers' Federation Film Unit in the 1950s (Docker 2001, pp. 164–167; Milner 2003, p. 42).

In 1941 my mother and father married in Bondi, Sydney, my father being many years older and widely travelled, including attending in Moscow in 1935 the Comintern's Seventh Congress and the International Lenin School. My mother brought to their relationship her specific history as an inheritor of longstanding Jewish dissident traditions, with her own international and diasporic consciousness, committed to Jewishness as an ethical universalism, intensely aware of what was happening to Jews all over the world, especially in the 1930s in relation to the rise of fascism, including in her own 'diasporic home' in England.

As I see it, my father and mother met in deeply troubled times in a world communist movement that was a kind of commodious cosmopolitan tent. In this essay I wish to think about how growing up in a communist family committed to internationalism and opposed to nationalism and racism may have influenced my writings from the New Left 1960s onwards, including my critiques of Zionism.

As befits ego-histoire with its strong archival interests, I think about what my parents have left me, in books, pamphlets, documents, letters, photos, memories. From these textual sources I try to imagine what my parents were like before I was born in 1945, for their histories, separate and together, have informed my upbringing. In this essay I talk about both my father and mother, though to write about my mother is a challenge. I haven't even a photo of her when she was young. How I wish I had a photo of her, or a diary, or letters she might have written during that time.

As it has turned out, however, I do have some reading material of hers. Stretching from the 1930s into the 1960s, they consist of three books, a pamphlet, and an inner Australian Communist Party document. I will focus on one of the books, William Zukerman's *The Jew in Revolt: The Modern Jew in the World Crisis* (Zuckerman 1937), which she must have acquired when she was still Elsie Levy living with her parents in Bondi.

I admire Walter Benjamin's insight, in his well-known essay 'Unpacking my Library: A talk about book collecting', that to a 'true collector the acquisition of an old book is its rebirth'. After World War Two, Hannah Arendt chose the essay, originally published in 1929, as the opening chapter of *Illuminations* (Benjamin 2007, pp. 61, 66).

My mother, born in 1912, and Hannah Arendt, born in 1906, were of the same generation; my mother married a communist and non-Jew, Ted Docker, and Hannah Arendt married a communist and non-Jew, Heinrich Blücher (Kohler 1996). References to Arendt will be like a silken thread throughout the essay; Arendt as part of a long post-Enlightenment tradition of liberal Judaism (Curthoys, 2013).

## My Father, Ted Docker: From the IWW to the Communist Party

Here I must record some contradictory reflections on my father, including, perhaps inevitably, conflicting views of the Soviet Union, which from 1920 till he died was central to his life. Just as my father rebelled against his family's legacy of values, in my late teenage years I rebelled against certain features of his legacy—but not, I think, all. There are continuities as well as discontinuities in historical passages from the IWW to the Communist Party to the New Left of the 1960s and 1970s.

The main continuity concerns anti-racism and anti-nationalism, which early-twentieth century radical groups inherited from nineteenth-century anarchist and socialist movements. Internationalism features in historians' accounts of the IWW. Verity Burgmann points out that the IWW's striving for the One Big Union would not be complete without the workers of all nationalities and races. The IWW consistently opposed the White Australia policy (Burgmann 1995, pp. 79–91).

There is a striking degree of continuity between the IWW and the Communist Party from 1920 in terms of internationalism and opposition to racism and nationalism. I think this continuity is evident in my father's attitudes and actions. In the early 1970s Ann Curthoys and I persuaded my father to write about memorable episodes in his life, and we were especially struck by his vivid reminiscences of the Kalgoorlie Riots of 1934, a shameful episode in Australian labour history, in some ways, if in far more minor key, sharing features of a pogrom as in *Kristallnacht* in Germany in 1938, and also anticipating the anti-Lebanese race riots in Cronulla in southern Sydney in 2005. My father's reminiscence, 'The 1934 Kalgoorlie Riots', was later published in *Labour History* (Docker & Gerritsen 1976, pp. 78–82). I'll reprise it here.

My father begins by saying that, as a member of the Political Committee, he was sent to Western Australia to investigate 'differences in the Yugoslav branch' in Kalgoorlie, 'which had two factions'. My father was given the task of restoring unity to the Yugoslav branch, but when he arrived in Kalgoorlie on 27 January, 1934 he had no opportunity to contact them as the riots started that same day. 'The death of the young Australian Jordon [Jordan]', wrote my father, 'precipitated the explosion'. He attended a meeting of the miners, held in a hall in Kalgoorlie, where the 'main complaint of the Australian workers', repeatedly made, was that 'their sons couldn't get jobs, but foreign-born workers could'. The 'Australian workers' sacked and set fire to buildings in Kalgoorlie, those identified as belonging to 'foreign shopkeepers', and then crowded on trains to travel to the nearby town of Boulder in order to continue the riots, which lasted

## 12. Genealogy and Derangement

for two days. In Boulder, a lorry was stationed on top of a hill by the miners' union officials in charge, with a crowd numbering in the 'thousands (but no women)'. My father says that 'two comrades who were young miners (one only about 20)' had helped him get out a roneoed leaflet which he'd written, and he gave them out to the miners as they walked up the hill towards the lorry. At the meeting speakers 'attacked the mining companies for employing so many foreigners, while Australians were unemployed'. My father continues:

> The tone of the speakers was very racist. We decided that one of us should mount the lorry and strive to change the direction of the discussion to the following. Opposition should be directed against the mine-owners over wages and conditions. A log of claims had been presented to the owners, who had not given their consent. This should be our main attack, and to achieve these demands the unity of all workers irrespective of race is needed.
>
> I mounted the lorry but it was considered unwise for me to attempt to speak, because I was not a miner, and I was unknown to the gathering.
>
> I jumped up on top of the lorry and stood there; the oldest of the two comrades jumped up and addressed the crowd. He put forward the correct position and was well received.

There is a warm portrait of Ted Docker in Katharine Susannah Prichard's *Winged Seeds*, published in 1950. A sympathetic character, Dinny, relates of the Kalgoorlie riots that 'a little bloke name of Docker' and Tom, a local Party member, were 'out all that night, helpin' foreign women and children to get away from their burning houses' (Prichard 1984, pp. 30–31).

The main discontinuity between the IWW and the Communist Party concerns a historic choice for radicals in the twentieth century, between political cultures, between anarchist and libertarian thinking and activity on the one hand, and on the other the highly structured political organisation associated with Marxism-Leninism and loyalty to the Soviet Union. When the IWW was defeated in 1917, it must have seemed clear to many radicals such as my father that what was now historically needed was the kind of hierarchical and tightly organised party whose model was provided by Lenin's Bolshevik revolution, creating the Soviet Union, the first society in history successfully to overthrow capitalism. Only a tightly organised Communist Party could survive destructive persecution by the state, including in illegal periods. The Marxist-Leninist model of a tightly organised party necessitated, however, a culture of internal policing and expulsion, especially as it turned out of intellectuals and writers. My father, I recall, said more than once when I was young that intellectuals could not be trusted in a revolutionary situation, they had no fixed class position and so could always waver. And, indeed, in the historical literature on the Australian Communist Party, my father's hostility to anyone who disagreed with the 'correct line' the Party prescribed at any one time, especially when exhibited by intellectuals and writers, has become almost legendary (Macintyre 1998, pp. 164, 178; Ferrier 1999, pp. 2, 66; Sparrow 2007, pp. 247–253).

Here was an acute difficulty for me, since in my late-teenage years as an English literature student at Sydney University I was becoming part of the very intelligentsia my father distrusted as historical betrayers of the working class. It pains me to recall my Oedipal harshness when my father and I, in the small Bondi flat, would have arguments about the Soviet Union. I felt impelled to point out that Stalin put people in forced labour camps, and would shout: 'Stalin *killed* people! How can you defend someone who killed people?' (Docker 1984a, pp. 77–81) How depressing it must have been for my father to register that his son who he hoped would be his heir as a revolutionary was rebelling against him and all his generation stood for. Further, my father, a very ascetic man, didn't drink or smoke (or own a car or house), and yet here was his son coming home late at nights on weekends in a state of disrepair.

Yet my father, I know from family stories, had rebelled against his father, indeed to such an extent that to my knowledge he never once mentioned or talked about him. I was repeating a father/son generational pattern. I was on my way to becoming an intellectual parricide, an activity in which, I have to confess, I became a repeat offender.

Looking back now, I think my bouts of late-teenage and early-20s drunkenness related to what Rimbaud's phrases and images suggested, where drinking myself silly was perhaps the rough equivalent of Rimbaud saying that to find the unknown we must derange ourselves. The unknown was a future as an intellectual outside my father's framework of values. Pierre Nora suggests in 'L'Ego-Histoire est-elle Possible?' that ego-histoire exists unresolvably between the social and the psychoanalytic, and here I will attempt some uncomfortable self-psychoanalysis, or at least a jittery journey into self-reflexivity. I recall a friend once visiting in the late-1980s and saying with commendable frankness, something like: 'We know what you're like, John; you like something and then suddenly you turn against it, why?' Challenged by ego-histoire, I'll attempt an uncertain answer here.

In learning to become a Leavisite literary critic in my student years, yearning for the supposed finer cultures of the pre-industrial English past, I was trying to displace my Marxist father, with his overriding interest in the political and economic and faith in the Soviet Union, with a critical father, F. R. Leavis, and a new belief system. Yet the infatuation with being a Leavisite did not last. I turned sharply, satirically, almost savagely, against Leavis's kind of criticism, as I recorded in a later essay, 'How I Became a Teenage Leavisite and Lived to Tell the Tale', first published in *Meanjin* in 1981 (Docker 1981) and then as the prologue to my *In a Critical Condition* in 1984 (Docker 1984b). Much of my intellectual life has involved a very similar repetition-compulsion, attraction to an intellectual interest or approach or figure followed a few years later by sharp critique and disengagement: the Sydney Libertarians, Derrida, popular culture, Australian literature (Docker 1972, pp.40–47; 1998, pp. 24–28; 2007, pp. 263–290).

Looking back at a strange life, I would have to say that I'm considerably less than sane.

Yet, I now think, my father's legacy is surely mixed. I rebelled against his particular optimism about history, his utopian certainty that the Soviet Union would become humanity's future; yet perhaps I've always also retained an intense optimistic desire, almost messianically enthusing about postmodernism or Mikhail Bakhtin's notions of carnival and carnivalesque. Yet, disengaging, I'm also often drawn to pessimism, dystopian visions, melancholia, concerning the idiocies, cruelties and absurdities of history; humanity as a species given to genocide and massacre; or finding myself in the Australian society I live in.

In political terms, I rebelled against a centralised, authoritarian Communist Party, attracted for a while to the Sydney Libertarians and becoming part of a New Left intelligentsia whose anti-hierarchy, anarchism and pluralism was a kind of theatrical Dadaist reprise of the IWW (see Sparrow 2007, p. 290). I didn't and don't wish to join any political party, nor indeed any organisation, even once declining to join an organisation for independent scholars. I can't 'join'. The cultural theorists I enduringly like, Mikhail Bakhtin and Walter Benjamin, are also as it were non-joiners. In their biography *Mikhail Bakhtin*, Katerina Clark and Michael Holquist create a portrait of an intellectual personality who in effect disliked being agreed with (Clark & Holquist 1984, p. 2). Hannah Arendt writes in the introduction to *Illuminations* that in her view Benjamin during the 1920s and 1930s was never going to commit himself, however tempted, either to Zionism or to joining the Communist Party, given his 'bitter insight that all solutions … would lead him personally to a false salvation, no matter whether that salvation was labeled Moscow or Jerusalem' (Arendt 2007, p. 36).

Nonetheless, I think I have inherited from my father his internationalism and anti-racism and perhaps also a certain fierceness, a willingness to overturn critical institutions and theories just as he was willing to defy the racist Australian workers about to attack Yugoslavs and Italians in Kalgoorlie in 1934. I hope so. Of course, it is that same ill-mannered truculence that ensured I would become an academic failure. But then, as Pierre Nora ponders in 'L'ego-histoire est-elle possible?', failure is intrinsic to ego-histoire.

# My Mother, Elsie Levy: A Diaspora Consciousness

In 1937 in Bondi in a semi-detached house which I would later know as my grandparents' home, a 25-year-old woman, Elsie Levy, was reading William Zukerman's *The Jew in Revolt: The modern Jew in the world crisis*, published in London (Zukerman 1937). Now I think: why was she reading this book? What did it mean to her? Did she agree with it? Who in Zukerman's view was the Modern Jew? What would she have read in *The Jew in Revolt* concerning the Palestinians? That she had kept it all the subsequent years of her life must mean it was important to her, and that she hoped one day it would be read again in her family.

I'd never heard of William Zukerman. I looked up Elizabeth Young-Bruehl's biography, *Hannah Arendt: For love of the world*, which tells us that Zukerman was the editor of the *Jewish Newsletter*, which he had begun in 1948, and was an outspoken organ of dissent within the American Jewish community. He was a disciple of Judah Magnes, and he knew that Arendt also admired Magnes, as she had made clear in a eulogy for him on his death in 1948 (Young-Bruehl 2004, pp. 290–291; Zukerman 1964). Now I had some bearings. Judah Magnes (1877–1948), a founder and first president of the Hebrew University in Jerusalem, was an associate of the philosopher Martin Buber. In their view, Zionism was not a political movement but primarily spiritual and cultural. Buber believed that the land of Palestine should be shared between its indigenous people and the incoming Jews from Europe; there could be autonomous Arab and Jewish communities living amicably together and cooperating in the one bi-national state (Docker 2013, pp. 86–116; Mendes-Flohr 1983, pp.112, 148–149, Young-Bruehl 2004, pp. 225–227).

Perhaps Elsie Levy had acquired Zukerman's red-covered 1937 book because she already knew of Zukerman and was enjoying reading and talking about articles he was writing for *Harpers Magazine* with other young, eastern suburbs radicals in Sydney in her circle of friends, including in the Jewish Youth Theatre. What she could ponder in *The Jew in Revolt* were the book's very strong likes and dislikes, in relation both to the impact of Hitler and Nazism on Europe, and political Zionism in Germany as well as Palestine. *The Jew in Revolt* is rich in arguments, attitudes, predictions and prophecies.

Zukerman was particularly apprehensive about the rise of nationalism in the 1920s and 1930s, and nationalism's ways of attaining, or attempting to attain state power. Here he puts forward what we might call the Zukerman thesis concerning the nexus of nationalism and anti-Semitism so visible in fascism and Nazism. Their anti-Semitism is not, he believes, a simple continuation of previous outbursts of anti-Semitism in European history, during the Crusades and the Inquisition (Zukerman 1937, pp. 19–22). In my mother's copy, there is a line in the margin next to Zukerman's argument that what is historically new is that the Nazis have made anti-Semitism 'the chief tool with which they have hewed their way to power'. Zukerman then contends that such a political use of anti-Semitism has become 'the feature of Nazism that is most widely imitated abroad', not only in countries of Eastern and South-Eastern Europe such as Poland and Romania but in the Western democratic countries of Europe, in France, Belgium and England (Zukerman 1937, pp. 23–24, 29–31, 34–38).

In an analysis that must surely have interested my mother, Zukerman writes that in England 'anti-Semitism has become the chief if not the only programme of British fascists', with 'vile anti-Semitic meetings' and 'anti-Jewish demonstrations in the East End of London and other thickly populated Jewish districts'. Mosley's speeches are 'tirades against the Jews, full of bitterness and hatred as though he had been a pupil of Julius Streicher all his life'; and there is a 'streak of sadism' in these speeches and those of his lieutenants 'which is actually frightening' (Zukerman 1937, pp. 39–41).

Yet, and here is part of his thesis, Zukerman feels there is a kind of historical hope in the way the fascists and Nazis have identified themselves so completely with anti-Semitism, for the struggle against fascism and Nazism by the liberal democratic world must also mean a simultaneous fight against anti-Semitism. If fascism and Nazism can be defeated, Zukerman predicts, anti-Semitism also will be defeated (Zukerman 1937, pp.42–48). We are, says Zukerman, in the midst of a battlefield, the 'new Armageddon'. However, and here is Zukerman's prophecy, when the 'final battle of Armageddon is over', anti-Semitism is bound to be defeated: 'If democracy is to live, anti-Semitism must perish. Fascism itself has made the destruction of Jew-baiting a condition for the survival of civilization' (Zukerman 1937, pp. 49–51).

My mother would surely also have been intensely interested in what Zukerman thought about Zionism, as controversial an issue in the 1930s as it is in the contemporary world. In *The Jew in Revolt*, Zukerman is highly critical of Zionism when it associates itself with nationalism. In the spirit of Martin Buber and Judah Magnes, he makes a sharp distinction between political Zionism which enshrines nationalism, and what he considers to be true Zionism, which is cultural and spiritual, emphasizing agriculture and productive labour. For Zukerman, true Zionism, all that is 'attractive, sympathetic and great in the movement', was brought to Palestine in the late-nineteenth century by Russian Jews escaping persecution by the state as well as fleeing the Ghetto itself. The 'first Jewish settlers in Palestine' in the 1880s were imbued with the 'great social, moral and idealistic tendencies' which were fermenting in pre-Revolutionary Russian society at that time, an idealism they shared with the general Russian intelligentsia; this was the 'age of Tolstoy' when Russian humanitarians 'sought various escapes from industrial civilisation and its evils' (Zukerman 1937, pp. 139–141).

Zukerman regards the Zionism initiated by Herzl in the 1890s, with its 'political schemes' and 'nationalistic sentiments', as a betrayal of true Zionism. He is astonished by the manifestations of political Zionism in Germany, from 1933 onwards, for it not only shares much with Nazism in terms of ideas but also actively co-operates with the Nazi regime. Incredibly, Zukerman observes, the Nazi plan of a 'Jewish exodus' has found favour and support in the Zionist movement. In Nazi Germany the Nazis have shown a 'remarkable readiness to work together with the Zionists in this particular enterprise', the emigration of Jews to Palestine. The Zionist Organisation is the 'only political party' other than the Nazi which is permitted in Germany; Zionist newspapers are 'flourishing'; Zionist meetings are 'encouraged' while meetings of non-Zionist Jews, even of the 'Jewish ex-soldiers', are 'suppressed' (Zukerman 1937, pp. 110–114, 117, 141).

The chief Jewish promoters of the scheme of exodus and of 'partnership' with the Nazis, Zukerman writes scornfully, are the 'extremist Zionist-Revisionists who represent the nearest organised approach to fascism made by Jews as a body'. Zukerman is scathing of the behaviour of the Revisionists, led by Vladimir Jabotinsky, in Palestine in the 1930s, where they functioned as a 'fascist party', with 'Brown Shirts, Storm Troops, and all the paraphernalia of fascism'. The Revisionists hounded out from the Zionist movement 'every Liberal and Labour leader', while in 1933 they assassinated the 'able Zionist Labour leader, Dr Chaim Arlosoroff'. They spoke openly of 'transferring the several hundred thousand Palestine Arabs' to Arab States and of 'establishing a Jewish State' on both sides of the Jordan (Zukerman 1937, pp. 113, 116, 127, 155, 161, 172–173).

Nevertheless, Zukerman believes that from 1933 onwards, with the assassination of Dr Arlosoroff, moderate Zionists have turned against the Revisionists: 'Revisionism in all its manifestations is dead in the Zionist world'. By the middle of the 1930s, Zukerman is sure, Palestine's Zionists are returning to true Zionism (Zukerman 1937, pp. 174–176, 179, 205).

I can only speculate on what Elsie Levy thought of *The Jew in Revolt*. She would most likely have been very interested in Zukerman's ideal of the modern Jew, who has 'tended mostly towards the radical political parties' and brought to them 'enthusiasm, genius and devotion'. There is now, he writes in his eloquent conclusion, a Jewish trend towards 'social radicalism', a 'turning leftward' especially by young Jews in Europe and 'even in the United States' (and even in Australia, she might have thought to herself). In more general terms, Zukerman reflects, a revolt, moral, spiritual, social and economic, is observable amongst the mass of Jewish people against the 'economic evils of Capitalism', nourishing a 'Social-Revolutionary movement' that is opposed to 'racial and nationalistic' incitements (Zukerman 1937, pp. 250–254).

Yet Elsie Levy could also have reflected that Zukerman's book gives ground for fear as well as hope; fear that nationalism might overpower the cultural values he admires. Zukerman believes that in Palestine the Zionist trade union body Histadruth is torn between two loyalties, of international labour as against 'nationalistic Jewry', and that nationalism always 'proved the stronger', for example, in Histadruth conducting 'strikes against the employment of Arabs in Jewish enterprises' (Zukerman 1937, pp. 179–181, 185). He writes scornfully that the political Zionists in general refuse any 'social and intellectual contact' with the Arabs, based on 'human equality and friendship' (Zukerman 1937, pp. 162–164).

As the years went on, during the perilous time of World War Two and later, my mother would have observed the fate of Zukerman's predictions and prophecies. Zukerman's thesis, that when the democratic forces defeat fascism and Nazism, 'anti-Semitism is bound to be crushed' as well (Zukerman 1937, p. 50), was supported by Hannah Arendt in her 1944 essay 'New Leaders Arise in Europe'. Here Arendt hails the development of a militant Jewish underground movement against the Nazis, saying that it was only possible because William Zukerman was right ('one lonely preacher in the wilderness'), there has indeed been a 'fast disappearance of antisemitism all over the European continent'; were it not for this, she adds, 'a Jewish underground movement, Jewish fighting units, and so forth would never have come into existence' (Kohn & Feldman 2007, p. 256).

Elsie Levy could well, however, have begun to suspect Zukerman's confident claim that from 1933 onwards, with the assassination of Dr Arlosoroff, Revisionism 'in all its manifestations is dead in the Zionist world' (Zukerman 1937, p. 205). On 4 December, 1948, when Menachem Begin, who inherited Jabotinsky's Revisionist ideals and would one day become prime minister of Israel, visited the United States to gain support for his newly formed Freedom Party, an open letter of protest was published in the *New York Times*. Drafted by Hannah Arendt and co-signed by her, Albert Einstein and others, it pointed out that while Begin's party now presents itself as a party of freedom, democracy, and anti-imperialism, it betrays its true character by its actions, as in the massacre of the Arab village of Deir Yassin earlier in 1948 (Arendt, Einstein *et al*. 2007, pp. 417–419; Young-Bruehl 2004, p. 232). Zukerman's prophecy here was proving increasingly wrong.

Zukerman's claim in *The Jew in Revolt* that there was active cooperation and partnership between the Zionists and the Nazis became a motif in Hannah Arendt's 1963 book, *Eichmann in Jerusalem: A report on the banality of evil*. Arendt points out that in the trial of Eichmann, the prosecution, fearing its case against him would be weakened, was careful not to bring into the open the 'cooperation' of the Jewish leaders throughout Nazi occupied Europe in the Final Solution. Eichmann received such cooperation 'to a truly extraordinary degree', with 'Jewish help in administrative and police work', including the 'final rounding up of Jews in Berlin' being done 'entirely by Jewish police' (Arendt 2006, pp. 42, 116–120, 125, 132, 143, 199).

Arendt's comment on the whole story of collaboration and betrayal by one's own resonates with pathos and horror: 'To a Jew this role of the Jewish leaders in the destruction of their own people is undoubtedly the darkest chapter of the whole dark story' (Arendt 2006, p. 117). What my mother thought of Arendt's *Eichmann in Jerusalem*, which caused a worldwide controversy when it came out, I don't know. My feeling is that she would have agreed with Arendt's view that many more Jews died because the recognised Jewish leaders enforced passivity by cooperating with the Nazis, and many more Jews would have lived if they had 'really been unorganised and leaderless' and had gone underground: 'there would have been chaos and plenty of misery but the total number of victims would hardly have been between four and a half and six million people' (Arendt 2006, p. 125).[1]

# Conclusion

When I was a child and teenager, my mother would fondly recall her childhood in the East End, frequently staying with her grandmother nearby especially when her father the family patriarch became too dictatorial. She would also recall anti-Semitism, in the way a primary school teacher in her London school 'would pronounce my name, Levy', and she would refer to how disgusting Oswald Mosley the English fascist leader was, but would then comment that 'we' in the East End would not let him and his Blackshirts in to destroy our community. I was always puzzled by the way she would say 'we in the East End in the 1930s', as if she still lived not in Sydney but in faraway London. I was, of course, being obtuse. It took me a while to realise that in diaspora consciousness, as I note in the preface to my *1492: The poetics of diaspora*, time and space are doubled (Docker 2001). Diaspora consciousness inheres in a sense of relating to more than one history, to more than one time and place, more than one past and future.

My mother's legacy has proven very powerful for me, in terms of diasporic consciousness, historical consciousness, my becoming a literary and cultural critic, and, from early adulthood, opposition to Zionism. I can't recall my father

---

[1] See also Part IV of *Hannah Arendt: The Jewish writings*, for example, '"The Formidable Dr. Robinson": A Reply by Hannah Arendt' (Kohn & Feldman 2007, pp. 496–511); also Zertal 2011, pp. 136–139.

ever reading anything except political texts. I admired my uncles for their intense cultural interests and passionate arguing over ideas, and my uncle Jock for his lifelong association with theatre and film. I've always been drawn to a sense of the world as theatricality, the *theatrum mundi*, as Walter Benjamin wrote in 'The Storyteller' (Benjamin 2007, pp. 106). Growing up, my mother left me a precious memory related to her reading, that she loved the stories of Sholom Aleichem, the Russian and then American Jewish writer (think *Fiddler on the Roof*); an interest I can now trace back to the 1930s and the Jewish Youth Theatre.

If my father revealed a straightforward optimism about history centred in the Soviet Union, my mother's legacy provided a more divided, ambivalent historical consciousness; history as optimism also in belonging to the Communist Party and fealty to the Soviet Union, and yet history also as shadowed by danger, fear, betrayal, and catastrophe. I've always remembered my mother saying how much she liked Sholom Aleichem, but I never got around to reading his stories; I felt a slight prejudice against Aleichem as possibly a writer of simple comical tales. I have begun to read him now, and have been surprised by how disturbing they are. 'The Haunted Tailor', for example, creates a portrait of extreme poverty for the Russian Jews in the village of Zolodievka, where the story's main character Shimon-Eli lives: 'the moon gazed down at Zolodievka's gloomy half-ruined houses that stood squeezed together without courtyards or fences or trees, looking for all the world like a cemetery … they were bowed so perilously that they would long ago have toppled over if they had not been propped up'. The tailor seeks to please his wife by buying a milking goat at another village, but the goat appears to be a golem, a possessed creature, a demon, changing its gender from female to male and back to female, bringing ridicule to the tailor, who by the end drifts into a catatonic state of madness, disintegration, near death (Howe & Wisse 1979, pp. 2–36).[2] On reading this story, I thought, here I am reading a text of an author admired by my mother that brings to mind Rimbaud's phrases about 'derangement of all the senses'.

In her 1943 essay, 'We Refugees', Hannah Arendt admires a Jewish tradition of 'Heine, Rahel Varnhagen, Sholom Aleichem, of Bernard Lazare, Franz Kafka, or even Charlie Chaplin', who prefer the status of conscious pariah (Kohn & Feldman 2007, pp. 274, 275–297).

Growing up, I can't remember my mother ever saying anything about Zionism or Israel. When, however, Ann Curthoys and I were living in London in the early 1970s, my mother sent a letter, dated 2 October, 1973, which included the interesting sentences: 'It looks as if the Israeli Arab War is going to be a long

---

2   In their introduction to *The Best of Sholom Aleichem*, Irving Howe and Ruth R. Wisse relate that in reading Aleichem's stories they are drawn to a modernist interpretation of how disturbing they are, which almost certainly explains why 'The Haunted Tailor' is placed at the beginning of their selection (Howe & Wisse 1979, pp.vii–ix, xxi, xxiv). Clearly, I am agreeing with Howe and Wisse in my reading.

one. I am disgusted with the Israelis.'[3] Looking back now, I can't remember any particular moment when young that I decided to be anti-Zionist. I feel as if I have always known how profoundly wrong it was that Zionists came from Europe to brutally dispossess Palestine's indigenous people of their sovereign rights and install themselves in their place; and that Zionism in its nationalism and ethnic exclusiveness represents an historical assault on universalist traditions of Judaism, of internationalism and anti-racism, exemplified in radical Jewish traditions and in my own family. I feel as if I have always felt that these radical traditions have to reply to Zionist nationalism, have to reprise an honourable history (Docker 2012b, pp. 1–32; 2012c, pp. 241–284). Internationalism and anti-racism figure in both my mother and father's values, they are a dual legacy. In that sense, my parents' legacies have come together.

## References

Arendt, H 2007, 'Walter Benjamin: 1892–1940', in W Benjamin, *Illuminations*, Schocken Books, New York, pp. 1–55.

Arendt, H 2006, *Eichmann in Jerusalem: A report on the banality of evil*, Penguin, London and New York.

Arendt, H, A Einstein, *et al.*, 2007 'New Palestine Party: Visit of Menachem Begin and aims of political movement discussed', in J Kohn & R H Feldman (eds), *Hannah Arendt: The Jewish Writings*, pp.417–419

Benjamin, W 2007, *Illuminations*, Schocken Books, New York.

Burgmann, V 1995, *Revolutionary Industrial Unionism: The industrial workers of the world in Australia*, Cambridge University Press, Cambridge.

Clark, K & M Holquist 1984, *Mikhail Bakhtin*, Harvard University Press, Cambridge.

Curthoys, A 2012, 'Memory, History, and *Ego-Histoire*: Narrating and Re-enacting the Australian Freedom Ride', *Historical Reflections*, vol. 38, no. 2.

Curthoys, N 2013, *The Legacy of Liberal Judaism: Ernst Cassirer and Hannah Arendt's hidden conversation*, Berghahn, New York.

---

3   My mother's letters to me in London are amongst the documents that Ann Curthoys and I have deposited in Mitchell Library; in late-2010 and early-2011 I spent some months reading our papers there.

Docker, J 2013, 'Dissident Voices on the History of Palestine-Israel: Martin Buber and the bi-national Idea, Walid Khalidi's Indigenous perspective', in J Evans, A Genovese, A Reilly & P Wolfe (eds), *Sovereignty: Frontiers of possibility*, University of Hawai'i Press, Honolulu, pp.86–116.

Docker, J 2012a, 'The Origins of Massacres', in P G Dwyer & L Ryan (eds), *Theatres of Violence: Massacre, mass killing and atrocity throughout history*, Berghahn, New York, pp. 3–16.

Docker, J 2012b, 'Instrumentalising the Holocaust: Israel, settler-colonialism, genocide (creating a conversation between Raphaël Lemkin and Ilan Pappé)', *Holy Land Studies*, vol. 11, no. 1, pp. 1–32.

Docker, J 2012c, 'Orientalism and Zionism: Dismantling Leon Uris's *Exodus*', *Arena Journal*, New Series, no. 37–38, pp. 241–284.

Docker, J 2008a, 'Are Settler-Colonies Inherently Genocidal?: Re-reading Lemkin', in A Dirk Moses (ed.), *Empire, Colony, Genocide: Conquest, occupation, and subaltern resistance in world history*, Berghahn, New York, pp. 81–101.

Docker J 2008b, *The Origins of Violence: Religion, history and genocide*, Pluto Press, Melbourne.

Docker, J 2007, 'The Question of Europe: Said and Derrida', in N Curthoys & D. Ganguly (eds), *Edward Said: The legacy of a public intellectual*, Melbourne University Press, Melbourne, pp. 263–290.

Docker, J 2001, *1492: The poetics of diaspora*, Continuum, London.

Docker, J 1998, 'How Close Should Writers and Critics Be?', *Australian Book Review* no. 202, pp. 24–28.

Docker, J 1984a, 'Father and Son: From old left to new', *Island Magazine*, vol. 18–19, pp. 77–81.

Docker, J 1984b, *In a Critical Condition: Reading Australian literature*, Penguin, Sydney.

Docker, J 1981, 'How I Became a Teenage Leavisite and Lived to Tell the Tale', *Meanjin*, vol. 40, pp. 411–422.

Docker, J 1972, 'Sydney Intellectual History and Sydney Libertarianism', *Politics*, vol. 7, no. 1, pp. 40–47.

Docker, J & A Curthoys 2006, *Is History Fiction?*, UNSW Press, Sydney.

Docker, T & R Gerritsen 1976, 'The 1934 Kalgoorlie Riots', *Labour History*, no. 31, pp. 78–82.

Ferrier, C 1999, *Jean Devanny: Romantic revolutionary*, Melbourne University Press, Melbourne.

Howe, I & R R Wisse (eds) 1979, *The Best of Sholom Aleichem*, Weidenfeld and Nicolson, London.

Kohler, L (ed.) 1996, *Within Four Walls: The Correspondence between Hannah Arendt and Heinrich Blücher, 1936–1968*, Harcourt, New York.

Kohn, J & R H Feldman (eds) 2007, *Hannah Arendt: The Jewish writings*, Schocken, New York.

Macintyre, S 1998, *The Reds: The Communist Party of Australia from origins to illegality*, Allen & Unwin, Sydney.

Mendes-Flohr, P R 1983 (ed.), *A Land of Two Peoples*, Oxford University Press, New York.

Milner, L 2003, *Fighting Films: A history of the Waterside Workers' Film Unit*, Pluto Press, Melbourne.

Nora, P 2001, 'L'Ego-Histoire est-elle Possible?', *Historein*, vol. 3, pp. 19–26.

Prichard, K S 1984, *Winged Seeds*, Virago, London.

Rimbaud, A 2005, *Complete Works, Selected Letters*, translated by W Fowlie, University of Chicago Press, Chicago.

Sparrow, J 2007, *Communism: A love story*, Melbourne University Press, Melbourne.

Young-Bruehl, E 2004, *Hannah Arendt: For love of the world*, Yale University Press, New Haven.

Zertal, I 2011, *Israel's Holocaust and the Politics of Nationhood*, Cambridge University Press, New York.

Zukerman, W 1964, *Voice of Dissent: Jewish problems, 1948–1961*, Bookman Associates, New York.

Zukerman, W 1937, *The Jew in Revolt: The modern Jew in the world crisis*, Martin Secker and Warburg, London.

# 13. Art Works From Home, Out of Place

## Helen Idle

> '... art is never an end in itself, it is only a tool for blazing life lines ...'
> (Deleuze and Guattari 2004, p. 208)

At the entrance to the exhibiton of Australian Indigenous art in the German city of Cologne in 2011, 'Remembering Forward: Australian Aboriginal Painting since 1960', I can just see over the shoulder of the gallery guard collecting tickets and into the first room. On a near wall I see something familiar. I recognise colours, texture and shape, and am brought to tears. I've sat on the ground in Gija country with my hand resting on the ochres of pink, white and yellow, similar to those used in the painting I see now. In Purnululu, under a deep overhanging rockface carved out of towering striated rocks, I sat with my sandwich and listened to the Indigenous guide sing the hymn 'How Great Thou Art' so it echoed through the cave-like surround. My uncle was being cremated at just that moment 1,000 miles to the south in Perth. I recall grief and the ache of mourning on first sight with this painting in Germany and am pulled into a dialogue with it.

The painting is a white ochre square disrupted by a black-filled curve entering the painting from one corner, bounded by white dots, and a smaller white-filled curve framed in black with a white dot border entering part way across one edge. Opposite are two circles. One, painted white, is entirely enclosed by the central area and the other is floating into the far edge with a black frame holding it. The inner white area is smeared with pink ochre, coming from a darker intense spot and pulled out in many directions, over and over again blending outwards in multiple layers. Short brushstrokes appear to flicker outward from this darker pink centre creating a sense of movement, gradually occluding the under white and black ground. Short, sharp, small movements imitating the flicker of fire. The painting is *Old Bedford* (2005) by Gija artist Paddy Bedford of the Kimberley region of north Western Australia.

In this intense moment of being, while genuinely experiencing the abiding now, *nunc stans*, I am alive to the present, the future, and the past. The call for an ego-histoire in 2013/14, if I've understood correctly, counters this experience by asking the writer to attend to her past. In the act of identifying aspects of my ego-histoire for this paper, I am challenged to narrow my perspective. My English version of ego-histoire dulls the senses with its demand to work within conventions of history making. How can I account for my transnational, global and even planetary histories? Should I declare a magpie-like intellectual journey from secondary school existentialism to undergraduate phenomenology and post-structuralism to post-colonialism and interdisciplinarity some 20 years later as a master's student? As the sole student in a secondary school French class, I read Camus and Sartre and tangled with existentialism—teenage angst writ large. This influenced my understanding of the world, and created an ontological reality that separated me from my family and friends. Passerini and Geppert note that most of the participants in the ego-histoire edition of *Historein* 'consider themselves as outsiders. Even Pierre Nora', and they ask whether we should consider 'Self- fashioned marginality, then, as a *leitmotiv* of the entire genre?' (Passerini & Geppert 2012, p. 14).

I am the outsider, white Australian in Cologne, looking at Indigenous painting in a modernist white cube art museum. Considering Mieke Bal's idea that a viewer can engage more deeply with a work of art by entering into a dialogue with it, by hearing what it 'says' or what theory it can make—listening to the art rather than talking over the experience—I am minded to work where 'thought processes emerge in the dynamic between the works as objects, their viewers, and the time in which these come together' (Bal 2010).

This viewing moment initiates a dialogue about beauty, pain, disruption, and terror. It creates a space of loss, grief, mourning, and shame. The painting tells me a story that is confusing, painful and appropriately full of loss. The work refers to the fire lit during the Bedford Downs Massacre in the 1920s. A group of Aboriginal men were accused by settlers of killing a bullock, they were chained and forced to fell trees that were then used to make a pyre upon which they were thrown after being fed poisoned food (Clement, 2003, p. 8). Paddy Bedford and other Gija artists paint this event and other massacres in the Kimberley region of Western Australia. The exhibition 'Blood on the Spinifex' displayed the work together in Melbourne and the catalogue interview with Paddy Bedford, in reference to another of his paintings, *Two Women Looking at Bedford Downs Massacre*, reports the massacre: 'Well this is the place where my old boss killed lots of people at one time, the killing place near the emu dreaming at Mount King.' (Starr 2002, p. 25).

My immanent moment with Bedford's work is further complicated by a blush of—is it shame, insecurity, a sense of not knowing where I should be? Elspeth Probyn has proposed using shame to 'generate new ways of thinking about how we are related to history and how we wish to live in the present' (Probyn 2005, p. 162). In that instance of the blush I am caught looking at the massacre and am confused by where to place myself in relation to it: I am made 'alive' to 'my relations to others' (Probyn 2005, pp. 34–35). These are not relations that can be resolved or solved, but enlivened by the act of looking. I'm being asked to consider my relation to Gija people and to that event in 1920s, as well as to my uncle's death.

My area of research is the experience of viewing contemporary visual art by Indigenous Australian artists in exhibition in western Europe. I'm working towards new methodologies and frameworks for critical analysis of this work—in particular 'out of country'—that may contribute to ways of exhibiting Australian Indigenous art in Europe. I am a PhD candidate at King's College London. This paper endeavours to show how I come to this area of study and demonstrates one way in which the immanent moment of contact between the viewer (me) and artwork—both of us away from 'home' and 'out of place'—may generate a deeper understanding of my relationship to country as a non-Indigenous Australian, and freshly negotiate my relationship with Australia from afar.

The obvious question is: why do I focus my research on Indigenous Australian art rather than non-Indigenous or plain Australian art displayed over here? The display of Indigenous art troubled, and still troubles, curators: the authenticity of the works is under scrutiny and too often no one knows where it should be displayed—in an ethnographic museum or a white cube? Where does it belong?

> … within whiteness's regime of power, all representations are not of equal value: some are deemed truthful while others are classified as fictitious, some are contested while others form part of our commonsense taken-for-granted knowledge of the world. (Moreton-Robinson 2004, p. 76)

The British artist Grayson Perry, broadcasting to the UK through the Reith Lectures on BBC Radio 4, commented on particular Indigenous work shown in the Royal Academy exhibition 'Australia' (a display including Emily Kngwarreye, John Mawurndjul and Rover Thomas):

> … they're powerful ethnic items, but are they contemporary art? You know, they look like abstract specialist paintings, but are they, you know, because do they know about the contemporary art world? I don't know (Perry 2013).

On hearing the ignorance expressed so clearly and shamelessly, on hearing long-established artists being insulted and their existence in effect denied, I am tipped into anger. I feel defensive of Indigenous artists, of Australia, and of myself. There are so many problems with Perry's observations yet they are helpful as a high-octane example of the racism which fixes Indigenous Australians into the ancient past. This questioning of your ontological reality, the essence of self, is a sure route to conflict. Being questioned as to whether you are real or not, to account for your very existence, is a daily challenge when living away from home, and in the capital city of colonialisation, London. The marginal and unsettling nature of the work in display and associated discourse, resonate lightly with my own out of placeness. I acknowledge that this in itself could be a problematic white strategy of using the other to interrogate self, something I write to elsewhere.

So where do I belong?

I come to my area of interest because I am a white Australian of settler-colonial heritage, born and raised in Noongar country, Western Australia, living in London. I live with an attachment to, and disconnection from Australia created by the 'tyranny of distance' (Blainey 1967), one that forges a space for me to examine my relationship to Australia through these works of art, where the artworks look back at me in my 'out of placeness'. Although choosing to live in the UK, I yearn for Western Australian country, for what is now, some 30 years after my first leave-taking as a young adult, an imagined place. This never to be fulfilled desire to be at home in country, in Balardung country east of Perth, where as a young white girl I had the freedom to roam and explore, protected partly by being recognised as the headmaster's daughter and partly by not yet being old enough to be prey for bored teenagers. It's a pretty ordinary story of a sandy-haired kid from country Western Australia, of Protestant colonial-settler heritage. 'Your girls read too much!' I recall my maternal grandmother whispering to her teacher-daughter, my mother. She was right. I read too much and learnt of places beyond the boundaries of my physical, emotional and psychological limits. Beyond the limits of niceness and pressed tea towels and freshly laundered dresses for 'best'. I grew to question the rules of 'best' behaviour and what made 'good girls' by speeding in cars on dirt roads with boys after school, or playing loud rock music on a bright orange record player (now in the care of a musician nephew), and reading about anarchy and feminism in the back of the secondary school's driving lesson car whilst my friends sat in the front learning to drive. All these ideas from countries far away—I barely heard anything of Indigenous stories, only those interpreted and sanctified by book publishers.

Our family moved every two years. My girlhood was largely formed in country Western Australia. Although we were free to roam in Balardung country, east of Perth, as far as a bicycle and the heat would allow, in Kaniyang country (south-west) we were bounded by a sense of foreboding and threat from the bush at the end of the orchard, 'so thick a dog can't bark in it'. Our parents, both West Australian born—a city slicker and a country girl—shared what they knew and loved of the bush by teaching us the English names of the plants and showing us secret places to find wildflowers: donkey orchids, spider orchids, prickly bacon and egg plants. Although at the age of seven my mother could catch, skin and cook a rabbit far from the farmhouse where she lived, she never taught me or my sisters. At the age of seven I was eating at a diner in New York City, in casual conversation with a publicity manager for the Beatles and Rolling Stones (accompanied by parents, I hasten to add). We'd been living in Seattle for 12 months.

My teacher-parents presented books for birthdays and Christmas. I read Enid Blyton, Ruth Park, Alistair McLean, Arthur W. Upfield, Henry Lawson, Banjo Patterson, Robert Frost, and John O'Hara. At school my father introduced me to Henrik Ibsen, Gerard Manley Hopkins and T. S. Eliot while he was my final year literature teacher, reading aloud long passages, performing his love of the ballad form. Combined, these experiences allowed me to imagine somewhere else, somewhere beyond country Western Australia. Yet day-to-day I attached myself to my immediate natural world by learning to note its changes and variety as taught by my country-grown mother, thus making a felt connection to wherever we were living at the time. It is country that I hear and smell. My heritage is not *of* that country, I don't hold the custodianship of it in any formal way as my fellow Indigenous schoolchildren may. But I have a yearning for it, especially from far away.

As an adult now living in London for more that 20 years, my imagined home is still of country Western Australia, Balardung country, places that are flat, golden-brown with a rustling lizard, and have vast blue skies with a soaring bird. My inner landscape is filled with these smells, sounds, and memory of a physical body heated by sun and brushed with dust. In some essential way, this is where I believe I belong. I look for connection to home in my London life through looking and experiencing artworks from 'home', here out of country. My research project considers the display and exhibition of Australian Indigenous artworks in Europe and, in seeking critical approaches shaped by the fact that they are being displayed 'outside' country, I am called to think about myself out of place as well. In fact, my non-Englishness, or non-Britishness, is underlined and my accent provokes endless enquiries as to where I am from. With the benefit of living in a huge cosmopolitan centre I am not seeking to fix my identity to any one type, despite some British people's subtly expressed anxieties at my being just that little bit different.

*\*\*\**

My grandmother played the church organ. My grandmother played golf. My grandmother made cheesy twists in a wood stoked oven surrounded by apple trees. My grandmother was connected to the country, to Noongar country, from a *wadjela* settler family, we are told.

As children grown in the country we heard tales of forebears, settling as freemen in south Western Australia: hardworking people who faced physical and emotional challenges that long sea voyages between England and India, or between Ireland and Van Diemen's Land may have prepared them for. We heard of the successes and of some losses. We learned of mental health crises, of the world wars separating families. Of a great uncle buried at the roadside where he fell while fighting in France.

Our women carried the stories and fluffed them into good shape while we grew untended in the bush behind the house. We didn't hear of the massacres, the conflicts and confusion here/there on Noongar soil. The hospitality of our Indigenous hosts was unrecognised.

In the moment of looking at artworks brought from Australia for display in Europe I want the representations of longed-for home to afford me a heartfelt experience. On occasion the works touch me and make a connection for me to the land, even if not my specific country—Noongar country—but country I have been in and lain upon. And I can sense the space, and air and light that feed the gap between here and there. I want this art to work as a bridge to somewhere else, and to the other, and to me, holding me in relation to Australia and to being alive.

***

Mine is an ordinary, mongrel-style, colonial-settler story.

I could be the great-great-granddaughter of an Irish-Australian's love affair with a Spaniard, resulting in a love child born in 1869, or was it 1897, named Augustus Ricardo. I could be the descendent of a gold miner, robbed of his nugget in the goldfields of Western Australia in 1890s by his American partner, who he then chased on foot some 600 kilometres to the port, only to see the ship leaving.

I could be the great-great-granddaughter of a woman from Nhill near Glenrowan who rode with Ned Kelly. I could be the great-granddaughter of a shopkeeper and drunk.

I am the granddaughter of an electrician and a clerk. I am the daughter of teachers.

I am connected to a beach between Cottesloe and Fremantle, Leighton, named for my paternal great-great-grandmother who managed the railway gates there where the new surf club crouches.

I am connected to the land by barefoot stubbed toes and sun-scarred eyes. I am connected to place by a longing to lie down in the hot red dirt and dive into the deep blue sky.

My body cells were struck under the Southern Cross in a springtime romance by people connected to the bursting of rough wildflowers and the swell of the Indian Ocean.

In a white cube in a city shaken by war I am overwhelmed with a sense of loss as my eyes light across chalky white and soft pink surfaces of a painting from home. A tingle of anticipation; am I going to be comforted? No. Everything is not going to be alright now.

## Acknowledgements

I'd like to thank the referees and Anna Cole for their guidance, and the editors for their commitment to this project. With thanks also to Ian, Jan, Lesley and Joan for their feedback during the writing of this paper. All errors are mine alone.

## References

Bal, M 2010, 'After-Images: Mere Folle', *Nomadikon*, Available at: http://www.nomadikon.net/ContentItem.aspx?ci=172 (accessed 22 October, 2010).

Blainey, G 1967, *The Tyranny of Distance: How distance shaped Australia's history*, Sun Books, Melbourne.

Clement, C 2003, 'National Museum of Australia Review of Exhibitions and Public Programme Submission', National Museum of Australia. Available at: http://www.nma.gov.au/about_us/nma_corporate_documents/exhibitions_and_public_programs_review/submissions/.

Deleuze, G & F Guattari 2004, *A Thousand Plateaus: Capitalism and schizophrenia*, translated by B Massumi, Continuum, London.

Kalgoorlie Western Argus 1905, 'Extensive Horse Sale', *Kalgoorlie Western Argus*, 1 August, 1905, p. 15. Available at: http://nla.gov.au/nla.news-article33026480 (accessed 23 December, 2013).

Konig, K, E Joyce Evans & F Wolf (eds), 2010, *Remembering Forward: Australian Aboriginal Painting Since 1960*, Museum Ludwig and Paul Holberton Publishing, Cologne and London.

Moreton-Robinson, A 2004, 'Whiteness, epistemology and Indigenous representation', in Moreton-Robinson, A (ed.), *Whitening Race: Essays in social and cultural criticism*, Aboriginal Studies Press, Canberra, pp. 75–88.

Passerini, L & A Geppert 2001, 'Historians in Flux: The concept, task and challenge of ego-histoire', *Historein*, vol. 3. Available at: http://www.historeinonline.org/index.php/historein/article/view/96/94.

Perry, G 2013, 'Playing to the Gallery', Reith Lecture, BBC Radio 4, 22 October, 2013.

Probyn, E 2005, *Blush: Faces of Shame*, University of Minnesota Press, Minneapolis.

Starr, B (ed), 2002, *Blood on the Spinifex*, The Ian Potter Museum of Art and the University of Melbourne, Melbourne.

# 14. From Bare Feet to Clogs: One Aboriginal Woman's Experience in Holland

### Rosemary van den Berg

'Like myself, my ego. Half wants to belong to the white world; the other yearns for the black of my mother's people.' Thomas Corbett. (van den Berg 1994, p. 2)

Aboriginal life stories during the 1980s and 1990s changed the face of Australian history and literature. Aside from a few important exceptions, prior to these times Aboriginal life stories had not emerged as a genre and the majority of life stories at this time were penned by white writers and were semi-fictional. Sally Morgan's book *My Place* (Morgan 1988) marks the beginning of a new genre of Aboriginal life writing and other Aboriginal people followed her lead by publishing their stories. These stories made a significant intervention into Australian history, telling first-hand how Aboriginal people survived under the strict state government laws enforced upon them. It was something of a time of enlightenment for many of Australia's literati and the general public as Aboriginal people penned their way to a new genre. Now there are many life stories told by Aboriginal people and a developing critical literature growing up around Aboriginal life writing. Oliver Haag has written a comprehensive study of Aboriginal biography and autobiography in his paper, 'From the Margins to the Mainstream' (Haag 2008) and traces Aboriginal writing from David Unaipon in 1951, and Theresa Clements in 1954, to the current times. Anne Brewster's two books on Aboriginal autobiography and biography, *Literary Formations: Post-colonialism, nationalism, globalism* and *Reading Aboriginal Women's Autobiography* (Brewster 1995, 1996), are significant contributions to the field. Both books give insights into Aboriginal writing of life stories, especially the latter, which studies Aboriginal women's life-story writers such as Ruby Langford and Doris Pilkington (Langford 1988; Pilkington 1991). Drawing on these surveys of the field, I argue that Aboriginal autobiographies are conceptually different from western forms of autobiography in that they spring from prior Indigenous sovereign traditions.

Aboriginal life stories are based on the experiences of the writer's life, with life experiences forming an archive for Aboriginal history. Many Aboriginal autobiographies do not delve intimately into their protagonists' individual selves. They do not have an ulterior motive driving them to uncover, for example, an intense existential relation with the past, nor to examine in-depth their reason for being. Their primary intention seems to be to write their story, identify with their respective Aboriginal cultures, their old people, and, to quote Pierre Nora, 'give a definite continuity to their own existence' (Nora 2001, pp. 19–26). Aboriginal autobiography and biography seek to inform the reader of the struggles faced to survive the massive changes to their Aboriginal world. I argue that differences can be seen in the European conception of ego-histoire and the autobiographical style of Aboriginal writing. My reading of Nora's introduction to his original ego-histoire collection suggests it can be seen in some ways as a warning to other western historians attempting to write their memoirs to beware of the pitfalls involved in writing an autobiography. Drawing on these themes, Remond reminds historians that they, like other mere mortals, can fall into the trap of elaborating on their life stories, parts of which may be untrue (Remond 1987). Jeremy D. Popkin's review of ego-histoire explains:

> A long tradition has taught [historians] to be on their guard against subjectivity, their own as much as others. They know from experience the precariousness of recollection, the unreliability of first-person testimony. Their professional training has taught them that everyone has an unconscious tendency to introduce a factitious coherence into the path of his life. They have no reason to believe that they are better armed against these distortions. They have no reason to think that they have any better chance to avoid the tricks of memory that they have learned to spy out in others. (Popkin 1999, pp. 725–748)

This is where the difference or the comparisons between western writing and Aboriginal writing of autobiography is most profound or acute, because the western criterion of objectivity and thus historical truthfulness, however contested, relies often upon written archives, whereas Aboriginal concepts of autobiography rely mainly on memory and oral traditions. The papers I have read on ego-histoire talk of European countries and the impact of other western cultures on their transnational experiences, and the writing of their histories. Pierre Nora writes of his own ego-histoire and mentions two characteristics of his personal situation: 'It's singular and unclassifiable character on the one hand … and on the other, the belated character of my own historical work' (Nora 2001, pp. 19–26). In comparison, the only characteristic formulation of my writing in this area was informed by my desire to relate my husband's and my own history to our children. Like other Aboriginal story-telling/autobiographies, our stories are directly related to our own experiences, and reinforce my stance on Aboriginal storytelling as different to ego-histoire. Aboriginal people often tell their life stories chronologically or as their lives unfolded, without thought to the literary or theoretical implications placed on those stories by white academia.

In writing *Clogs and Bare Feet* (van den Berg 2009), I drew on my own and my husband's memories to write our stories with the express purpose of leaving our children a record of their parents' respective histories: my husband's childhood in Holland, my early life in Australia, and our lives together. I related my autobiography through memory, and my husband's biography is based on his memories. Our stories work in conjunction with each other, because they are related with intergenerational reminiscences (Brewster, 1995, pp. 51–53). My book relates intercultural and interracial memory. One instance is when my husband fought his boss for calling me derogatory names. Stephen Muecke points out that Aboriginal truth regimes and 'historical objectivity' rest on personal and intergenerational witnessing (Muecke 1983, p. 85). Telling biographies, in an Aboriginal context, means unfolding genealogies, personal memories and history, and is an important element to Aboriginal storytelling which aligns to Aboriginal modes of history. However, although ego-histoire and Aboriginal life stories emerge from different traditions, they both invite scholars to ponder their own life stories in relation to their research. My essay below is an example of the concept of ego-histoire meeting my attempt at Aboriginal life-story writing, thereby, I hope, extending what I consider the Eurocentric origins of Nora's ego-histoire.

Aboriginal culture was an oral culture and had been for millennia before colonisation and the British–style education that was foisted on Aboriginal people. Traditionally, Aboriginal people had to learn, digest and remember all the information they received from their elders. Their very lives could depend on this knowledge. Given these cultural reasons for sharp memory retention, when some Aboriginal people write their life stories, their memories can be acutely focused. I do know that when my elderly father permitted me to write his biography, *No Options No Choice: The Moore River Experience* (van den Berg 1994), he was alert and aware of what I was writing. If he thought I was deviating from his story, he would tell me so in no uncertain terms and I would have to rewrite a paragraph or sentence until he was satisfied. When my father died at 81, he was lucid. My family applauded the fact that our family history would contain the truth of our father's life. Reports in the Native Welfare Department's files were impersonal, but now we would have a personal account and knowledge of our father's life and times. His words were coming from his Aboriginal experiences, not from the perspective of a government bureaucracy. Writing my father's biography prepared me for always adhering to the truth of the story-teller in my research and subsequent writing and publications. In this case, this meant to tell his story 'like it is', without elaboration or distortion.

When I wrote *Clogs and Bare Feet*, I had retired from lecturing and tutoring at Murdoch University. With plenty of spare time on my hands and boredom setting in with mundane tasks around the home, I decided to write my story.

I wanted to give my children a sense of continuity in their lives with my history, so they would know their place in life and their history. But then I thought, 'Why just write my story?' I would write about my husband's early life in Holland as well, to give our children a clearer picture of both their parents' early lives, as well as combining the two stories after we married. Our children would know and understand their father's Dutch culture and heritage and their mother's Aboriginal culture and heritage. Suffice to say, details of our personal lives would remain private, but I would write about our respective childhoods in Holland and Australia, combined with stories of our married life which included our children. In effect, I wrote my husband's biography and my autobiography as a single book, with the title referring to 'clogs' for my husband's Dutch heritage, and 'bare feet' for my Aboriginal heritage. I thought the title represented our stories in a simple and concise way, without too many frills and fancy words.

My husband and I have a cross-cultural marriage. When we fell in love and married, we knew next to nothing about each other's cultures, but with time we learned to accept our idiosyncrasies. It is funny, but the issue of skin colour never came into our relationship. They say love is blind and in our case this was definitely the case. I personally think that our difference in character was the reason why our marriage lasted so long. Jack is an extrovert; I am an introvert, which is why we complement each other. In our case, opposites do attract. However, although our respective families did not take kindly to our marriage at first, in time, they came to accept we had married for life. We have been married for 47 years. We've had a good marriage; we have our five children, 26 grandchildren and 22 great-grandchildren, with four more on the way. They are all healthy, so we have much to be thankful for and to appreciate in life. We are not rich, but our lives are enriched by loving and caring for each other. What more can anyone ask for in this life? By writing our stories, I wanted to convey to our children the hardships their parents faced within a cross-cultural marriage, while living in a very racist country from 1966 onwards. Back then, Australia did not have a very good reputation in human rights and both Jack and I battled to find an easier path for our children to be accepted into the white world as people with as much right to live in Australia as anyone else.

Although I relied on my and my husband's memories to relate our stories in *Clogs and Bare Feet*, I realised that I had to conduct research for my book, including family photographs, and consulting historical and geographical texts in order to ensure ship movements and travel were correctly related in my husband's story. I did so with the purpose of authenticating his movements so there would be no mistake in his storyline. His memories coincided with the ships he named and the routes taken in relation to his work. I was satisfied that our memories held the guts or the essential parts of our stories.

# 14. From Bare Feet to Clogs

Now I will speak about the formative experiences of the time we lived in Holland in 1978–1980. Following are excerpts from my manuscript, later published as the book *Clogs and Bare Feet*:

> In early October 1978, with four of my children, I left my homeland, Australia, to travel to Holland, my husband's country. Jack had already gone on ahead and had sent for us to join him in Rotterdam. Our oldest daughter, Leanne, who had won a scholarship and was going to college at the time, was joining us as soon as the school term ended. Our younger children, Diane, Sharon, Peter and Valerie were so excited to be flying in an aeroplane to see their father again, and while I too was excited, I was filled with trepidation at the thought of going to a country that was so alien to us. Sitting there on the plane I wondered what lay in store for us. We were going to a strange land where English was not the spoken language, the currency was different from ours, where the climate was too cold and the people would all be white. White faces, white places. I hoped the kids would settle down but for myself, I had my doubts about whether I'd be able to adjust. I was an Aboriginal woman, my people were Aboriginal people, I would miss the sunshine and everything that was Australia. But for my husband's sake I would try living in Holland. It would be an experience for all of us and I sincerely hoped my husband's family would accept me as his wife and give me the respect that I hoped for. Jack and I had been through so much together and I didn't want his family to come between us. It would be a test for our love and relationship as husband and wife. Jack had shown himself to be a fair man when it came to meeting and mixing with my family and friends. He wasn't racist and treated everybody as he himself wanted to be treated. But if anyone of each other's cultures, white or Aboriginal did or said anything derogatory to me or our children, he would stand his ground and let people know his thoughts on the situation even if it meant fisticuffs. But that was in Australia. Would he be any different in Holland amongst his own people? As I sat in the plane contemplating these issues, I knew, in my heart, that Jack would not act any differently. He would stand by us and protect us come what may. As the plane came in to land at Schiphol Airport, Amsterdam, I couldn't wait to see my husband again and to meet his family.

My thoughts on the plane while travelling to Amsterdam show the uncertainty I felt when leaving my homeland, family and friends behind. Yet I had faith in my husband's ability to look after us while we were living in Holland. My main concern was for our children should anything happen to Jack or me. However, on our arrival at the airport, and having passed through customs, more concern and uncertainty awaited me and my children:

> I looked around for my husband among the waiting crowd of people eager to see their loved ones again. I could not see Jack anywhere and after awhile, Diane and Sharon started to worry as well. So we waited and waited in that strange place where language was a barrier to communication and everything was foreign and unsettling. Peter and Valerie were in their element playing and while I did not want them to be a nuisance to other people, I was glad their minds were occupied with playing. I didn't know what to do. After nearly an hour I tried to ring his mother's place, but not being wise in the ways of the world, I made a hash of the telephone call, so I just decided to wait and worry. Every so often I would go to the entrance of the airport and see if I could see him coming, and after a while I thought I'd better go to some official for help. Even my two youngest kids had given up playing their game and were sitting quietly waiting.

All sorts of things were going through my mind, none of them complimentary to Jack or his family, but I kept my frustration to myself for fear of upsetting my children, for I could see the worry on their faces with traces of the fear I felt inside.

> Finally we saw Jack and his mother and sister and a couple of other people walk through the door. I breathed such a sigh of relief that I'm sure people nearby heard me. The children rushed up to their father and amid the hugs and kisses, we were able to meet Jack's family and hear his explanation of why they were late in meeting us. Apparently they were held up in a traffic jam on the main highway from Rotterdam to Amsterdam and just had to wait for it to clear before they could move. I was so glad to see Jack. All my worries had disappeared now that he was with us.

This was our introduction to Holland and the Dutch side of our family—the initial transnational experience that is so clear in my mind; it was like it happened yesterday. The impact of living in Holland and the experiences it afforded me were like nothing I had encountered in Australia.

> As we made our way out of Schiphol Airport, I looked around for my first real look at Holland. We piled into two cars to accommodate all of us and then we were on the road to Rotterdam. I saw grey skies, leafless trees and picture post-card farms and villages with church spires so high one could see them for miles around. And the countryside was so flat. There was no comparison between my homeland and Jack's country. I marvelled at the Dutch road systems which had overpasses, underpasses, tunnels, concrete highways and cobblestone roads and canals; and everyone drove on the right hand side of the road. I would

have to teach my children the reverse road rules to that in Australia. On second thoughts, I had to learn about these rules myself; besides learning the language and currency, and other things about the Dutch that I didn't know. I knew then that I would be living a life-changing experience, starting right at that very moment. I wondered if it would change me and my outlook on life. Living in Holland would reveal a whole new world of 'whiteness', one that I, as an Aboriginal woman, would live in for who knew how long?

Australia at this time, in 1978, did not even have 200 years of British history behind it, yet here was Jack's homeland steeped in European history. His family was proud of their country and heritage and their independence as a nation. It was so different from the English traditions that were brought to Australia, with their ideas of white supremacy, racism and bigotry; and the pomp and ceremony and class system among their own people. They had no thought for the Aboriginal people whose lands they were claiming as their own. While the Netherlands did colonise some countries, such as Indonesia, Suriname and many Caribbean Islands, were they as harsh with the indigenous people as the British were to the Aborigines? I didn't really know. At this time, I only knew my world in Australia and the ugliness of the 'native' policies that were developed for the Aboriginal people. At this time, I was a housewife and mother. My entry into the world of academia came later, after we returned to Australia. So my experiences in Holland were based on emotive feelings and common sense, not the logic or analysis I was to apply to a situation after I studied for my degrees. That in itself would dictate the terms of my living in Holland. I was a novice in overseas travel and transnational experiences, with only my husband to guide me in the ways of the Dutch world. I was soon to discover that people the world over were human beings with all their foibles and frustrations regardless of the colour of their skin. All the fancy trappings of culture, class and affluence meant nothing when it came to the interactions of human relationships.

> When we first came to Holland our family was divided with my two older girls Diane and Sharon remaining with their grandparents while Jack, Peter, Valerie and I were to stay at his sister's place with her husband and four children (they had the bigger house). When our eldest daughter Leanne arrived a month later, she stayed at Oma and Opa's house as well, so overcrowding and lack of privacy occurred. At first, everything was fine, but then, after the New Year, the vagaries of human nature between two women who were totally different in all aspects of inter-family relationships surfaced and mayhem ensued. We left Jack's sister's house and lived in a caravan where my husband worked. Even living in the caravan, I felt the freedom of having our own place, of being mistress of my own domain. Living here would suffice

until the government house my husband had applied for when we first arrived in Holland, became available. Not long after we were informed of the availability of a house and when we moved in, it was the happiest of days. My husband and I with our five children were together again under the one roof!

Once we were settled in our new home, a two-storey four bedroom place, life in Holland became more interesting for me. Jack had a good job and our children were attending school. When they first commenced classes at their respective schools (high school and primary), they became quite the celebrities because they came from Australia and could speak English. Yet all of them learned to speak Dutch; a language that I could not roll my tongue around. While I could understand Dutch if I listened really carefully, I felt so embarrassed trying to speak it that I gave up altogether and if Jack wasn't present I would have the kids translate for me. Eventually Jack bought a car which made life even more interesting and on weekends we could travel to places around Holland. Once we followed the Rhine River to Heidelberg in Germany, drove to Antwerp in Belgium and even to Paris, France.

In Holland, as in the countries we visited, I found the Europeans were polite and courteous; Jack and I being together, with our children, did not raise an eyebrow. Maybe there was racism, but I was treated as a human being, not as someone of dubious character because I was Aboriginal, a black person. I found this extraordinary. Perhaps this next excerpt from my manuscript would give a better comparison of the differences between Holland and Australia in their acceptance or denial of the human condition in each:

> Those trips to Paris and Heidelberg opened up my mind to different people and cultures throughout the world. I found that living in Holland, with its acceptance of the various races that had migrated here from Turkey, Suriname and Indonesia, to name a few, was how people could live together without too many hassles. They were free citizens in every sense of the word, providing they obeyed the laws of the land. I thought about the way we Aborigines were treated in Australia and realised that racism played such a huge part in life in my country. Being a decent person was based on the colour of your skin. If you were any colour but white, you were looked on as inferior and had to try doubly hard to be accepted by mainstream Australians.

Although racism, bigotry and prejudice were a way of life for Aboriginal people in Australia, I found the Dutch and other Europeans more liberal in their thinking on matters of race. In these countries I found respect and concern for a fellow human being.

We had been in Holland for nearly a year when a sense of isolation began to sink into my psyche. Outwardly I was happy because I knew that Jack and our children were happy and they loved our life in Holland. There was plenty for them to do at work and school, and at home, but I was lonely. Although we had made friends with Jack's sister after the argument we had had earlier in the year; and my husband argued with his mother, but were reconciled later, I started to feel homesick for my own family. I felt a loneliness and isolation that went deeper than anything I had known before. I missed visiting my father and my siblings, the hills of home near Perth, and the sunshine on my bones, warming my whole outlook on life. In effect, I missed my homeland — Australia. Homesickness is a debilitating condition and at times I became nervous and scared and wondered what I was doing so far from my homeland and my own Aboriginal people. Every day I would look for letters from home in the letterbox or maybe receive an unlikely telephone call, but weeks would go by while I grew more depressed. My homesickness was like a toothache; it would not go away. I was happy when my husband and children were around me, but more and more I would sink into despair of maybe dying before I saw my father, sisters and brothers again; and of leaving my children in a strange land. I longed for the casual and carefree way we were in Australia without having to be on my guard all the time, afraid of saying something that would upset Jack's family. In my mind I was living in limbo, not belonging anywhere.

And so the weeks passed by. While there were days when I enjoyed being in Holland, the shopping, the visiting and having my husband and children around me, I kept getting sick. Jack was getting more worried by the day. My moods would change in a flash; one moment I'd be full of the joys of life, the next I would be miserable and morose, not saying much, crying when alone, and not sleeping. In our travels all over Holland, the flower markets of Amsterdam, Koekenhoff, Nijmegen, Haarlem, Hook of Holland, Den Haag, Delft, the Zuider Zee, and several of the seaside resorts, and even when we went to a place where the Dutch and Spanish fought back in the 1700s, I forgot my woes. I loved seeing historic places. Besides English, I'd loved history and geography at school. To learn how other people lived throughout the ages and where they came from gave me much pleasure. It was so interesting seeing these places, like the site of this old battle, the house in Amsterdam where Anne Frank and her family sought shelter from the Germans, and the historic sites around Paris, brought to life how people struggled for freedom and justice. But while Jack took me and the children to these places, for all his love and concern, when I returned home I could not shake this feeling of doom or that I would die in Holland. In hindsight, I think I was on the verge of a mental breakdown. I just wanted to go back home to Australia.

One day, Jack and his mother came home, smiling from ear to ear. When I looked at them, I saw Jack waving some papers in his hands and when he told me they were tickets home to Australia for me and our children, I cried like a baby. I was so happy! I couldn't thank Jack and his mother enough. They had gone to the Australian Consulate in Den Haag and enquired about repatriation back to Australia for me and the children. After stating ill-health as the reason and convincing the Australian Embassy that I was in dire straits health-wise, the Australian government via the Embassy granted me and my children a free passage back to my homeland. My children and I were going home to Perth, Western Australia, the following week. In the flurry of readying for departure, I packed our cases. Although Jack had to remain behind until he finalised our affairs, I would miss him terribly, but I was so glad that I would once again see my family. And when I saw the Western Australian coastline from the plane, my joy knew no bounds.

My time spent in Holland with my family is an experience I will never forget. It remains stark in my memory. For me, it was a time of change, of growing and of looking at the world through a wider focus instead of being insulated or slotted into a pigeon-hole of invisibility because I was an Aboriginal person. In Holland I had a freedom in a white world that I could never hope to attain in my homeland. It opened my eyes to the worth of a human being, an individual, and not being judged by my race or the colour of my skin. It was an exhilarating experience. I was seen as a person in my own right, a human being, not as a nonentity in the country of my birth. Nevertheless, I knew the circumstances I would be returning to in Australia, the racism that would see me grind my teeth in frustration at being a second-class citizen. I knew that the Aboriginal people now had the right to vote with the Referendum of 1967; I knew that the federal government had enacted the *Racial Discrimination Act of 1975*, and that Australia was trying to implement other laws and statutes that would improve the lot of the Aboriginal people, but there would always be that element of insidious racism that was present in Aboriginal/white Australian relationships. Insidious racism is hard to explain but, to my way of thinking, it is a deliberate indifference to Aboriginal people that constitutes an invisibility of being. To the dominant culture, Aboriginal people are present but their presence is not acknowledged (except as nuisance value) because they have been relegated to the background as being of no consequence to white society. However, back in 1980, when my children and I returned to Australia, I could not foresee the racist attitudes towards Aboriginal people changing in the near future, but I did not care. I was going home to my homeland and I would fight for my right to be treated with respect for what I was, an Aboriginal person.

In hindsight, my own experiences in Europe in 1978–1980 have stood me in good stead for my writing as an Aboriginal person and as an academic with a PhD. During my studies for my MA in English and PhD, I gave several papers at conferences in Nijmegen and Utrecht in Holland and at Klagenfurt in Austria, and another paper in Delhi, India, in 2004. So my time in Holland gave me a grounding in international travel, meeting different peoples and cultures and, in essence, gave me the incentive to promote Aboriginal culture and people overseas and at home. My writing this paper on ego-histoire has enabled me to understand myself in a much more academic or objective way, instead of accepting my interlude in Holland as an inexperienced novice in writing auto/biography.

My writing for the past few years have been pro-Aboriginal and I make no apologies for it. I write about Aboriginal/Australian history, make political comment about the treatment Aboriginal people receive at the hands of the Australian governments, both federal and state, and generally promote Aboriginal people in a positive light. And yes, I did view Australia differently on my return from living overseas: I wondered why it was so racist towards Aboriginal people, which spurred me on to attain a higher education and to seek integrity and maturity in my writing abilities. This, in turn, would enable me to voice my concerns through literary and media outlets regarding the historical and contemporary injustices suffered by Aboriginal people in Australia since colonisation. Through my writing, I have tried to make readers see a different side to Aboriginal people and their cultures, a side that is not witnessed in the media. There definitely are some Aboriginal people who shed a negative light on our people, but there are many more who believe in the Dreamtime tenets of our ancestors and have not permitted 'living white'—that is, being integrated into white society by government policies and laws—to interfere with our fundamental psyche of being Aboriginal. I want to show that the majority of Aboriginal people are a decent and law-abiding people from traditional times to this contemporary society. That is the reason for my writing.

The Aboriginal autobiographies/biographies I have written and read are stories of people who have been repressed and subjected to the harsh realities of colonialism and nationalism in Australia. What has emerged from their writing is that Australian history has had to recognise that this country has a 'Black History' as well as their own white history. Aboriginal literature speaks for itself. What can I say to future or emerging writers of Aboriginal auto/biographies? What can I say except follow your own truth, research background information and believe in yourselves and be proud of what you are doing for your people and your country.

# References

Brewster, A 1995, *Literary Formations: Post-colonialism, nationalism, globalism*, Melbourne University Press, Melbourne.

Brewster, A 1996, *Reading Aboriginal Women's Autobiography*, Sydney University Press, Sydney.

Haag, O 2008, 'From the Margins to the Mainstream: Towards a history of published Indigenous Australian autobiographies and biographies', in F Peters-Little, P Read & A Haebich (eds), *Indigenous Biography and Autobiography*, ANU E Press, Canberra, pp. 5–28.

Langford, R 1988, *Don't Take Your Love to Town*, Penguin, Ringwood.

Liakos, A 2001, 'History Writing as the Return of the Repressed', *Historein*, vol. 2, pp. 47–58.

Morgan, S 1988, *My Place*, Fremantle Arts Centre Press, Fremantle.

Muecke, S 1983, 'Ideology Re-iterated: The eses of Aboriginal oral aarrative', *Southern Review*, vol. 16, no. 1, pp. 86–101.

Nora, P 2001, 'L'Ego-Histoire est-elle Possible?, *Historein*, vol. 3, pp. 19–26.

Pilkington, D 1991, *Caprice: A stockman's daughter*, University of Queensland Press, St Lucia.

Popkin, J D 1999, 'Historians on the Autobiographical Frontier', *The American Historical Review*, vol. 104, no. 3, pp. 725–748.

Remond, R 1987, 'Le Contemporain du Contemporain', in P. Nora (ed), *Essais d'Ego-Histoire*, Gallimard, Paris, pp. 293–346.

van den Berg, R 2009, *Clogs and Bare Feet*, RoseDog Books, Pittsburgh.

van den Berg, R 1994, *No Options No Choice: The Moore River experience*, Magabala Books, Broome.

# TALES OF MYSTERY AND IMAGINATION

# 15. Home Talk

Jeanine Leane

## Beginnings

This is a story about how I came to write. In 2010, when I was in my late 40s, I completed a PhD and wrote a volume of poetry and a novel. This is a story. It is not an essay or an article or a treatise or anything else that 'scholarly' writing is called in western literature. This is a story because Aboriginal people live for and by stories. This is the story about how I came to write all that I did and how I came to find my place and my voice in a nation that until the early 1970s was dominated by an official White Australia Policy. It can be argued that, even in the twenty-first century, vestiges of the 'white nation' still prevail.

As Pierre Nora intended, I write this as a combination of personal history set against the broader socio-political contexts of the late-twentieth and early-twenty-first centuries in Australia. In this way, I hope to shed some light on how growing up Aboriginal has informed my historical practice and why the relationship between my personal life and professional research is inseparable. The value of Nora's method for me is that it allows me to self-reflect on how my understandings of western culture were shaped and formed through my home culture *and* how Anglo-Australian understandings of Aboriginal people were shaped and formed in the classroom and how this continues to inform my research. As I write this, I have at the forefront of my mind ongoing issues of non-Aboriginal editing of Aboriginal works that continually ask Aboriginal scholars to justify their 'facts' against or in relation to a body of Anglo-western knowledge that is accepted and assumed as factual.

I am a Wiradjuri woman. In Australian English, Wiradjuri means 'of the rivers' or 'river people'. My country where I was born and raised is situated between three rivers. I grew up on the Murrumbidgee River near a small country town called Gundagai, which is also a Wiradjuri word, meaning 'bend in the back of the knee', as the town is situated on a bend in the river. I was born in the early 1960s in a larger town called Wagga Wagga situated on the same river. In 1961 my mother was very young and had a difficult relationship with my father who was of Irish descent. Two unmarried Aunts raised my sister and me. In 1961, Australia fiercely, proudly and loudly called itself a 'white nation'. Since 1901, when the colonies became the federated nation of Australia, the *Immigration Restriction Act* was officially introduced and enforced under the White Australia

Policy. The policy was not officially dismantled until the Whitlam Government came to power in 1972. The policy restricted the entry of all immigrants who were not British. The original inhabitants of the land, whom the British called 'Aborigines', were entrapped within the imposed white nation and everything about us was inferior, in deficit, and undesirable.

My Grandmother, like many Aboriginal girls, worked in the homes of wealthy white people. She attracted the attention of a Devonshire settler who came to Australia to farm. He was an austere protestant and a fierce and proud supporter of British colonial interests. He was staunchly patriotic and had intended, had the war not ended, before he was old enough to enlist, to join the British in South Africa during the Boer War (1999–1902). One of his many concerns, related to me time and time again through story, was that England and Europe were being 'ruined by liberalism'. He deplored universal suffrage for women and those with no property and condemned any movement related to economic independence for women. 'Politics', he said, 'should be left to the men with interests to protect'. He was well suited to nineteenth century colonial Australia and followed a well-worn but greatly understated pattern of settler farmers in Australia marrying Aboriginal women, because the expectations for the treatment and up-keep of such women were far less than that of white women. Marrying an Aboriginal woman provided many settlers with a slave, a concubine and a workforce of children who could be educated or not at their white fathers' discretion.

Many people have asked me as an adult why such a man would marry an Aboriginal woman and I say to them that she was a perfect choice in keeping with his socio-political and religious views because she had no rights and therefore no recourse for anything he did. He could keep her in complete isolation as a slave and no one would think anything of it. Also, as Kim Scott's novel *Benang* starkly illustrates, white colonists thought that Aboriginal blood could be 'bred out' in a few generations and Aboriginal women became part of individual eugenics schemes as well as those imposed by the states (Scott 1999).

My grandfather was bitterly disappointed that of his 12 children, only four were boys. But for my grandmother it was the beginning of the secrets that were the stories she had never been allowed to tell—our history through her memory. My grandfather ruled the women with an iron fist as he did not trust women left to their own devices or intellect. My grandmother's hair had to be braided and pulled tightly back at all times, she was only allowed to wear brown, and could have no bare skin showing apart from her face and hands. The first two children born were girls and my grandfather chose names from the Old Testament, which my grandmother secretly deplored. Fortunately, when two sons arrived in quick succession after that, named of course after English kings, he lost interest in the girls, except for making them slaves on his farm, and my grandmother named the other six girls herself after her favourite flowers. I grew up with a garden of aunties.

## Keepers and Tellers

Seven of my eight aunties were sent for a time to a small school in the area called 'the creek school'—a tiny one-room building on the outskirts of the main town. My grandfather decided that if they could read and write, they would be more useful to the husbands and 'masters' he would place them with. At school, my aunties were ostracised and made to feel ashamed of their dark skin, but they did learn to read and write. Because they were marginalised and isolated they spent a lot of time alone thinking about what they read—history in particular; the public, national history in the classroom and the personal secret history at home.

As I write this piece, it strikes me how much history within my family has repeated itself. Three of my aunties were sent to domestic service and three were made to stay and work the farm. Of those sent to domestic service, one suffered and survived sexual assault. She was one of the aunties who raised me almost 25 years later. My sister and I had similar experiences at school of being teased and shamed for our Aboriginality as my aunties had decades earlier. It is a common assumption of western history that the passing of linear time somehow equates to improvement, progress or advancement but, as this story shows, this was not the case for Aboriginal people.

After I was born my mother left me in the care of her two older sisters. One was in her early-40s and had never married. She said she was part of the 'war-generation', lots of women from that generation were left unmarried. But later on as an adult I pieced together the events of another colonial tragedy—a farming accident that left her unable to have children. She was almost broken-hearted, except my sister and I came along. My elder aunt was in her late-50s and was single by design. She had little patience for men in general, based on her observation of her own mother in particular, but also some of the settler women that she worked for. She always said: 'Marriage is not for better or for worse—it's for worse only.' She was fiercely independent and once her father passed away she was determined never to have to answer to any man again. And she didn't. She died when she was 93. When I was a teenager in the 1970s she developed a keen interest in the Women's Liberation Movement, as it was known at the time. Once my grandmother expressed some reservation at a scene we saw on our battered second-hand television of women burning their bras. Aunty Boo said: 'I don't care about their underwear as long as they stand up to the men!'

My two aunties were both a complement and a contrast in my life. They were the balance and symmetry that grounded me. My younger Aunty Bubby was shy and romantic. Her favourite books were *Wuthering Heights,* the story of another country where land, people and spirits are also intricately intertwined, and *To Kill a Mockingbird,* because it spoke to the power of children. She said if she ever got married it would have to be someone who looked like Heathcliff and acted liked Atticus Finch. When we were little she told us the reason she never got married was because there never was such a man. It was years later that I learnt the real reason why.

Aunty Bubby took my sister and me out walking and taught us how to love the land. She taught us about the flora and fauna. We knew the name of every single wildflower that quilted the hills where we lived, as well as the stories of the animals. Both my aunties loved animals, both native and introduced, and our home was always a menagerie of injured and unwanted animals. She loved other people's children and all through my childhood she was usually looking after white children as well as my sister and me, because she did it for free. There was one child in particular who used to spend weeks on end at our place while her parents worked to build up their business. The three of us used to keep my grandmother entertained for hours running around and playing boisterous games, pretending to be some of the white folk in town that the aunties talked about in the privacy of our home. The aunties used to call us 'the magpies' because we were 'always running round laughin' an' singin' an' makin' a lotta happy noise'.

My older Aunty Boo was feisty, practical and as a grown woman with no authorities to fear any more, very blunt. She was tiny and oozed energy. My earliest and most endearing memory of her was pushing a wheelbarrow around the paddocks. Nothing went to waste and no farm animal died in vain. Every time she came across a dead sheep she would take the wheelbarrow and a pair of hand-held shears and take off the fleece to sell and give the sheep a decent burial, which was a challenge, given how hard the country baked the earth. She walked the fence lines and picked off every tuft of wool snagged to the barbs. When she wasn't walking the paddocks, she gardened. I grew up in a ramshackle house built from bits and pieces, but the garden was magnificent. It still is, even though the old house is falling down around it.

Aunty Boo was a night owl. I asked her once why she stayed up for hours after everyone else. She said she liked to listen to the ghosts of the place that only came out when it was quiet. At school they told us there was no such thing as ghosts, except the Holy Ghost. But when I go back to the old place, I hear for ghosts too.

Aunty Boo was a great hoarder of all sorts of things that took her fancy. Her bedroom was an elephant's graveyard of old things discarded by the settlers she had worked for: feather boas, fox-fur stoles, pictures of crisp European winters with hounds and horses, a grandfather clock, washstands, pitchers, tea chests of Victorian underwear, crystal bowls full to the brim of costume jewellery, porcelain dolls, gollywogs, teddy-bears, bits and pieces of chipped floral china, brass candlesticks, and ornaments of all different shapes and sizes. Her favourite possession was a white elephant. It was a huge fine ceramic elephant, with garnet eyes and tusks of real ivory charging across a piece of deep green jungle, trunk held high as if trumpeting. My aunty always said that elephants with their trunks in the air meant good luck.

'Looks like a tough one, this one', she remarked more that once while fondling her treasure. 'That's how ya gotta be sometimes … chargin' forward … meet the trouble head on … like ya mean business.' She got the white elephant from an elderly woman she once cared for. It was a gift from the old lady on her deathbed. 'This white elephant ain't useless!' Aunty was adamant about this. 'His ol' head be full 'o things that only an elephant 'ud remember. I got a memory like an' elephant an' r'member an elephant never forgets!' Her favorite saying, which my sister and I grew up with, was: 'There's no such thing as can't! Ya can do anything if ya put ya mind to it! Can't is jus' for lazy, weak people an' that ain't you an' me babe!'

The balance between my two aunties has been one of the most influential experiences of my life. I know how to dream, be romantic and have a soft touch, but I also know how to charge head-on, trunk up, when I need to confront something, or face my fears. And I know that there's no such thing as can't.

At home the women who raised me always told stories about people and places. They were like magpies too, gathering bits and pieces of lives known, things seen and heard, gems of wisdom carefully and lovingly hoarded in the archive of memory, to be shared as precious stories—lessons for life. 'Home-talk', we used to call it, because it was the talk that made us feel at home and the talk that had to stay at home. Most of these stories were shared at night, around a fire in winter or at the kitchen table in summer. Some of these family stories were told openly to us as children and some were told after we were meant to be sleeping, but I was a precocious child and I would pretend to be asleep on my makeshift bed, which was really an armchair, and listen for as long as I could. They weren't traditional Dreaming stories that many people associate with Aboriginal storytelling, they were the stories of how my grandmother and my many aunties had lived as black women and remembered who they were despite national and local efforts to 'breed out the blackness'. Some of the stories were funny, some confused me, and some were very sad, but one thing that emerged through all of these stories is that the women were talking about a different Australia to the one we learnt and read about at school. The public Australia presented by my non-Aboriginal teachers and in my textbooks was a different place to the one the women talked about. The textbooks, teachers and my aunties were talking about many of the same events, such as the 'discovery of' and subsequent 'peaceful settlement' of Australia, the federation of the colonies to become one nation, the crossings of mountains and rivers by settlers who were 'unlocking the lands for industry and wealth', Australia as a 'workers' paradise' and a land of opportunity freedom and hope. But my aunties' experiences of and opinions on these and other historical events and narratives which formed the public discourse of the nation were very different from that of my white educators. As children we were always told to 'keep these stories at home', so people at school wouldn't laugh at us and so we wouldn't get into trouble for some of the cunning things the women did to get by. I picked up on a lot of common threads in these stories and I also heard whispered secrets—stories that were unfinished because the women sometimes stopped talking when they got to a certain point.

When they weren't telling their own stories, my aunts used to read to us from books they loved, usually by well-known writers such as Emily and Charlotte Bronte, Charles Dickens, George Eliot and J. R. R. Tolkien. One of our favourite stories was *The Wizard of Oz*, because the heroes, Dorothy, Toto and their friends, were the least likely people to be heroes. I noticed a lot of the stories they loved had unlikely heroes—usually someone who appears to be powerless or in a diminished position, like a servant, a child or a dog. At home I used to write stories too. Because very few other children from school were allowed to or wanted to play with us, my aunts used to give us scraps of paper from grocery deliveries and tell us to 'go and write a book or a story'. I used to lose myself in the activity of writing stories and harboured secret ambitions of becoming a writer. But I didn't tell anyone.

## The Western Classroom

In the 1960s and 1970s, Australia was a very unforgiving place for all those who were not white. My first novel, *Purple Threads,* is an episodic narrative that focuses on events, places and people (Leane 2011). I recalled an incident that happened to me as an Aboriginal child in school in the late 1960s which illustrates an all too common experience for Aboriginal people. It goes like this. One day in a small country school in Gundagai, where I was never accepted by my peers because my sister and I were the only Aboriginal children at the school at the time, a group of girls my age called my Aunties 'black witches'. I cried and thought it was all too hard. My aunties in their wisdom tried to console me. One of my aunts had worked as a maid in the homes of wealthy white Australians and had become the companion of an elderly Irish woman. One of her many tasks was to read to this elderly woman. This gave her a tremendous insight into the colonial mind and a great appreciation of their stories. She told me Epictetus's story of the purple threads in the white Roman togas, which were rare but special, 'that small part which is bright and makes everything else graceful and beautiful' (Leane 2011, p. 109).

But I couldn't appreciate it at the time and I went to bed thinking:

> I couldn't tell them I wanted to be white then. But if I was white I'd see myself everywhere. In the classroom, when I opened up a book or looked at a picture. In the crowded playground, laughing, skipping and jumping between elastics. Down the main street of town. Or on the movie screen. I'd not stand out from the rest. But purple? Black? Too hard. Too ugly. Too different. (Leane 2011, p. 109)

I'm ashamed to say that I wanted to be white then, because if I was white things would have been so much easier and if I was white I would have been considered normal. All I can say in my defence is that I was young and when I was young I wanted to be like everyone else. But I realised that this was never going to be and this is the story of how I came to accept who I was, who I am, and who I continue to be. I am and will always be indebted to those who helped me navigate this path.

Aboriginal presence has always made itself felt in the minds and imaginations of settlers. This has been evidenced through the representations of us in settler literature. Literature and stories are the window to national consciousness at any given time, for both Aboriginal and non-Aboriginal people. Aboriginal scholar Aileen Moreton-Robinson notes in relation to Aboriginal representation in settler discourse: 'Representations are more than just symbols. They are a means by which we come to know, embody and perform reality' (Moreton-Robinson 2000, p. xxii). Since the early-nineteenth century we have been constructed and reconstructed in the Anglo-western literary canon as the exotic, the primitive, the noble savage, the innocent, the child-race, the barbaric, the depraved fringe dweller, the violent demonic aggressor, the tragic half-caste, the 'Venus Jezebel', and the militant trouble-maker. Continuing almost entirely uninterrupted until the second half of the twentieth century, explorers, sailors, soldiers, clergymen, farmers and even some convicts wrote of us. While some of these authors sort to be sympathetic, all of their depictions were embedded in difference and caste us always in deficit to Euro-British immigrants.

I sat in western-style classrooms and heard all this. What Aboriginal people were meant to look like and how we were meant to act were firmly entrenched in settler psyche. My experiences of being Aboriginal were made deficit or invisible to my teachers and peers, as were the experiences of the women who raised me. In 1979, I was 17 years old, an age where questions of who I was and how others saw me were paramount in my mind. Sitting at my desk in a Senior Catholic High School in Wagga Wagga, however, there was suddenly no space to retreat. All eyes were on me. The class teacher had decided that we would read *Coonardoo*, Katharine Prichard's 1929 novel about relationships between Aboriginal women and white men on the north-western frontier where white settlement had more recently encroached on traditional Aboriginal lands (Pritchard 1990). I was the only Aboriginal student in the class. Thus my peers' gaze sought me out and scrutinised me, as they were encountering their first iconic literature dealing with Aboriginal Australians. The book's representation impacted on me, how I felt about myself and how others saw me and related to me. It was an alienating experience. My sense of myself, my knowledge of Aboriginal women, was savaged under the onslaught of the book's images.

The representation of Aboriginal women in the narrative stood in complete contrast to the way I saw myself and other Aboriginal women I knew. Although set 50 years earlier, I was raised by Aboriginal women who were the contemporaries of the woman Coonardoo, after whom the narrative was named. These women were strong, independent, outspoken and most of all ambitious for the next generation, my generation, to enjoy the same rights and privileges as white Australians and to be educated to the standard of our colonisers. Yet all this was undermined by the representations within Prichard's novel and the authority and status given to a body of white authors to represent Aboriginality. Coonardoo was promiscuous, helpless, totally lacking in intellect, dependent and defeatist. She was incapable of the abstract thoughts, reason and conceptualisations that the white characters displayed in the narrative.

Another thing that really perturbed me about my education was the western preoccupation with objectivity. I loved history and literature, even though it was always not kind to my people. I saw the gaps and spaces as sites that could be rich with alternative voices and experiences, if only I could find a way to open up these spaces and make different voices heard.

As a child and an adolescent I was fascinated by the story of Hannibal, told to me first by Aunty Boo who had read the story aloud many times to her elderly charge. Hannibal, whose homeland was Carthage, stormed the Roman Empire, wreaked havoc for 15 years and his siege and guerrilla warfare tactics have made it into every western-authored history text on the Roman Empire and every military manual ever since. He invented and mastered what is still referred to today in military circles as 'the art of turn'.

Years later, as a student of ancient history at senior high school our class studied the Roman Empire. My aunt's interest in this story was not so much Hannibal's military genius, although she did refer to it; her interest was in his courage and genius in using elephants as the forerunners of heavy artillery, and his sense of memory and justice to his father, Hamilcar, who died in an earlier conflict against Roman encroachment, to his country under threat from Rome, and his ancestors who died defending this cause. She said it was a black history because Hannibal, his ancestors before him, and his descendants after were black.

And so I wrote once in an essay: 'I wonder why every time I read about Hannibal, he is depicted as "the threat", "the problem" and the "thorn in the side of Rome".' My teacher didn't answer these questions. Instead they proceeded to admonish me for using the pronoun 'I', and for writing a history essay in the 'first person'. The teacher told me that I should be more objective and to 'leave myself out of the picture and just focus on the facts!' But I wondered, despite the fact that the historian I was reading never mentioned 'I' or 'me' (themselves) as part of their take on the Punic Wars, how objective were they really? I remembered that Aunty Bubby said: 'This history is a funny business. You can get into a lot of trouble for touting the wrong heroes.' And I did.

## Finding My Way

I managed to make it through high school and, at that time, I was the only one from a large extended family of many cousins who did so. I did so because I was encouraged and supported by my aunties, who said: 'One day you'll get to say something else.' But that day was a long way away then. I left school still wondering how I could 'fit into the grander scheme of the western order of things' (see Foucault 1970), and how we can shift the paradigm if we can't own the position from which we speak or write. Why is it that western historians and authors can just write without locating themselves within the bigger picture that they are writing about and without acknowledging the cultural platform from which they speak? Does this make their narratives objective? Maybe, truth is not universal. Maybe there are many truths that have their origins in where the one remembering stands and who and what they are remembering. How can I even begin to fill the gaps and give some voice to historical silences if I can't place myself and identify the position from which I speak?

So I left school perturbed and disturbed about western notions of objectivity, and the fact that Aboriginal people only make appearances in the meta-narratives, the 'big picture' of history and literature, when we were needed to make a point about how we were making our presence felt in settler consciousness at any given time. The novel I referred to earlier, *Coonardoo*, is a good example of this. Prichard constructs an Aboriginal woman in order to write a white man's tragedy. The greater concerns of the narrative are legitimacy and inheritance in the north-west of Australia (see Hodge & Mishra 1990, p. 54). *Coonardoo* is the story of a white man who loses his wealth, his property, and his mind because of his love for an Aboriginal woman who dies in tragic circumstances before her time.

Despite some not so happy memories of my school days, when I left school in the late-1970s the socio-political climate had changed due to the election of the Whitlam Labor Government. In the lead up to the election, the Australian Labor Party's election slogan was: 'It's time for a change!' And it was. Gough Whitlam and his cabinet were elected in November 1972. Within a short time, Whitlam implemented radical changes: the Anti-Discrimination Act, the abolition of tertiary education tuition fees, and the introduction of the Tertiary Education Assistance Scheme, a means-tested allowance that would allow children from lower socio-economic backgrounds to attend universities en masse for the first time in Australia's history. Without the election of this government and the monumental changes it managed to implement before it was sacked by Governor General Sir John Kerr on November 11, 1975, I would never have gone to university and I would not be where I am today.

At my first lecture in English Literature at the University of New England, Armidale, in 1981, the Professor of the Department stood up and delivered his welcoming speech in his best Oxbridge accent. It wasn't too welcoming for some of us: 'For those of you who are the first generation in your family to attend university, you will struggle and be challenged, because it takes more than a generation to appreciate the language, the nuance of this fine body of literature.'

It reminded me of a poem I'd studied in High School by T. S. Eliot. Like J. Alfred Prufrock, I felt ill at ease and wondered how I presumed to come. But I did come and one of my Aunties said to me before I left: 'Good on ya babe. You'll be able to talk to the gov'ment and lotsa 'portant people. But doncha forget ya home talk when ya learnin' to be flash.'

So I came, however presumptuous, and I stayed.

30 years later I am still challenged by the English and Australian literary canons. But I do appreciate them, and I have engaged with them passionately on a number of fronts. I stopped writing poetry and short stories while I was attending university; I was so intimidated by the critiques many of my lecturers made of the writings of others and of what constituted 'good literature' in the first place. But I kept a journal where I jotted down ideas and memories. It also struck me how those among my lecturers who considered themselves as 'scholars of English literature' were very scathing of Australian literature. Despite being told it was second rate, I chose to study Australian literature and it was there that I encountered many more representations of Aboriginal people that reflected the mindset of settler society at any given time and our

containment within settler literature and thus settler imagination. In particular, I encountered Patrick White, whose 1961 representation of Aboriginality was a tragic and marginalised one. His 1976 representation of noble savages practicing ritual cannibalism never left me and drove me years later to write a PhD on this and other representations.

Through the 1980s and 1990s I taught high school in Canberra and introduced my students to my favourite literature. Classrooms are important sites for change. It was amidst the contestation for the telling of Australia's past, termed 'the history wars' during the Howard Government (1996–2007) that I entered the tertiary sector as a lecturer working with students who were studying to become teachers in 2000 at the University of Canberra. While I found most students were eager to understand and help Aboriginal people, it was mainly on their own terms, and these same students were reticent to teach against the narrative of Australian settler history that they were familiar with. Many grappled with the idea that I wasn't asking them to teach against, I was asking them to teach Aboriginal perspectives alongside the dominant settler histories. It was tough going, but once again this was an important site for change.

In 2002 I was encouraged to present a paper at an Indigenous Researchers' Forum at the University of Western Australia, Perth, and I wrote and presented a paper that was on something dear to my heart, 'Representations of Aboriginal Presence in the Australian Literary Canon'. An Indigenous scholar, Professor Martin Nakata, heard this paper and he suggested that I write a proposal to be admitted as doctoral candidate. I remember saying, 'I can't do it because I can't write about this according to western expectations of objectivity. I can't leave myself out of this discussion.' As soon as I said this, I felt my aunties' words coming back to me: 'There's no such thing as can't.'

I thought I couldn't be like my aunt's elephant then, charging head on to confront my foes and fears. The professor's response was that I didn't have to, and, in fact, that to identify my position and perspective within the research would make it a stronger thesis. This was a revelation and I thought seriously about writing a proposal. Then, in 2003, as I was developing this proposal, my eldest aunt passed away. I was devastated as I thought of all the memories and stories I had stored; these needed to be told because they are the important threads missing from the tapestry of recorded Australian history, like the purple threads in my aunt's story. They were the secrets that needed to be told.

I was accepted as a candidate for a doctorate at the end of 2004, at the University of Technology, Sydney, but I found I was paralysed and couldn't move forward with the research because the stories I grew up with were playing on my heart and mind. How could I write anything else until I found a way to tell these important stories? How could I write of the misrepresentations of Aboriginal people in the nation's literature until I could testify to the agency, resilience and determination of my people, without whom I would not even be in a position to attempt this doctorate? By early 2005, when I had left my job, was on a scholarship to study full-time, and had still done nothing, my supervisor began to wrap me over the knuckles. I woke up one day, midway through 2005 and knew I had to just start writing the stories I was raised with, no matter how rough and how emotional I had to make a start. Now she was gone, I had to be like my Aunty Boo's elephant.

So I abandoned my academic research and started writing. When I sat down to write, I thought about other good stories I knew, particularly those with the unlikely heroes, such as Bilbo Baggins who single-handedly outwitted a dragon, but the real battle was fought in the tunnel, alone, before he even faced the dragon. And I thought of Toto, my Aunty Boo's favourite character, who worked out that the wizard was a hoax with the help of the cowardly lion, the brainless scarecrow and the heartless tin man, who were really brave, intelligent and compassionate, but had been told otherwise. All these characters felt powerless but they conquered what they feared most, even though they felt small and helpless at the time.

I thought about the most respectful way to tell some of the stories. I chose to use the literary devices of poetry and short story because I could focus on certain episodes that were significant and that were situated at the intersection of public history and personal memory, as this divergence was (and is) a fertile site for telling the stories and experiences that had been selectively left out of settler discourse. I thought that literature, works commonly described as fiction, was the best way of presenting a truth, because it gives a face and a voice to such truths. Also, it allows the use of pseudonyms, so that people's experiences of events and times can be spoken of respectfully. I also considered that much of the non-fiction I had read in history was not the truth either. An Aboriginal writer whom I greatly admire, Alexis Wright, said in relation to her decision to use fiction to tell the stories of her people: 'I felt literature, the work of fiction, was the best way of presenting a truth—not the real truth, but more of a truth than non-fiction which is not really true either. Non-fiction is often about the writer telling what is safe to tell' (Wright 2002, p. 13).

Another one of my favourite writers, Gunter Grass, said when he won the Nobel Prize for Literature in 1999, 'a writer is someone who writes against the currents of time'. The stories I grew up with were very much like this.

I thought about the stories I'd heard in terms of threads and secrets. I had to think very hard about some of the haunting memories that were whispered late at night, and some of the things that were never fully explained to me as a child because they were too hard to talk about. I wrote the poetry first because, as I remembered, I became angry with some of the things I'd heard and the mysteries I'd pieced together as an adult. The main strengths of poetry for me are its brevity and evocative imagery, and I wanted to be really blunt and explicit about the things that had happened, that the family had carried as shameful secrets when the shame was really that of white Australia.

The name *Dark Secrets After Dreaming: A.D. 1887–1961* came to me very quickly once I started writing, as this slim volume of poetry deals with some of the very early experiences of the Wiradjuri as settlers encroached on traditional lands. It is also a play on western time. As an adult, through my friendships with other Aboriginal women of my generation I knew that many of the secrets of the women I grew up with had not just happened to them but to many Aboriginal women. Inferences to physical, emotional and sexual abuse, exploitation and lost children were all too common a theme. So I chose to make the voice within the poetry that of the 'Black Woman' who speaks of the 'White Woman' as the epitome of colonial presence. For example:

> The White Women sigh and seethe.
> We are a burden with our dark faces
> unreadable eyes and lithe limbs.
> ('White Woman's Burden', Leane 2010 p. 18)

> White women surround themselves with fruits
> and flowers from their own land.
> They call it a garden!
> ('Agony in the Garden', Leane 2010, p. 26)

I wanted to be a medium for speaking out against the country's past. I was deliberately generalising because as a people we have been generalised about, and I wanted settlers to read about themselves in this way because for too long our stories have been talked over. I use the pronouns 'they' and 'them' to position whiteness as otherness. I wanted to offer a fresh insight into the brutality of domestic slavery in colonial Australia, and for people to consider the intergenerational effects of abuses perpetuated there. But I also wanted to show the resilience, intuition and determination of those I wrote about.

Although the poetry in *Dark Secrets* is based on events that happened before I was born, and ends with a reference to my birth, I deliberately used the first person singular 'I' to link the present to the past. Even though the incidents referred to were very much unfinished business. When people have survived abuse, the aftermath can and will continue to resurface. One reviewer wrote: 'Non-Indigenous Australian readers must forgive Leane for lumping us all together' (Whittle 2010, p. 20). But I don't want forgiveness; I want non-Aboriginal readers to consider what it is like to be placed on the 'other side' of the cultural divide and how it feels to be described in such unflattering, general and brutal terms.

By the time I came to write *Purple Threads,* 12 months later, I felt that I had dealt with some of the intergenerational trauma that I was experiencing; not that it will ever go away, but to find a medium to express it that was respectful to those involved was cathartic. When I thought about writing *Purple Threads,* once again I thought about important incidents, but these things related more to memories and stories about the land and what connected people to land. My grandmother and all of my aunties were born post contact; my grandmother in the first 100 years of occupation, in 1887, and my aunties from 1907 onwards. Yet while none of the women lived a 'traditional' (if you take the conventional white definition of those who speak an Aboriginal language and live in a community) Aboriginal lifestyle, they had an innate capacity to 'read' the land and the seasons like a book or a map. The women I grew up with were always amazed that the settler farmers, in particular, couldn't read the land and were always surprised, stressed and dismayed by the weather and that they tried so hard to live against the land. The farmers were illiterate according to the Aboriginal order of things. The Wiradjuri landscape where I grew up is as much a character as any of the people, because it is living and resilient like the women in the stories. Flowers too, both native and domestic, are a strong motif, because they are as reliable and vibrant as the women who raised me. Flowers and stories can live forever. As my aunties always said: 'Country turns and turns again, resilient.'

I chose to narrate the stories through the eyes of a child. I did this because that was the way I heard many stories and I didn't fully understand some things at the time so I didn't try to interpret them from an adult perspective. I've re-told memories and allowed my adult readers to think about what I didn't say or think at the time. An undercurrent that an adult can read through the language of a child pervades many of the stories. The river is a continual motif of what appears on the surface, not always reflecting or fathoming the depths below. There is also the undercurrent of secrets that will never be told and things unresolved. Another reason I chose the voice of a child was because, like some of my favourite characters mentioned earlier, children are both powerless and powerful. At the time I could do nothing but listen, watch and remember. But as an adult I realised that to remember and to tell is powerful.

So I wrote a collection of inter-related poetry and an episodic novel as a testimony to the power of memory, the impact this can have on public history, which is never a closed book, and the importance of 'Home-talk' in connecting the secrets and threads for the telling of the nation's past. They are not autobiography or biography, they are collective memoir—history as stories, stories as history. Only then could I get on with my PhD.

# References

Baum, L F 1900, *The Wizard of Oz*, George M Hill Company, Chicago.

Foucault, M 1970, *The Order of Things: An Archaeology of Human,* Tavistock, London.

Hodge, B & V Mishra 1990, *Dark Side of the Dream: Australian literature and the poet-colonial mind,* Allen & Unwin, Sydney.

Leane, J 2011, *Purple Threads,* University of Queensland Press, St Lucia.

Leane, J 2010, *Dark Secrets After Dreaming: (AD) 1887–1961,* PressPress, Berry.

Moreton-Robinson, A 2000, *Talkin' Up to the White Woman: Aboriginal women and feminism*, University of Queensland Press, St Lucia.

Prichard, K 1990, *Coonardo*, Angus and Robertson, Sydney.

Scott, K 1999, *Benang from the Heart,* Fremantle Arts Press, Fremantle.

Whittle, M 2010, 'Review: *Dark Secrets after Dreaming: (AD) 1887–1961*' ,*Poetry Matters,* vol. 11, pp. 20–21.

Wright, A 2002, 'Politics of Writing', *Southerly,* vol. 62, no.2, pp. 10–21.

# 16. True Ethnography

Gillian Cowlishaw

## Anthopologist Needed

It is autumn 1999 and the vigorous crashing of the metal knocker on the front door of my house in Glebe has me in a state of alarm as I leave the quiet study and run downstairs. I open the door to a dark, dishevelled figure, wild hair, lean and edgy. A gravelly, menacing voice says, 'I've come to make a land claim on this property'. The grim expression dissolves as I exclaim, 'Frank Doolan!' He shakes my hand with a flamboyant black man's double gesture, still tense, ready to cut and run, ready for a fight—or fun. 'How are you?' I ask, and he says, 'I'm still goin'. But more important, [dramatic pause] how are *you*?'

He stays all afternoon. Frank was a friend from earlier research in Bourke and university in Bathurst, but I had not seen him for some years.[1] He explains that Mt Druitt in western Sydney is now his home. 'This is my tribe now', he says. 'True warriors they are too. Despite what you think.'

I leave it, knowing what he means (Cowlishaw 1988).

Frank has much to tell. He is in town to deliver a document to the District Court to support a young fellow's appeal against his 18-year sentence for murder—he killed a man when out 'cruisin' for a bruisin''. Frank explains, with care and precision, the reason for his plea to the court—his belief that this boy does not deserve the long prison sentence. With passionate feeling breaking through in his language, Frank places the boy's plight within the specific violence and pain that the family experienced. These are Aboriginal experiences. It is Indigenous conditions that made this lad vulnerable to becoming a victim of his own anger, violence and confusion. Punishment on top of punishment, a wasted life that could be reclaimed. Frank has a handwritten statement that he has presented to the court, but does not offer it to be read. Does he not trust me? I am conscious that my comfortable terrace house in Glebe could appear a place of wealth and self-indulgence, well protected from the rigours of life as Frank knows them. Yet there is no accusation or comparison in Frank's importuning, no disguised moralising about whitefellas' practices. He knows I am interested in what he tells me and that I could make something of it.

---

1 In 1980, I began long term ethnographic research in Bourke, a country town notorious for tempestuous race relations. I conducted further research there in the 1990s (Cowlishaw 1999, 2004).

His stories are elaborate, attempts to reveal complex and profound social meanings. They also reveal Frank's creative vision—each event is vested with emotional immediacy. He dangles anecdotes as hooks that link elements of his world to contrasting public and political perceptions.

Frank's talk is challenging and beguiling because his intentions are never obvious. He seems more purposeful and in control than he's been at some times in the past. He shows a mordant wit, is often charming and usually dramatic. Again and again, between his poetry and parables, and large mugs of black tea, he urges me to come and work in Mt Druitt. He says he does not want to eat, but when I make myself a sandwich for lunch, I make one for him too, and eventually he eats half of it. Food seems a distraction, a necessary fuel for the body only. Smoking rollies, cradling his tea, he sits outside on the back step, but is never still for long. He paces, building a narrative, anxious to complete a particular point, to show the significance of an event, or a life, or a report in the paper. I have little control over the conversation, but there is no passive listening. If I lose track, I am likely to be ambushed with a question. But like all true storytellers, Frank will also readily retell the tale; these are not material artefacts to be fashioned once and then fixed in time, like written words.

## The Great White Hope

20 years earlier in Bathurst, I was teaching one of the early courses, called 'Aboriginal Studies'.[2] After politely asking my permission, Frank Doolan, who I had recently met in Bourke and who was enrolled in other courses, sat in on a tutorial to support his mate who was making a presentation. I engaged in some critical discussion with the students and later, in the winter dusk, I heard Frank shouting contemptuously outside my office: 'You think you're the great white hope, but you're just another white woman who does not understand.' Frank's perception of a slight to his mate was, needless to say, unintended. I don't know if Frank's mate felt slighted, but I was made sharply aware of sensitivities that I had given little thought to. When I got over the hurt and anxiety caused by this one-man demonstration, I saw that other Koori[3] students also displayed sore spots that needed to be taken into account. What was liberating, anti-racist, controversial, funny or subversive exposé for Anglo students was not necessarily seen in the same way by Aboriginal students. Rural and urban students also responded very differently to topics and issues in Aboriginal studies. Further, Frank's anger abated and the incident furthered our budding friendship.

---

2   An explosion of academic interest in Aborigines had evoked demands for generalist courses, often concentrated on historical sources rather than studies of classical Aboriginal traditions by anthropologists.
3   Local designation for Aboriginal.

Frank was right to be wary of the well-meaning whitefellas, armoured with their goodwill (Berlant 2004). I could not be seriously affronted at being put in this category, as the Great White Hope is a familiar figure, and one with whom I have quite a lot in common. There are many who have offered advice, assistance and solutions to the difficulties Aboriginal people regularly experience. Many Aboriginal people are also now on this treadmill, co-opted into proffering insider expertise to solve what is often seen as the nation's problems with Indigenous people, or at least the statistical evidence of these problems.

While Aborigines everywhere are familiar with whitefellas, the reverse is not the case. Despite their assertive symbolic presence and the familiar claim that Aborigines are the most researched people in the world, the lives of Aboriginal Australians are largely concealed from the urban majority. They are 'known' through shocking images, worrying statistics and concerned discourses that flood the press. As well, Indigenous art is renowned. Public consciousness remains stubbornly oblivious to anthropologists' accounts of intricate kinship systems, philosophical sophistication, intriguing social structure and the rich Indigenous language environment.

## Anthropology

'You're an anthropologist? How *interesting*.'

And later, 'Did they accept you?'

This frisson of excitement evokes what is now absurd nineteenth-century imagery about what is us and what is other, but also hints at a deeper interest and desire. It is hard to think of an appropriate answer to the old images of hostile natives. I want to say, 'There is no "they" there'. Perhaps it is the guilty knowledge of dispossession that leads so many to imagine Aborigines as unwelcoming. Or maybe it is simply the difficulty of understanding why people would accept a curious stranger into their lives, especially one who was actually studying the abject hosts as depicted in the satirical film *Babakiueria* (BBQ area). When working in remote Arnhem Land I could quip, 'They loved my 4WD', hoping the irony was understood. Or explain, 'Lorna and Nellie are my sister and cousin, blackfella way'. Or tell a long tale of how they have come to know us.

So what was that question again?

But later I had to answer the question, 'Where do you work?', with 'Bourke', and more puzzled, anxious responses emerged, often a sympathetic, 'How bad is it now?'—people know about the racism that defines the country town of Bourke.

Nowadays, when I confess that I am working with Aborigines in the outer Sydney suburb of Mt Druitt, a certain sceptical discomfort relieves me of further explanation. It is assumed that I am on some kind of mission to do good, to expose injustice, to offer a sympathetic account of pathetic lives in Sydney's own suburban western desert. All these responses are ordinary outcomes of public 'knowledge' of anthropology, of Aborigines and of Australia. I am both contributing to, and contesting, that knowledge and the anxieties and ideologies that suffuse it.

When the 'invasion of Aborigines' country' began to take a central role in the interpretation of Australian history, anthropologists' interest in traditional Aboriginal culture came under scrutiny. Had that interest adequately represented contemporary Aborigines? The verdict, to which I made a small contribution, was a resounding no. Had it added to Aborigines' burdens? Yes. Historians, glowing with virtue at having belatedly included Aborigines in Australia's history, were seldom concerned with cultural questions. Cultural studies scholars severed their work on Indigenous issues from the contaminated ethnographic studies; Aborigines' traditions were their own and western scholars should not be undermining their authority (Mudrooroo 1997; McDermott 2002). One implication was that others' traditions were not relevant to interpreting the past or the present of Australian society. As an impassioned rewriting of the contours of Australian history emerged, the scribes of the day were interested in old wounds and brave new worlds cleansed of a superseded racism. Warnings against whitefellas messing in Indigenous matters became part of public discourse in the 1980s and anthropology is the discipline seen as most marred by this transgression.

## Ethnography

I was a student during the 1970s groundswell when the epistemological underpinning of anthropology—to understand and legitimise traditional cultures—was abruptly inverted into just another form of hegemony. Anthropologists studied these people (what arrogance); anthropologists took knowledge from them without recompense (how exploitative); anthropologists wrote books about them to advance their own careers (so dominating). In popular and much academic discourse, the desire to understand was judged to be a misunderstanding, an enterprise fundamentally flawed by its underlying condition: colonial dispossession.

Yet few appreciate or grapple with the messy core of ethnographic practice—immersion in, and intimacy with another social world, in my case a remote Arnhem Land community in the 1970s and since, Bourke in the 1980s, and Mt Druitt from 2000. Ethnographic writing does not seek a quantifiable truth. Its empirical evidence is a melange of recorded speech and action, opinion and emotion and evidence of material and imagined realities. Emotional judgments and moral reactions are always present as the observer participates and the participant observes and the informant and researcher share their interests. Let me be clear. Disciplined and careful observation is central to this, as to any research. Part of what I tried to reveal in *The City's Outback* is the unique strengths—as well as the limitations—of informal, idiosyncratic and subjectivist ethnographic practices, such as my relationship with Frank Doolan. I deliberately depict early stages of the process of loitering with intent in other people's lives. This practice has something in common with other kinds of social encounter, although the intent and the consequences differ in important ways.

Ethnographic research consists of practices that many forms of enquiry pride themselves on avoiding: immersion and intimacy with a particular social domain over a long period of time. Personal relationships are at the core, with all the risks and responsibilities they entail. The ethnographer willingly experiences a destabilisation of her familiar everyday world and some loss of self. As the social sciences have increasingly affirmed, subjectivity, affect and complexity can be the objects of methodical analysis. This approach rejects the fantasy of 'finding order in events by putting events in order' and accepts 'the inseparability of knowledge from its knower' (Comaroff & Comaroff 1992).

In the course of her analysis of white hegemony in Australia, Aileen Moreton-Robinson makes the pointed claim that 'Indigenous people have been among the nation's most conscientious students of whiteness and racialisation. Participant observation was our method' (Moreton-Robinson 2004). I endorse her assertion that Indigenous people have a specific way of knowing whiteness because it supports a view of knowledge as positioned while allowing that legitimate knowledge is not confined to the identity position of the knower. We can know something of others' worlds initially and primarily through everyday personal interaction, discovering otherness at the subjective interface of the social world. This is the epistemological foundation of anthropology's basic method.

Anthropology always nurtured much greater ambitions than simply recording the culture of others. At the core of the discipline was a desire to overcome the barriers that cultural difference erects to human understanding. When we examine the term 'radical alterity', we find it refers not to different human beings, but to radically different ways that equivalent human beings live in the world. Ethnographers provide evidence of amazing variation in the social worlds human beings have created, encompassing dramatic differences in everyday habits, material creations, authority structures, and systems of knowledge and belief. The discipline was thus founded on a powerful humanism which asserted that cultural, class, racial and other systemic differences are not insuperable barriers to shared knowledge or to sharing the social world. Aware of their interest, to me at least, the Mt Druitt informants opened themselves to be seen in ways they retained control of, at least until I picked up my pen. While bookish pursuits mark a realm of power that my informants have little knowledge of, this does not preclude their pleasure in being represented in that world. Few of them are likely to read this work, yet the consciousness of one or another of them looking over my shoulder as I write has spurred me on with nervousness and excitement.[4]

Now that categories of primitive and civilised, prehistoric and modern have partially dissolved, fieldworkers come from anywhere and study everything. Those who were once others now study us. The boardroom and the clinic, minority groups and cults, remote places, the suburban street and the internet are all objects of ethnographic attention. What remains central to these renewed, robust and inquisitive forms of anthropology is ethnography, that is, the researcher's insistence on experiencing particular social conditions and specific social relationships. The ethnographer goes among people and relates to them as far as possible on their own terms. S/he tries to live as they do in order to use this personal experience as the foundation for describing, analysing and explaining social phenomena. This is a close-up experience of people who are likely to change your mind.

# Frank

Frank Doolan changed my mind. I see Frank as embodying a crucial dynamic in Australian public life. He represents one among a range of subjective orientations concerning Indigenous identities, as these struggle to be expressed and implanted. He wants the Indigenous world to remain one where social relations are valued more than individual achievement. I perceive in Frank a blackfella struggling to reject, eject and disempower the white man within himself, refusing recognition and respect to its alien inhabitation. Frank's vision of what it is to be Aboriginal is fired by the sense that Aboriginal people are being drowned, submerged, swallowed by a largely indifferent world. He resists the aspirations people read into him—to be a leader, a political strategist, a social worker.

The internalised shadow of the white man means that Frank knows how the white world works; he has had various romances with elements of that world and has sought ways to deal honourably with its people and its institutions. He has had some stunning successes, but he has also been repeatedly disappointed

---

[4] Mudrooroo and, quite differently, McDermott have explored the difficulties Aboriginal writers face in having to write for the world of the invader (Mudrooroo 1990; McDermott 2002).

and despairing. It is not the whiteness in white men that troubles him; they are what they are. It is the black man that interests Frank, and his considerable passion, intellect and poetry are focused on being and becoming one and, perhaps, inspiring others to do so.

The significance I take from Frank's endeavours, and the stories he helped me obtain, is not just about the damage done to Aboriginal people in the past; it is also about how selves are formed, reformed, sometimes deformed, in conditions of social upheaval. There is a sharp contradiction between the way the nation is so ready to plead guilty to specific crimes in the past and its inability to cope with their effects. In *The City's Outback* I document some of these effects in a fragmented community, in broken kin networks, in individualised lives.

## The Untidy Backyard

Frank's visit to Glebe led me to toy with and then develop the idea of a research project in western Sydney after my Bourke book was completed (Cowlishaw 2004). I was in profound agreement with Frank that these lives are as meaningful as any others, and that there is tremendous and unrecognised significance in the definitively Aboriginal drama they are living out. Not that Frank would put it quite like that. I wanted to explore Frank's vision further. For one thing, was he fair dinkum? His sense of mission and his talk of warriors and struggles often seemed like romantic hyperbole rather than any realistic sense of what people want or need. His criticisms of the Mr Bigs in Aboriginal affairs seemed unfair: 'If he came out to Mt Druitt we'd find him a black girl. He doesn't need that white one', said in a tone leavened with humour and with ironic self-awareness of his own past liaisons. But it was his pained and explicit search for meaning in everyday events that I found utterly compelling, and which led to the research project of 2000.

There is an often cited statistic that the largest concentration of Aboriginal people in Australia lives in western Sydney, yet the people who live there are largely unknown. Is this 'bogan' area, among 'westies' and the cultural deserts of western Sydney, the place where the culturally deprived of the Aboriginal population belong, out of sight among the least fashionable people of the city? What do such unspoken evaluations hide? And do these Aboriginal people form a defined community, despite being scattered among the suburban streets populated by other public housing tenants and people of many ethnic backgrounds? Of what significance is being Aboriginal, or for that matter, not being Aboriginal? Such questions underlay the research I undertook in 2000.

A year after the western Sydney research began, and after months of visiting, recording and photographing, driven by my 'informant' Frank Doolan (although I drove the car), I became strung out and depressed, intellectually and emotionally. The research terminology about 'the intricate dynamics of everyday life in Mt Druitt' began to seem incongruous and the research had ceased to make sense. Frank was involving me in tragic personal dramas he believed to have immense significance: Annette, for instance, whose life-long distress seemed to be abating, recorded an account of her life of pain and stubborn hatred, of family destruction and minimal comfort, trying, she said, to love, and asking for my help. I hurried to transcribe the story she told me, but when I took the pages back, shaped into a coherent sequence, I found the house deserted, with bits of broken furniture strewn in the front yard. I tried but failed to locate her.[5] What was I to do with that?

What was *research* to achieve? Was this what Aboriginal lives were about?

It took some years and a series of false starts to see coherence and value in that research project. In the end I told the story of the research, its failures and its successes, with other purposes in mind, particularly to infiltrate and disturb the public discourses that assume we know how to know these lives. In *The City's Outback*, I explored the practice of ethnographic fieldwork in western Sydney in tandem with certain aspects of Indigeneity, relying on depiction and minimising sociological explanation.

## The Research Story

The ethnography of *The City's Outback* was shaped by Frank and by the people he took me to visit and to record. At the end, I felt obliged and driven, haunted by the sense that these stories meant more than appeared on the surface and that my experience of them also had significance beyond the mere fact of recording them. 'Stories' seemed such an inadequate term for the fragments of memory, the brief recorded disclosures of these extraordinary lives.

It will be clear to academic readers that I have a very bad case of the 'diary disease' (Bourdieu 2003; Geertz 1988). This self-induced condition exists because a reflexive, diary-like form can break down a common distinction between the research practice and the findings or data. The relationship between Indigenous and non-Indigenous worlds, their overlapping and interweaving, their co-constructedness, their self-knowledge, and their everyday reality, has been my focus independent of the research site (see, for example, Cowlishaw 1999).

Long threads of disciplinary frameworks, institutional histories, ideological and theoretical paradigms, connect any research project to its past. One beginning is

---

5   Annette's story appears in chapter three of *The City's Outback*.

the grant application where we present our intellectually cogent and confident intentions as sincere, objective—and modest. Outlining my intended research in 1999, I became convinced of the significance, indeed the magnificence of the investigation I was proposing. With contacts from the Bourke research, and infected by Frank's fervour, I felt I could achieve a good deal in Mt Druitt. Only when the work began was the construction revealed as artificial and brittle in the face of the world's complexity and recalcitrance. My plans were too elaborate and ambitious for the 12-month project I called 'Urbanising Aboriginality: The dynamics of racial identities in urban and suburban Sydney'. I intended to conduct

> extensive ethnographic research in Mt Druitt, western Sydney. This project will document what it means to be an Aboriginal person in urban conditions and what external obstructions or internal resistance exists to the full realisation of indigenous citizenship … At the heart of this research is the notion of organic intellectuals, that is, those who articulate conceptions of the past, present and future of Aboriginality as it emerges within the community.[6]

These words are appropriate for the seminar room, but their presumptuousness was out of harmony with this fieldwork. 'Urban Aboriginality' and 'what it means to be an Aboriginal person' refer to labile, dynamic entities, matters of contestation and assertion, rather than self-defined things waiting to be observed and described. While Frank fitted the idea of an 'organic intellectual', what he 'articulated' would require considerable translation to fit the rest of the description.

The application also assumes a congruence between the value of the research to the researched and to the funding bodies. I promised to 'shed light on a recognised national problem', assuming the desire and the ability to solve or ameliorate these problem lives. The nation's 'recognition' is cunning, and does not deliver what it promises for reasons that are both complex and intractable (Lea 2002, 2008; Povinelli 2002). Nor is the nation a unified entity with unitary intentions, separate and independent of the university, the Australian Research Council, the citizenry and all who might identify as 'us'. Can the mythic 'we' actually offer Aborigines, 'them', equality, self-determination, 'our' respect? Or even much in the way of understanding? Frank clearly thinks we could do much better with a little help from our Indigenous friends.

---

6   Some elements of this project were incorporated into a successful application for an Australian Professorial Fellowship to continue the Mt Druitt research. The new project began in 2006, leading to the writing of *The City's Outback*.

## Racialised Knowledge

More directly, the application assumes that the 'characteristic self-images, discourses, cultural forms' of Indigenous people are available in recognisable form. In Arnhem Land, it was soon clear that the 'experienced realities' of Indigenous people had to be translated to become meaningful to a wider audience. But the lives and language of western suburbs Aboriginal people are not recognised as in need of translation because they are using familiar tools such as English. Thus, rather than render them familiar, I wanted to show their mystery and strangeness.

While there is a clear contrast between Frank's poetry, stories and essays and the kind of writing I do, we both pursue something I think of as truth. These truths illuminate social dynamics by counteracting accepted understandings of the social world, understandings that reify and normalise the forms of power and authority that appear to bind it together. Frank's work remains closely linked to those it is about and for, whereas mine is produced within an academic and establishment framework that it is Frank's deliberate political practice to avoid. Frank writes by hand on paper and has no desire to revise his words. The 'word processing' has gone on in his head beforehand. Interestingly, though, there were moments in our informal interaction where each of us hinted at a suppressed desire to embrace the other's audience.

Ethnography is well placed to illuminate the cultural politics that enables some people to be heard and condemns others to 'talking under water'. It does this by bearing witness to the significance of lives so often assumed to have none, other than as objects of the aesthetic or sentimental interest of those closer to the powerful forces that shape all our worlds. While none of us can avoid what Moreton-Robinson called 'racialised ways of knowing' (Moreton-Robinson 2004, p. 2), I aim to bring elements of these racialised ways into focus and wonder whether our desire to condemn and expunge them may not create further silence and mystification. The boundaries between these specific ways of knowing are part of asymmetries that were established in an earlier era, but are not fixed and/or stable. Recognising them has the potential to dissolve barriers to relationships of exchange and debate. The work done by me and Frank is located where social, ethnic and racial identities are intertwined.

Besides the importuning of Frank Doolan, I have reasons for invading the Indigenous realm that go far beyond that realm itself. I do not seek the details of Aboriginal culture or Indigenous lives for their own sake; what I seek is an understanding of how social differentiation works. How is a racial dichotomy reproduced when the concept of race is rejected? How does a social identity work in itself and for itself? How does Australian history get settled?

How is what I think of as the white neurosis about Aborigines expressed in this suburban environment?[7] These questions are as germane to non-Indigenous people as they are to self-defined Indigenous people, and to the extensive interaction between them.

Given the general acceptance that colonial history was destructive of Aboriginal society, how is it that destructive effects are only recognised in general and impersonal terms? Should there be attention to the identification, diagnosis or treatment of wounded Aboriginal people, as Judy Atkinson recommends (Atkinson 2002)? Is it patronising or arrogant for others to identify particular historical damage, and will such exposure feed negative racist stereotypes? Is the sympathetic public now sated with stories of Aboriginal suffering? Professionals who are closely embroiled in the cultural dynamics of health and other service delivery have internalised these anxieties. But since the Commonwealth Emergency Intervention of June 2007, such perceptions have been superseded by a rhetoric that demands urgent responses to what is now stamped with the label of social pathology following publication of a plethora of horrendous images and stories (Altman & Hinkson 2010).

## Auditing Ethnography

The ethnographer becomes dependent on the people whose lives she is discovering—in this case Frank and those he is sure will cooperate in my desire to know them. They are given the technical term 'informants' in ethnographic research because they allow the researcher some way into their social lives and become co-researchers, to a degree determined by their interest and engagement. Ideally these are people with something of a sociological imagination, a sense of the contingencies of their own social worlds. Far from being informers, disloyal to their own realm, they are, like the ethnographer, interested to represent, semiotically, their own social world.

The rewards for those who participate, interact and engage with the ethnographer and the research are multiple and complex. For some there is the fun of it, or the serious pleasure of recording their own opinions or stories. Many, in my experience, enjoy a chance to talk, explain and perform before an outsider who is eager to listen. A rare few might find absorbing interest in the work as work, and become inspired to think differently and to engage with transcripts and with further analysis. My rewards are obvious: I get to know people whose lives are different from my own and sometimes form longstanding relationships that continue to enrich my life, and, I venture to say, those of these friends.

---

[7] I use the term 'neurosis' to refer to the intense attention, emotional weight and confusion that surrounds Aboriginal issues in public and in private debate.

My ethnographic fieldwork in Mt Druitt proceeded in a fluid and unstructured way, shaped by forceful individuals and willing participants as well as those more reluctant or hostile and those who went missing. I found no 'objects of study', but human beings pursuing social objectives through complex attachments. Rather than me being the active fieldworker in a passive field, my 'informant' Frank has been an active agent in the research process. This was a negotiated encounter, in which all parties were engaged in different ways. The caricature of the fieldworker as colonial master may reflect one element of structural relations but has little relevance down among the interpersonal relationships that constitute fieldwork.

Thus, university ethics committees, particularly the superintendents of Aboriginal research protocols, are seriously misguided when they try to judge the moral trustworthiness of the fieldworker without taking the views of the subjects of research into consideration. The ethnographic research itself is threatened by attempts to legislate some formula to control researchers' practices. Ethical judgments are part of a constant process of reflection about living relationships with people who are themselves engaged in other ethical domains. The normative regimes that ethics committees seek to impose try to take responsibility away from the researched as well as the researcher and foreclose on the dilemmas that confront both in their encounters. Were they successful, the whole endeavour would cease to be a dynamic relationship, with moral, emotional and political contradictions, and would instead become a formal playing out of a set of pre-ordained rules, producing nothing original.

This particular ethnography is part of a disciplinary history at the same time as it is trying to overcome some of its evasions by being quarrelsome and awkward. For instance, I want to know why this social realm attracts less interest and analysis than others. Why does a small army of anthropologists, myself included, work with black people in the north of the continent while virtually none have been attracted to places such as Mt Druitt. Perhaps it seems obvious that the suburbs are not a fascinating cultural domain of difference. Is this a judgment the social sciences stands by? Perhaps a more significant question is why ethnographers take virtually no interest in the suburban population that is not Aboriginal?

At the least, *The City's Outback* is a reminder that a quite other social realm is right here on the city's doorstep. The western suburbs are not separate from the wealthy city of Sydney that conceived and bore them. But this mother seems ashamed of her western offspring. Heading for weekends in the Blue Mountains, city dwellers speed past on the motorway, neatly avoiding any relationship with these vast suburban reaches. These suburbs are the focus of a certain cosmopolitan concern and periodic deprivation scandals, but they represent what and where the city's sophisticated citizens do not want to be.

\*\*\*

Frank's liaison work did not stop when he moved from Mt Druitt to live in an old caravan on the riverbank outside Dubbo, acquiring the nickname Riverbank Frank. On Police Remembrance Day in November 2006, he walked into the Dubbo police station and asked the nervous young sergeant at the desk for 'one of them ribbons' that officers wear on this day to mourn colleagues who have died in the line of duty. Frank wore the chequered ribbon all day, saying, 'If we want them to respect our pain and our rituals we have to show that we respect theirs'.

# References

Altman J & M Hinkson (eds) 2010, *Culture Crisis: Anthropology and politics in remote Aboriginal Australia*, UNSW Press, Sydney.

Atkinson, J 2002, *Trauma Trails: Recreating song lines*, Spinifex, Melbourne.

Berlant, L 2004, 'Compassion (and Withholding)', in L Berlant (ed.), *Compassion: The culture and politics of an emotion,* Routledge, New York.

Bourdieu, P 2003, 'Participant Observation', *Journal of the Royal Anthropological Institute*, vol. 9, pp. 281–294.

Comaroff, J & J L Comaroff 1992, *Ethnography and the Historical Imagination*, Westsview Press, San Francisco.

Cowlishaw, G 2009, *The City's Outback*, UNSW Press, Sydney.

Cowlishaw, G 2004, *Blackfellas, Whitefellas and the Hidden Injuries of Race*, Blackwell, Oxford.

Cowlishaw, G 1999, *Rednecks, Eggheads and Blackfellas: Racial power and intimacy in north Australia*, Allen and Unwin, Sydney and Michigan.

Cowlishaw, G 1988, *Black, White or Brindle: Race in rural Australia*, Cambridge University Press, Sydney.

Geertz, C 1988, *Works and Lives: The anthropologist as author*, Stanford University Press, Stanford.

Lea, T 2008, *Bureaucrats and Bleeding Hearts: Indigenous health in Northern Australia,* UNSW Press, Sydney.

Lea, T 2002, 'Between the Pen and the Paperwork', unpublished PhD thesis, University of Sydney.

McDermott, D 2002, 'Bare Feet, Broken Glass: Aboriginal poetry and the leaving of trauma', in X Pons (ed.), *Departures: How Australia reinvents itself*, Melbourne University Press, Melbourne.

Moreton-Robinson, A (ed.) 2004, *Whitening Race: Essays in social and cultural criticism*, Aboriginal Studies Press, Canberra.

Mudrooroo 1997, *The Indigenous Literature of Australia*, Hyland House, Melbourne.

Povinelli, E 2002, *The Cunning of Recognition: Indigenous alterities and the making of Australian multiculturalism*, Duke University Press, Durham.

# 17. Lands of Fire and Ice: From Hi-Story to History in the Lands of Fire and Ice—Our Stories and Embodiment as Indigenous in a Colonised Hemisphere

May-Britt Öhman and Frances Wyld

This article brings together two Indigenous scholars who have come to better know their Indigenous history as they story it alongside their work as historians and academics. We find that the historical landscape changes when family history is better understood: time and space become embodied, history becomes personal. Sámi scholar May-Britt Öhman speaks of singing to the hillside in a 'Sound of Music' style, and then feeling forced to break out of song and into yoik.[1] Similarly, Aboriginal Australian scholar Frances Wyld writes about her connection to land and family history, including a visit to desert Australia where she no longer saw a world of silos, but of solace. Through embodiment comes a new identity, shared and understood. As scholars understanding the power-laden binaries of colonised and coloniser, writing at the intersection of personal and public using ego-histoires, we find shared methodologies to tell stories of the self inhabiting lands of fire and ice. Applying ego-histoire, we argue for a new version of history as academic discipline: a discipline which includes the Indigenous peoples' embodied vision and experiences; a history discipline which challenges the coloniser's current Hi-Story, within which Indigenous peoples are made the other, the exotic, primitive and invisible 'vanishing race'; a history which empowers and strengthens ourselves as scholars and at the same time provides our students (Indigenous as well as non-Indigenous) with a history which takes into account Indigenous peoples visions, experiences and stories.

## Prelude

Öhman and Wyld are from two different countries and met in a third country: at the 2011 Native American and Indigenous Studies Association conference in

---

1  Yoik is traditional Sámi singing/recital where the story being told is an inherent part of the music produced. Identified by the Swedish state church as heathen, the tradition has disappeared in many families, while kept secret in others. With Sámi cultural revitalisation taking place over the last two decades, the tradition has started to regain force.

the USA. They exchanged contact details with the plan, which many conference delegates have, to collaborate at a future date. Ongoing communication between these two scholars resulted in Wyld travelling to Sweden to attend the First Uppsala Supradisciplinary Feminist Technoscience Symposium in 2011, which was convened by Öhman. They went on to collaborate further in producing this chapter. In 2012, Wyld participated in the second symposium via Skype, presenting the following story with Öhman. The two met again in 2013 when Öhman held the Third Uppsala Supradisciplinary Feminist Technoscience Symposium, which had now grown to a week-long event with a strong Indigenous focus attracting scholars from all over the world. Wyld hopes to return to Sweden again to visit Öhman's ancestral home and see the Northern Lights, and also hopes to be able to host Öhman in Australia.

Both storytellers have Indigenous heritage and work in academia. We speak from a voice that is created in a hybrid space, joining the lands of Sápmi and Australia, working across disciplines, including words of both colonised and coloniser. But we follow a tradition of storytelling, a narrative evident in many Indigenous cultures and used as a teaching tool. It is also a device recognised by historians in the use of ego-histoire. Popkins states: 'Historian-autobiographers are uniquely placed to show that the historian's subjectivity is not arbitrary but rather a result of choices among a historically defined range of possibilities. (Popkin 1996, pp. 1166–1167). We choose to tell our stories.

May-Britt: I want to start with a story of my first embodied meeting with yoik. In my family, the Sámi heritage was shamed away; language, religion and cultural traditions washed away by a state policy of assimilation to a Swedish–European positivistic industrial modernity. Yoik was proclaimed by the church as blasphemous. Forest Sámi were judged to not be real Sámi—the real Sámi were the Mountain reindeer herding Sámi. My family was supposed to become Swedish, modern. My mother fiercely denied any Sámi heritage. It was only at the age of 42 that I was told that we were Sámi (Öhman, 2010). Aged 23, in the fall of 1990, just before leaving my hometown Luleå to start my studies in the history of science and ideas at Uppsala University, I visited the mountain Loktaćohkka/Låktatjåkka (350 kilometres from Luleå towards Narvik) with friends. The air was so fresh, the mountain so majestic. I wanted to sing to it. Trained to sing the European way, in a church choir, I started singing, 'The hills are alive, with the sound of music'. But after the first tones I had to stop. I felt like I was swearing loudly in a church and the mountain was hushing me. I felt like the only way of singing to the mountain was through yoiking. I had never learnt how to yoik. In my family no tradition of yoiking was ever passed on to me. Still, I did yoik, a low almost mumbling respectful vuolle.[2] Not to the mountain. I actually yoiked the mountain and the view. It felt right. It felt good.

---

2 'Yoik' means 'to sing'. 'Vuolle' is the song/narrative. (See Stoor, 2007).

The memory and feeling has followed me ever since. But not until this very moment have I mentioned this event to anyone. I yoik my memory of this event now, to you, the reader.

Frances: The autobiographical element for me in this chapter is the storying of my connection to land and the journey back into my Aboriginal history, in particular my reactions to my family story, an autobiography written by my aunt, Doris Pilkington Garimara, which is being used within the curriculum of history teaching (Garimara1996). My autobiographical moments may seem fragmented and this is because the connection is fragmented. The removal of Aboriginal children in Australia from their families has created generations of people removed from culture and identity. If I had grown up within Aboriginal culture I would have a matriarchy of elders to call upon for wisdom. I can still choose to practise this within my workplace, within a colonised space. I can turn to the work of senior Aboriginal woman and academic Irene Watson who discusses colonisation and the rejected law of terra nullius:

> Franz Fanon saw the 'smoking ashes of a burnt-down house after the fire has been put out (but) which still threatened to burst into flames again'. I ask the reader: in relation to Australia, has there even been an attempt to put the fire out. Or have we witnessed merely the illusion of change? (Watson 2007, p. 17).

The fire still burns. There is somehow still a connection for me to my Aboriginal ancestry even though I am also tied to the old imperialist structures.

# Introduction

The land is a story place; its history is open to the gaze of those who can see. We share stories, we travel from hemisphere to hemisphere, returning to our own country with new perspectives, new ways to construct the stories of our pasts. The etymological definition of history can be placed within two languages: in old French we have the word *estoire* or *estorie* meaning 'chronicle, history or story', and in Greek the word *historia*, meaning 'a learning or knowing by inquiry; an account of one's inquiry, history, record, narrative'. For Indigenous peoples this connection to story is important, for we are storytellers. But our worldview differs from that of what is commonly perceived as the objective, disciplined history, predominantly written by the colonisers. This mode of establishing history—or as we prefer to call it 'Hi-Story'—has not been kind to us.[3]

---

[3] In feminist writing, History has been challenged as 'His story': history being produced from a male perspective. The concept of 'Herstory' was introduced in the 1970s to emphasise the role of women or history told from a woman's point of view, as well as a piece of historical writing by or about women.

When searching for the 'pure' definition of Indigenous Peoples, as Maori scholar Linda Tuhiwai Smith observes, the 'othering' by historians and anthropologists is seen as a desire to know and define the 'native' (Smith 2005). This desire of the dominant culture fixed Indigenous identities to the past, disallowing the development and change afforded to modernist cultures. Binaries developed and doors closed to the pursuit of a sharing of knowledge as inquiry through storytelling. This paper will examine a pathway across the disciplines made possible by ego-histoire; the situating of culture that evolves, of myth used to explain everyday life, of knowledge embodied and remembered. The land is a history place, whether it is the ice-scapes inhabited by the Indigenous people of the Arctic, or the desert-scapes of the Indigenous people who inhabit lands the colour of fire in Australia.

## Locating Ego-Histoire Alongside Yoiking and Indigenous Storytelling

Starting with the memory of yoiking the mountain, May-Britt raises a fundamental issue in regard to history—as opposed to Hi-Story—when evoking this integral part of Sámi culture, expression, history, and storytelling, which, despite recent efforts, is still far from being recognised within the social sciences and humanities (see Stoor 2007). First of all, it tells about the yoiking being silenced because it is considered blasphemous by the colonising state church, leading to an eradication of this tradition, and an important part of the Sámi culture. But here May-Britt shows how it comes back to her, as a force from the mountain, and from within. While such embodied encounters are not recognised within current Hi-Story, it is recognised as part of the Sámi culture, and could be part of a new version of history in which Indigenous perspectives are voiced. In this way, yoiking could be considered to be playing a role as ego-histoire. The yoiking can be described as the creation of a picture or photo expressed in phrases and song. Sámi author Johan Turi wrote in 1910:

> Sámi singing is called joiking. It is a practice for recalling other people. Some are recalled with hate, and some with love, and some are recalled with sorrow. And sometimes such songs concern lands or animals: the wolf, and the reindeer, or wild reindeer. (Turi 2011, p. 161).

In 2007, the Swedish Sámi yoik artist and Indigenous scholar Krister Stoor published his dissertation, 'Yoik Tales: A study of the narrative characteristics of Sámi yoik' (Stoor 2007). Stoor argues that the yoik tradition is not just music or song, and that the story told is of equal importance: 'The way of presenting a vuolle is also a part of the yoik tradition and one has to consider both the spoken and the sung messages in order to understand what the performer means.

In short, yoik must be recognised as verbal art or storytelling' (Stoor 2007, p. 177). Another currently active Sámi yoiker and scholar of law, the Norwegian Ande Somby, also discusses yoik from a social science perspective. He states that there is a difference between yoiking and other European/western musical tradition. You don't yoik about something. You yoik something or someone, the yoiker becoming an integral part of what he or she is yoiking: 'In a manner of speaking, a yoik has no object. In fact, it is altogether impossible to envision yoik in terms of subject and object' (Somby 1996, p. 1). Yoiking can thus be considered a form of production of history, ultimately challenging and possibly overthrowing the proclaimed objectivity criteria of Hi-Story, in which only documents and recorded stories collected and dissected by colonisers and power-holders in society are recognised (see Haraway 1991b).

Storytelling is a tradition within many Indigenous cultures (Archibald 2008; Martin 2008; Kovach 2010); it is a way to pass on a worldview as a respectful process between storyteller and listener. Traditions are built upon this exchange and the stories are valued. With the introduction of the written word through colonisation and the developed technologies that go with writing, many Indigenous people chose to write down their stories for publication. One of the most popular genres has been autobiography or life writing, as stated by Moreton-Robinson in *Talkin' Up to the White Woman* (Moreton-Robinson 2009). Smith also discusses this theme:

> Indigenous peoples want to tell our own stories, write our own versions, in our own ways, for our own purposes. It is not simply about giving an oral account or genealogical naming of the land and the events that raged over it, but a very powerful need to give testimony to and restore a spirit, to bring back into existence a world fragmented and dying (Smith 1999, p. 28).

Smith speaks of a desire to be self-naming, and of shifting identities and hybridities (Smith 2005). Hybrid space recognises the legacy of narratives from two sides of the world. In speaking of his own hybrid space, Indigenous scholar Ian Anderson found that by listening to the stories of his people he had become a 'voyeur of [his] own history' (Anderson 2003, p. 44). As Indigenous peoples we can become disconnected from our own stories because they are used for education or research purposes, or are written by the coloniser. As Indigenous people working in the world of the coloniser, there is a danger that we can forget to follow the protocols of an Indigenous worldview. The use of preludes as introductions and life-writing as story telling, and by working alongside respectful academics using ego-histoire can remedy this.

The term hybrid is controversial, and we use it in the way that Donna Haraway uses her Cyborg Manifesto (Haraway 1991a): it is blasphemous. We use it in recognition that our work is a meeting of our biological and cultural selves. It is a hybrid space connected to sites of memory, 'enveloped in a Möbius strip of the collective and the individual, the sacred and the profane, the immutable and the mobile' (Nora 1989, p. 19).

It is a challenge to develop a voice that can speak autobiographically, to develop the life writing voice of the self, within a field that asks for an objective voice based on written sources, collected by the colonisers in state or church-supported archives. Both our cultures have honoured themselves in not leaving traces, or marks behind. There are no or very few documents left showing our ancestors' point of view, whereas there are massive amounts of information collected by outsiders visiting, colonising and dissecting our ancestors lands and lives. So how then to write our own history? In this paper we speak of an Indigenous worldview, an ontology and epistemology documented by a growing number of Indigenous academics (for example, Martin 2008; Arbon 2008).

To make this hybrid space that mixes history and life writing, to argue that this voice is important, is to look back in time and to be connected to place, to speak not as a generalisation but as the self. Smith warns that 'social science cannot simply develop grand narratives of the silenced without including the voices and understandings of marginalised and silenced communities' (Smith 2005, p. 91). We create a hybrid space to look back in time to see how the subject is created and think that, like Nora, we make history that will one day require a chapter in a book. It is a time when we challenge universities to situate Indigenous studies within their departments where the teaching of history is still very important. As Indigenous people we challenge all historians to include the subjectivity into this scholarship. To us, what happened and still happens through colonisation is personal, and it is a matter of life and death—of both cultural and physical survival and mental wellbeing. In Australia this subjectivity has been questioned, declared a distortion, as stated by Frances Peters-Little, who says that 'the whole basis for wanting to become a historian in the first instance comes from a place deep inside me, from a desire to understand, acknowledge and come to terms with what has happened to my ancestors, my culture and my land' (Peters-Little 2010, p. 2).

A story wants to be told here, one that speaks to the issues of who writes history and why the personal can invade the academic space. Life-writing invades the academic format; the Indigenous worldview cannot be kept out. We tell our own stories.

Frances: When I think of speaking back to the historian who has spoken about my family in public, I think not in academic arguments, I think of a day in time. It was the day of Australia's National Apology to the Stolen Generations. I chose not to attend one of the public events where it would be televised, I chose to teach. I gave myself no time for reflection as I heard the words from our Prime Minister, I drove past the place of my own birth, a place far from my peoples' cultural home because child removal practices had affected the generations before and my birth was elsewhere, in this suburb that I drive through. My lecture would be on Aboriginal history in education; it was passionate. I held in my hands the newspaper that was using images of the film made from the biography of my grandmother. I spoke about the historians who would call this story a myth. The last activity of the teaching day was a role play. Halfway through I lost my voice. A student stepped forward to read the prepared script and I knew then that spending the day teaching instead of attending the public events was the right choice. On that day, I chose to listen to the apology on the radio in my car, but I also chose to speak, to not necessarily be amongst the masses making history, but to tell a history.

Frances Peters-Little as Aboriginal woman and historian recognises that the discussion on remaining dispassionate in her work is a luxury she has 'not been afforded'; for her and other Aboriginal people, 'the past and present are linked indissolubly through place and belonging' (Peters-Little 2010, p. 2). It is timely for historians to place themselves in their work through life-writing and autobiography. Connections to the past must be maintained to continue the work of decolonising academic spaces.

## Colonised Lands of Ice and Fire

We write about lands storied as extremes, as elements in opposition to each other. The land inhabited by the Sámi people is known as Sápmi and shares the historical title of terra nullius with their Australian Aboriginal cousins. Sápmi extends across four current nation states: Norway, Sweden, Finland and Russia. This view of Sápmi is a colonising one, whereas a gaze provided by Sámi people shows you a land that has no borders, a map seen from the top of the world, extending over the Arctic and sub-Arctic regions of the Scandinavian peninsula and the Kola peninsula (Öhman 2007). This colonising gaze was also extended to Australia, now seen as one country, not as it was over 200 years ago: a patchwork of language groups similar to the continent of modern Europe. To story these descriptions we see the art of cartography moving in opposite directions, the scattering of one Indigenous group and the homogenising of another. If the land could story itself it would not speak as a cartographer or as a study in elemental oppositions. The land would speak of seasons, of lands with no boundaries. As we write it is winter in the land of fire and summer in the land of ice. And they were not the land of no-one prior to colonisation.

May-Britt: I learnt in school, and it is still taught to school children, that the Scandinavian Peninsula was completely covered by an ice-cover up to three kilometres thick, leaving no possibility for human or non-human life in this area. We learn that 10,000 years ago the ice started melting away and that today we can find traces of the first human settlers who migrated here. Archaeological investigations are plentiful in Sápmi. They have been conducted throughout the twentieth century, partly financed by the Swedish state power company (Vattenfall) obliged to finance archaeological investigations before inundating our lands and damming our rivers (Öhman, 2007). Somehow, for some reason, it is very important to find out what the Sámi are. Why so different from the Swedes? The archaeologist C-G Ojala, himself a person with roots in this region with its mixed groups of Sámi, Finns and Swedes, writes:

> The origin of the Sámi people has been one especially consistent theme in the history of scientific interest in the Sámi. At times, it has been the dominant theme, overshadowing other ways of studying and understanding the Sámi past. Throughout the centuries, many ideas and views on the origin of the Sámi have been put forward by different researchers — Lappologists, historians, archaeologists, linguists and anthropologists — who have connected various older sources and new findings in their search for origins. Moreover, the origin of the Sámi has very often been presented as being a great mystery and a riddle waiting to be solved (Ojala 2009, p. 11).

Who was here first, after the ice melted away? The question of who the first human inhabitants were has become a controversial political issue, with archaeologists called to provide testimonies in courts over disputes of traditional land rights between Sámi reindeer herders and other local inhabitants who have been—despite probably being related to one another—categorised as Swedes and having bought or inherited land areas (see Ojala, 2009, p. 155). Searching in literature for information so that I can understand and communicate how this land of ice would have looked, I find something revolutionary. Well, it is a revolutionary insight to me. I was told and had learnt to believe that nothing could have lived here with this immense ice-cover, that my ancestors had to migrate here at some point after the ice-age. But in March 2012 a group of researchers at my own university published an article stating that trees lived here: 'Our findings imply that conifer trees survived in ice-free refugia of Scandinavia during the last glaciation, challenging current views on survival and spread of trees as a response to climate changes' (Parducci *et al.* 2012).

They talk about trees. And now I remember Astrid Cleve von Euler, the first female PhD of natural sciences in Sweden, and how as a young student writing my first essay, I discovered her work and her rejected claims of the ice age survival of Sámi on the Norwegian coast (Cleve von Euler 1936; Öhman 1991).

I was so thrilled back then, but I never heard of any such ideas again, until now. I start to see humans and animals. Fish. And I remember a film, by a Sámi film maker, that I saw long ago, the first full-length film in Sámi language and based on an old Sámi myth—a Stallo (Stallú) tale. The Stallo, half human, half demon, is evil and cunning, and hates humans for no reason and tries to kill them and eat their flesh, and kidnap children and women. In most narratives, the human ('Sámi' refers to 'human' in Sámi languages) tricks the Stallo into falling into a hole in the ice, or leads him, naked, to a mountain or forest to freeze to death (see Cocq 2008, p. 157). In the film *Pathfinder*, it is Aigin, a Sámi boy living on the ice and snow whose family has been killed by a band of mean men, and who is being forced to be their pathfinder—also the name of the film—who shows them the way to other fleeing Sámis (Gaup 1987). He manages to trick them and thereby save his people. The Stallo has been beaten again. But what I remember most of all is the overwhelming ice and snow. How could they have lived there? What was the director telling us by showing us all this ice and snow? I remember experiencing -42°C this last winter in Jokkmokk, and I think about my Inuit friends in Greenland, who still live in a region covered by ice, in some parts up to three kilometres thick. And I think, 'maybe we were actually always here', just as the Sámi author Johan Turi states in his 1910 book (Turi 2011). Maybe we too, like our Aboriginal friends in Australia, have been here for at least 60,000 years. Surviving on and by the ice, despite it seeming impossible, until now, when scientists find evidence that certain trees survived. I feel hope. I don't know why. But I feel hopeful. I will reclaim my past. I, who used to hate the cold and snow, will reclaim my understanding of living with and enjoying the ice and snow. I yoik the ice. I yoik the snow. I yoik our past, our present and our future. The Stallo of today is the ongoing depletion of our nature, ever expanding greed for minerals, electricity, energy. They may call it 'development', 'job opportunities' and 'renewable energy resources', but it actually is another invasion by the Stallo. The animals, the reindeer, lose their grazing lands, our fish die, our waters get poisoned, they train shooting at missiles over our heads, and electricity production turns our rivers into death traps for humans and animals. But we won't give up. We survived the ice age; we will not be beaten by the Stallo. We will not perish, we won't vanish. We were always here. We will always remain here.

In the sixteenth century, Gustav Vasa established the Swedish state and began the colonisation of Sápmi (see Öhman 2007). Within this period of enlightenment and through the birth of structuralism as a method to study the other, Sámi people became subject to several scientific studies and, in particular from the nineteenth century, were depicted as being primitive, or closer to nature. These investigations were paralleled with an industrial exploitation of the Sámi territories in what was considered as making use of 'dormant' natural resources within the Swedish nation state—hydropower exploitation, mining, and forestry. From the 1950s, the region became the arena for state-approved testing of military weapons, including nuclear bombs. In the twenty-first century, as the post-cold war situation led to cutting down on military spending, these military test bases were turned into commercial test fields where NATO and any interested and well-paying foreign nation may test out missiles and shooting techniques above and on the reindeer grazing lands before making use of them elsewhere in the world. In the public relations imagery of power companies and the military, the area is described as unpopulated, uninhabited wilderness. The Sámi, the humans, just aren't there (see Öhman 2007).

Australia was colonised in 1788, and all that the colonisers had learnt in previous efforts of colonisation would be applied to this new endeavour. Australian Aboriginal peoples also became the object of studies and, like their paler-skinned cousins in Sápmi, were assumed to be a vanishing race. Richard Broome speaks of the use of Charles Darwin's theories on evolution and how they was taken up by other theorists to describe human development. Broome states that 'evolutionary theory led to worldwide scientific interest in Australia's Aboriginal peoples, deemed the most 'primitive' of all' (Broome 2010, p. 103). European museums became the recipients of artefacts and remains, grouping together the 'vanishing' people, the Sámi and Indigenous Australians. Aboriginal history became a story of domination and segregation, with the underlying thought being that Aboriginal peoples would eventually cease to be. We were denied the chance to evolve as any other culture does, to make use of the technologies brought by the new inhabitants to build new lives. We are storied as relics of the past, without a right to maintain culture and create hybrid spaces. Our lives became debates about the truth, as is evident in the 'history war': the battle between non-Indigenous academics taking either liberal or conservative views on the writing of history in Australia. Tony Birch, an Indigenous scholar sums it up well:

> This cultural war does not involve Indigenous people beyond objectification. Nor does it represent the interests of Indigenous people. The self-styled liberal historians, who have recently engaged in their 'war', believe otherwise and appear to be offended when Indigenous people disagree with them — even within the nominally pluralist environment of the academy. The history war has in fact been a phony war, a brand name and logo to sell books and promote insecure egos as much as it claims to be an engaging and necessary examination of the past (Birch 2007, p. 108).

As Indigenous peoples we need to move beyond objectification. When we travel to our lands of ice and fire our memories return. But it is the discontinuation of the binaries of northern and southern hemisphere and the borrowing of place we take from Pierre Nora that gives us the ability to move beyond objectification.

Australia and Sweden—unlike Nora's storying of the United States—have yet to become sites of 'plural memories' (Nora 1989, p. 10). To do so they must embrace an instructive history to hold onto national identity. A life history cannot be written under these circumstances, instead we must escape to the place made possible by the work of Pierre Nora, we move 'Between Memory and History: Les lieux de mémoire' (Nora 1989), because we know that the land is a site of memory.

Nora defines a difference between history and memory: 'History, because it is an intellectual and secular production, calls for analysis and criticism. Memory installs remembrance within the sacred; history, always prosaic, releases it again' (Nora 1989, pp. 8–9). He adds that memory is owned by many groups; it can speak of the collective and the individual.

## The Embodiment of History

May-Britt: Two decades after my first embodied encounter with yoik, I walk through the forested lands of the forest Sámi, along the small road from my mother's birth place—nowadays a house empty of inhabitants, which I live in when I come to the area to do interviews for my research project—towards the Lule River. As I walk, inspired by learning about yoiking and vuolles, and recently having followed a short course in yoiking, I try out my own yoik capacity. First it just sounds weird. I can't find my voice. As I continue to walk and try to yoik, I am suddenly attacked by a vuolle. It is an old woman's vuolle surprising me. It is deep in tone, it feels almost ugly and aggressive. It scares me. I stop walking. I stop chanting. At once I realise that the very spot where the old woman's vuolle attacks me is at the crossroads between the old road along the river, at the place of my maternal grandfather's birthplace, and also the home of the last recognised 'real' Sámi in our family. I imagine that it is my grandfather's grandmother, Sigmora (1835–1919), who has spoken to me. She is powerful and somewhat scary. I feel confused. Is it really possible to be attacked by a vuolle? Later the same day I talk to my research colleague, who also knows the Sámi world and whose partner and sons are Sámi. I tell her briefly about the incident, saying that a vuolle came over me. I somehow expect her to dismiss my feeling. Yoik attacks aren't something I can really speak about within the academic world and be taken seriously. When yoiking is discussed in academia, it is as a study object, something to be analysed, something that can be dissected. But instead she asks: 'What kind of yoik was it?'

Again, I am shocked. I am stunned by the recognition of my experience. I thought we would laugh at it together and dismiss it as something funny but not real. So I hesitate. Then I answer, 'I don't know', and quickly change subject.

I feel I need to contemplate what has happened. I don't have the words to explain it, even to myself. But in all cases, even though I might not be ready just yet, I have heard a—my own?—Sámi voice breaking through. When I am ready I will yoik again. I think Sigmora wants me to be proud and trust myself.

Phenomenologist Maurice Merleau-Ponty, in speaking of his homeland France, said that 'history takes still more from those who have lost everything, and gives yet more to those who have taken everything. For its sweeping judgements acquit the unjust and dismiss the pleas of their victims. History never confesses' (Merleau-Ponty 1964, p. 4). As scholars using autobiography or life writing, we find shared methodologies to tell stories. Through embodiment comes a new identity, shared and understood through the reworking of European philosophical traditions.

The nature of our academic research has taken both authors close to our ancestral lands. In such incidents we were overtaken with a need to write stories of inquiry. These episodes introduce a memory and a change in identity. May-Britt, in her urge to yoik, illustrates a deeper embodied need to use her ancestral traditions to yoik the hillside and the forest, to recognise the landscape as a memory place, a place of decolonisation. Nora described an era of historiography in an 'epistemological age', where historiography becomes a site for memory (Nora 1989). We can then embody these ancestral memories and use them to construct stories. We re-learn a set of knowledges and discourses, our habits change. We see a world that is colonised, but we also see under it a site that still holds its memory and can tell its stories to those who can listen. Frances experienced this phenomenon when travelling through desert country on her way back to her city workplace, a structure that consists of small offices along a corridor which can be described figuratively as a workplace of silos. Silos, in the literal and non-figurative sense, are large cylindrical buildings that store grain. To 'whitewash' was a term used throughout the 'history wars' in Australia to denote a re-storying or censorship by the dominant, in this case white, culture. Whitewash in its literal sense is a type of low-cost lime-based paint. The author, in the passage below, uses the literary method of metaphor to draw parallels but also to speak of the joy in knowing her desert origins and the solace that it provides:

> In the land of silos, every year you get new information to whitewash your sense of knowing in a way that denies you the truth as you sit in a world dominated by western science. You believe that like the ones who paint the silos white you make your own knowledge strong, you are re-imagining your own dominance on the landscape where your truth must be loud to affirm your own survival. In the land of solace you only have to listen to yourself and the truth that comes from being to survive (Wyld 2011, p.66).

If history will not confess, then sites of memory must have an equally loud voice to bring balance. We are turning again to Merleau-Ponty and his recognition that 'the main concern of our time is going to reconcile the old world and the new' (Merleau-Ponty 1964, p. 4). As collaborators from different hemispheres, we have learnt our commonalities and how we had to learn new sets of knowledges to reconcile old and new theories within our academic work. To meet this goal, we use the work of Nora and his 'new genre, for a new age of historical consciousness' (Nora 1984, p. 4). We use story and an understanding that our histories are embodied within us, we use memory because the past refuses to be forgotten.

Frances: I perch like a bird on my balcony on the 23rd-floor room of an Auckland hotel. I am in Auckland for an Indigenous research methodology conference. This is a culturally safe space that acknowledges the need to use multiple disciplines that has Indigenous knowledge at its base. It is timeless, incongruous with the discipline of history. Indigenous voices are here, there was even a yoik delivered during the cultural events. I presented today, choosing to tell a story of motherhood, not the documented story of my family history, although I did choose to include an image depicting but not naming my aunt and grandmother. In question time, someone asked how my grandmother got home. I paused before answering, telling the questioner that my answer will sound like the title of a book and film, because it is. Then I went on to say that I have already written about the impact this has had on my working life (Somerville, Somerville and Wyld, 2010), and the objectification that non-Indigenous colleagues have committed when using the film in teaching without having conversations with me, without acknowledging the connection. After the presentation, an Indigenous elder came to me, kissed me, and whispered, 'you told my story too'. I perch on the balcony, like a bird wanting to fly back to its homeland. I watch parts of the film on YouTube. It is pure Hollywood, it is dramaticised and has been criticised in the media, and my goal now is to find another perch from which to teach Indigenous content. Now on my home campus a week later I am in the library researching European scholars once again. I want to look into the idea of auratic perception used by German Jewish scholar Walter Benjamin (Benjamin 2005). I want to teach cultural studies to students in a way that acknowledges other people who believe in a connection to place, and that it isn't just within an Indigenous worldview. I find the book I want, and above it on another shelf is the book penned by my aunt poking out amongst other books, as if someone had looked at it and not put it back properly. I take it and in re-reading am reminded that it is a gentle re-telling of history. It tells me that we are forced within this academic space to become critical, to be in crisis—as the etymology of critical describes—to be in a diseased place. This is not a way to be, it is not the ontology of Indigenous peoples. In reading my grandmother's story, written by my aunt, I am reminded that Martu women are often 'quiet' and 'dignified' (Garimara 1996, p.76) and I wonder if this is because we know how to carry a sense of history within us?

## Conclusion

As authors, historians and Indigenous scholars we are in support of the idea of ego-histoire because it fits an Indigenous worldview; we challenge the production of the winners' Hi-Story of the current existing nation states. We argue for the idea of ego-histoire as it can bring forward a so-far silenced history, not available in the documents in the coloniser's archives. Together we dare to rely on our Indigenous traditions. We are daring to recognise stories and memories coming to us—not through coloniser's archives and archaeological findings only, but through our embodied encounters with myths, landscapes and memories passed down—as well as our own traditions on how our history is told and retold. Ego-histoire asks the historian to look back at themselves and to write the self into their work. We also support Nora's work into lieux de mémoire because it fits with the Indigenous connection to land. Our title claimed a binary of hemispheres but our collaboration is only made possible because of a belief in a single sphere that is currently colonised by dominant cultures, a sphere that wants Indigenous people to remain primitive, to vanish, and fade away as exotic museum relics. We are historians and academics, and we create a new vision of history, which could be on display in museums. The history we need to write and transmit in our present is of our own lives and circumstances. We are voices that want to be heard after decades of being objects on the dissecting plate of the winning historians' gaze where our stories were considered as curiosities. Our lands of fire and ice are returned to us through stories, alongside winners' side historians who are brave enough to write themselves into their own work, and challenge Hi-Story. We started our work with a prelude, should we end it with an epilogue? No, because the story doesn't end, it is the Möbius strip folding back on itself creating what Indigenous people have always had: a sense of timelessness, of always being here, and the determination to always remain here.

# References

Arbon, V 2008, *Arlathirnda Ngurkarnda Ityirnda: Being – knowing – doing: De-colonising Indigenous tertiary education*, Post Pressed, Teneriffe.

Anderson, I 2003, 'Black Bits, White Bits', in M Grossman (ed.), *Blacklines: Contemporary critical writing by Indigenous Australians*, Melbourne University Press, Melbourne, pp. 43–51.

Archibald, J 2008, *Indigenous Storywork: Educating the heart, mind, body, and spirit*, University of British Columbia Press, Vancouver.

Benjamin, A 2005, *Walter Benjamin and History*, Continuum, London.

Birch, T 2007, '"The Invisible Fire": Indigenous sovereignty, history and responsibility', in A Moreton-Robinson (ed.), *Sovereign Subjects: Indigenous sovereignty matters*, Allen & Unwin, Sydney, pp. 105–117.

Broome, R 2010, *Aboriginal Australians: A history since 1788*, fourth edition, Allen & Unwin, Crows Nest.

Cleve von Euler, A 1936, *Komsakulturens Ålder*, Lindesberg.

Cocq, C 2008, Revoicing Sámi Narratives: North Sámi storytelling at the turn of the twentieth century. unpublished PhD thesis, Umeå Universitet. Available at: http://urn.kb.se/resolve?urn=urn:nbn:se:umu:diva-1598.

Fanon, F 1971, *The Wretched of the Earth*, Penguin, London.

Garimara, D P 1996, *Follow the Rabbit-Proof Fence*, University of Queensland Press, St Lucia.

Gaup, N 1987, *Pathfinder*, Norwegian Film Institute, Norway.

Haraway D 1991a, 'A Cyborg Manifesto: Science, technology and socialist-feminism in the late twentieth century', in D Haraway (ed.), *Simians, Cyborgs and Women: The reinvention of nature*, Routledge, London and New York, pp. 149–181.

Haraway, D 1991b, 'Situated Knowledges: The science question in feminism and the privilege of partial perspective', in D Haraway (ed.), *Simians, Cyborgs and Women: The reinvention of nature*, Routledge, London and New York, pp. 183–201.

Kovach, M 2010, *Indigenous Methodologies: Characteristics, conversations, and contexts*, University of Toronto Press, Toronto.

Martin, K 2008, *Please Knock Before You Enter: Aboriginal regulation of outsiders and the implications for researchers*, Post Pressed, Teneriffe, QLD.

Merleau-Ponty, M 1964, *Signs*, Northwest University Press, Evanston.

Moreton-Robinson, A 2009, *Talkin' Up to the White Woman: Indigenous women and feminism*, University of Queensland Press, St Lucia.

Nora, P 1989, 'Between Memory and History: Les lieux de mémoire', *Representations*, no. 26, pp. 7–24.

Öhman, M-B, 2010, 'Being May-Britt Öhman: Or, reflections on my own colonized mind regarding hydropower constructions in Sápmi', in Elovaara, Sefyrin, Öhman & Björkman (eds), *Travelling Thoughtfulness: Feminist Technoscience Stories*, Department of Informatics, Umeå University, Umeå, pp. 262–292.

Öhman, M-B 2007, 'Taming Exotic Beauties: Swedish Hydropower Constructions in Tanzania in the Era of Development Assistance, 1960s–1990s', Stockholm Papers in the History and Philosophy of Technology, Royal Institute of Technology, Stockholm. Available at: http://kth.diva-portal.org/smash/get/diva2:12267/FULLTEXT01.

Öhman, M-B, 1991, 'De Första Naturvetenskapskvinnorna vid Uppsala Universitet', unpublished undergraduate essay, Department of History of Science and Ideas, Uppsala University.

Ojala, C 2009, 'Sámi Prehistories: The politics of archaeology and identity in northernmost Europe', Occasional Papers in Archaeology no. 47, Department of Archaeology and Ancient History, Uppsala.

Parducci L, T Jorgensen, M M Tollefsrud, E Elverland, T Alm & S L Fontana 2012, 'Glacial Survival of Boreal Trees in Northern Scandinavia', *Science*, vol. 335, no. 6072, pp. 1083–1086.

Peters-Little, F 2010, 'Introduction', in F Peters-Little, A Curthoys & J Docker (eds), *Passionate Histories: Myth, Memory and Indigenous Australians*, ANU E Press, Canberra, pp. 1–6

Popkin, J D 1996, 'Ego-Histoire and Beyond: Contemporary French historian-autobiographers', *French Historical Studies*, vol. 19, no. 4, pp. 1139–1167.

Smith, L T 2005, 'On Tricky Ground: Researching the native in the age of reason', in N Denzin & Y Lincoln (eds), *Sage Handbook of Qualitative Research*, Sage, London, pp. 85–107.

Smith, L T 1999, *Decolonizing Methodologies: Research and Indigenous peoples*, University of Otago Press, Dunedin.

Somby, A 1996, 'Joik and the Theory of Knowledge', in M Haavelsrud (ed.), *Kunnskap og Utvikling*, Universitetet i Tromsø, Tromsø.

Somerville, C, K Somerville & F Wyld 2010, 'Martu Storytellers: Aboriginal narratives within the academy', *The Australian Journal of Indigenous Education*, vol. 39, supplement, pp. 96–101.

Stoor, K 2007, Juoiganmuitalusat — Jojkberättelser: En studie av jojkens narrativa egenskaper, unpublished PhD thesis, Umeå University. Available at: http://urn.kb.se/resolve?urn=urn:nbn:se:umu:diva-1323.

Turi, J 2011, *An Account of the Sámi*, Nordic Studies Press, Chicago.

Watson, I 2007, 'Settled and Unsettled Spaces: Are we free to roam?' in A Moreton-Robinson (ed.), *Sovereign Subjects: Indigenous sovereignty matters*, Allen & Unwin, Sydney, pp. 15–32.

Wyld, F 2011, 'In the Land of Silos', *Journal of Australian Indigenous Issues*, vol. 14 no. 1, pp. 63–66.

# 18. Turning into a Gardiya

Stephen Muecke

**Stephen Muecke, Chinatown.**

Source: Dieter Kirchner, 1977.

Well, it was a long time ago now—
when I was in Halls Creek—
I'd been there a few times—
different times,
coming and going, you know—
bits of research, this and that—

Or sometimes I was just passing through—
that good old country, you know—
I couldn't keep away!—

Well, anyway, this one time—
there's some kind of ceremony going on—
that time the camping ground was just north of the highway—
right in town—
nothing there now—
just servos there today—
all those humpies musta been pulled down—
you know, cleaning up the town—

Archie Singpoo had had a few—
but he was still in control—
says, 'I can cut you, if you want?'—
looking at me up close, grinning—
oh, he had the authority and everything—
he'd told me about how his uncle—
used to run the business around here—
down to Balgo, back up through Nicholson station west to Christmas Creek—
and back again to Halls Creek—

'I know one gardiya got that'—
I say—
'that Kim Akerman, you know him?—
cicatrices across his chest—
might be that Wongai mob down in Kalgoorlie bin cut-im'—

(I was talking Pidgin, you know—
just to fit in—
your language slips around like that—
Anyway, that's another story I'll tell you later—
about researching Aboriginal English)

I wasn't sure—
'What for—?
how you gonna cut me?'—

## 18. Turning into a Gardiya

'Longa didjun'—
Archie says—
grabs one empty stubbie—
stone right there for break-im—

'Oh! No, no,' I say—
'I think not right—
not really right for me—
gardiya and everything'—
I was just a youngfella, then—
didn't want to be 'scarred for life'!—

Tracey Moffatt, I think, had a photo series—
called Scarred for Life—
wonderful photos of Koori and Murri kids—
adolescents—
being punished for this or that—
wondering how they fit in—

Oh, Archie knew what he was doing, you know—
even if we'd done the run—
down to the pub—
brought back a slab of Emu Bitter—
and that ceremony still going on—
people drinking—
I felt shame—

He was fitting me in—
simple as that—
(loud) 'Alright,' he says—
'I gonna call you "brother"—
I'm tjungarrayi, that mean you gotta be tjungarrayi, too—
and that woman you with?—
You gotta call her nambitjin, wife—
Straight. That's the Law—
the Law—
that one over there too,' pointing with his lips—
and all the guys sitting around have a good laugh—
that old girl—
not young, she really old!—
one oldfella sitting next to me whispering, 'he like-em gardiya, that old girl, oh yes, any kine'—

So, that's the finish, of my story—
'bout how I got made into a gardiya—
well, not really the finish—
I got a lotta story like that—
different ways—
but finish now, I gotta go back to Sydney—

Because there's another Stephen Muecke who isn't a gardiya, who works at the uni, writes lots of weird stuff. It is a question of style—I want to argue the point, and I can't do that in Paddy Roe's narrative style (Roe 1983) that I have just been reproducing, respectfully—you have to shift your language if you want move your argument along and take it somewhere where it does seem to matter. There are no new thoughts without some kind of new style, as Nietzsche said (Nietzsche 1996, p. 342). And there is a geography as well, styles have their regions and countries; if I started in a Kimberley English style, it is because it belongs up there, just as this kind of English belongs to other places, pretty universal, maybe not academic, and if I get too colloquial the editors have to reject it. Regional Englishes that belong in their places, then, that seem to thrive and not disappear because the teachers in primary say 'stop talking that mixed-up English!' No, the smart students just acquire another language; they are all multilingual, and why not?

In Sydney there are no gardiya. You might be a gubba, just as in the Top End you are a balanda, and there must be many other names for whitefellas. So I can't become a gardiya unless I cross the invisible border into the Kimberley. And I do each time I go there, just like all the other whitefellas who have been given a place in Indigenous Australia that they are more or less aware of, more or less accepting of. They are, in fact, more or less assimilated. This is no trivial thing. It is a powerful connection, creating, without any pressure, the kind of loyalty that normally goes with family.

'Teeb, Teeb!'—
kids in the bushes outside pub—
'Teeb, teeb'—
Until I realise it's my name—
they are calling—
(yelling) 'Tomorrow—
we gotta go la riber!'—

When you got that—
Toyota—
you a driver—
for anyone—

And if one day you—
take a mob of kids—
swimming la river—
lotta fun, cute kids—
singing aaall the way—

That Creedence:
Don't go around tonight, Well, it's bound to take your life, There's a bad moon on the rise.[1]

Cute alright—
But lotta humbug goin' on—

Turning into a gardiya. Metamorphosis is the ancient philosophy of this country: that range of hills is always becoming a woman lying down is always becoming a blue-tongue lizard (Muecke 2004, p. 4). What if metamorphosis, and everything that it implies about the interrelatedness and persistence of life forms, were as rational as any other system?

I can sing you that song—
if you like?—
Nalyak—
that blue-tongue lizard—

If you turn into a gardiya you can turn back again, soon as you head south. Don't even try to talk straight! Because speech turns, like good stories, talk has to take a detour to get somewhere. You don't become fully Aboriginal, any more than that mob becomes whitefella when you call them names.

Let's not get sentimental about being a gardiya, it can be killer work if you are hired to administer or teach in some remote community. 'Kartiya are like Toyotas', Kim Mahood reports a Western Desert woman saying. 'When they break down we get another one' (Mahood 2012). There are 'the mad, the bad and the incompetent' (the classic 'missionaries, mercenaries and misfits'), as well as the well-meaning idealists who get ground down by the isolation and pressures. For these ones, Mahood's tough account is required reading. And in her story, the new admin. woman is happily inducted as a nampitjin (my 'wife' by the way), meaning she can only 'belong' to a certain section of the community: 'She doesn't understand that she is colonised territory. Invisible to her, power struggles of ancient lineage and epic proportions are being played out. This is our kartiya—hands off.'

---

1   I didn't realise it at the time. Poverty stricken kids singing joyously about strange fears sweeping across the country: 'I know the end is coming soon/I fear rivers overflowing/I hear the voice of rage and ruin'.

One other time—
I was starting my PhD work—
running around looking for stories—
just like this one I guess!—

This would be, ooh—
late 70s?—
and I start in Broome—
oh, I'd been there before—
before, plenty of time—
in and out of there—
stayed six weeks one time—
that time I was working for Susan Kaldor—
and Ann Davidson was my offsider—
on language stuff—

You know what I was saying just now?—
those primary school teachers—
couldn't understand why kids—
couldn't talk that High English—
you know—
they didn't have an ear for that Creole—
teachers never understand—
teachers back in those days, anyway—

Alright, so I'm looking for Paddy Roe—
coupla people said he was good for story—
even old Prof Berndt from UWA—
I was a student there then—
few other people—

So I find him—
in the middle of Broome—
he's right there—
oh, I had to go to mamabulandjin first—
and they sent me on—
he's at the old Anne St Reserve—
that time—
working—
oh, it was—
just about before dinner time—

And I asked him if he can help me with story—
'What's that?' he yells out—
he's on toppa the roof—
with crowbar and everything—
pulling off the old iron—
corrugated iron—
you know, that one got ramu[2]—

'What kine?'—
he climbs down from the roof—
shakes my hand and everything—
'University, eh? Down in Perth—
jus' story and all that kinda thing—
you want me to tell-im story?—
oh, I can do that!—
no worries, young fella—
bye 'n' bye—
might be after tea time?'—
then he looks at me straight—
'things gotta go both ways, you know'—
I didn't understand—

'They closin' this reserve—
all my old people gotta move—
most of them gone now—
(lifts a gnarled finger) I'm only one man here (laughs)—
so I'm taking this all stuff Block—
Coconut Well—
millibinyari we call-im—

So I gotta take all this old iron out there—
you can give me a hand?—
alright, chuck-im that lot longa truck—
I only got this truck coupla day—
then yunmi can drive out there—
tell story—
(under his breath) two ways, you know.'

Who said economies were just about cold hard cash? People get traded too, and that fine storytelling had me seduced, seconded and permanently attached to the Roe mob.

---

2  This gardiya building material has an aesthetic that crosses over. The corrugations are like the parallel grooves incised in old boomerangs and shields.

Position description:
Driver.
Minder for old Butcher Joe (back then).
Official paperwork.
Scholarship: numerous articles and two books for Paddy Roe.
What's my name? Paddy calls me 'Madya' (boss).

Economics is about entanglement. Philosopher and anthropologist Bruno Latour highlights what a mad construction economics is, that pride and joy of us westerners and our most powerful export. It is providence itself, a second nature, a religion that presides over the distribution of all that is good and evil. For the sake of comparison, Latour talks of anthropologists who might read Marcel Mauss on the gift and look at 'primitive' economies in the Pacific and 'recoil in horror at the imbroglios which are described among these others, "Oh dear", they sigh, "these poor people will never get out of this mess, they are always tied up, attached, indebted, hooked, mixed up, entangled."' Whereas, Latour goes on, in our modern economies 'with long practice we have gotten used to being hardened to the idea of settling up with those we enter into transactions with … we get out of such imbroglios by adding the exact opposite: "And now we are even; I owe you nothing; we have exchanged the equivalent; see you later!"' (Latour 2012, pp. 446–447, my translation).

An ideal of turning someone close into a stranger, of wanting to close deals, as if getting away were the aim, But in fact people don't live to the ideal and this economy, that sees itself also as a hard science where equivalent values are precisely and coldly calculated, is just as mixed up and intimate as any Pacific bartering system. And the cold hard gaze? Far from it, it is full of sales surprises and marketing tricks, testosterone and stimulant-fueled traders, fictional goods, cooked books and outright lies.

My first son was named for Butcher Joe—
Joe Muecke—
1983, he was born—
in Adelaide—
I musta gone back to the town I was born—
pick up a nice Adelaide girl!—

So that connection was always there, after that, crossing over into my family—
One of my old relatives might have got a bit of a shock—
(What? They called him after a black man?)
but we never worry—
me and Patience—
we never worry—
very happy when that beautiful little boy come along—

Joe, like Butcher Joe, like Joseph Roe—
All gumbali, namesakes—

Now, that gumbali—
here's the thing—
when you are namesake for someone—
that's a special relationship—
not like brother-in-law or granny or cousin-brother
but a little bit the same—

You not a straight-up relation through family—
oh you might be, but—
you share something different with your gumbali—
like every time I go to Broome—
when I head up there—
I might see Stephen Albert—
you know, Baamba, the actor?
he used to be in the bands too, playing music —
Broome Beats, singing—
he was in Bran Nue Dai as well, Uncle Tadpole—

Anyway, he always says hello to me—
walkin' round Chinatown—
'Hey, Gumbali!'—
we have a chat—
some sort of relationship we got—
I don't know what it is, but!
And when me and Patience went back to Broome—
after Joe was born—
this might been—
ooooh—
nineteen-eighty-five or -six?—
we had that little boy with us—
only one kid then—

We was down at mulabulandjin—
came along to see old Lulu[3]—
a bit too early in the morning I think—
he was still in the house—
so we waited—
Teresa had some puppies—
and little Joe was playing around with the puppies—
I got a photo of that somewhere—

---

3  3 Paddy Roe's family nickname.

When Lulu come out of the house—
he was all happy—
you know like he is—
full of energy—
he calls out 'HELLO!'—
with his arms out wide—
and little Joe ran and jumped into his arms—
straight away—
soon as he called him—
and that was the first time he ever met Lulu—
you know—
it's a thing like that—

So having been magically captured ('colonised' as Mahood said) this one gardiya, me, is still a loyal member of the Goolarabooloo mob, still working for Paddy's grandsons 40 years later. In the Land of Metamorphoses, you get possessed by psychogenic forces. You begin to understand that economics is about trading values, it's not just accumulation for profit's sake, surely? If it is not about things that really matter to you, what is the point? Another idea that Latour gets from Gabriel Tarde: What if 'to have' were more important than 'to be'? So you can philosophise about having or not having, as you are being possessed by country, as much as by its custodians. This is philosophically miles away from being about identity or being. So 'being' a gardiya is about having tradable values. You have certain ideas, skills, know-how, attached to you, and you are attached to them, they matter to you. So when you become in turn attached to some mob, they have these values too, on call. And from them the gardiya gets knowledge, skills, know-how. Two ways.

So that is why, in these stories about metamorphosis and 'skill transfer' as they say in the jargon, I have wanted to stress how lives are at stake, with the refrain of CCR's old song in my head, that the kids sang all those years ago, reminding us about the 'rage and ruin' spreading across the country. That can happen, sure, if too many people don't ask themselves what really matters to them.

# References

Latour B, 2012, *Enquête sur les Modes d'Existence: Une anthropologie des modernes*, La Découverte, Paris.

Mahood, K 2012, 'Kartiya Are Like Toyotas: White workers on Australia's cultural frontier', *Griffith Review*, vol. 36.

Muecke, S 2004, *Ancient and Modern: Time, culture and Indigenous philosophy*, UNSW Press, Kensington.

Nietzsche, F 1996, *Human, All Too Human*, translated by R J Hollingdale, Cambridge University Press, Cambridge.

Roe, P 1983, *Gularabulu: Stories from the West Kimberley*, (edited and with an introduction by S Muecke), Fremantle Arts Centre Press, Fremantle.

# 19. Tales of Mystery and Imagination from the Tweed River: Shaping Historical-Consciousness

## Philip Morrissey

The invitation to submit an essay as part of this collection on ego-histoire has enabled me to reflect on a series of intra-Aboriginal narratives between different peoples along the Tweed River that I had been exposed to in my early childhood. Over the passage of time, I have begun to understand how these narratives (and vivid fragments of story) have formed my basic dispositions, in a manner analogous to the Bourdieuan concept of *habitus*. Bourdieu sees *habitus* as 'a system of lasting, transposable dispositions which, integrating past experiences, functions at every moment as a matrix of perceptions, appreciations, and actions' (Bourdieu 1990, pp. 82–83). The dialogic, quasi-magical world represented in these stories has intrinsically shaped my historical-consciousness and underscored my subsequent work in the academe, both in bringing Aboriginal epistemologies to the fore of pedagogy in Aboriginal studies at the University of Melbourne, for example, and in exploring notions of the uncanny in Aesopic philosophy (Morrissey 2011).

In what follows I quote Martin Buber from his preface to *Tales of the Hasidim: The Early Masters* about the significance of the 'naked story' as a framework for reflection (Buber 1968, p. ix). For, like Buber's Hasidic tales, what I relate here are not 'prosaic facts' but 'illuminative tales' suggesting hidden realities and addressing fundamental structures of human life. For Buber, the form of the naked story is an epistemology in itself. This is resonant, too, with Aboriginal practices of story-telling, including in relating historical stories. In offering these stories as a form of ego-histoire I deploy Buber's edict of presenting the unadorned story as a theoretical frame, inviting the reflexivity of the reader.

A personal legacy of the stories I include below, such as in 'Dancing Curlews,' is an enduring and profound belief in the extra-dimensional qualities of existence and the uncanny integrity of animal life. These themes also thread though my research and my teaching. Other stories below, such as 'The Fight'—the title is a reference to the famous William Hazlitt essay of 1822 (Hazlitt 2000)—imprinted me with an intuition of the connection of sex with violence, and love with death. This may have run counter to the banal platitudes of political correctness but it did provide a pathway to understanding great art and literature, so that when I read, as I relate at the end of the essay, Richard Hughes' *A High Wind in*

*Jamaica*, in the Tweed River, its dark themes, enunciated within the immediate and disquieting world of post-slavery, were a continuation of what I had already began to understand through story. Finally, the story 'Uncle Tommy Norley' and its tale of intra-Aboriginal violence introduced me to an early form of self-reflexivity and individualism. It was clear to me even then that there were no unified narratives of communal resistance to colonisation. Rather, the colonial world I experienced through the stories of my family was one of individuals working, fighting and dying. And it is this that influences what I teach and what I write.

This collection of stories is one I've written down for the first time. They are stories that were told to me by my mother, my grandmother or my uncles, or stories that were told by them in my presence. The exception is 'The Dave Sands Story', which was told in a communal setting by a senior Aboriginal woman from Kempsey, New South Wales. In retelling that story I've attempted an atmospheric, interpretive mode of writing. I've related all the other stories in plain English because with the passage of time I'm unable to do justice to contexts in which I heard them and the specific vernacular used by the story-tellers. The stories which feature my mother and uncles as children take place in the 1930s. 'The Fight' is set in the late-1930s. The incidents described in 'Uncle Tommy Norley' took place in the late-nineteenth century. In each instance, I believe that I was the sole living repository of the story at the time of writing it down.

What has been amusing for me is the consideration that, while my professional life as an Aboriginal scholar in the academe has not depended on me presenting myself as an elder or custodian of an oral tradition, I somehow metamorphose into that stereotypical role when writing down these stories. In contradiction to this stereotype, I feel strongly that the stories I recount below have individualised me rather than contributed to the production of a generic Aboriginal subject. In this regard I am ambivalent with respect to Deleuze's and Guattari's thesis on a 'minor literature' as 'deterritorializing one terrain as it maps another', in its presupposition of a collective enunciation (Deleuze & Guattari 1986, p. 18).

The radical content of the 'Uncle Tommy Norley' story, for example, disrupts other Indigenous and non-Indigenous histories of the frontier, some of which have become almost normative in the way they represent the coloniser/Aboriginal binary. The 'Uncle Tommy Norley' story challenges us more broadly to think of the extreme violence of the Queensland frontier and how that could also translate into intra-Aboriginal violence; of the emerging affiliative relationships between coloniser and Aboriginal, often based on work; and the conflict between tradition and modernity within the Aboriginal world itself.

My experience of the storytellers and stories coincides with that of the Italian playwright and Nobel Laureate, Dario Fo, when he writes of the *fabulatori*, the storytellers of his childhood who, 'with their language and tales made an indelible mark on my future choices and on my way of judging events and characters in both fantasy and reality' (Fo 2005, p. 62). The fantastic, or the uncanny, became for me part of the fabric of an everyday reality that could never be simply prosaic, shaping the current of my subsequent work.

The Tweed River, where many of the stories are set, is a tidal river on the New South Wales/Queensland coastal border. The stories set along the river all take place in a time when there was a hybridised community of Aboriginal and South Sea Islanders living there. The generic term *Dugai* was used to refer to white people; the community of Aborigines and South Sea Islanders referred to themselves as *Goories*. Where appropriate, I have deployed these terms in my essay. It would be a mistake to attempt to frame these stories with a contemporary discourse of 'traditional owners' and 'country', for these concepts were not in use at that time and 'skin colour' was the critical point of difference between *Dugais* and *Goories*.

Paddy Roe's *Gularabulu: Stories from the West Kimberley,* edited by Stephen Muecke, provides a further useful frame of reference for thinking about the stories I've made public here. In his introduction, Stephen Muecke classifies Paddy Roe's stories as *trustori* (true stories), *bugaregara* (stories from the Dreaming), and *devil stori* (stories about devils and spirit-beings) (Roe 1983, pp. vii–viii). The stories that played a role in forming my worldview fall mainly into the categories of *trustori* and *devil stori*. The Dreaming was never an overt factor in understanding the river or the country that surrounded me. The strange and miraculous found in some of the stories was logically related to the super-abundance of nature itself. If the river was full of sharks and overflowing with fish, oysters, and crabs, why would its riparian surrounds not include spirits and other strange beings?

## Devil Storis

The following *devil storis* are set on Greenbank Island. Greenbank Island was once an island on the Tweed River, but is now joined to the shore and has transformed into a banal suburb of Tweed Heads. Greenbank Island was home to a succession of Aboriginal families in the early-twentieth century. People lived in houses, widely spaced over the island, and there were never more than a few families living there at any one time. The last Aboriginal family lived on the island in the 1960s, and for this particular family, as for my family, the island seems to have functioned as a transitory space when first moving to the Tweed River from Queensland. It is quite possible that those families who lived there in the early part of the twentieth century were seeking lives with maximum freedom from state control. In the 1930s the Tweed River was still full of freshwater sharks and the island was resonant with the uncanny 'energies' of an earlier time. The only way to get to the island was by rowing a boat. My mother told of rowing across the river with warm bread purchased from the bakery and, on one occasion, of the bread falling into the water on the floor of the dinghy. When my family left the island sometime after World War Two, a young fisherman named Matt Philp rowed the family's furniture in a dinghy up the Tweed River to their new home. Here are the *devil storis* from that period.

## Tiger and Patchy

At certain times all the adult males in the family would have travelled away from the Tweed River seeking work. My grandmother and younger family members would be at home alone. Indoors, in the evenings, they would hear the family dogs outside barking, growling, and yelping, and then some spirit or being would throw the dogs—and sometimes the family goats—onto the roof. Occasionally, my mother and uncles would see the dogs, Tiger and Patchy, growling and flinching away from these invisible or imaginary creatures.

## The Size of a Calf

My Uncle Darcy was walking though the bush once with another boy when they encountered a four-legged animal the size of a calf. The creature entered the river and began to swim, but instead of dog-paddling it swung its forelegs in the manner of a freestyle-swimming human.

## Shaking Bushes

One day, as dusk was setting in, my mother was with Uncle Darcy on the river hunting for sand crabs. The technique involves pinning the crab to the sandy river-floor with a thin pole and then picking it up by its rear legs before it can escape. My mother was after one especially large crab while Darcy, who was becoming impatient, waited. Finally she gave up and ran to join him. As she ran, the bushes on the side of the bush track began to shake and quiver, without any sign of wind or other intervention.

## Dancing Curlews

Curlews figure in stories from many Aboriginal communities across Australia, often as portentous omens. My mother told stories of curlews seen dancing around camp fires, and of being confronted on lonely bush tracks by dancing curlews with coal-red eyes. Here the suggestion is that curlew is almost like a medium—open to possession by a spirit. It is intriguing as to why such an inoffensive bird has acquired such a reputation.

## The Chain Man

The Chain Man was a dreadful being that walked the mangrove islands and estuaries of the Tweed River carrying a clanking chain. There was never any report of the Chain Man actually harming anyone but, like the fabled Medusa, he was so terrible in aspect that anyone encountering him was liable to die of fright. When I was in a relatively isolated part of the river with other boys, we would mock-frighten each other with stories of the Chain Man. The one person who I had heard of as actually encountering The Chain Man was an old non-Indigenous fisherman, named Mr Alvin. After the encounter he returned to Greenbank Island in a state of shock, and was nursed for several days until his recovery by my grandmother. This was told to me by my mother. The Chain Man was an actual being who lived on the river, not a spirit. Mr Alvin believed that he had seen the Chain Man, but might the original story have been based on nineteenth century encounters with an escaped convict from the nearby Moreton Bay Penal Settlement? Chains and leg irons were worn by convicts.

# *Trustoris*

## The Fight

Bare-knuckle fights bore no relationship to brawls or street fights and were fought under classic London 'Prize Ring' rules, with fights ending when a combatant was unable to rise from a knockdown, or in the Aboriginal way, with real-time arbitration. Spectators might intervene when they thought points of honour and precedence had been adequately satisfied. Fights were usually scheduled for a Sunday morning when people had free time. Many of the challenges, I assume, were issued on the Saturday night when people were socialising and drinking. In a spirit of sportive violence, Eddie Cavanagh, the key figure in 'The Fight', as the Sunday events were known, would challenge the crewmembers of the coastal steamers docking into Tweed Heads in the early part of the twentieth century. As a small boy I witnessed a fight in the classic bare-knuckle style. No punches were thrown but I was impressed by the fierce menace of hissing breath, rolling fists, circling, and flatfooted shuffling of the fighters. My grandmother related the story of how her oldest and favourite son, Eddie, arranged to fight a rival who was attended by his extended family, while she was the only person who turned up to support Eddie. My mother, less into the romance, provided the background: the fight was over an enchanting woman, though it was more about honour than anything else. Eddie had refused to marry the woman in question and she had commenced a parallel relationship with another man. Whether the combatants consciously realised it or not, the fight was about orderly transition in personal relationships. A comparative understanding from the Kimberley region of Aboriginal Australia is seen in the late Paddy Roe's narrative, 'We better go back to country' (Roe 1984, pp. 106–112). After running away with another man's woman, Paddy returns to face punishment from her former partner. The punishment is administered publicly and the matter resolved.

Uncle Darcy was also a noted bare knuckle fighter and, as it was related, would not tell anyone if he had a fight arranged but would simply get up at dawn and head off. The better the fighters, the more serious the fights. Once, a noted bare-knuckle fighter, a white[1] challenger from somewhere else, turned up drunk one evening, issuing Darcy a challenge that was accepted for the following morning. Both fighters damaged each other and 'Sonno' (Darcy's nickname) was spitting blood for days after the fight. This was an agrarian world, in many respects closer to the Wessex of Thomas Hardy's novels than the world of the Protectors of Aborigines, which left me with an acute awareness of the body as the locus of individuality, sex, love and violence. In this world this violence could sometimes extend to crimes of passion, ending in death.

## Professional Boxing: The Dave Sands Story

This is the one story in this collection that was told by a non-family member. The storyteller was an old woman, the grandmother of the last Aboriginal family to live on Greenbank Island, and it was told with a deliberate point to be made. In content the story was simple: Dave Sands (1926–1952), an internationally renowned Koori boxer during the early 1950s, unable to get a world title fight, went timber-cutting with his brothers and was killed when the truck he was driving ran off the road. His untimely death, as the manner in which the story was told made clear, was causally related to the injustices the Aboriginal fighter suffered throughout the latter portion of his boxing career, as well as more generally to his destiny as an Indigenous Australian. As an appendix to the story, the old woman also spoke of Ron Richards (1910–1957), a great Aboriginal fighter of the 1930s and 1940s, who was a precursor to Dave Sands as Aboriginal Australia's first national hero. She narrated her encounter with Richards as an old man, telling of finding 'this old fulla' on the street and taking him home for a meal. After eating in silence, the old man identifies himself:

---

1   1 I use the term 'white' here because it was an important element in the original telling of this story.

'I'm Ron Richards.' The Richards story, however, did not have the impact of the Dave Sands story: it was too easy to visualise. I could picture the old man eating quietly, possibly lost in his own thoughts, and then, as a gesture of thanks for the meal, revealing his identity: 'I'm Ron Richards.' That story's message was simpler: decline after success, weakness after strength. Richards' destiny was a common one for Aboriginal men: a good man destroyed by alcohol. Therefore the evident point of the story was simpler. But the Sands story was mysterious, pointing at something beyond its immediate content. Sands had achieved, at the time of his death, an unheard-of level of success and acceptance in the non-Aboriginal community. The force of the story came from its warning that success was a property of settler society and, like fire, unstable and dangerous in its effects. But along with caution, the story spoke of desire; Sands' inspirational achievements, accomplished in daring relation to settler society, are remembered and presented by the storyteller a decade after his death as a programme of self fulfilment as well as risk. In its compression of themes of success, mortality, and agency, the story served as a parable addressing the policy of assimilation and the inevitably increased level of interaction between settler and Aboriginal Australians.

## Uncle Tommy Norley

This is the only story I know of that deals with intra-Aboriginal violence on the frontier. The story is incredibly dense, and is deserving of extended analysis from the listener. In writing it down I've tried to keep in mind the following from Martin Buber: 'the anecdote, as well as the short story, is a species of condensed narrative concentrated in one clearly outlined form. Psychology and adornment must be eschewed. The more "naked" it is, the more adequately it fulfils its function' (Buber 1968, p. ix). The story was told to me by my mother.

Uncle Tommy Norley was travelling with his (white) boss in North Queensland. They camped outside a town, and Tommy's boss went into town to buy food. While the boss was away, an Aboriginal warrior came out of the bush with a tomahawk and attacked Tommy. Tommy took the axe off him and killed him.

When the boss returned and learned what had happened he said to Tommy, 'Don't tell anyone about this or we'll get into trouble'. They took the body and tied it to the roots of a mangrove tree, underwater. That night a big wind came up. The dead man's spirit emerged from the water and tried to roll Tommy and his boss into the campfire.

## The View from Terranora

Terranora is now listed as a suburb of Tweed Heads but at one stage was made up of small crop-farms growing beans, peas, or tomatoes. The relation between *Goories* and *Dugais* was negotiated around work, and the *Goories* had a sense of their own dignity, which masked the reality of the rapacious and disrespectful behaviour of white men in relation to Aboriginal women. In the early 1960s, when most Aboriginal people on the Tweed did not own cars, small crop-farmers would collect Aboriginal workers from their homes for bean and pea picking, usually in open trucks. This work was mainly done by women, although older men and men between jobs would also pick beans. I once heard one school teacher talking to another about the 'colourful clothing' of the women bean pickers: a local version of the Ceylon tea pickers. When I told my mother she simply laughed.

Taking the day off from school I would wait with anticipation to see who else was also not going to school that day. Each of the working parties had a 'ganger' who organised the work gangs and negotiated with the farmer. The names of farmers I recall include Burger, Strong, and Abernathy. The gang I remember most strongly was led by a senior woman, named Ruby Roberts, and I looked forward to the smokos and lunch break when I would have the opportunity to listen to older people such as Ruby talk. My usual mode of work was to pick beans until the sun had fully risen and it had become warm, and then start playing, returning for bursts of work. The supreme pleasure of the bean picking excursion, however, was the early morning drive up in to the hills from where I could look down on the mist rising off the Terranora Lakes. As well as the aesthetic dimension of such a sight, it gave me a sense of the more remote parts of the river where the Chain Man might still be encountered.

## Finally

One day in summer, roaming around the river I found two books that had been washed up by a high tide. I took them home and put them on top of a shed to dry in the sun. When I eventually remembered the books and went back to get them I found that they had dried in a readable state. One was an orange-covered Penguin paperback, John Buchan's *Greenmantle,* the other a hardback edition of Richard Hughes' *A High Wind in Jamaica*. I read *Greenmantle* easily, enjoyed and then forgot it. Richard Hughes was more problematic for a pre-adolescent. I still retain the details, as well as the major themes, including the relationships of the older girls with the captain and the mate, and the eventual perfidiousness of the children, against the backdrop of the immediate post-slavery world.

Perhaps the quasi-miraculous aspect of this—the two books dropped into the river somewhere, or possibly, even into the ocean, being carried together and then washed up by the tide—was a harbinger of what was to come.

# References

Bourdieu, P 1990, *The Logic of Practice*, Polity Press, London.

Buber, M 1968, *Tales of the Hasidim: The early masters,* Schocken Books, New York.

Buchan, J 1916, *Greenmantle*, Hodder & Stoughton, London.

Deleuze G & F Guattari 1986, *Kafka: Toward a minor literature,* University of Minnesota Press, Minneapolis.

Fo, D 2005, *My First Seven Years (Plus a Few More),* Methuen, London.

Hazlitt, W 2000, *The Fight and Other Writings,* Penguin, London.

Hughes, R 1929, *A High Wind in Jamacia,* Chatto & Windus, London.

Morissey, P 2011, "'Old Cobraboor': Colonial violence and Aboriginal modesty', in P Morrissey (ed), *Aesopic Voices: Re-framing truth through concealed ways of presentation in the 20th and 21st centuries,* Cambridge Scholarly Publishing, Cambridge, pp. 358–368.

Roe, P 1984 'We Better Go Back to Country', in K Benterrak, S Muecke & P Roe, *Reading the Country: Introduction to nomadology,* Fremantle Arts Centre Press, Fremantle, pp. 106–124.

Roe, P 1983, *Gularabulu: Stories from the West Kimberley*, (edited and with an introduction by S Muecke), Fremantle Arts Centre Press, Fremantle.

# 20. Nourishing Terrain: An Afterword

## Gillian Whitlock

Ego-histoire is an unlikely import into Australian Indigenous studies. At least so it seemed to me in Paris in December 2011 at the conference that became a prehistory to this collection of essays. I listened as a non-Indigenous Australian researcher, sharing a concern for ethical ways of living, researching and teaching in Aboriginal country, and wondered why it was that ego-histoire was so confronting, and so unfamiliar in its address to Indigenous Australian studies. A number of writers here reflect this uneasiness, and in Pierre Nora's essay 'Is "Ego-Histoire" Possible?' (translated here in the Appendix) we see why this is so. Nora highlights the features of the intellectual environment in France that led to ego-histoire: 'the return of the subject', the historiographical turn, and the new regime of historicity in France in the late-1970s and early-1980s. The transposition of each of these to Australian Indigenous studies now immediately unsettles the gendered, national and individualist presuppositions of the project—limits of the genre that remain unremarked in Nora's essay. As a 'bemused' Jane Haggis suggests, Nora's cool, encompassing, explanatory gaze and its singular unitary history of the nation is unsettled in contemporary Australian studies. Like a number of other writers here, Haggis turns to 'entanglement' to understand the relations between self and other, the history of the narrator and the narrated, that circulate in contemporary Australian autobiographical writing, a writing that draws the contact zone and the incommensurability of Indigenous and settler histories into thinking about the self and its professional conduct as a humanities scholar. There is, Gillian Cowlishaw argues, a messiness in thinking about 'us' and 'other'. In response, Cowlishaw turns to the diary as a genre that personalises the professional life, as do a number of other writers here (see, for example, Jan Idle's 'field notes', and Ros Poignant's journal). This self-reflexive form of writing breaks down the distinctions between 'research practice' and 'findings or data', and what emerges is an 'entanglement' of Indigenous and non-Indigenous worlds that is both personally felt and professionally practised. The diary grasps that intimate immersion of the self in other worlds, a destabilising and disorienting knowledge and experience of otherness that recurs in this 'provincialisation' of ego-histoire into postcolonial space and time. More generally, these essays practise forms of autobiographical writing that enable a performative sense of self,, a working through memory and recognition, and what Franca Tamisari calls 'a personal way of knowing others' that finds expression in the classroom as well as in research practice: a 'methodology of encounter', Jan Idle suggests, where observing 'self out of place becomes part of the project'.

To some extent this style of academic memoir is familiar in contemporary life narrative. Feminism, postcolonialism, and critical race theory, among other methodologies, have fostered an introspective and autobiographical turn in academic writing internationally for some time now. In Australia this took a particular form late last century, and in association with a politics of reconciliation and 'the history wars' (Macintyre & Clark 2003; Clendinnen 2000; Read 2000). This produced what David Carter called 'the conscience industry': a style of public intellectual activism energised by national issues concerning land rights and native title, the Apology, frontier violence, child removal and genocide (Carter 2004, p. 17). A particular style of autobiographical narrative appeared: memoirs, essays and histories 'exercising forms of "interiority" or "ethical self-reflection"' and an intense focus on issues of national conscience and civic virtue (Carter 2004, p. 33). The ethical force of bearing witness and engaging with history through personal responsibility reappears in the turn to ego-histoire on occasion; for example, the coming into knowledge of whiteness as a racial identity that is conventionally unmarked or transparent recurs, and 'haunted' white memoir presents a relocation of self in relation to settler ancestors and a previously unacknowledged Indigenous presence. But different styles of 'Turning into a Gardiya' emerge in ego-histoire, and these accommodate Stephen Muecke's turn to metamorphosis, with its bracing critique of sentimentality and its 'respectful' reproduction of Paddy Roe's Kimberley English and its ground-breaking language of reciprocity and storytelling. Similarly, Barry Judd's remarks on the practical usefulness of critical theory to deliver useful and practical outcomes for the elders of Papunya reflect back on discourses of reconciliation and benevolence with a critical eye on various forms of hegemony in settler cultures.

For Nora, ego-histoire was about the nation, and citizenship. Here it takes a very different turn. It is, as Oliver Haag suggests, a project inspired by a transnational approach to Indigenous studies. Recently, Graham Huggan has written critically of the assumption that Australian literary, historical and cultural studies represent a collective national project. Huggan's idea of work in the Australian humanities is global: its geographical and cultural horizons are expansive, and it is 'accountable to the wider world' (Huggan 2008, p. 13). There has been an implicit assumption, Huggan argues, that Australian literature and history is still primarily a matter to be debated among Australians: 'while it may not be strictly necessary to be Australian to write Australian literature, it certainly helps if one wants to do Australian literary criticism' (Huggan 2008, p. 145). Is this one reason why ego-histoire seems so strange as it draws together a new transnational community of scholars? The American critic Wai Chee Dimock remarks that literary studies conducted as citizenship studies is reflex action for many of us, for the national literature is a doxa: 'All the more reason, then, to bracket it, to experiment with other groupings less automatic and more generative of knowledge, if only because of the methodological self-awareness it requires.' (Dimock 2006, p. 226) This draws attention to the different jurisdictions of texts beyond or below the horizon of the nation.

This is exactly what ego-histoire does. It puts Australian texts and contexts in transit, into new expansive and transnational networks; it moves from Paris to Papunya, Mullimbimbi to Venice. I am using 'transit' here in the terms suggested by Jodi Byrd's *The Transit of Empire*, which envisages Indigenous critical practice as particularly open to the possibilities of comparative studies. Indigenous literature, she suggests, moves as an active presence, 'in multiple synchronic formulations' (Byrd 2011, p. xvii). Byrd acknowledges that transit is a provocative association, more commonly suited to diaspora studies than work on Indigeneity, but she means to emphasise how Indigeneity troubles sovereignty and citizenship, most particularly that of the nation, both close to home and further abroad. For Byrd, like other critics concerned with Indigenous critical theory (such as Povinelli and Moreton-Robinson), the nation invites disaggregation. The limited and provisional kinds of citizenship and belonging that become available to indigenous people in and through the nation, and the always troubled 'management' of Indigeneity by the settler state invites alternative concepts of sovereignty and belonging. Outside country, the transits of Indigenous writing trouble the thresholds of sovereignty and citizenship within Australia and offshore. 'Country' is a key word of Aboriginal English, used all over Aboriginal Australia to name the place where a person belongs in terms of kinship, which imposes mutual responsibilities of caring and keeping upon land and people (Bonyhady & Griffiths 2002 p. 2).[1] In the terms of Melissa Lucashenko's 'earthspeaking', 'known country' is a sacred ground of Indigenous language, culture, nurture, sanctuary, responsibility and safety; every landscape of this country has its Dreaming Law (Lucashenko 2006, p. 28).[2] The anthropologist Deborah Bird Rose describes Country as 'nourishing terrain':

> Country in Aboriginal English is not only a common noun but also a proper noun. People talk about country in the same way that they would talk about a person: they speak to country, sing to country, visit country, worry about country, feel sorry for country, and long for country. People say that country knows, hears, smells, takes notice, takes care, is sorry or happy. Country is not a generalised or undifferentiated type of place, such as one might indicate with terms

---
[1] 'Country' in this sense is an Australian Indigenous term that refers to what is elsewhere understood as the distinctive claims to land, kinship communities, native languages, and traditional practices that are foundational to first nations' identity and belonging.
[2] 'Known indigenous country is healing, nurture, sanctuary, responsibility and safety. Unknown country is frightening, inhabited by dangerous spirits, liable to violent defence by its true people. Yet in an indigenous sensibility, there is (or was prior to the massacres and removals) no wilderness, no barren land and no dead heart. The land is not cursed and nor are its human inhabitants. Resurrection is not required where there has been no Fall' (Lucashenko 2006, p. 28).

like 'spending a day in the country' or 'going up the country'. Rather, country is a living entity with a yesterday, today and tomorrow, with a consciousness, and a will toward life. Because of this richness, country is home, and peace; nourishment for body, mind and spirit; heart's ease (Bird Rose 1997, p. 7).

Bird Rose astutely grasps the difference of 'country' in Indigenous epistemologies and the 'country' we find in Raymond Williams' *Keywords,* a definition shaped by the history and culture of western modernity (Williams 1985). Interpretations of country as living presence with its own set of memories permeate contemporary Indigenous writing and criticism. Country is nourishing terrain of Indigenous sovereignty. In these essays Indigenous land and people are recalled with an affective force that affirms country as a shared heritage of belonging: in Philip Morrissey's 'Tales of Mystery and Imagination from the Tweed River', for example, which translates country in terms of a hybridised community of Aboriginal and South Sea Islanders that imaginatively reaches across to the Kimberleys, as well as the storytelling of Paddy Roe and Stephen Muecke.

The turn to ego-histoire opens a new space for thinking about the transits of Indigenous literature, art and film in Europe, and it suggests how European Australian studies emerges as a distinctive presence. Transits such as this raise questions about what kinds of agency become available to Indigenous texts in 'foreign' country, and it opens up ways of thinking about the nation itself as 'foreign' terrain. These new affiliations include connections between Indigenous and European histories, as ego-histoire turns to traumatic memories that circulate in the wake of its civil wars, genocides, partitions and terrors, and explores how these connect to Indigenous archives of memory. We see this, for example, in Oliver Haag's essay on Romany Europe and Indigenous Australia. Or, very differently, in the transnational imaginary that emerges in Philip Morrissey's invocation of nostalgic memory connecting the Tweed River to the agrarian Wessex of Thomas Hardy. This voice of 'Home Talk' that responds to ego-histoire can experiment with embodiment and voice in an expansive transnational world, such as the conversation between May-Britt Öhman and Frances Wyld, which translates 'discipline' not in terms of conventional institutional practice but as Indigenous embodied and remembered language and experiences. Like Jeanine Leane, for Öhman and Wyld, ego-histoire is an invitation to depart from scholarly languages that cannot give voice to Indigenous embodiment and experience; 'this is a story', says Leane, and for her, like Morrissey, ego-histoire becomes an opportunity to write in an expansive transnational frame 'in the first person', a story that incorporates the canon of English literature and the history of ancient Rome as well as Australian literature. The Wiradjuri landscape and epistemology of Leane's storytelling refuses to be contained by the imaginary of the settler nation, and its generic Aboriginal subject.

In this way, ego-histoire generates new filiations on different scales of citizenship and belonging, kindled by the agency of Indigenous culture, history and literature to reach outside country and beyond the nation. These are not merely amiable reflections of the work we do as citizens of the nation in immediate proximity to country, and tenuously reconciled with it. This is genuinely and interestingly a 'foreign' country, generative of new subjects and sovereignties. And so it is that ego-histoire brings us home other-wise, in a productive unsettlement of citizenship that calls into question our scholarly disciplines, and to think anew about what it means to practice them here, nourished by the terrain of Aboriginal country.

## References

Bird Rose, D 2004, *Reports from a Wild Country: Ethics for decolonisation*, UNSW Press, Sydney.

Bird Rose, D 1997, *Nourishing Terrains: Australian Aboriginal views of landscape and wilderness*, Australian Heritage Commission, Canberra.

Bonyhady, T & T Griffiths (eds) 2002, *Words for Country: Landscape and language in Australia*, UNSW Press, Sydney.

Byrd, J A 2011, *The Transit of Empire: Indigenous critiques of colonialism*, University of Minnesota Press, Minneapolis.

Byrd, J A & M Rothberg 2011, 'Between Subalterneity and Indigeneity', *Interventions*, vol. 13, no. 1, pp. 1–12.

Carter, D (ed.) 2004, *The Ideas Market*, Melbourne University Press, Melbourne.

Clendinnen, I 2000, *Tiger's Eye: A memoir*, Text, Melbourne.

Dimock, W C 2006, 'Scales of Aggregation: Prenational, Subnational, Transnational', *American Literary History*, vol. 18, no. 2, pp. 219–228.

Huggan, G 2008, *Australian Literature: Postcolonialism, Racism, Transnationalism*, Oxford University Press, Oxford.

Lucashenko, M 2006, 'Not Quite White in the Head', *Manoa*, vol. 18, no. 2, pp. 23–51.

Macintyre, S & A Clark 2003, *The History Wars*, Melbourne University Press, Melbourne.

Read, P 2000, *Belonging: Australians, place and Aboriginal ownership*, Cambridge University Press, Cambridge.

Whitlock, G 2004, 'Becoming Migloo', in D Carter (ed.), *The Ideas Market*, Melbourne University Press, Melbourne, pp. 236–258.

Williams, R 1985, *Keywords: A vocabulary of culture and society*, Oxford University Press, Oxford.

# APPENDIX

# Is 'Ego-histoire' Possible?[1]

## Pierre Nora

## Translated by Stephen Muecke

The book *Essais d'Ego-Histoire* seems to have been a belated success. The idea behind the book, even though it didn't appear until 1987, because of delays in production, dates for me from the same period as *Lieux de Mémoire*, that is, from the end of the 1970s and the early 1980s, and it shares the same kind of intention. But while *Lieux de Mémoire* had an immediate success, the *Essais d'Ego-Histoire* were, at the time, an intellectual and publishing failure. This was no doubt a relative failure because the expression (like that of 'lieu de mémoire', by the way) was very quickly taken up and used. But the criticisms were hardly extensive, and were even ironic or annoyed in tone. I put this reaction down to a saturation effect. In the previous decade, historians and history had seen a triumphant breakthrough, and now here they are, seemingly going beyond the bounds of their university discipline to make themselves actors on the social stage. Georges Duby became president of a new TV channel and was inducted into the French Academy. Emmanuel Le Roy Ladurie was appointed director of the Bibliothèque Nationale. René Rémond became a television commentator on election results. They were everywhere, and their success was enough to cause some irritation. To cap it all of, instead of doing their job and telling us stories, all they were doing was turning themselves into history.

So *Ego-Histoire* had an underground existence for quite a while, not quite clandestine, but unclassifiable, a little like Philippe Ariès' *L'Historien du Dimanche*, which dates from 1980 and was a great inspiration to me. Philippe Ariès is a historian who was for a long time marginal to academic pursuits, and central to the Annales school. A Maurassian and inheritor of a tropical fruit business, he is the very personal author of a extremely good book on attitudes towards life, death and childhood. He was picked up belatedly at the time by the Ecole des Hautes Etudes en Sciences Sociales, and Michel Winock, who did more or less the same thing at Seuil that I did at Gallimard, had the good idea to suggest to him that he put a book of interviews together on the direction he took, on his sensibility towards time, present and past; his relation to history. I must emphasise this last point, because it is central to understanding ego-histoire. Ariès certainly shared with the Annales historians the tendency towards total rupture with the past, of a definitive break with 'the

---

[1] Originally published in 2001 as 'L'ego-histoire est-elle possible?', *Historein*, vol. 3, p. 19–26.

world we have lost', to use the expression of English demographer Peter Laslett. This is what distinguished him from the traditional, academic, university history. But coming from a traditionalist and monarchist family, this feeling of loss induced in this reactionary an intense existential relation with the past, the need to understand it in its difference, to re-establish a way of being derived from it. What made him an historian was part of his very being. History was not a career or a curiosity for him, but a reason for living, he had the need to inscribe his own existence into a definite continuity. To my mind, ego-histoire was no different.

So what was it all about exactly? An experimental trying-out, a laboratory procedure. Could the historian make an historian out of himself? Can he or she who has material and memorial documentation on themselves that no-one else will ever have access to put this internal documentary material into service for an external gaze? Can she become her own object of study and under what conditions? Can one describe oneself in the same way one has described so many others? Doesn't the fact of being an historian allow one to have a specific view on oneself, which is neither that of the autobiographer, nor that of the writer, the friend, the psychoanalyst, or the confessor? The question is worth asking. The result, even if a part failure, will be revealing and instructive. The development of this project would obviously need to be in relation to the intellectual environment of the time, highlighted, it seems to me, by three main points.

The first is what has come to be known, albeit in a rough approximation, as 'the return of the subject'. What is meant by this is that, after the great period of structuralism, semiology and textualism, the human person was put back in the centre of action and thought. In history, this meant attention was refocussed on the role of autonomy, will, and freedom in the thinking and acting individual, in relation to the structures, the collective determinations, and the global conditionings to which history seemed to have been entirely devoted. It was also the moment when a new and powerful interest in biography arose. This phenomenon is certainly linked to the philosophical tendency for a 'rehabilitation' of the self, and a 'repossession' of the subjective role of individuality. It is also linked, for the historian, to a sign of the times that was more properly French: the end of communism, the rise of interest in national history, and, to be perfectly frank, the growth in strength of the historical image of General de Gaulle. While such a statement may seem excessive, it still has some truth in it. De Gaulle certainly contributed to the rehabilitation of the idea of subjective will in historical action; the idea of the great man which we historians so much wanted to forget about. Let's not make comparisons to the point of caricature. But there was, in the 1980s, a profound intellectual transformation, which came to link a philosophical problematic, this 'return of the subject', to an historical problematic and a national problematic.

A second sign of the times, deeply felt by myself, and which belongs to the constellation of things in which ego-histoire was born, was the arrival of the historiographical dimension of history.

In a country like France, historiography took a long time to take root, in its broadest sense, or rather in its double sense: on the one hand, the general study of the conditions and modalities of the development of historical science, on the other, the fact that if the word 'history' itself designated both the reality of the past and the way in which we make sense of it, then the discourse of the historian as a whole is about historiography. In France, where history as exercise of the intelligence of the past has been an equally active agent as history as the reality of the past, historiography in the modern sense of the word has taken on an almost subversive character. It has appeared in the form of a dismantling of traditional grand national history. I'm happy to locate its beginnings in Georges Duby's *Le Dimanche de Bouvines*, which appeared in 1973 in Gallimard's series 'Thirty Days Which Made France'. When I commissioned the book from Duby, his first reflex was to refuse. He was quick to understand the challenge and interest that was in planting the flag of 'new history' on one of the most prominent outcrops of 'history's battleground', the very battle that could be seen as founding national unity. The causes, unfolding and consequences of Philippe Auguste's 1214 victory on the Bouvine Plain have been extensively narrated, especially by Achille Luchaire in Ernest Lavisse's *L'Histoire de France*. Duby did something quite different. He tried to follow, through the centuries, how the immediate perception of the lived fact was propagated in successive waves to build the massive block of a national representation, through stories, manuals and commemorative events. What was born there was a type of history which I have spent a lot of time on myself, since the historiographical dimension lives in the heart of the *Lieux de Mémoire* project. What is has in common with ego-histoire is its capacity to defamiliarise a subject which we spontaneously inhabit. To direct a type of historiographical gaze on oneself, at a time when the whole period was undergoing a generalised penetration of the idea of history such that it was almost a case of everyone becoming historian of himself, could not be much more in tune with the zeitgeist.

This was especially because—and this is the third fact I want to stress—those years were also those in which history entered what one might call its reflexive age, one could even say its epistemological age. Of course, reflection on history was never absent from its practice. Nevertheless, history conquered and installed its knowledge base [*scientificité*] on a refusal of 'philosophy of history'. What is new is the integration of theoretical reflection into the very practice of what Marc Bloch called the historian's vocation. What is new is the consciousness of an 'historical operation', as Michel de Certeau put it, in the very heart of the historian's work. Hence the title, borrowed from an article by

Michel de Certeau, 'Faire de l'Histoire' (doing/making history), which Jacques le Goff and I gave in 1974 to the three edited volumes in which we wanted to see the beginnings of this new type of historiography, the historical expression of a new regime of historicity.

If I have permitted myself the repetition of the name of Michel de Certeau (the Jesuit historian who went through Lacanian psychoanalysis), it is because the refusal he sent me in opposition to his participation in the *Essais d'Ego-Histoire* is, on its own terms, highly revealing of the nature of the project: 'I was tempted by the project', he wrote, 'to the extent that it might permit—or permit me—to articulate my debts in the course of a historical project, debts which have sustained and oriented it ... I would feel uneasy in this kind of writing, even though I have studied it extensively, and it is fascinating. So having been divided between the interest in acknowledging debts and the (stubborn?) refusal to write a chronicle about 'me', I don't think I can meet your cordial request. I am very sorry, especially ... as the question is, in itself, a fundamental one.'

Should I go further into the actual content of each *Essais d'Ego-Histoire* and the reasons for which I approached Maurice Agulhon, Pierre Chaunu, Georges Duby, Raoul Girardet, Jacques Le Goff, Michelle Perrot, and René Rémond? Should I try to characterise the way in which each of them confronted the difficulty? I will allow myself, rather, to go back to the book itself and the conclusions I believed I was able to draw from it, to quickly go over the sequels and off-shoots this highly engaging project had, and has provoked. They are proof of its seminal and fertile character. They are of two sorts.

The first concerns the refusals to write for it, of which three are particularly significant: those of Annie Kriegel, Pierre Vidal-Naquet et François Furet— three leading lights of French historiography, three close friends whose track records, whose motivations as historians and writing talent made them the first to be approached for this experiment. All felt squeezed by the constraint to keep it under 50-odd pages, but each embarked on writing their memoires. The inspiration paid off handsomely for two of them.[2] For the third, the inspiration has to be guessed at. Because that is how *Le Passé d'une Illusion* (1995) has to be read, for the most part. It is François Furet's intellectual autobiography which adds the weight of his lived experience to his historical analysis of the communist idea, and the sadness in his personal recollections made the violence of his critical incisiveness acceptable to the understanding of many communists.

---

2  They were gracious enough to remember in their prefaces: 'Here is my contribution [to *Essais d'Ego-Histoire*] wrote Annie Kriegel. Years late and several hundred pages too long.' *Ce que j'ai cru Comprendre*, Robert Laffont, Paris, 1991. And Pierre Vidal-Naquet: 'For a long time I resisted those who would have me write such a book of "ego-histoire" by an historian.' *Mémoires, 1: La Brisure et l'attente, 1930-1955*, Seuil-La Découverte, Paris, 1995.

Again, it is the autobiographical character which explains that, for the main part, the analysis stops in 1956, the date when the communist idea, in its Stalinist form, was denounced by the twentieth congress of the USSR Communist Party, by Kruschev, at the time the world's highest communist authority. *Le Passé d'une Illusion* is an example of a particular genre, that of memoires thought through historically.[3]

*Essais d'Ego-Histoire* also generated a series of books, most often in the form of interviews,[4] in which the authors have developed or completed that which they were only able to announce in the initial essays. The comparison is instructive. The individual work gains no doubt in terms of the wealth of information and freedom of expression, but it only underscores what it was that *Essais d'Ego-Histoire* had that was unique and original, a group portrait, and what it reveals about the difficulties of the enterprise.

Here the choice of participants was key. It had to have enough variety to allow the expression of strong personalities within the incorporated group. Enough balance to represent, even roughly, a broad palette of political families; centred enough so that the unity of a post-war generation might appear, which also knew both the blowing up of the disciplinary frontiers and the opening of society onto the political world, onto administration and onto the media. As different as each of these essays is, bringing them together really throws light on the internal cleavages that have traversed the discipline over the last 30 years: the split between historians marked by the Annales school and others; the split between Marxists and non-Marxists; the split between those who did a thesis and those who refused to.

But the lessons to be learnt from the whole set of accounts only make clearer the difficulties that each of the participants faced, in their own way, in applying the rule of the game: to see oneself as an historian. There lie the limits of the genre. I am not speaking of the obvious difficulties: scruples about speaking of oneself, the impossibility of reporting on one's own qualities; the fear of individualising oneself in relation to one's colleagues. I am speaking about the difficulties inherent in the exercise itself. After having seen only individual lives followed in traditional histories, historians have gotten used to only being historians through their sense of the collective. Witness to this is the evolution of the genre

---

3 One would have to add to this series of productive refusals the wonderful text which Mona Ozouf wrote spontaneously, and who I had been too discreet to approach, as the preface to her collection on revolution, utopia and teaching. *L'Ecole de la France*, Gallimard, Paris, 1984. It was entitled 'L'Image dans le Tapis' (Image in the Carpet).

4 Pierre Chaunu and François Dosse, *L'Instant Éclaté : Entretiens*, Aubier, Paris, 1994; Georges Duby, *L'Histoire Continue*, Odile Jacob, Paris, 1991; Raoul Girardet and Pierre Assouline, *Singulièrement Libre: Entretiens*, Perrin, Paris, 1990; Jacques Le Goff, *Une vie pour l'Histoire: Entretiens avec Marc Heurgon*, La Découverte, Paris, 1996.

of biography, which has been powerfully renewed.[5] Witness also the dead-ends reached by the attempts at historical psychoanalysis. Caught between the social capture of the self and intimate hypersubjectivism, is ego-histoire possible? It is perhaps its vain efforts, its secondary benefits and its failings which give rise to the immense interest; its half-failures are the real successes.

If I had to sketch my own ego-histoire—which mistakenly I did not permit myself to do at the time because of misplaced discretion—I would no doubt have begun with two obvious characteristics of my personal situation. Its singular and unclassifiable character on the one hand: Editor? Historian? Professor? Journal editor? On the other, the belated character of my historical work. These are the two things I would have tried to clarify and explain.

If, in fact, I had one word to define myself, I would be happy to say that I am 'centre-marginal'. A marginal, who did not follow a classical career, nor academic, editorial or literary. I would be wrong, however, not to recognise that between Hautes Etudes and Gallimard I occupy a crossroads position which has put me at the heart of French intellectual life for 30 years. Hautes Etudes is a special institution created to herd together sheep with five legs who do not have the qualifications to hope for a place in a classical university; at the same time, it is the most vibrant and creative amongst them. It is true I am not a professional editor, but directing the human sciences department at a publisher like Gallimard is hardly a minor clerical job. I have edited *Le Débat* for 20 years, but it has not made me a leader of a movement like *NRF* did for Gide, or *Les Temps Modernes* for Sartre, *Esprit* for Emmanuel Mounier, or even Raymond Aron with *Commentaire*, but I am certainly a band leader. The problematic of memory, to which I have devoted myself, is perhaps not about history in the classical and traditional sense of the word, but it is one of the newest and most fertile fields in the discipline. And even *Lieux de Mémoire*, this very collective work indeed, with 130 authors, is at the same time recognised as a personal work. In all my fields of activity can be found this same mix of centrality and marginality, this sideways crab movement, this retreat towards engagement. Is this by chance? I would go even further: this way of being both on the inside and on the outside is part and parcel of my intellectual nature. I am not an imaginative soul, an artist. I belong entirely to the tradition of critical intelligence. This is what makes me an historian and an editor.

This vital disposition I would certainly put down to my being the youngest in my family. A numerous and warm family, liberal and even tribal. A strong-willed surgeon father, an older brother who had everything; I would have trouble impressing him at first, and, later, as his peer, in making my mark. So I began to

---

5   See especially Jacques Le Goff's introduction to *Saint-Louis*, Gallimard, Paris, 1996, where he reflects on bibliographical method.

play the part of the precocious child very early on, the little genius I was not. Because at age eight I had to write plays in verse and draft constitutions, it was said, once and for all, that I would be a writer. Being a professor and an editor was only a small change from a half-achieved, half-missed profession. So I was the youngest, the one who listens and observes more than he can participate, the one who criticises and judges. The war which I experienced from ages nine to 13, only exacerbated this failure to fit in. And because we were Jewish we had to flee to a free zone, to Grenoble, then hide in the Vercours district, at a peasant's place, and then at the end, with the Resistance.

Such experience is maturing and contributes to being out of step with one's generation, distancing one from school-mates who were not able to know, as I did at a decisive age, what tragedy there can be in history and in life.

The other characteristic of the person in question is the long, drawn out indecision about being an historian. First the indecision about becoming one. I had plans to be a philosopher, a doctor, a psychiatrist, an economist, a film director, before deciding to do history. After graduation [*l'agrégation*], I imagined I could be an Americanist or something in Arabic studies, before falling back, like going home, on the history of contemporary France. Maybe some fundamental questions on this strange country were tapping into my unconscious all this time. They could only have been born during the war, from the unbelievable defeat, from the exclusion of Jewish people from the Resistance. And afterwards they could only have been reinforced, between communism, Gaullism and through to the colonial wars.

There was not a single episode, any tiny event, which (despite the intellectual Marxism in the air) did not relate to the mysteries of the nation. French passions have always fascinated me.

We were very badly trained for this type of study. It was the big gust of wind brought by the Annales which drew me towards history. This gust blew us a long way from political history, from national history, from contemporary history, towards the open spaces, the weight of long periods, and economic and social determinations. The political, the national and the contemporary seemed to be tarred by the same brush. It was as if there was a hiatus between our lived experience and our intellectual training. I struggled for a long while with this contradiction. What kind of scientific approach could best respond to the demands of our civil and historic conscience? It was clear that the political dimension was more than just a simple superstructure, a simple matter of power, but was the very form of our being together; and that a new political history would no doubt be this 'total history', precisely the one the Annales historians had wanted to construct against the narrowness of traditional political history. It was also clear that a national history would have to give up the chronological account to draw food for thought from what all the human sciences might bring. But, in point of fact, what the human sciences brought to the study of France, its demography, its economy, its regions, its peoples, had ended up dissolving the model of a unitary France, to the point of wondering what one was talking about by speaking of it in the singular.

Where, then, is the unifying principle of a fragmented national idea? And how can one give a 'contemporary' history the intellectual and scientific dignity which it seems to be refused? For 20 years I played my part with those who kept turning around these questions. For me they were linked. I felt more or less clearly that the history of present times was not the simple temporal prolongation of the history of the recent past, but that it was governed by another regime of historicity, dominated by the category of the present linked to that of memory, and that it called for other types of relations to the past and other ways of coming to terms with them. But what method could plug the singularity of the present directly into weighty heritage of long periodicity?

In order that this whole set of questions might find one set of answers (in the framework of the historian, that is) and that a general problematic of memory might come to me, the one with which I am identified, I needed to wait for a veritable explosion of memory to happen. There was and needed to be, at the end of the 1970s, a fundamental memorial wave crashing onto a France in full upheaval, and that the whole period be grasped, as it were, by memory. It was history itself, as always, that made me into an historian.

I would be the first to admit that these two paths are not more likely than others to put me on the tracks of whatever the ego-histoire that had been hoped for, might be. Should one conclude on the impossibility of the exercise? Perhaps. But isn't that another reason to keep at it?

www.ingramcontent.com/pod-product-compliance
Lightning Source LLC
Chambersburg PA
CBHW040934240426
43670CB00029B/2979